'Surya P. Subedi offers a scholar's diagnosis of what is wrong with the international human rights system and a practitioner's suggestions to fix it. Drawing on his experiences as an activist, an academic, and as a UN Special Rapporteur, he shows the possibilities and the limitations of this vital body of norms and how they might translate from words to deeds.'
Professor Simon Chesterman, National University of Singapore and Secretary-General, Asian Society of International Law

'An effective UN addresses and remedies human rights violations. At present the organization does not deliver. In this accessible book Professor Subedi provides a competent and comprehensive assessment of the UN human rights system which culminates in a compelling plea for reform including concrete and feasible suggestions for change.'
Karin Arts, Professor of International Law and Development, ISS, The Hague, The Netherlands

The Effectiveness of the UN Human Rights System

The UN human rights agenda has reached the mature age of 70 years and many UN mechanisms created to implement this agenda are themselves in their middle age, yet human rights violations are still a daily occurrence around the globe. The scorecard of the UN human rights mechanisms appears impressive in terms of the promotion, spreading of education and engaging States in a dialogue to promote human rights, but when it comes to holding governments to account for violations of human rights, the picture is much more dismal.

This book examines the effectiveness of UN mechanisms and suggests measures to reform them in order to create a system that is robust and fit to serve the twenty-first century. This book casts a critical eye over the rationale and effectiveness of each of the major UN human rights mechanisms, including the Human Rights Council, the human rights treaty bodies, the UN High Commissioner for Human Rights, the UN Special Rapporteurs and other Charter-based bodies. Surya P. Subedi argues that most of the UN human rights mechanisms have remained toothless entities and proposes measures to reform and strengthen them by depoliticising the workings of UN human rights mechanisms and judicialising human rights at the international level.

Surya P. Subedi, OBE, QC (Hon), is Professor of International Law at the University of Leeds, member of the Institut de Droit International, former UN Special Rapporteur for human rights in Cambodia and barrister at Three Stone Chambers, Lincoln's Inn, London.

Human Rights and International Law
Series Editor: Professor Surya P. Subedi, OBE, QC (Hon)

This series will explore human rights law's place within the international legal order, offering much-needed interdisciplinary and global perspectives on human rights' increasingly central role in the development and implementation of international law and policy.

Human Rights and International Law is committed to providing critical and contextual accounts of human rights' relationship with international law theory and practice. To achieve this, volumes in the series will take a thematic approach that focuses on major debates in the field, looking at how human rights impacts on areas as diverse and divisive as security, terrorism, climate change, refugee law, migration, bioethics, natural resources and international trade.

Exploring the interaction, interrelationship and potential conflicts between human rights and other branches of international law, books in the series will address both historical development and contemporary contexts, before outlining the most urgent questions facing scholars and policy makers today.

Available titles

Human Rights and Charity Law
International Perspectives
Kerry O'Halloran

Human Rights and Development in International Law
Tahmina Karimova

The Emerging Law of Forced Displacement in Africa
Development and Implementation of the Kampala Convention on Internal Displacement
Allehone M. Abebe

Business and Human Rights
History, Law and Policy – Bridging the Accountability Gap
Nadia Bernaz

Extracting Accountability from Non-State Actors in International Law
Assessing the Scope for Direct Regulation
Lee McConnell

Socio-Economic Human Rights in Essential Public Services Provision
Marlies Hesselman, Antenor Hallo de Wolf and Brigit Toebes

About the Series Editor

Professor Surya P. Subedi, OBE, QC (Hon), is Professor of International Law, University of Leeds, member of the Institut de Droit International and former UN Special Rapporteur for human rights in Cambodia.

The Effectiveness of the UN Human Rights System

Reform and the Judicialisation of Human Rights

Surya P. Subedi, OBE, QC (Hon)

DPhil (Oxon.); Barrister (Middle Temple)
Professor of International Law, University of Leeds, United Kingdom
Member, Institut de Droit International
Former UN Special Rapporteur for Human Rights in Cambodia

Routledge
Taylor & Francis Group
LONDON AND NEW YORK

First published 2017 by Routledge

2 Park Square, Milton Park, Abingdon, Oxfordshire OX14 4RN
52 Vanderbilt Avenue, New York, NY 10017

Routledge is an imprint of the Taylor & Francis Group, an informa business

British Library Cataloguing in Publication Data
A catalogue record for this book is available from the British Library

Library of Congress Cataloging in Publication Data
Names: Subedi, Surya P., 1958– author.
Title: The effectiveness of the UN human rights system : reform and the judicialisation of human rights / Surya P. Subedi.
Description: Abingdon, Oxon ; New York, NY : Routledge, 2017. | Series: Human rights and international law | Includes bibliographical references and index.
Identifiers: LCCN 2016052913 | ISBN 9781138711532 (hardback)
Subjects: LCSH: Human rights. | United Nations—Evaluation. | United Nations. Human Rights Council—Evaluation. | United Nations. Office of the High Commissioner for Human Rights—Evaluation. | International agencies—Evaluation.
Classification: LCC K3241 .S83 2017 | DDC 341.4/8—dc23
LC record available at https://lccn.loc.gov/2016052913

ISBN: 978-1-138-71153-2 (hbk)
ISBN: 978-0-367-22424-0 (pbk)

Typeset in Galliard
by Florence Production Ltd, Stoodleigh, Devon, UK

Contents

Preface

The first real encounter that I had with human rights was when I was a student leader in the late 1970s, fighting for democracy in my native country, Nepal. I was imprisoned twice for challenging effectively a one-party system of government known as the party-less panchayat system. As a law student, I asked myself what rights did I have under international human rights law, what the UN could do for me and what legal remedies I had so that I could challenge the administrative order in their detention of me in jail without a trial. When I was eventually released from prison I resumed my studies and upon the completion of my law degree I began to practise law as an advocate. Again, I realised all the imperfections of the national and international legal system in protecting fundamental rights of my clients as individuals. When I later joined the judicial service of Nepal I was entrusted with the task of writing the periodic reports of the country on human rights to various UN and associated agencies. This gave me an opportunity to see the challenges faced by the government of a least-developed country in realising human rights. It indeed was a tall order for an impoverished country, Nepal, to realise many human rights and especially those relating to economic, social and cultural rights.

After spending many years in academia in the UK studying, researching and publishing in human rights, I was appointed as the UN Special Rapporteur for human rights for Cambodia and had to deal with the cases of everyday violations of human rights in the country, another least-developed and impoverished country, and the challenges it faced in realising human rights. After being on the receiving end of human rights violations during my early career, I myself was now in a high-level UN position responsible for monitoring and documenting human rights violations and doing my utmost to protect and promote human rights in another Asian country, Cambodia, similar in many respects to Nepal in terms of political upheaval. While the people of Cambodia had high expectations of me, I realised that in reality I had no real powers to protect people from the human rights violations they faced. For instance, I would regularly receive individual petitions from those whose rights were violated or were facing the threat of violation, but I had neither the powers nor the resources to entertain such petitions. Of course, I would use all means at my disposal, such as writing directly to the people in the government bringing the matter to their attention in the forms of urgent appeals or allegation letters, and sometimes the violation would stop or the threat of eviction from their land would not be carried out. However, if the government ignored the communication and the eviction proceeded, resulting often in the burning down of the dwellings of the villagers and forcible eviction of families, there was little I or the UN system of human rights could do about it. It was basically from the high altars of morality, reason and persuasion that I was expected to make my contribution to the promotion and protection of human rights in Cambodia by influencing change in policy or the conduct of the various branches of the government. I also realised that I was not alone in this respect: the effectiveness of most of the UN human rights mechanisms was also based on the use of soft power and this power was not adequate to deal with the harsh realities of human rights violations of a contemporary world that is dominated by multi-polarism in international relations.

While I was trying to tackle human rights issues in Cambodia and digesting the limitations of the UN human rights mechanisms, the Arab Spring or the Arab Awakening of 2011–2012 brought to the fore the weaknesses of these mechanisms in the face of the high expectations of the people of the Arab world who wanted to bring about substantial change in their countries. As a person with a keen interest in the work of the various UN human rights mechanisms and especially the Human Rights Council, I observed for hours and hours the proceedings within the Council to gain first-hand experience of the workings of this principal UN human rights body. I also had the privilege of working as a member of the Advisory Group on Human Rights to the British Foreign Secretary between 2010 and 2015 during which attempts were made to tackle global human rights challenges. During this experience too I realised the limitations of the UN human rights system. It was in the context of these various experiences that I decided to write a book critiquing the workings of the UN human rights mechanisms and analysing their strengths and weaknesses with a view to putting forward proposals to address the weaknesses. This book is the product of that endeavour.

While this book is based primarily on the research that I carried out into workings of the UN human rights regime from its inception to 2016, it does draw on my own personal experience of work in human rights as a human rights activist, an advocate and a barrister, an advisor on human rights to several governments, and the UN Special Rapporteur for human rights in Cambodia for 6 years. Thus, I believe that I bring to bear in this book my experience of theoretical and practical work in human rights law, in different capacities, spanning some 30 years in both the developed and developing world.

I have many people and institutions to thank for their assistance in writing this book. First of all, I would like to thank the School of Law at the University of Leeds for granting me study leave in the first half of 2012 and to the American University Washington College of Law in Washington, D.C., for inviting me to spend my sabbatical as a Visiting Professor there. It was during my stay in Washington, D.C., that this book was conceived and designed.

My special thanks go to Dean and Professor Claudio Grossman for his numerous acts of kindness in hosting me and providing me the intellectual support that I needed. As a leading academic and as the Chairperson of the Committee of the Chairpersons of UN treaty bodies, his seasoned and distilled views have had a profound impact on my own thought process.

I would like to extend my sincere thanks to Ms Louisa Riches, a PhD scholar at the University of Leeds, for her research assistance, to Ms Olga Nakajo at the Office of the UN High Commissioner for Human Rights in Geneva for her support, and to Mr Henderik Tan of Singapore, an LLB student at the Leeds University Law School, for his assistance in scouring for me the human rights law collection at the Brotherton Library at Leeds. I also thank the staff at the UN Library at Palais des Nations in Geneva for their assistance in locating various research materials not readily and easily available elsewhere. Last but not least, very many thanks are due to my family and especially my daughter, Anita, herself a recent Oxford law graduate, for her assistance in going over the manuscript and suggesting how it could be made more accessible to law students like her.

Leeds, 24 October (UN Day), 2016
Surya P. Subedi

Introduction

Human rights are guaranteed for all in international law, but sadly such rights are not a reality for many people around the globe. The objective is universal, but not the practice. Law, whether national or international, is of course breached all the time all over the world. Generally speaking, law does not lead, it follows. Therefore, the effectiveness of the law is not judged by whether it is breached or not, but by the ability of the mechanisms to adequately address such violations. When it comes to international human rights law it is the effectiveness of the UN human rights institutions and their activities that come under close scrutiny. This is especially so when the UN human rights agenda has reached the established age of 70 years and many UN mechanisms created to implement this agenda are themselves in their middle age.[1] The score card of the UN human rights mechanisms appears impressive in terms of promoting human rights, spreading the education of human rights and engaging States in a dialogue to promote human rights, but when it comes to holding governments to account for violations of human rights the picture is rather dismal.

Of course, the UN human rights institutions are not designed to provide a direct remedy to the victims of human rights violations and cannot thus be judged against this criterion. They are primarily about monitoring compliance of a promise made by States, through various international human rights instruments, to the people of the world that human rights are inherent and inalienable to them and their rights and dignity will be protected and assisting States in realising human rights. The primary responsibility of protecting human rights rests with the States and the national institutions within the governance structure of the countries concerned. What the UN human rights mechanism is entrusted with is the monitoring of the activities of these State institutions

1 The UN as an international organisation established in 1945 is now 70 years old. The Universal Declaration of Human Rights adopted in 1948 is fast approaching that age. The 1966 Covenants on Civil and Political Rights as well as on Economic, Social and Cultural Rights are now 50 years old. Even the relatively new Human Rights Council is now 10 years old, which is a long enough time to assess its effectiveness.

and making recommendations to ensure that enjoyment of human rights becomes a reality for all. Thus, most of the UN human rights mechanisms interact mainly with States rather than with individuals (the exception being in the cases of examining individual petitions against specific violations of human rights by treaty bodies).[2]

Since most UN mechanisms for monitoring and implementing human rights treaty provisions were developed in the second half of the last century, and in a political context marked by the bi-polar nature of the world as seen in the Cold War, they reflect that mindset. Most of them are largely political bodies rather than judicial. Consequently, they are facing tremendous challenges in today's multi-polar world. Simultaneously, the third pillar of the UN, that is human rights, lacks the leadership and resources enjoyed by the other two pillars (peace and security, and development) and the gap between idealism and reality remains wide. Both the law and the institutions designed to enforce or implement the law have to change with time. Yet that has not been the case in terms of the UN institutions designed to protect human rights. The mindset and the framework of the 1960s and 1970s are still in existence without having gone through any appreciable degree of reform to respond to the challenges of the contemporary world.

2 See generally, Philip Alston, *The United Nations and Human Rights: A Critical Appraisal* (Clarendon Press, 2nd edn, 2013); Philip Alston and James Crawford (eds), *The Future of Human Rights Treaty Monitoring* (Cambridge University Press, 2000); Philip Alston and Frederic Megret (eds), *The United Nations and Human Rights: A Critical Appraisal* (Oxford University Press, 2nd edition, 2013); M. Cherif Bassiouni and William A. Schabas (eds), *New Challenges for the UN Human Rights Machinery: What Future for the UN Treaty Body System and the Human Rights Council Procedures?* (Intersentia, 2011); Anne F. Bayefsky (ed.), *The UN Human Rights Treaty System in the 21st Century* (Kluwer, 2000); Maria S. Becker and Julia N. Schneider (ed.), *Human Rights Issues in the 21st Century* (Nova Science Publishers, 2008); Kevin Boyle (ed.), *New Institutions for Human Rights Protection* (Oxford University Press, 2009); Hilary Charlesworth and Emma Larking (ed.), *Human Rights and the Universal Periodic Review: Rituals and Ritualism* (Cambridge University Press, 2015); Rosa Freedman, *The United Nations Human Rights Council: A Critique and Early Assessment* (Routledge, 2013); Felice D. Gaer and Christen L. Broecker (eds), *The United Nations High Commissioner for Human Rights: Conscience for the World* (Martinus Nijhoff, 2013); Angela Hegarty and Siobhan Leonard (eds), *Human Rights: An Agenda for the 21st Century* (Cavendish Publishing, 1999); Helen Keller and Geir Ulfstein (eds), *UN Human Rights Treaty Bodies: Law and Legitimacy* (Cambridge University Press, 2012); Julie Mertus, *The United Nations and Human Rights: A Guide for a New Era* (Routledge, 2005); Gerd Oberleitner, *Global Human Rights Institutions: Between Remedy and Ritual* (Polity Press, 2007); Michael O'Flaherty, *Human Rights and the UN: Practice before the Treaty Bodies* (2nd edition, Martinus Nijhoff, 2002); Bertrand Ramcharan, *The United Nations High Commissioner for Human Rights: The Challenges of International Protection* (Martinus Nijhoff, 2002); Bertrand Ramcharan, *The United Nations High Commissioner in Defence of Human Rights* (Brill, 2004); Bertrand Ramcharan, *The United Nations Human Rights Council* (Routledge, 2011).

Questions that arise

Speaking for the last time to the Commission on Human Rights, the then UN Secretary-General Kofi Annan had stated that 'the era of declaration is now giving way, as it should, to an era of implementation.'[3] The question that arises is whether this has been the case since then or since the establishment of the Human Rights Council in 2006? How well equipped is the UN system of human rights, designed essentially for the twentieth-century Cold War epoch marked by bi-polar politics, to deal with the violations of human rights in the contemporary world? If States with varying degrees of respect and conviction for human rights can operate within the UN system on an equal footing, how truly universal are 'universal' human rights in the first place? How can States with autocratic, dictatorial and authoritarian systems of governance operate as they currently do with impunity? Without universal (and therefore, uniform) acceptance or ratification and implementation of human rights treaties, how can the rights enshrined therein be regarded as belonging in equal measure to each individual?

On the other hand, if there is no universal compliance, how are the UN human rights mechanisms created to uphold such universal human rights responding to it? How well equipped and effective have they been in discharging their responsibilities? If they have not been effective, what reform is necessary to make them better equipped to ensure universal compliance with universal human rights standards? What lessons can be drawn from the experiences of the struggle for human rights and democracy in the Arab world and elsewhere, and the failure of the UN to address serious violations of human rights in countries such as Syria, North Korea or Iran?

Scope of this study

It is in light of the above-mentioned questions that this book is designed to assess the effectiveness of the UN system of human rights and propose measures to reform and strengthen it by depoliticising the workings of UN human rights mechanisms and judicialising human rights at the international level. In doing so, this study provides a critical bird's eye view of the political and legal landscape of the UN system of protecting human rights created largely in the second half of the twentieth century. It demonstrates that while the political landscape of the world has changed since then, the ideology behind the creation of UN human rights mechanisms has not changed significantly and most of the UN human rights mechanisms have become effectively toothless entities.

3 Kofi Annan's address to the UN Commission on Human Rights, Geneva, 7 April 2005, available at http://www.un.org/sg/STATEMENTS/index.asp?nid=1388 (accessed 28 December 2015).

The system as it stands brings to mind the Shakespearean phrase, 'much ado about nothing'.

There is a plethora of under-resourced and outdated UN human rights institutions with often overlapping competencies. In order to promote and protect human rights, a frenzied attempt has been made in the last 70 or so years to adopt more human rights instruments and create far more human rights institutions within the UN system, leading one to wonder whether by doing more the UN is actually doing better. For instance, if it is a developing country like Brazil, Cambodia, Colombia, Guatemala or Nepal the government of the country is likely to receive a request for visit by a range of UN institutions ranging from the UN High Commissioner for Human Rights down to the Deputy and Assistant High Commissioners, treaty bodies, and a variety of special procedure mandate holders. All of them are quite eager to make recommendations regardless of how actionable they are. A developing country is often inundated with too many reports and recommendations numbering in the hundreds if not thousands from these UN human rights agencies. Therefore, the main objectives of this study are to present a comprehensive examination of the effectiveness of the UN human rights mechanisms and the need for de-politicisation of the workings of these UN mechanisms and the judicialisation of human rights at the international level. In doing so, it casts a critical eye on the rationale and effectiveness of each of the major UN human rights mechanisms and argues that these mechanisms should be streamlined and consolidated and they should be supplemented and complemented, if not replaced, by an international judicial mechanism.

Reform of the UN system and judicialisation of human rights

In this book, the author argues that the time has come for a major shift in the approach to the protection of human rights in order to address the gap between idealism and reality. Propositions include de-politicisation of the workings of various UN human rights mechanisms and judicialisation of international human rights in order to hold governments and individuals in positions of public authority to account for violations of human rights. There is a need to establish a direct link between the promises made in the UN human rights instruments and the intended beneficiaries of such promises, i.e. the individuals. The individuals should have direct access to an international judicial body, albeit under narrowly defined conditions, so that the international system is not overwhelmed by a floodgate of cases and frivolous claims. The conditions could include the requirement of exhaustion of domestic remedy prior to resorting to the international mechanism. Since not many individuals would be able to afford such access, this could perhaps be accompanied by an international fund.[4]

4 See generally on the judicialisation of human rights or the establishment of an international court of human rights: Sean MacBride, 'The Strengthening of International

Unlike in international criminal law or international humanitarian law in which individuals can be held to account for violations of such laws under narrowly defined conditions, in international human rights law there is no provision for holding individuals to account for violations of human rights. Even when an individual submits a petition to a UN treaty body or to the Human Rights Council, all they can do is to ask States to explain the situation and make recommendations to rectify the law, policy or situation.

The UN treaty bodies or the Human Rights Council or any of the UN human rights institutions cannot hold individuals to account for human rights violations, nor can they provide any direct remedy to the individuals whose rights have been violated. In the absence of an international judicial mechanism, human rights have been politicised and States have often applied double standards. It has weakened the credibility of the international regime of human rights and UN human rights institutions and made it easier for many governments to undermine human rights and the work of UN human rights bodies. For instance, countries like North Korea, Syria and Iran have thus far got away with systematic, widespread and grave violations of human rights in spite of being a party to many human rights treaties. An Independent International Commission of Inquiry on the Syrian Arab Republic appointed by the UN published its report on 11 February 2016 stating that 'flagrant violations of human rights and international humanitarian law continue unabated, aggravated by blatant impunity'.[5] But no concrete action has yet been taken to hold the Government of Syria to account for such flagrant violation of human rights and humanitarian law. Thus, most of the human rights promises have remained empty promises for millions of people around the globe living under oppressive regimes.

When the Universal Declaration of Human Rights was adopted in 1948 by the UN it was only a 'soft law' instrument of programmatic character. The European Convention was the first major international instrument that converted the 'soft law' principles into 'hard law' principles, binding on all States parties to the Convention and created the European Court of Human Rights to enforce such rights. Both the European Convention and the Court have since

Machinery for the Protection of Human Rights', *Nobel Symposium VII: The International Protection of Human Rights*, Oslo, 25–27 September 1967; Julia Kozma, Manfred Nowak, and Martin Scheinin, *A World Court of Human Rights – Consolidated Draft Statute and Commentary* (Neuer Wissenschaftlicher Verlag, 2010); Manfred Nowak, 'It's Time for a World Court of Human Rights' in M. Cherif Bassiouni and William Schabas (eds), *New Challenges for the UN Human Rights Machinery: What Future for the UN Treaty Body and the Human Rights Council Procedures?* (Intersentia, 2012); T. Meron, *Human Rights Law-Making in the United Nations: A Critique of Instruments and Process* (Clarendon Press, 1986).

5 A/HRC/31/68, p.1 (Summary). See also the report entitled 'Out of sight, Out of Mind: Deaths in Detention in the Syrian Arab Republic', A/HRC/31/CRP.1 of 3 February 2016.

their inception expanded the scope of human rights and made it possible to hold European governments accountable for the violation of human rights. The European Convention was followed by the Inter-American Convention on Human Rights and the African Charter on Human and Peoples Rights. However, no such attempt to judicialise human rights at the international level has taken place.

After taking a rather softly-softly approach to protecting human rights for the past 70 or so years, it is time to address this unsatisfactory state of affairs in international human rights law, if human rights are to be taken seriously. It should be submitted that de-politicisation of the workings of the UN human rights mechanisms and the judicialisation of international human rights alone will not bring human rights violations to an end, but the possibility of being found guilty by an international human court through its binding decision as opposed to by a political body within the UN system will deter many people in government and positions of authority and provide better and concrete legal remedy to the victims of human rights violations.

Limitations of the International Criminal Court

Although there is in existence the International Criminal Court (ICC), its jurisdiction is limited to only very serious cases of violations of human rights and humanitarian law amounting to crimes against humanity. Further, the ICC is largely a State-centric or State-driven court. Individuals have no direct access to the Court. No matter how credible the evidence might be, non-official individuals cannot sue the individuals in government or in other positions of public authority for committing crimes against humanity before the ICC. All they can do is to appeal to the prosecutor of the ICC to investigate such crimes – and such appeals can often fall on deaf ears for a number of reasons, including political considerations.

The number of States parties to the Rome Statute which created the ICC is not impressive and the ICC can do very little about crimes against humanity in States which are not party to the Rome Statute. Of course, the Security Council of the UN has the powers to refer matters relating to crimes against humanity committed in States not party to the Rome Statute, but as we have seen in the cases of Syria and North Korea,[6] the Security Council is often crippled by the veto power wielded by its permanent members. What is more,

6 Following a report by a commission of inquiry led by Justice Michael Kirby (A/HRC/25/63) documenting the systematic, widespread and grave violations of human rights in North Korea, the General Assembly passed a resolution in December 2014 inviting the Security Council to consider referring the matter to the International Criminal Court. The resolution was passed by 116 votes to 20, with more than 50 abstentions. This resolution was adopted upon the recommendation of the Third Committee of 14 November 2014. A/C.3/69/L.28/Rev.1 of 14 November 2014.

since three of the five permanent members (China, Russia and the US) of the Council themselves are not party to the Rome Statute, any decision by them to refer matters concerning crimes against humanity in other States to the ICC will raise the question of legitimacy. After all, the Security Council itself is a political body often driven by political considerations rather than objectivity. Therefore, there is not really any meaningful international judicial mechanism to hold governments and individuals in positions of public authority to account for violations of human rights no matter how grave such violations are. This really is simply an unsatisfactory state of affairs in the twenty-first century.

Limitations of the powers of reason and persuasion

Much of the UN human rights agenda relies on the use of soft power and powers of reason and persuasion for its implementation. It is from the altar of morality that the UN calls on States to comply with their human rights obligations. This approach has its limitations. One reason for adopting a softly-softly approach in the implementation of human rights was that some of the international human rights treaties and the Universal Declaration of Human Rights itself spoke of the progressive realisation of human rights by States within available resources. Realising human rights was regarded as an incremental process. But that was 70 or so years ago. The world has moved on since then and the UN human rights mechanisms should now be expected to have a robust system of protecting human rights. It should be able to grant direct access to an international judicial body to individuals who are the actual victims of human rights violations, rather than making them rely on the cooperation of States, many of which are authoritarian themselves, to have their rights protected and enforced, or rely on political bodies such as the Security Council of the UN to have legal proceedings commenced against the perpetrators of gross violations of human rights.

De-politicising the workings of the UN system of human rights mechanisms

This book has two objectives: first, to provide a comprehensive and thorough analysis of the effectiveness of the current UN human rights mechanisms and, second, to offer a number of measures designed to reform these mechanisms by depoliticising their work and making them more adequately equipped to address the challenges and opportunities brought about by the emergence of a multi-polar world, and to hold governments and individuals in positions of public authority to account for violations of human rights. The proposals include empowering the Human Rights Council to impose diplomatic and economic sanctions; streamlining the work of human rights treaty bodies; revamping the special procedures system; and enhancing the status and powers of the UN High Commissioner for Human Rights. These proposals look to enable these bodies to hold governments and individuals in positions of public authority to account for violations of human rights. To this end, this book seeks to argue for the judicialisation of human rights at the international level under the auspices of the UN. Despite its imperfections, the UN is the only credible organisation that we have and our endeavour should be to reform it and perfect it rather than abandon it, condemning it as an inefficient or ineffective bureaucratic organisation not fit for purpose, or an organisation designed to promote and sustain Western political agendas, or an institution led by people not up to the challenges in hand. After all, the UN is a body where all States, regardless of what political system they adhere to, come together to debate and participate in its activities.

Although the UN appears divided on issues relating to countries and territories such as Syria, North Korea, Ukraine, Palestine and Iran, it is less divided than during the Cold War period. The deep division during the Cold War period was along ideological lines. That is not the case today. Neither the East–West nor the North–South divide is on ideological grounds. It is on economic or strategic grounds. Whatever division there is today among States is tactical and along the lines of national interests of individual countries. There are no major global agendas at this juncture that divide nations within the UN. Therefore, this is the most opportune period in history ever to overhaul the UN system of human rights.

Organisation of this study

This study will begin by analysing some of the key challenges and themes pertinent to the operation of the UN human rights project in the contemporary and globalised world. It traces the conceptual and international development of human rights and the rationale for the universality of human rights. In doing so, it explores the evolution of human rights from a national concept to an international one and presents an overview of the current regime of the international human rights system led by the UN. Next, will be an analysis of the strengths and weaknesses of each of the main human rights mechanisms, namely, the Human Rights Council, the Office of the High Commissioner for Human Rights, the Special Procedures, the General Assembly and other associated agencies, within the UN system created to implement and ensure compliance with international human rights law. Finally, this study will present arguments for reform of the UN system of human rights and suggest measures to this effect, including de-politicisation of the workings of the UN mechanisms and judicialisation of human rights at the international level.

Inspiration for this study

Much of this book is inspired by the present author's own firsthand experience both personally and professionally, and in particular working closely with the UN as part of its human rights machinery. The present author is of the view that as someone with personal exposure to the workings of some of the UN human rights agencies at both a practical and theoretical level, and personal experience on the ground spanning some 30 years in both the developed and developing world as a human rights activist and advocate, an academic, a barrister, a senior UN official, and an advisor to several governments,[7] he has a 'moral and professional obligation', to borrow the notion and words of Meron,[8] to conduct an analysis of the effectiveness of the UN human rights system and suggest proposals for reform. The measures recommended in this book are the results of such an endeavour.

7 The present author began his career in human rights as a human rights activist in the late 1970s; he was imprisoned twice in his native country, Nepal, for campaigning for human rights and democracy prior to the country becoming a democracy. He was the longest serving UN Special Rapporteur for human rights in Cambodia between 2009 and 2015. He also was between 2010 and 2015 a member of a high-level Advisory Group on Human Rights to the British Foreign Secretary. In addition, he has worked as a legal advisor to the Ministry of Foreign Affairs of Nepal and represented the country in the UN General Assembly and is currently Professor of International Law at the University of Leeds and a practising barrister in England.

8 T. Meron, *Human Rights Law-Making in the United Nations: A Critique of Instruments and Process* (Clarendon Press, 1986) 291.

1 The place of human rights in the contemporary and globalised world

1.1 Introduction

Prior to examining the effectiveness of the UN human rights mechanisms in making the application of human rights truly universal in the chapters that follow, this chapter aims to assess the place and role of human rights in the contemporary and globalised world, and the role of the UN in promoting and protecting human rights, and introduces by way of a general overview some of the key challenges and themes pertinent to the operation of the UN human rights project in the current century. These issues will then be explored in more detail in subsequent chapters.

1.2 Human rights as embracing modernity and redefining democracy

The modern concept of human rights, known largely as civil rights and liberties until the advent of the United Nations, has evolved over a long period of time as an integral part of the concept of the rule of law. It has redefined the concept of democracy itself in the sense that even after winning an election a government enjoying the support of the majority, even an overwhelming one, cannot breach the core rights of individuals, including minorities. Such matters are monitored not just politically, but also judicially. These checks and balances have the aim of preventing tyranny.

In most countries, except for a few Islamic States, mainly in the Gulf region, and certain parts of Africa, embracing human rights has meant embracing modernity in the approach to life and in social relations. Human rights are about advancing civilisation – enabling people of any background, origin, race, colour, nationality, creed and sexual orientation to lead a more dignified and sophisticated life. Just as society changes and humans become more refined in their lifestyle and thought processes, the greater the demand there will be for the respect and protection of human rights. The concept of 'human rights' is organic and will keep evolving with the evolution of society, with the recognition and addition of new rights, or the new or expanded definition of existing rights. The concept of human rights is by its very nature anti-feudalist and is based on individualistic foundations of Western political philosophy in general – and Anglo-Saxon notions of individual autonomy in particular – the latter being grounded on common law principles including fairness, justice, equity, and the individual right to property. The common law notion of the Anglo-Saxon world was that law emanated from the people, rather than being imposed from on high by government. In this respect, the law belongs to the people, not the State; rights are taken, not granted; the law should be there not to control the individual but to free and empower them, with the State being the servant, not the master, of the individual, oiling the wheels of human creativity and ingenuity whether through the upholding of rights, or providing security of property and inviolability of private contract. These common law principles have contributed to the evolution of human rights – the notion of personal freedom inherent in the individual later evolved into the concept of human rights.

Although a number of group rights, such as those relating to minority rights and the rights of indigenous peoples, are an integral part of the international human rights agenda, when we speak of human rights we are speaking, in essence, of the rights of individuals. This is because group rights stem from individual rights. Until the Middle Ages, when people spoke of a society, it was understood to be an association of families, rather than of individuals, where inequality within a family or society was accepted. It was the earlier natural rights or civil rights, and later the human rights agenda, which sought to address this inequality arising from domination by the patriarchal family structure, and the oppression of priests operating within an authoritarian church.[1] The human rights agenda sought to empower the individual first, and then women, by freeing them from the clutches of feudal and theocratic societal relations rooted in inequality. This agenda enabled the concept of the individual to gradually displace the family, tribe, clan or caste as the basis of social organisation. The concepts of both secularism and human rights were instrumental in advancing the interests of the individual, and undercut traditional inequalities of status. Thus, the concept of human rights is by its very nature and origin a progressive and emancipating concept.

Originally developed as a defence of individuals against the State, and inspired later by other developments such as the jurisprudence of the Nuremberg[2] and

1 For a review of the history and development of legal philosophy and history with reference to the move away from religious law during the enlightenment and beyond, see for example, M. Koskenniemi, *From Apology to Utopia: the structure of international legal argument* (Cambridge University Press, 1989; reprinted 2005), for a broader scope, see Stanley N. Katz, *The Oxford International Encyclopaedia of Legal History* (Oxford University Press, 2009).

2 Ann Tusa and John Tusa, *The Nuremberg Trials* (Skyhorse Publishing Company, Inc, 2010). On 11 December 1946, the UN General Assembly unanimously adopted Resolution (95) 1 'Affirming the Principles of International Law recognised by the Charter of the Nuremberg Tribunal' and the judgment of the Tribunal. One of the lasting effects of the Nuremberg Tribunal was the adoption of the Genocide Convention of 1948 by the UN.

Eichmann[3] trials, human rights have, over the decades, come to encompass a variety of socioeconomic and cultural issues, including entitlement to citizen welfare in the form of economic justice, and not only the equality and the empowerment of women but also of other groups of individuals and minorities.[4]

1.3 Human rights as a means of preventing revolutions

Unlike some political ideologies which often call for armed revolutions (such as certain manifestations of Communism), the human rights agenda seeks to bring about change in an orderly, gradual and peaceful manner. There is no need for revolution or outside intervention in countries where human rights are respected. In modern times, revolutions or foreign interventions have taken place in countries where the rulers have not respected human rights. Revolutions and foreign interventions in a given country do not guarantee a better quality of life for the citizens of the country concerned, or greater respect for human rights in the aftermath. Egypt and Libya are examples of countries where a revolution has brought about more misery for the people, as well as more chaos and further violations of human rights. In Egypt President el-Sisi has turned out to be a more brutal dictator than the former President Hosni Mubarak, who was overthrown by a revolution.[5] Libya, Iraq and Afghanistan are examples of countries where foreign interventions have led to situations which are worse than what had prevailed prior to such interventions. More people have been killed in these countries after foreign interventions than before.

Foreign intervention does not seem to work in a country which has not readied itself through a gradual process of embracing democratic culture and respect for human rights. An imposition of democratic values from outside does not seem to be the answer to the problems resulting from bad governance. It is clear that to be truly successful, the international human rights agenda requires States to make gradual and incremental progress in protecting and promoting human rights – the UN human rights mechanisms are one such group of processes that are designed to ensure that States do deliver on their promises to do so, and thus reinforce this sense of gradual, but nonetheless continuous, progress. This process removes the need for a revolution or foreign intervention. For instance, by implementing the recommendations of the author in the capacity of UN Special Rapporteur for Human Rights in Cambodia concerning the reform of State institutions, the country avoided further violence in the aftermath of the 2013 general election and embarked

3 David Cesarani, *Eichmann: His Life, Crimes and Legacy* (Vintage, 2005); Hannah Arendt, *Eichmann in Jerusalem : A Report on the Banality of Evil* (Penguin, 1994)

4 See generally, Aryeh Neier, *The International Human Rights Movement: A History* (Princeton University Press, 2012).

5 Roger Boyes, 'Goodbye, Arab Spring. We like dictators now', *The Times* (London), 3 December 2014, p. 34.

on the road to peaceful political transition. Those countries which have committed themselves to respecting human rights and reforming their system of governance have witnessed more stable governments, economic growth and a maturing democracy peacefully.

1.4 Human rights as part of social engineering

The UN human rights programme is part of an attempt at social engineering at an international level, designed to ensure that events like the ones experienced during the Second World War are not repeated. The atrocities committed by Nazi Germany against the Jewish population of Europe during the War provided the backdrop, and impetus, for the creation of the UN human rights agenda. This may be one reason why the UN human rights agenda was traditionally perceived as a programme designed to protect the rights of minorities.

1.5 Human rights as the mantra of the modern world

All major religions of the world including Buddhism, Christianity, Hinduism, and Islam, have in the past occupied huge swathes of land in order to spread and cement their influence. Big cathedrals, mosques, temples and pagodas were built to spread the *mantra* of the religious values of the day. Yet, the mantra of the modern human rights movement is not about building large physical structures, but about building ideas and temples of knowledge and enlightenment in the minds of the people. Thus, the human rights treaties, declarations, resolutions and the mechanisms created to promote, protect and implement these rights and freedoms arguably provide the structures of a modern day religion. Since the notions of the rule of law and human rights are evolving and are intertwined, the journey of both will long continue even if the UN or the international legal order in its present form were to cease. Both the rule of law and human rights are now associated with human civilisation and as long as humans continue to advance their civilisation, these concepts will continue to be part of that process, even if they may be known by different names in the future.

1.6 Human rights as a check on the excesses of capitalism

Since human rights are premised on individual freedom, autonomy of the individual and personal liberty, they work hand in hand with democracy and capitalism. However, neither democracy nor capitalism is free of its own pitfalls. Karl Marx built his Communist philosophy on the back of the pitfalls of capitalism, highlighting its exploitative character. He offered an alternative that numerous States subscribed to. However, that alternative did not succeed and Communism collapsed altogether, for all practical purposes, after being in existence for only approximately 70 years. Of course, countries like China, North Korea and Vietnam still profess to practise Communism. But having made a wholesale subscription to a capitalist economy it is doubtful whether China and Vietnam can still be regarded as Communist countries. They are holding on to the word 'communism' or 'socialism' in order to deny the people in the country the civil and political rights to which they are entitled under international human rights law and to prolong the monopoly of power for the Communist parties in these countries. North Korea is a different case altogether. It is an isolated totalitarian State, brutally governed by a regime which does not seem to believe in any international norms. Regardless of the situation in countries such as China, North Korea and Vietnam, it can be submitted that Communism is dead as a political philosophy and is no longer capable of mounting a challenge to the notion of human rights and personal liberty. What the human rights agenda has sought to do is to temper both capitalism and democracy, and offer a certain degree of protection to people from the excesses of capitalism and from the repercussions of the malfunctioning of democracy. In other words, the philosophy of human rights provides the middle path, or the third way, by which people are free to do what they wish to with their life, knowledge, ingenuity, or property; but in exercising their freedom they are to pay due respect to the rights of others. This due respect applies to State and non-State actors, to individuals and to communities, to corporations and other organisations and, not least of all, to governments.

1.7 Human rights as underpinning democracy

Democracy without human rights can become a mobcracy, kleptocracy, chumocracy, technocracy, theocracy and even an autocracy. Democracy is viewed primarily as a system based on periodic free and fair elections, albeit there is more to it than that. Yet, the governments thus elected can become dictatorships if the system of governance is not underpinned by human rights and the rule of law. Indeed, as stated candidly by Joseph Goebbels, Nazi Minister of Propaganda (1933–1945), 'This will always remain one of the best jokes of democracy that it gave its deadly enemies the means by which it was destroyed'.[6] Democracy can be demolished by popular will – the very ideal on which democracy is based – but not if it is underpinned by the principles of the rule of law and human rights. If democracy is not underpinned by human rights and the rule of law it cannot remain a democracy in the real sense of the term. Thus, human rights and democracy are concepts that are intertwined. The international human rights instruments and especially the 1966 International Covenant on Civil and Political Rights, contain provisions which

6 See in G.H. Fox and G Nolte, 'Intolerant Democracies', 36 *Harvard International Law Journal* (1995), p. 1.

in effect support the idea of a right to democratic governance without explicitly mentioning it.[7]

1.8 Supremacy of human rights

The advancement of the international human rights agenda has meant that neither parliament, nor a State's constitution, nor its highest domestic court is supreme any longer. The situation of human rights is a matter of legitimate concern of the international community, challenging as it does State sovereignty. Human rights and their norms reign supreme. No parliament can enact laws undermining those human rights that are internationally recognised. To say that even the most powerful of parliaments, such as the British parliament, is sovereign or supreme is a fiction. Nor can a domestic constitution curtail people's rights enshrined in international human rights instruments. Therefore, the claim of constitutional supremacy in countries such as the US is no longer valid. The same is the case with the claim of supremacy of the supreme courts of countries such as the US or India, which have the ability to repeal a law deemed to be inconsistent with the constitution of the country. Although it has been said that the law is what judges say is law, and that 'the Constitution means whatsoever a majority of the Supreme Court says it means',[8] such a majority is not free to interpret the provisions of a constitution in a manner that undermines the rights of people guaranteed in international law. While the rule of law is an abstract concept, human rights have sought to accord a concrete meaning to the ideas behind the supremacy of the rule of law or its empire.[9]

1.9 Human rights representing a silent revolution led by the UN

For our time, and for the purposes of this study, human rights are taken to be those that are enshrined in a number of international human rights treaties adopted under the auspices of the UN. Greater respect for human rights has spurred a revolution in societal ideas and values, and resulted in the transformation of many traditional societies. The international human rights agenda of our time has helped accelerate the globalisation of ideas, instilled

7 Thomas M. Franck, 'The Emerging Right to Democratic Governance', 86 (1) *American Journal of International Law* (January 1992), pp. 46–91.

8 Justice Antonin Scalia, 'Justice Scalia's Tribute and Thoughts on Human Rights' in Jo Carby-Hall (ed.), *Essays on Human Rights: A Celebration of the Life of Dr Janusz Kochanowski* (Ius et Lex Foundation, 2014) 24.

9 For more on the 'law's empire', see Ronald Dworkin, *Law's Empire* (Harvard University Press, 1988). See also, Patrick Macklem, *The Sovereignty of Human Rights* (Oxford University Press, 2015).

confidence in people to not only engage in cross border trade and investment, but also to develop a global outlook in carrying out business or simply travelling for pleasure. It has played an important role in encouraging people to build international supply and service networks, and in empowering individuals to demand fairness and justice of, and from, their governments. The confidence of the global citizenry that their basic rights, their universal rights, will be respected in those countries they wish to visit for business or pleasure, continues to develop. This confidence permits the global citizenry to benefit from the opportunities offered by global mobility brought about by advances in science, technology and affordable travel.

What has been witnessed since the establishment of the UN is nothing less than a silent revolution. Under UN leadership, human rights have become part of a global moral movement in which civil society organisations, human rights defenders, academics, journalists and ordinary men and women with an articulated sense of right and wrong, have actively participated. The march towards greater freedom is on, and the organisation that has led this march, and is capable of continuing to do so from the high altar of morality is the UN.

1.10 The UN human rights agenda as an agent of change

Since its establishment, the UN as a world organisation has come to be the standard bearer for human rights. The drive to promote human rights under the auspices of the UN has been regarded as an effort to establish a universal set of moral norms that transcend battles, ideological or otherwise, between States. The inception of the UN was focused on creating an international order based on the rule of law and stability. As Brownlie states, a major achievement of the draftsmen of the Charter of the UN was 'the emphasis of the provisions on the importance of social justice and human rights as the foundation of a stable international order'.[10]

Although the Charter of the UN nowhere explicitly provides authorisation for the political organs of the UN to assume monitoring powers, let alone enforcement powers, in the field of human rights, it does lay down certain values and principles of the international community, including respect for human rights. Under Articles 55 and 56 of the Charter, States pledge to work towards materialising these values and principles.[11] This was, and still is, the popular will of the peoples of the UN. States which join the UN are required to abide by this popular will of the international community. Consequently, no member State of the UN is allowed to invoke national laws or national practices against

10 Ian Brownlie and Guy S. Goodwin-Gill (eds), *Brownlie's Basic Documents on Human Rights* (6th edn, Oxford University Press, 2010), 1.

11 Charter of the United Nations and Statute of the International Court of Justice, 1945, available at https://treaties.un.org/doc/publication/ctc/uncharter.pdf (accessed 8 October 2014).

another State's obligations under the UN Charter.[12] Therefore, even if human rights can be time and country sensitive, no member of the UN can negate the human rights developed and recognised by the UN.

The UN values and the UN definition of human rights are the values of the international community of our time and are part of contemporary international law. These rights come in different forms – enshrined in the Universal Declaration of Human Rights, rights recognised as *jus cogens*, or simply rights recognised as general universal principles of international law. Regardless of whether they are conventional or customary, States which are members of the UN must accept those human rights as the minimum even if they are not party to any other international human rights treaties. Naturally, in the case of States that are party to other international human rights treaties, they have an additional obligation to abide by the human rights commitments they have made.[13]

On the basis of the universal acceptance of the universality of human rights[14] – or at least with regard to the rights embodied in the Universal Declaration of Human Rights – and the *erga omnes* character of basic human rights as stipulated in the judgment of the International Court of Justice in the *Barcelona Traction*[15] case, it can be held that the law is settled that States have a right to express their concern about the violations of basic human rights in another State. Consequently, human rights matters can no longer be regarded as 'off limits' to the international community as 'matters which are essentially within the domestic jurisdiction of any State'.[16]

In the long history of human civilisation, the UN has made a profound contribution to the development of human rights within a relatively short period of time, spanning a mere six or seven decades, and has created mechanisms to promote and protect human rights. More so in fact, than any thinkers, philosophers, nations and other institutions. As a former UN High Commissioner for Human Rights observed in a statement issued to mark Human Rights Day on 10 December 2010, 'Since the United Nations was established over 60 years ago, there have been dramatic advances in crafting and implementing a system of universal human rights – rights which are, under international law, applicable

12 This would be a cumulative impact of several provisions of the Charter of the UN such as Articles, 1, 55, 56 and more importantly Article 103. Ibid.

13 See for a list and text of such core international human rights treaties, Office of the United Nations High Commissioner for Human Rights, The Core International Human Rights Treaties, http://www.ohchr.org/EN/ProfessionalInterest/Pages/Core Instruments.aspx (accessed 30 June 2014).

14 Such universality is not necessarily accepted, see Chapter 2.

15 Case Concerning the Barcelona Traction, Light and Power Company, Limited (New Application: 1962) (Belgium *v.* Spain) International Court of Justice.

16 Article 2(7) of the Charter forbids other States from intervening in the internal affairs of another State.

to each and every one of us: old and young, male and female, rich and poor, whoever we are and wherever we are from'.[17] Human rights have come to be a *mantra* and a yardstick in measuring the standing of a nation in international relations. For this reason, in the event of the UN being disbanded, its contribution and impact will be longer lasting, much in the same way that the works of great philosophers, past and present, continue to shape and mould current ideas and developments.

The human rights monitoring and implementation role of the UN evolved slowly through the practice of member States. Moving away from the initial attitude of having no practical power to act in the late 1960s and early in the 1970s, the UN Commission on Human Rights began to undertake monitoring measures through the appointment of country- or territory-specific Special Rapporteurs at the behest of developing countries. The trend towards monitoring continued with the adoption of measures such as the 1235 and 1503 procedures.[18] With the creation of the position of the High Commissioner of Human Rights in 1993, the appointment of a number of country-specific and thematic special procedures mandate-holders and the establishment of the Human Rights Council, the UN has now very much become a monitoring body for the implementation of human rights. It is not only the UN human rights bodies that have embraced the role of speaking out on issues of human rights, the UN Secretary General has become accustomed to contributing vocally to such matters, albeit the active involvement in this respect has varied according to the personality of the Secretary General of the time. The Security Council too has been involved in various human rights issues in a number of cases and has engaged with the High Commissioner for Human Rights on such concerns.

1.11 Promoting a rules-based international society through human rights

In terms of the pronouncement of human rights, our generation is living in exciting times. Huge advances have been made since the establishment of the UN in 1945 in the creation of a rules-based international society. Consequently, the international law-making process has come to be regarded as a useful tool in articulating a code of conduct governing relations between States themselves, and between governments and the people within a State. Frenzied attempts have been made during the past 60–70 years to introduce at the international level certain norms and rules of behaviour in many areas of human activity.

17 Statement by the UN High Commissioner for Human Rights, Navi Pillay, of 10 December 2010, http://www.ohchr.org/EN/NewsEvents/Pages/DisplayNews.aspx?NewsID=10585&LangID=E (accessed 18 July 2014.

18 Economic and Social Council resolution 1503 (XLVIII) of 27 May 1970 as revised by resolution 2000/3 of 19 June 2000, and Economic and Social Council Resolution 1235 (XLII) of 6 June 1967.

As part of that endeavour, the notion of human rights came to be recognised as a part of international law, determining that the way citizens within a given State were treated by the government of that State did not remain an exclusively domestic matter, but was rather a matter for international regulation and concern.

The surrender of certain sovereign rights is an inevitable side effect of UN membership. Membership of the UN involves accepting the exception to the principle of non-interference in the internal affairs of States contained in Article 2(7) of the UN Charter.[19] For instance, the Vienna World Conference on Human Rights of 1993 unequivocally states that 'the promotion and protection of all human rights and fundamental freedoms . . . is a *legitimate concern* of the international community' (emphasis added).[20] The creation of the Human Rights Council in 2006 with explicit powers that it is entitled to exercise through, among other things, its new Universal Periodic Review (UPR) reporting and monitoring mechanism, implies that for the first time in the history of human rights all member States of the UN have become the subject of scrutiny of their internal human rights affairs, and that the scrutiny is primarily conducted by other member States means that not only is the UPR a periodic review, but it is also a 'peer' review.[21] Whilst this review is designed to be cooperative and to focus on capacity building rather than remonstration, the UN has effectively devised a mechanism that permits the circumvention of the principle of non-interference in the internal affairs of States, albeit allowing only for a 'soft' type of intervention. This is a huge milestone in the history of public international law and in the journey of international human rights.[22]

The Universal Declaration of Human Rights was ground-breaking; it pronounced for the first time in modern human history that all human beings were equal before the law. The Universal Periodic Review mechanism shares this 'ground-breaking' characteristic in its requirement that all UN member States are to have their domestic laws implementing State commitments and obligations to human rights scrutinised by all other member States, and civil society. Such commitments and obligations include those human rights treaties

19 Article 2(7) of the UN Charter 'Nothing contained in the present Charter shall authorize the United Nations to intervene in matters which are essentially within the domestic jurisdiction of any State or shall require the Members to submit such matters to settlement under the present Charter; but this principle shall not prejudice the application of enforcement measures under Chapter VII'.

20 Declaration and Programme of Action, World Conference on Human Rights, A/CONF/157/24, para 4.

21 Felice D. Gaer, 'A Voice Not an Echo: Universal Periodic Review and the UN Treaty Body System', *Human Rights Law Review* (2007) 7 (1), 109–39.

22 See GA Resolution 60/251 of 15 March 2006 forming the Human Rights Council and the subsequent GA Resolution putting flesh onto the bones of the UPR, GA Resolution, 5/1. Institution-building of the United Nations Human Rights Council, 18 June 2007.

that States have ratified, but also more broadly they encompass the provisions of the Universal Declaration, as this instrument does not have to be ratified, and is accepted and regarded as part of customary international law binding on all States, and other human rights ratified by the States concerned. Thus, both the 1948 Universal Declaration of Human Rights and the twenty-first century Universal Periodic Review mechanism are significant milestones in the evolution of human rights in modern times and in the acceptance of the universality of human rights.[23]

1.12 The corpus of international human rights law

Currently there are around 130 separate international human rights instruments (conventions, protocols, declarations, resolutions, codes of conduct and statements of standards and principles) which form the corpus of international human rights law. These instruments form the basis upon which the UN human rights institutions operate and which accord a universal character to human rights. It was the Vienna Declaration and Programme of Action of 1993 adopted by the World Conference on Human Rights[24] that settled the debate on whether civil and political rights should come before economic, social and cultural rights, or vice versa, by stating that 'All human rights are universal, indivisible and interdependent and interrelated. The international community must treat human rights globally in a fair and equitable manner, on the same footing, and with the same emphasis'.[25] When the heads of State and governments of the world met in New York in 2005 for a World Summit, also known as the Millennium +5 Summit, they accepted human rights as one of the three principal pillars (along with peace and security, and development)[26] of the whole UN system.

Thus, the debate today is less about whether the human rights values championed by the UN are universal, whether the international law of human

23 For critical appraisal of the UPR mechanism see, for example, Rosa Freedman, *The United Nations Human Rights Council: A Critique and Early Assessment* (Routledge, 2013); Dr Purna Sen (ed.) *Universal Periodic Review: Lessons, Hopes and Expectations* (Commonwealth Secretariat, 2011); Elvira Domínguez Redondo, 'The Universal Periodic Review of the UN Human Rights Council: An Assessment of the First Session' (2008) 7 (3) *Chinese Journal of International Law*, 721.

24 Adopted by the World Conference on Human Rights, 25 June 1993, http://www.ohchr.org/en/professionalinterest/pages/vienna.aspx (accessed 8 October, 2014).

25 Ibid., para 5.

26 The 2005 World Summit Outcome stated that human rights was one of the three major pillars of the UN system together with peace and security and development: 'We acknowledge that peace and security, development and human rights are the pillars of the United Nations system and the foundations for collective security and well-being. We recognize that development, peace and security and human rights are interlinked and mutually reinforcing.' A/RES/60/1 of 24 October, 2005, para 9.

rights is really law or whether human rights are part of international law, but more about what can be done to further strengthen and make effective the system of international protection of human rights, including through reports, legal remedies and monitoring within and around the UN system.[27] The debate as to whether international human rights are a means of pursuing a Western agenda carries less weight today, given that such rights have come to be regarded as universal by all UN member States through the Vienna Declaration of Human Rights of 1993 in general and the 2005 UN Outcome Document in particular. Although it is widely submitted that the concept of human rights is Western in its origin, non-Western developing countries have participated and played an important role in shaping and moulding the UN human rights agenda. As stated by Oberleitner:

> What once was utopian has indeed become practice: global human rights institutions meddle with national administrations; poke into ballot boxes, drag mass murderers before criminal tribulations, sponsor judicial education . . . and rummage around prison cells. They represent a practical, hard-nosed approach to spelling out community norms, shaping their content, realizing them on the ground and deterring deviant behaviour.[28]

Indeed, the author of the present study himself has carried out similar activities in his capacity as the UN Special Rapporteur for human rights in Cambodia.[29] As stated by the then UN High Commissioner for Human Rights, Navi Pillay, in her speech on 5 December 2013 marking the twentieth anniversary of the adoption of the 1993 Vienna Declaration of Human Rights and the creation of her own office:

> In the past two decades, much has been achieved, indeed more than people perhaps realize. The fundamentals for protecting and promoting human

27 Such institutions include not only those with a direct human rights mandate or responsibility such as the UN charter-based bodies, treaty bodies supported by the UN or created under the auspices of the UN, but also other UN agencies with a specific mandate to promote certain human rights such as the United Nations Educational, Scientific and Cultural Organisation (UNESCO). There are other UN agencies such as the United Nations Children's Fund (UNICEF) and the United Nations Development Programme (UNDP) which have mainstreamed human rights into their activities. Then there are other UN specialised agencies such as the International Labour Organisations (ILO), World Health Organisation (WHO) and the Food and Agricultural Organisation (FAO) which have a role in protecting and promoting certain social rights.

28 Gerd Oberleitner, *Global Human Rights Institutions: Between Remedy and Ritual* (Polity Press, 2007) 190.

29 See generally, Surya P. Subedi, 'The UN Human Rights Mandate in Cambodia: The Challenges of a Country in Transition and the Experience of the UN Special Rapporteur for the Country' (2011) 15(2) *The International Journal of Human Rights*, 247.

> rights are largely in place – the firm foundation of the Universal Declaration of Human Rights which is the basis for a strong and growing body of international human rights law and standards, as well as the institutions to interpret the laws, monitor compliance and apply these laws to new and emerging human rights issues.[30]

However, the main problem with the UN human rights system lies in the implementation of the standards set by the UN and recommendations made by various UN human rights institutions – these largely remain reactive rather than proactive.

1.13 The challenge of implementation and enforcement

The score card of the UN human rights mechanisms appears impressive in terms of promoting human rights, spreading the education of human rights and engaging States in a dialogue to promote human rights, but when it comes to holding governments to account for violations of human rights, the picture is rather dismal. As stated by the then High Commissioner, 'the key now is to implement those laws and standards to make enjoyment of human rights a reality on the ground.'[31] Indeed, in spite of the existence of a plethora of human rights instruments and institutions, there have been many setbacks and a number of tragic failures to prevent atrocities and safeguard human rights, 'in several instances where deplorable, large-scale violations of international human rights law were occurring, the international community was too slow, too divided, too short-sighted – or just plain inadequate in its response to the warnings of human rights defenders and the cries of victims.'[32]

In spite of the legally binding nature of human rights commitments and international human rights instruments, there is a tendency to regard the enforcement of UN human rights standards achieved via moral pressure rather than legal sanction. For instance, the then President Rajapaksa of Sri Lanka, whose government is under investigation by the UN for alleged violations of human rights in Sri Lanka during the bloody offensive against the Tamil Tigers, stated in his address at the Summit Conference of the South Association for Regional Cooperation in November 2014, that human rights were moral and ethical concepts which were being used as a political tool against his

30 'Human Rights: The Next 20 Years', Opening remarks by Navi Pillay at the Human Rights Day Event 2013, Geneva, 5 December 2013: Media Statement, OHCHR, Geneva.

31 'A 20-20 Human Rights Vision', statement by the UN High Commissioner for Human Rights Navy Pillay for Human Rights Day, 10 December 2013. Media Statement, OHCHR, Geneva, http://www.ohchr.org/EN/NewsEvents/Pages/DisplayNews.aspx?NewsID=14074 (accessed 9 October, 2014).

32 Ibid.

government. He went on to add that intervention in the internal affairs of States in the name of human rights was not permissible.[33] Although he was wrong in his assertions, his views provide an example of how people with authoritarian tendencies regard human rights. Human rights are perceived by the political elite in many countries as something to aspire to achieve rather than to be implemented here and now. The government of a country may ratify human rights treaties to obtain legitimacy of its rule, if it is autocratic, or for gaining popularity, or to signify to the world that the country is open for business, but not be serious about implementing them.[34]

This is partly because while the international human rights obligations and standards are global, their realisation and implementation must be at a local level. Human rights treaties set the international human rights standards, but not the standards for their enforcement. It is through national law and with the help of the national judiciary that UN member States that are party to various international human rights treaties are supposed to make human rights a reality for their citizens. This is what the human rights treaties stipulate. Under the concept of universal jurisdiction and particularly after the adoption of the UN Convention against Torture in 1984, States are not only entitled to but are obliged to prosecute people suspected of committing certain violations of human rights, including war crimes and crimes against humanity, even if the crime was committed in another State(s). A number of States have exercised universal jurisdiction to bring people to justice even when the crime was committed in another State(s), especially when the people suspected of

33 'Human Rights should be recognized by all as a moral and ethical concept rather than as a political tool. Sadly, however, we are witnessing motivated political agendas being thrust by extra regional entities, on some countries in our region, in the guise of human rights. Intervention in such form is being attempted with scant regard to the structures, and cultural traditions of societies, and ground realities. While SAARC practice has been to abstain from involvement in bilateral issues of a political nature, we must resist external manipulations. It would be morally in keeping with the SAARC spirit, to join forces against external threats on Member States.' Statement by Mahinda Rajapaksa, President Democratic Socialist Republic of Sri Lanka at the eighteenth SAARC Summit (South Asian Association for Regional Cooperation), 26 November 2014. Available at http://www.srilanka.no/press-release/media-releases/257-statement-by-his-excellency-mahinda-rajapaksa.html (accessed on 7 December, 2014).

34 There have been numerous studies and debates as to why States engage with the international human rights project and why they ratify human rights treaties, and the impact, if any, upon State action as a result – see for example, Ryan Goodman & Derek Jinks, 'Measuring the Effects of Human Rights Treaties' (2003) 14(1) *European Journal of International Law*, 171; Oona Hathaway, 'Why do countries commit to human rights treaties?' (2007) 51(4) *Journal of Conflict Resolution*, 588; Linda Camp Keith, 'The United Nations International Covenant on Civil and Political Rights: Does It Make a Difference in Human Rights Behavior?' (1999) 36 *J. Peace Res.* 95; Harold Hongju Koh, 'Why Do Nations Obey International Law' (1996–97) 106(8) *Yale Law Journal* 2599; Beth A. Simmons, *Mobilizing for Human Rights: International Law in Domestic Politics* (Cambridge University Press, 2009).

committing such crimes are found to be present in their territory. For instance, a French court jailed in March 2014 a former Rwandan spy chief, Pascal Simbikangwa, for 25 years in respect of the 1994 genocide in Rwanda.[35]

The UN treaty bodies created are not designed to provide legal remedy against human rights violations, but rather to monitor compliance and suggest correctional measures. Their recommendations are intended to encourage States to act, for example, by amending existing law and policy, or by introducing new laws and guidance, rather than to provide remedy for individual victims of human rights violations. The responsibility to provide appropriate legal remedy to victims of human rights violations rests with the national judiciary. However, since domestic courts in many countries with dictatorial or autocratic or authoritarian system of governance are unable to provide protection of human rights, the UN human rights institutions were created as a supplementary or complementary mechanism to monitor and ensure compliance with human rights obligations of States.

However, establishment of common standards for the protection of human rights and even a base for the protection of such standards in the form of various UN mechanisms has not protected millions of people from human rights abuses, be that in Syria or Iran, or Libya under Muammar Gaddafi, or Egypt under Hosni Mubarak or the Soviet Union under Communism. The UN human rights machinery has not been able to intervene effectively in internal affairs of States which abuse the rights of their citizens. Therefore, for these millions of people the 'promise' of 1948 made through the Universal Declaration of Human Rights and other human rights treaties remains unfulfilled. This is one reason why some eminent scholars of international law, such as Hersch Lauterpacht, criticised the Universal Declaration at the time because its status as a declaration meant it was non-binding and there was no provision for a system of enforcement.[36] As Boyle states, 'How might the human rights commitments made by States be translated into protection for individuals in practice? Sixty years after the [Universal] Declaration was proclaimed it remains the central challenge.'[37] It indeed is more so now than ever before because of the move towards an increasingly diverse, diffused, fragmented and decentralised system of international governance in general and the UN human rights system in particular.

35 'Rwanda ex-spy chief Pascal Simbikangwa jailed in France', BBC News (Africa, 14 March 2014) http://www.bbc.co.uk/news/world-africa-26587816 (accessed 9 October 2014).

36 H. Lauterpacht, *International Law and Human Rights* (Praeger, 1950), p. 575, as cited in Martti Koskenniemi, *The Politics of International Law* (Hart Publishing, 2011), p. 155.

37 Kevin Boyle, 'Introduction' in Kevin Boyle (ed.), *New Institutions for Human Rights Protection* (Oxford University Press, 2009), p. 1.

1.14 Human rights as the third pillar of the UN

Despite regarding human rights as one of the three major pillars of the UN system along with peace and security, and development, the institutional structure of the Charter of the UN itself does not introduce any institutions entrusted with the task of protecting and promoting human rights into the structure of principal organs of this world organisation. The first pillar, that is, peace and security, suffers from having too many 'leaders' such as the Secretary General and the Security Council and especially the permanent members of the Council. The second pillar, development, has one clear leader in the form of the head of the United Nations Development Programme (UNDP) with offices around the globe. Yet human rights, the third pillar, has no single leader. The public perception is that the UN High Commissioner for Human Rights is the UN human rights leader, but in reality this is not necessarily so given the limitations of this position. Indeed, the position is arguably politically inferior within the UN hierarchy, operating as it does under the supervision of the Secretary General (and experience has shown that some Secretary Generals are more 'secretary' than 'General').

Furthermore, the power and responsibility to promote and protect human rights is distributed and diffused amongst a myriad of bodies such as the human rights treaty bodies, the High Commissioner for Human Rights, the Human Rights Council and the Special Procedures, all of which work independently of each other. What is more, none of these bodies have the status enjoyed by the Security Council. Although, as we will see in various chapters of this study, the principal organs of the UN, including the Security Council, the General Assembly, the Economic and Social Council and the Secretary General have played an important role in the promotion and protection of human rights, the primary task of promoting and protecting human rights has been entrusted mainly to second tier institutions, that is, the subsidiary bodies of the principal organs of the UN. In this respect, the lack of institutional coherence and strength is therefore quite worrying.

It was the UN Commission on Human Rights, a subsidiary organ of the Economic and Social Council, which was the flagship UN institution for the promotion and protection of human rights between 1947 and 2006. When the decision was taken to establish a new Human Rights Council to replace the Commission on Human Rights as part of the reform programme of the UN, rather than establish the Human Rights Council as a stand-alone UN institution, it was established as a subsidiary agency of the General Assembly. This was despite the proposal of the then UN Secretary General Kofi Annan in his report entitled, *In Larger Freedom*, published in 2005, to accord the three principal fields of activities of the UN, namely, peace and security, development, and human rights, equal status in the organisation's architecture.[38]

38 UN GA A/59/2005, http://www.un.org/en/ga/search/view_doc.asp?symbol=A/59/2005 (accessed 8 October, 2014).

The Human Rights Council was not elevated to the status of the Security Council or to that of the Economic, Social and Cultural Council. Nor was an international court of human rights created to protect human rights by providing effective remedy to the victims of human rights. It was on the whole, very much a missed opportunity.

1.15 UN human rights mechanisms and their effectiveness

The setting of legal standards in the field of human rights and the establishment of mechanisms to monitor the implementation of those standards has been the primary means for pursuing the human rights objectives of the UN. Of the mechanisms put in place to monitor implementation of human rights standards are the UN Charter bodies such as the Human Rights Council, the Office of the High Commissioner for Human Rights, and the Special Procedures, as well as the several treaty bodies established under various human rights treaties.[39] More than 20 years have passed since the adoption of the Vienna Declaration and Programme of Action held under the auspices of the UN.[40] However, in spite of their best efforts, critics argue that these treaty or political bodies have not been effective in preventing human rights violations and in bringing human rights violators to account. An example offered to this effect is the non-compliance by States with the obligations flowing from the human rights treaties that they have ratified. This is because much of the UN system of human rights protection is based on periodic reporting under various human rights treaties, but many of the States parties to such treaties have not lived up to the relevant obligations; they have not submitted timely periodic reports or have submitted reports designed to cover up the real situation.

If mechanisms such as the periodic reporting of the record of promoting and protecting human rights by States and their review by various UN human rights bodies were more robust, the world would be a much better place for all to live in and people would not have to risk their lives to fight for their rights in countries such as Egypt, Tunisia, Libya, Syria and many other States as late as in 2014. It is important to bear in mind that the events of 2014 occurred nearly 70 years after the adoption of the Universal Declaration of Human Rights in 1948 and nearly 50 years after the adoption of the 1966 Covenants on Civil and Political Rights and Economic, Social and Cultural Rights. If the UN system was working effectively, the dictatorships in these countries would not have survived for so long.

The recent crises around the globe, whether in Syria or Iran or North Korea, have brought under the spotlight nearly 70 years of standard setting and

39 These matters are considered in more detail in subsequent Chapters. See for example, Chapters 3, 4 and 7.

40 Adopted by the World Conference on Human Rights, 25 June 1993.

institution building to ensure compliance of human rights obligations of States. Both the UN and the rule of international law, including the international human rights system, are in crisis. Their effectiveness is being questioned.[41] Such criticism escalated when the UN was unable to protect the people of Syria in spite of reports by various UN human rights agencies and fact finding missions[42] blaming the Assad regime for massive violations of human rights.[43] The UN Human Rights Council and the General Assembly passed several resolutions against the Assad regime, the UN High Commissioner for Human Rights pointed out a series of violations of human rights in several of her reports,[44] the heads of five major UN agencies issued a rare joint appeal to the international community in April 2013 to do much more to end 'cruelty and carnage' in Syria,[45] but in the end very little, if any, tangible progress has been made.

The crisis in Syria brings the inadequacies of the UN system of human rights and humanitarian law into sharp relief, arguably more than ever before. Another example is the report of the Commission of Inquiry on Human Rights in the Democratic People's Republic of Korea which was headed by Justice Michael Kirby, a distinguished jurist of Australia.[46] After submitting a credible and well-documented report on the violations of human rights in North Korea, the

41 See for example, the findings of the UN Human Rights Council Commission of Inquiry reports, statements and oral updates, http://www.ohchr.org/EN/HRBodies/HRC/IICISyria/Pages/IndependentInternationalCommission.aspx (accessed 01 July 2014).

42 See for example, 'G20: No Excuse for Inaction on Syria: Provide Urgent Aid, Halt Flow of Arms to Abusive Forces, Support ICC Referral', Human Rights Watch, 5 September 2013, http://www.hrw.org/news/2013/09/05/g20-no-excuse-inaction-syria. Melissa Eddy and Chris Cottrell, 'Human Rights Watch Criticizes Inaction on Syria' *New York Times*, 21 January 2014, http://www.nytimes.com/2014/01/22/world/middleeast/rights-group-assails-inaction-on-syria.html?_r=0; 'Syria's forgotten crisis: Enforced disappearances rife amid UN inaction', Amnesty International, 29 August 2014 (all accessed 9 October 2014).

43 However, action by the international community has been beset by difficulty; the UN Supervision Mission in Syria established by Security Council resolution 2043, 21 April 2012, and put in place to oversee the cessation of violence and monitor the Joint Special Envoy's six-point plan to end the conflict in Syria was unable to fulfil its monitoring mandate due to intensified armed violence in the region, see http://www.un.org/en/peacekeeping/missions/unsmis/ (accessed 01 July 2014).

44 See for instance, the Opening Statement of the UN High Commissioner at the 23rd session of the Human Rights Council on 27 May 2013 (Media Statement, OHCHR, Geneva, 27 May 2013) and her Opening Statement on the Urgent Debate on Syria at the 23rd session of the Council on 29 May 2013 (Media Statement, OHCHR, Geneva, 29 May 2013).

45 'Syria crisis: UN issues rare joint appeal for action', BBC News: Middle East, 16 April 2013, http://www.bbc.co.uk/news/world-middle-east-22163884 (accessed on 16 April 2013).

46 A/HRC/25/63 of 7 February 2014.

Human Rights Council was effectively prevented from taking any action. Not only North Korea, but China too rejected the report stating that it had not supported the establishment of the Commission in the first place and that this position remained unchanged.[47] With this opposition from China, the prospect of referring the violations of human rights and humanitarian law in North Korea to the International Criminal Court via the UN Security Council remained very slim, especially so because of China's veto power in the Security Council. Nonetheless, the General Assembly took up the matter and passed a resolution in December 2014 calling on the Security Council to refer the matter to the International Criminal Court, putting more pressure on reluctant States such as China and Russia.[48]

The architecture of the ICC itself is not satisfactory enough to deal with the challenges of the twenty-first century multi-polar world. Its jurisdiction is limited to only very serious cases of violations of human rights and humanitarian law amounting to crimes against humanity; individuals have no direct access to it and there is very little it can do about crimes against humanity in States which are not a party to the Rome Statute – and the number of such States is large. Of course, the Security Council of the UN has the power to refer matters relating to crimes against humanity committed in States not party to the Rome Statute, but the Council itself is often crippled by the veto power wielded by its permanent members.

1.16 The impact on the UN human rights agenda by the rise of multi-polarism

Another challenge in the hands of the UN human rights machinery is posed by multi-polarism in international relations. Much of the international system in general, and the UN human rights system in particular, was conceived,

47 A copy of the letter from the Chinese Permanent Mission to the UN in Geneva to Justice Michael Kirby is on file with the present author.

48 The resolution was passed by 116 votes to 20, with more than 50 abstentions. This resolution was adopted upon the recommendation of the Third Committee of 14 November 2014. A/C.3/69/L.28/Rev.1 of 14 November 2014. Following a report by a commission of inquiry led by Justice Michael Kirby (A/HRC/25/63) documenting the systematic, widespread and grave violations of human rights in North Korea, the General Assembly decided to 'submit the report of the commission of inquiry to the Security Council, and encourages the Council to consider the relevant conclusions and recommendations of the commission and take appropriate action to ensure accountability, including through consideration of referral of the situation in the Democratic People's Republic of Korea to the International Criminal Court and consideration of the scope for effective targeted sanctions against those who appear to be most responsible for acts that the commission has said may constitute crimes against humanity'. See also 'UN General Assembly seeks North Korea ICC charges' BBC News: Asia, http://www.bbc.co.uk/news/world-asia-30540379 (accessed on 19 December 2014).

designed and developed in the political context of the bi-polar political world of the Cold War in the twentieth century. The UN human rights system is very much the result of compromise between those countries placing a great deal of emphasis on an individual liberty-based theory of reserved natural rights of the individual, among others, and those Communist States adhering to the idea that sovereignty of the State is pre-eminent and there can be no international limitation on this sovereignty, or that international interference in any pretext in the internal affairs of the State cannot be accepted. The pre-eminence of the State was the idea that was advanced in the run up to the 1966 International Covenant on Civil and Political Rights (ICCPR) and International Covenant on Economic and Social Rights (ICESCR) and especially the ICCPR's Option Protocol. The rights enunciated and especially the monitoring mechanisms pursuant to the 1966 Covenants were influenced by the ideological and political divisions of the world at the time. For instance, the Covenants omitted certain rights such as the right to property, heralded as a cardinal right of any individual in the free-market world.

As we now live in an increasingly multi-polar world marked by the rise of emerging powers such as BRICS[49] – Brazil, Russia, India, China and South Africa – with different political systems and a varying degree of commitment to human rights – questions have arisen as to whether the UN system of protecting human rights is fit for the purposes of this new era. With the rise of new powers, 'the geometry of global power is becoming more distributed and diffuse',[50] as we have seen in the major international fora such as the UN General Assembly, the Human Rights Council, and the G20. While the Arab Spring or Arab Awakening that began in 2011 gave hope to millions of people across the Arab world, the crises in countries such as Syria, and the inability of the UN to protect the people from human rights abuses, have exposed the weaknesses of the UN system of human rights. The exercise of the veto power by Russia in the Security Council against resolutions designed to bring to account people suspected of committing serious crimes against humanity and human rights, demonstrated that a single State or a small minority of States can hold the majority to hostage and frustrate the object and purpose of the UN and the whole international human rights agenda.

The UN human rights agenda has largely been allowed to operate as a western dominated endeavour until relatively recently. Before now, much of the Communist world was on the defensive and not willing to stake a claim for leadership in this area on the international stage. Even leading democratic developing countries such as India and Brazil did not demonstrate their

49 In early 2014, the BBC ran a series of programmes focusing on the emerging economic powers of the 'MINT' countries, Mexico, Indonesia, Nigeria and Turkey, http://www.bbc.co.uk/news/magazine-25548060 accessed 1 July, 2014.

50 Hillary Clinton, 'The Great Power Shift', *New Statesman* (London), 16 July 2012, p. 28.

enthusiasm for the international human rights agenda because they too were somewhat inhibited by the situation of human rights in their own countries. Therefore, whether it was setting the international human rights standards or creating UN human rights agencies or making senior level appointments to such bodies, it was mainly western countries that dictated the agenda. This may not necessarily remain the case in the future. The growth in the domestic strength of countries which now play a significant role on the economic world stage has had a corresponding impact on the demands of the populations of those States for their countries to be democratic leaders and to play a key role in other international fora, including human rights.

1.17 Pitfalls of the middle path based on dialogue and cooperation

The Charter of the UN speaks of the *promotion* rather than the *protection* of human rights and other international human rights instruments speak of *cooperation* rather than *enforcement* of international human rights standards. Accordingly, the UN human rights system is premised upon cooperation as the means to advance the human rights agenda. This is all very well, but when real, substantive cooperation is lacking and international condemnation and pressure do not succeed, atrocities continue. The UN human rights institutions lack enforcement powers. The flagship UN human rights body, the Human Rights Council, is a political body. So is the position of the UN High Commissioner for Human Rights. In such a situation the credibility of the UN system and the international human rights agenda depends on either military intervention, whether under Chapter VII of the UN Charter, or under the auspices of humanitarian intervention.

The emerging rhetoric in this area is focused on action pursuant to the Responsibility to Protect, known as 'R2P', in situations where the government is engaged in committing atrocities against its own people (intervention in both Kosovo and Libya are examples), or through legal intervention by either national courts or international or regional criminal or human rights courts or tribunals such as the Yugoslavia Tribunal. It is accepted that there is a responsibility on the part of the international community to protect the citizens of such States.[51] Between these two methods of intervention (military and

51 See generally, Aidan Heir, *The Responsibility to Protect: Rhetoric, Reality, and the Future of Humanitarian Intervention* (Palgrave Macmillan, 2012); Alex J. Bellamy, *Global Politics and the Responsibility to Protect: from Words to Deeds* (Routledge, 2011); Anne Orford, *International Authority and the Responsibility to Protect* (Cambridge University Press, 2011); James Pattison, *Humanitarian Intervention and the Responsibility to Protect: Who Should Intervene?* (Oxford University Press, 2010); Jared Genser and Irwin Cotler, *The Responsibility to Protect: the Promise of Stopping Mass Atrocities in our Time* (Oxford University Press, 2012).

humanitarian) is the political or quasi-judicial method of intervention by the UN human rights mechanisms mainly in the form of preventative or correctional measures.

Military invention is always a last resort, controversial and dependant on the decisions of the Security Council, including unanimity among the P5.[52] Yet, intervention that seeks to hold individuals legally to account via the ICC or *ad hoc* tribunals operates mainly in the aftermath of the acts and atrocities concerned – that is, when people have already been murdered, maimed, tortured, raped, and subjected to other atrocities. Neither military nor humanitarian intervention has been perceived to be the role of the UN human rights mechanisms – it was between the idealists and realists that a 'middle-way' approach was adopted, based upon State cooperation to implement or enforce human rights. The utility of this middle-way approach itself has come under question in the wake of the crisis in Syria and defiance by States such as Iran and North Korea and the politicisation of the Security Council. Consequently, many people, including scholars, diplomats, and UN officials, have endeavoured to find a way to bridge the gap between the guarantee of rights in law and the guarantee of rights in reality and this study is an attempt to add to that discourse.

1.18 The legal status of human rights and the need for their judicialisation

A topical question debated in law schools around the globe as late as the 1960s and 1970s used to be whether international law was really law. But now the debate has moved on and whilst this question remains a live issue to some extent, it demands less time and attention. Now the questions debated are whether international law works, focusing on the effectiveness of international institutions created to enforce and implement this body of law. This is especially so regarding international human rights law and various UN human rights institutions. Very much like the Civil Rights Act of the US enacted in 1964, the rights proclaimed in international human rights law instruments, including the Universal Declaration of Human Rights, were premised on voluntary compliance by States.

The Charter of the UN does not explicitly provide for monitoring powers for the organisation in the field of human rights. It was expected that the community of 'civilised nations' led largely by 'gentlemen' would honour their own commitments through national legislative, administrative and judicial measures to implement the provisions of these instruments. That is one reason why these instruments, concluded in the aftermath of the Second World War and during the Cold War, did not include provisions for enforcement. Rather,

52 The permanent five members of the UN Security Council, China, France, Russia, United Kingdom, and United States of America.

they relied upon soft law or soft power and diplomatic mechanisms designed to remind States of their obligations, to achieve the desired objectives through cooperation and dialogue. This was so with the UN human rights treaty bodies and the UN Commission on Human Rights.

There was little change in this situation following the end of the Cold War and the collapse of Communism in Europe. The Office of the UN High Commissioner for Human Rights created in the immediate aftermath of the Cold War was not granted any real legal powers; only soft power was entrusted to the High Commissioner. The events of 9/11 shocked the world and prompted the UN Secretary General into action with an ambitious agenda for reform of the UN in general and its human rights mechanisms in particular.[53] The reform agenda resulted in the creation of the Human Rights Council to replace the Commission on Human Rights. Opinion on the merit of this change remains divided; the Human Rights Council is also lacking in any real legal powers for the protection of human rights. Similar to other UN human rights mechanisms and the beleaguered Commission on Human Rights that it replaced, the Council remains a largely political body reliant upon soft power.

The foundations of the international human rights agenda and the effectiveness of the UN human rights institutions were shaken once again by the events in the Arab World during the 'Arab Spring' – the massive violations of human rights in Syria and inaction of the UN Security Council and other UN bodies to come to the rescue of those people subjected to gross human rights violations raised global concern. During the present author's visit to Geneva to address the Human Rights Council in September 2014 a prominent ambassador from a developed country asked him the following question: why, in spite of the efforts made by the UN and its human rights agencies over the past 70 or so years, was the world regressing and witnessing the rise of brutal terrorist organisations such as the Islamic State of Iraq and the Levant (ISIL)[54] in the Islamic world? This is a pertinent question, to which a simple answer is not readily available, but much discussion abounds that failure on the part of the UN and its human rights mechanisms and other institutions has allowed extremist and fanatic groups such as those like and supporting ISIL to have come into existence. This failure is tied up alongside failed foreign policies and action, for example as can be seen in the current situations, in Iraq, Afghanistan and Syria, and the funding of extremist or terrorist organisations allegedly by States that are purportedly Western allies.

Indeed, it was the inaction of the Security Council and the use of the veto power against resolutions designed to take concrete and decisive action in the

53 In particular, see for example, the report produced by the then Secretary General of the UN, Kofi Annan, 'In larger freedom: towards development, human rights and security for all', 21 March 2005, UN GA A/59/2005, http://www.un.org/en/ga/search/view_doc.asp?symbol=A/59/2005 (accessed 8 October 2014).

54 Also referred to as IS or ISIS or Daesh.

face of the atrocities in countries such as Syria that is partly responsible for it. Had the autocratic and corrupt leaders in countries such as Afghanistan, Egypt, Iraq, Saudi Arabia, and Syria been held to account for the violations of human rights in their countries and had the Arab Spring succeeded it would have been difficult for the extremist groups such as ISIL to entice young Muslims to join them from these and other countries. When many of the youth in the Islamic world saw the Arab Spring failing and the UN unable to take any concrete and decisive action in support of those fighting for democracy and human rights they perhaps saw ISIL as an attractive alternative.[55] It is autocracy, dictatorship, corruption and bad governance in the Middle East and North Africa that has to take some responsibility for the rise of the IS supporters.

Another stark example is North Korea whose leaders have, thus far, got away with systematic, widespread and grave violations of human rights in spite of being a party to many human rights treaties including the 1966 Covenant on Civil and Political Rights. Report after report of UN Special Rapporteurs for the country and of the UN treaty bodies such as the Human Rights Committee and the recommendations therein have been ignored by the leaders of this totalitarian State as they know that these UN mechanisms are largely political toothless entities and there is no meaningful sanction for such violations. It is the failure of the UN system to judicialise human rights and hold the people in government and positions of public authority that is partly responsible for such an unsatisfactory situation whether it is in North Korea, Syria, Iran, Iraq, Saudi Arabia, China, Cambodia, Belarus, Egypt and so on and so forth.

1.19 Conclusions

The phrase 'human rights' conjures up political imagery in the minds of many people around the globe, even though human rights are now legal rights in international law and in the legal and constitutional systems of a large number of countries with democratic or semi-democratic systems of governance. The political nature of the mechanisms within the UN system designed to promote and protect human rights, reinforces the political imagery associated with the phrase 'human rights'. Further, since many human rights, such as certain economic, social and cultural rights, are aspirational or simply viewed as programmatic, to be implemented within the means of a government, political leaders in many countries with authoritarian or autocratic tendencies tend to regard human rights as political rather than legal. The thrust of the analysis and arguments presented in this study is that while there is universal acceptance

55 For example, see media coverage considering the appeal to women and girls to join jihad, Harriet Sherwood and others, 'Schoolgirl jihadis: the female Islamists leaving home to join Isis fighters' *Guardian* (London, 29 September 2014) http://www.theguardian.com/world/2014/sep/29/schoolgirl-jihadis-female-islamists-leaving-home-join-isis-iraq-syria (accessed 8 October 2014).

of human rights, their implementation is not universal. Most States do not take periodic reporting under various human rights treaties seriously, and national institutions and mechanisms for the protection of human rights themselves are weak, politicised and often ignored by the people in power. Of course, the judiciary is there in different countries and many of them are independent and effective in providing remedy against human rights violations, but the judiciary in many other countries can be frustratingly slow, corrupt, full of political cronies, and lacking in resources to enable them to dispense speedy, effective and impartial justice. Accordingly, the time has come for a major shift in the approach to the protection of human rights in order to address the gap between idealism and reality and to hold governments and individuals in positions of public authority to account for violations of human rights. This new approach would aid in adding clarity to the definition and meaning of human rights.

In the absence of an international supreme court or an international judicial body to flesh out the nature, meaning and scope of human rights there is a lack of consensus on the meaning and scope of human rights. For instance, what is meant by the freedom of religion? Whose definition of freedom of religion should be accepted? It is a hotly contested freedom not only in many Islamic countries but also in predominantly Hindu States such as Nepal or predominantly Buddhist States such as Myanmar (or Burma). There has been an attempt made by treaty bodies and various UN Special Rapporteurs to flesh out the nature, meaning and scope of various rights included in human rights treaties, but such bodies are not judicial, their pronouncements are not legally binding and are often contested and ignored by States. Therefore, there is a huge role and scope for an international judicial mechanism to advance and add credibility to the provisions in international human rights instruments. Human rights should no longer be left solely in the hands of political institutions within the UN system if the world is serious about protecting human rights in the multi-polar world of the twenty-first century. To conclude, human rights are indeed political, but the mechanisms for compliance with them do not have to be and should not be political. Human rights become worthless in many countries unless they can be enforced by a court of law, whether national or international.

2 The conceptual and international development of human rights

2.1 Introduction

We are often told that human rights are universal and the UN human rights mechanism was created with a view to ensuring that each and every human being is able to enjoy such rights. Yet, the question remains as to how genuinely universal human rights are and what is the basis for the claim of their universality? Are all of them justiciable? If not, do they still meet the test of universality? If rights are universal are they applied universally? Is there an effective mechanism to ensure universal compliance of universal human rights? If not, is the notion of universality of human rights an empty phrase? Do human rights represent the values of non-Western civilisations too, for them to be regarded as universally accepted norms? If not, are human rights universally accepted by States?

If human rights are universal are they of *erga omnes* character? If so, is there an obligation on the part of all States, acting individually and collectively, to ensure that they are respected and enforced universally? Do States such as Qatar, Kuwait and Saudi Arabia, whose economy is built and supported largely by migrant workers, have an obligation to extend and respect the universal rights of migrants? These are the questions this chapter aims to examine before proceeding to address the effectiveness of the UN human rights bodies in promoting compliance with such 'universal' rights. In doing so, this chapter will analyse the origins and evolution of international human rights law, the basis for the claim of universality of human rights and the framework and status of this body of law that is in existence today.

2.2 The concept of human rights in antiquity

The history of human rights, known as civil rights and liberties or natural rights prior to the advent of the modern era of human rights, can be said to be as old as the history of human civilisation itself. The concept of human rights was born out of an ordinary human sense of right and wrong and out of a desire to uphold what was right. The notions of the rule of law and the rights and liberties of individuals evolved together as integral parts of the same process. The idea behind both of these notions was to give to a man what was due to him and not to take away from him what was earned by him. The genesis of human rights was this sense of morality and the idea of right and wrong. Such precepts for human society were not coined as 'human rights' but existed in different forms, for example, the Hindu concept of *dharma* requires every human being to do what they are supposed to do in order to live an orderly and purposeful life in a civilised society.

One can trace the evolution of the modern concept of human rights and the rule of law to ancient documents and deeds such as the Code of Hammurabi (c.1792–50 BC), which is said to be the oldest surviving text establishing the basic tenets of the rule of law, the dicta of Cyrus the Great, King of Persia who died in 529 BC, proclaiming a policy of religious tolerance and prohibition on slavery, and the teachings of the Buddhist King Ashoka of ancient India (c.264–38 BC) which were designed to promote non-violence and tolerance, sow the seeds of welfare of the people at the heart of governance and establish a system of justice to prevent wrongful punishments.

Present-day international human rights law has come into existence through a long period of evolution and is based on the values which inspired various revolutions and the entailing declarations of rights that accompanied them, as well as the writings of thinkers and philosophers. Such individual rights and liberties have evolved over time and within various civilizations; the notions of rights and freedoms as developed and articulated by Western philosophers of antiquity, and further fleshed out by more recent ones and championed by visionaries from the East and West, such as William Wilberforce, Mahatma Gandhi, Martin Luther King, Nelson Mandela, Gloria Steinem, Huda Shaarawi, Simone de Beauvoir and Rigoberta Menchu, who have been canonised as part of the human rights movement we know today.[1]

2.3 Philosophical foundations of human rights

In philosophical terms, human rights are those rights that are inherent in every human being, or the rights that are needed for any individual to lead a life with dignity. They are founded on the law of nature and the principle of the rule of law.

The concept of human rights has its origins in the work of early philosophers and political thinkers. It was Greek thinkers such as Plato and Aristotle who developed the early notion of democracy, and it was the Romans who concretised the notions of the rule of law and a method of governance based on divided and, therefore, restrained government with three branches of the State.

Many philosophers argued that all men knew intuitively that they had natural power or instinct to make choices and the law had to be developed to

1 See generally Aryeh Neier, *The International Human Rights Movement: A History* (Princeton University Press, 2012).

recognise and respect such natural human conduct (or 'human will'?).[2] For instance, Immanuel Kant maintained that natural law, known to reason, rather than consent or consensus, was the basis of all rights and obligations as well as the basis of authority of those who made positive law.[3] The argument was that everyone had an innate right to freedom by virtue of their humanity and everybody had an obligation to acknowledge the dignity of every other person.

The origins of human rights rest upon concepts of protecting what is due to an individual. In other words, human rights originate from recognition of that which a person is entitled to, and the commitment to not taking this away. From this perspective, human rights are seen as more of a set of ideals of a society and forming part of the basis of good governance. Human rights are not necessarily rights 'given' by States to their citizens. As stated by Justice Scalia, human rights 'are not conferred by a beneficent State but predate the State and are to be protected by the State.'[4]

They are the rights that the State has agreed to uphold when a political settlement was reached concerning the political structure of a society, thereby enabling citizens to lead a life in peace. In other words, human rights are the result of a social contract and respecting human rights is honouring the contract made.

Thus, statehood and its entailing mechanisms encompass the duty to protect human rights. Be it the British Bill of Rights (1689), the American Declaration of Rights (1774) and the Declaration of Independence (1776),[5] or the French Declaration of Rights of Man and of the Citizen (1789), human rights bills appear in their content to have been inspired by the writings of philosophers such as John Locke, Montesquieu, Rousseau, Milton, Voltaire,[6] and the very tradition of human rights in Western Europe seems likewise informed by Greek

2 For a discussion of the nature and source of human rights see M.B. Dembour, 'What Are Human Rights? Four Schools of Thought' (2010): 32(1) *HRQ* 1.

3 For a discussion of Kant's work and legal theory see, for example, B. Sharon Byrd and Joachim Hruschka (eds), *Kant and the Law* (Ashgate, 2009); Paul Guyer, *Kant on Freedom, Law, and Happiness* (Cambridge University Press, 2000), Karl Ameriks and Otfried Höffe (eds), *Kant's Moral and Legal Philosophy* (trans. Nicholas Walker; Cambridge University Press, 2009).

4 Justice Antonin Scalia, 'Justice Scalia's Tribute and Thoughts on Human Rights' in Jo Carby-Hall (ed.), *Essays on Human Rights: A Celebration of the Life of Dr Janusz Kochanowski* (Warsaw: Ius et Lex Foundation, 2014) 21.

5 The American Declaration of Independence is the usual name given to a statement adopted by the Continental Congress on 4 July 1776.

6 For instance, John Adams, a leading figure of the American Continental Congress that prepared the US Constitution and the second President of the US, later remarked that the American Revolution was 'Locke, Sidney, Rousseau, and de Malby.' In other words, the Americans were putting into practice the ideas of European philosophers, as cited in Micheline R. Ishay, *The History of Human Rights: From Ancient Times to the Globalization Era* (University of California Press 2004), 96.

Philosophy, Roman law, Judaeo-Christian tradition, the Humanism of the Reformation and the Age of Reason or the Enlightenment.[7]

2.4 The nature and category of human rights

The concept of human rights is an evolving one. There is no consensus as to the definition of human rights. The definition varies from one society to another, and from secular societies to religious ones. What was not a human right in a given society yesterday has often become a right today and what is not a right today is likely to be a right tomorrow as the society advances. There is no internationally agreed or universally defined hierarchy of human rights, notwithstanding the right to life or other rights which can be included in the definition of *jus cogens*, and would likely sit at the apex of the list of rights. Indeed, this recognition of some type of hierarchy (however crude) has influenced discourse in the area. It can now be said that human rights could roughly be grouped into the following four categories: absolute rights, due process rights, qualified rights and more qualified rights.

The top category of rights, absolute rights, includes rights that affect a person as an individual, such as the right to life and liberty or the right not to be tortured or subjected to other inhumane and degrading treatment. In other words, negative rights, i.e. rights of protection from interference in the very life and dignity of the person, are situated within the first group of rights from which no derogation is possible under any circumstances, including a state of emergency. These are the inherent and inalienable rights of every human being.

Then there come due process rights, the second category, relating to the social survival of a person, such as the right to property. The third category of rights, qualified rights, are social rights designed to enable a person to perform or undertake activities freely in a society, such as freedom of speech and assembly. The fourth and final category of more qualified rights are economic and cultural rights, such as the right to work. Such rights tend to be implemented gradually in a society up to a point within its means.

While some human rights are to do with individual liberty, many of them are collective in character. Examples of the latter are the right to freedom of assembly, the right to education, the right against discrimination, environmental and cultural rights as well as the right to development. Human rights are about protecting and enhancing a human being's freedoms and the term freedom itself is time and country sensitive. Amartya Sen's definition of freedom includes the following five distinct types:

7 See for a more detailed account of the evolution of human rights, Micheline R. Ishay, *The History of Human Rights: From Ancient Times to the Globalization Era* (University of California Press, 2004); T. Meron (ed.), *Human Rights in International Law* (Oxford University Press, 1984): 69–113; R. J. Vincent, *Human Rights in International Relations* (Cambridge University Press, 1986), Chapter 2.

(1) political freedoms,
(2) economic facilities,
(3) social opportunities,
(4) transparency guarantees, and
(5) protective security.[8]

Indeed, the modern corpus of international human rights law seeks to protect and advance these types of freedoms. Since human rights are dynamic, evolving all the time and time-sensitive, new institutions and treaties will always be needed to recognise new rights and make provisions to ensure their implementation. We will now examine the evolution of the concept of human rights throughout modern history, and the new mechanisms that have been introduced to cement their evolution.

2.5 Evolution of the modern concept of human rights

2.5.1 The contribution of Magna Carta to the evolution of human rights

Human rights have historically been regarded as a check on the 'tyranny of the ruler' and they now also function as a check on the 'tyranny of the majority', even in countries with a democratic system of governance. The modern concept of human rights was born out of a struggle to restrain the rulers of the day from excesses or from interfering in the autonomy of an individual, and to empower and require the State to facilitate the promotion of equality, justice and fairness for all, and this continues to be so to this day. It was against those very laws that were unfair, and the legal authorities that derived their power from them, that the human rights movement grew. As noted by Hannan, early notions of personal freedom were already in the process of evolution in England during the tenth century,[9] and later found expression in Magna Carta granted by King John in 1215 to his barons. Indeed, it was in 1100 that Henry I, William the Conqueror's son, published the Charter of Liberties, to assure the barons he would deal with them more reasonably than his brother had done. Magna Carta was essentially a political settlement whose purpose was to provide certain guarantees against specific grievances to the free men of England.[10]

8 Amartya Sen, *Development as Freedom* (Oxford University Press, 1999), 10.

9 Daniel Hannan, *How We Invented Freedom and Why It Matters* (Head of Zeus, 2013) 75 and 87.

10 See Anthony Arlidge and Igor Judge, *Magna Carta Uncovered* (Hart Publishing, 2014); Dan Jones, *Magna Carta: The Making and Legacy of the Great Charter* (Head of Zeus, 2014). See also for a succinct account of the significance of Magna Carta, the Lord Chief Justice, Lord Judge, 'The Foundations for a Great Democracy', *Counsel*, London, August 2013, 21–22.

It was a radical and revolutionary yet at the same time a conservative document. Since Magna Carta of 1215 was basically coerced out of the King by the barons, and was subsequently declared null and void by the Pope, there were various later versions of Magna Carta adopted, and the most prominent of them was the one issued in 1225 since it was adopted out of the free will of the ruler in favour of the people.

Magna Carta and other landmark documents such as the Habeas Corpus Act of 1679 and the Bill of Rights of 1689, the Declaration of Rights of 1774 by the first Continental Congress of the United States and the French Declaration of the Rights of Man and of the Citizen of 1789 formed the basis of modern day human rights. It can be said that the British Glorious Revolution seems to have inspired the American Revolution and the latter seems to have inspired the French Revolution, and the European philosophers seem to have inspired the evolution of democracy and the modern notion of rights and freedoms.[11]

Magna Carta itself is a document that the nobility of England demanded from the King of the country at the time to sign in favour of the people. It was an attempt to readjust the balance of power between the King and the barons and was made at a time when due to these power conflicts society was verging on an outright revolt by the barons due to poor and arbitrary government by the monarch, heavy tax demands by the monarch to finance wars and crusades, and quarrels with the Pope. This political settlement between the feuding classes formed not only a political peace, but in practice constituted the formal beginning of the modern concept of human rights and of the notion of a constitutional monarchy. As President Franklin Roosevelt said in his third inaugural address, 'The democratic aspiration is no mere recent phase in human history . . . It was written in Magna Carta'.[12]

The informal beginning of what has evolved into contemporary notions of rights and liberties goes much further back into history. According to Sir James Holt 'Magna Carta was not a sudden intrusion into English society and politics. On the contrary, it grew out of them . . . Laymen had been assuming, discussing and applying the principles of Magna Carta long before 1215.'[13] Some of the provisions in Magna Carta guarantee to the citizen freedom from imprisonment or from dispossession of his property and freedom from prosecution or exile 'unless by the lawful judgement of his peers or by the law of the land.'[14] Thus,

11 A. Goodwin (ed.) *The New Cambridge Modern History. Vol. 8, The American and French Revolutions*, 1763–93 (Cambridge University Press, 1965); Alexander Grab, *Napoleon and the Transformation of Europe* (Palgrave Macmillan, 2003); R. R. Palmer, *The Age of the Democratic Revolution: A Political History of Europe and America, 1760–1800* (Princeton University Press, 1964).

12 Third Inaugural Address of Franklin D Roosevelt, 20 January 1941.

13 As cited in Tom Bingham, *The Rule of Law* (Allen Lane, 2010) 12.

14 Some of these provisions read as follows:

> (39) No free man shall be seized or imprisoned, or stripped of his rights or possessions, or outlawed or exiled, or deprived of his standing in any other way,

Magna Carta has been regarded as a document that symbolises the rule of law in England, protecting the rights of the individual. On its 750th anniversary in 1956, Lord Denning stated that Magna Carta was 'the foundation of the freedom of the individual against the arbitrary authority of the despot.'[15] Writing in 2010, Lord Bingham said that in Magna Carta 'was the rule of law in embryo.'[16] The basic principles of this historical document have influenced the framing of the constitutions of the Commonwealth and other countries worldwide, including the United States.

2.5.2 The common law notions of fairness and justice and the evolution of human rights

The common law of the Anglo-Saxon world – law that could not be altered either by judges or politicians – has had a profound impact on the evolution of human rights.[17] It was built around personal freedom and the adjudication of disputes by an independent magistracy. Since the common law emanated from the people, as opposed to being a top-down imposition by the government, judges could not make new law by their decisions. Their job was limited to declaring what the common law was or what the personal freedoms of the individuals were which had existed since time immemorial.[18] This included a robust defence of the individual right to property and inviolability of private contracts. This is one reason why it is said that an Englishman's home is his castle.

nor will we proceed with force against him, or send others to do so, except by the lawful judgement of his equals or by the law of the land.

(40) To no one will we sell, to no one deny or delay right or justice.

(45) We will appoint as justices, constables, sheriffs, or other officials, only men that know the law of the realm and are minded to keep it well.

(52) To any man whom we have deprived or dispossessed of lands, castles, liberties, or rights, without the lawful judgement of his equals, we will at once restore these.

15 As cited in Francesca Klug, Keir Starmer and Stuart Weir, *The Three Pillars of Liberty: Political Rights and Freedoms in the United Kingdom – The Democratic Audit of the United Kingdom* (Routledge, 1996) 3.

16 Tom Bingham, *The Rule of Law* (Allen Lane, 2010) 12.

17 W. W. Buckland and Arnold D McNair, *Roman Law and Common Law A Comparison in Outline* (Cambridge University Press, 2008); R. C. Caenegam, *The Birth of the English Common Law* (2nd edn, Cambridge University Press, 2008); H. Patrick Glenn, *On Common Laws* (Oxford University Press, 2007).

18 Note that this was the position in *Courtney v Glanvil* (1615) in which it was held that the Chancery Court in England was unable to intervene if the Common Law Court had determined the matter, *Blond's Civil Procedure* (Aspen Publishers, 2007) 122. However, see *Earl of Oxford's Case* (1615) 21 ER 485 – in which the decision of the Common Law Court was set aside by the Chancery Court, providing that equitable principles prevail, Gernot Biehler, *Procedures in International Law* (Springer, 2008) 21.

Protected by common law, an Englishman's right to his home and property was sacrosanct and could not be interfered with by the State – no share in it could be claimed by anyone else including his own children and he was free to enjoy it in the manner which he deemed appropriate, including selling it or giving it to whatever person or organisation he chose through his will. This notion of personal freedom inherent in the individual can be discerned in the notion of human rights inherent in every individual.

2.5.3 The Glorious Revolution and the English Bill of Rights

Another major chapter in the history of the evolution of rights was the English Bill of Rights of 1689, adopted following the Glorious Revolution in 1688 (it is called 'glorious' mainly because it did not result in any bloodshed) which established the supremacy of parliament over the British monarchy. The Revolution replaced the reigning king, James II, with the joint monarchy of his protestant daughter Mary and her Dutch husband, William of Orange. However, before they were offered the crown, William and Mary were asked to consent to a document called the Declaration of Rights, later enshrined in law as the Bill of Rights. It affirmed a number of constitutional principles, including the prohibition of taxation without parliamentary consent thereby setting Britain on a firmer path towards constitutional monarchy and parliamentary democracy. Recalling their 'ancient rights and liberties' the parliamentarians declared that 'the pretended power of suspending the laws or the execution of laws by regal authority without consent of Parliament is illegal' and that 'levying money for or to the use of the Crown by pretence of prerogative, without grant of Parliament, for longer time, or in other manner than the same is or shall be granted, is illegal'.[19]

As can be seen from the provisions of Magna Carta and the Bill of Rights they are basically declarations about the relationship between Parliament and the monarch. Magna Carta and the Bill of Rights together with the Habeas Corpus Act of 1679,[20] all of which emerged from struggles between the king and a group of lords and aristocrats and which would develop into the modern Parliament of England, provided the foundations for the development of a modern concept of human rights, particularly with regard to the checks and balances put in place to restrain the ruling elite. Highlighting the far-reaching impact of the Glorious Revolution, Ferguson states that it was about 'the protection of individuals from arbitrary expropriation by the Crown.'[21] It freed

19 Available at legislation.gov.uk: http://www.legislation.gov.uk/aep/WillandMarSess2/1/2/introduction (accessed 16 December 2014).

20 Available at legislation.gov.uk: http://www.legislation.gov.uk/aep/Cha2/31/2/contents (accessed 16 December 2014).

21 Niall Ferguson, 'The Human Hive', The BBC Reith Lectures: The Rule of Law and Its Enemies, first broadcast 19 June 2012. http://www.bbc.co.uk/programmes/b01jms03 (accessed 1 July 2014).

up people's minds, leading to the creation of new civil society organisations, as well as the expansion of existing ones into new spheres of activity. The Revolution instilled confidence in people to go out and do creative things, including focusing on wealth creation.

2.5.4 The American Revolution

The American Revolution against British rule was led by rebellious Britons, mainly from Scotland and England, who had emigrated to the colonies.[22] The American revolutionaries were largely conservatives. When the American colonists initially began their struggle against the excesses of British rule and later for independence, they invoked the rights contained in the early English documents. They were asking the British establishment to do what the British people themselves had asked their kings a century earlier. The colonists asserted that they possessed all the rights of Englishmen; no taxation could be levied on them without representation; without voting rights, the English parliament could not represent the colonists; only the colonial assemblies had a right to tax the colonies; and they had a right to trial by jury.[23]

When Thomas Jefferson drafted the American Declaration of Rights in 1774,[24] the document asserted that Americans were a 'free people claiming their rights as derived from the laws of nature'. However, what is noteworthy here is that the 1774 Declaration claims its authority for the rights proclaimed for the colonists from both (1) the law of nature, and (2) the provisions of the English constitution, referencing by implication documents such as Magna Carta and the English Bill of Rights. Many of the leading Colonists were English citizens when they departed England for the new territory, and remained English citizens in the colonies, so the view being pursued was that English law, including the provisions in Magna Carta and the English Bill of Rights,

22 See Arthur Herman, *How the Scots Invented the Modern World: The True Story of How Western Europe's Poorest Nation Created Our World & Everything in It* (Three Rivers Press, 2001).

23 Through the Declaration of Rights of the Stamp Act Congress of 19 October 1765 and the Declaration and Resolves on Colonial Rights of the First Continental Congress of 14 October 1774 the American colonists asserted that they possessed all the rights of Englishmen; no taxation could be levied on them without representation; without voting rights, English parliament could not represent the colonists; only the colonial assemblies had a right to tax the colonies; and they had a right to trial by jury. The 1765 Declaration of Rights and Grievances was a document passed by the Stamp Act Congress, declaring that taxes imposed on British colonists without their formal consent were unconstitutional. It asserted that the people in the American colonies were entitled to all the same inherent rights and privileges as those available to the people within the kingdom of Great Britain.

24 The Declaration and Resolves of the First Continental Congress, 14 October 1774: available at http://www.ushistory.org/declaration/related/decres.htm (accessed 16 December 2014).

travelled with them and applied to them wherever they happened to reside and carry on their business. The provisions of Jefferson's 1774 Declaration of Rights constituted the foundation of the American Declaration of Independence of 1776 and ultimately the bills of rights were incorporated into the American constitution.

The difference between the 1774 Declaration of Rights and the Declaration of Independence of 1776 was that the latter invoked 'the Laws of Nature and of Nature's God' to entitle the colonists to independence on the basis that 'all men are created equal, that they are endowed by their Creator with certain unalienable Rights, that among these are Life, Liberty and the pursuit of Happiness.'[25] Thus, reliance was made not only on the law of nature but also on a Christian religious foundation of rights. The colonists appear to draw inspiration from the work of philosophers of the sixteenth and seventeenth centuries. Although provisions, such as the ones in the 1774 Declaration of Rights, did not feature in the original federal Constitution of the US drafted in 1787, the 12 amendments to the Constitution drafted by the First Congress in New York in September 1789, just 1 month after the French Declaration of the Rights of Man and of the Citizen, included a set of rights which came to be known as the Bill of Rights.

2.5.5 The French Declaration of the Rights of Man

Another major advancement in the evolution of human rights was the adoption of the French Declaration of the Rights of Man of 1789. The French people fighting against the tyrannical rule of Louis XVI asserted in the French Declaration of the Rights of Man and of the Citizen of 1789 that 'The aim of all political association is the conservation of the natural and inalienable rights of man. These rights are: liberty, property, security and resistance to oppression.'[26]

25 There is a long list of grievances of the people of America against the King of Great Britain in the 1776 Declaration of Independence which were relied upon to justify the declaration of independence. It read in part as follows: 'That all men are created equal, that they are endowed by their Creator with certain unalienable Rights, that among these are Life, Liberty and the pursuit of Happiness. That to secure these rights, Governments are instituted among Men, deriving their just powers from the consent of the governed, that whenever any Form of Government becomes destructive of these ends, it is the Right of the People to alter or to abolish it, and to institute new Government, laying its foundation on such principles and organizing its powers in such form, as to them shall seem most likely to effect their Safety and Happiness.' For more on this subject see, for example, Edward G. Gray and Jane Kamensky, *The Oxford Handbook of the American Revolution* (Oxford University Press, 2013); *American Independence, Events to 1776: Facsimiles of Documents* chosen by D.L. Thomas (HMSO, 1976).

26 Article 2 of the French Declaration, http://www.conseil-constitutionnel.fr/conseil-constitutionnel/root/bank_mm/anglais/cst2.pdf (accessed 10 October 2014).

This assertion was informed mainly by the belief that every man is born free and it is natural for him to defend his autonomy and dignity. The French Declaration stated that the representatives of the French people, organised as a National Assembly, 'have determined to set forth in a solemn declaration the natural, unalienable, and sacred rights of man'. Accordingly, the National Assembly went on to 'recognize' and 'proclaim', the rights of man and of the citizen. The following were some of the rights recognised and proclaimed:

1. Men are born and remain free and equal in rights. Social distinctions may be based only on considerations of the common good.
2. The aim of all political association is the preservation of the natural and imprescriptible rights of Man. These rights are Liberty, Property, Security, and Resistance to Oppression.

[. . .]

4. Liberty consists in the freedom of being able to do anything that does not harm others; thus, the exercise of the natural rights of every man has no bounds other than those that ensure to the other members of society the enjoyment of these same rights. These bounds may be determined only by law.
5. The Law has the right only to forbid those actions that are injurious to society. Nothing that is not forbidden by law may be hindered, and no one may be compelled to do what the law does not ordain.
6. The law is the expression of the general will. All citizens have the right to take part personally, or through their representatives, in its making. It must be the same for all, whether it protects or punishes.

[. . .]

9. As every man is presumed innocent until he has been declared guilty, if it should be considered necessary to arrest him, any undue harshness that is not required to secure his person must be severely curbed by the Law.
10. No one may be disturbed on account of his opinions, even religious ones, as long as the manifestation of such opinions does not interfere with the established Law and order.
11. The free communication of ideas and opinions is one of the most precious rights of man. Any citizen may therefore speak, write, and publish freely, except what is tantamount to the abuses of this liberty in the cases determined by Law.

[. . .]

17. Since the right to property is inviolable and sacred, no one may be deprived thereof, unless public necessity, legally ascertained, obviously requires it, and just and prior indemnity has been paid.[27]

27 Declaration of the Rights of Man 1789; available at http://avalon.law.yale.edu/18th_century/rightsof.asp (accessed 16 December 2016).

These core rights of man enunciated in the French Declaration have served as the basis of the civil and political rights guaranteed in many national and international human rights instruments today. Two progressive nations of the time, France and the newly independent America, were inspired by similar ideals and sought to found a new system of governance based on fundamental rights and freedoms of the citizenry derived from western philosophical foundations and the law of nature. The leading intellectuals at the time such as Thomas Jefferson and James Madison, fighting for American independence and seeking to establish a democratic system of governance in the post-independent America, had studied Locke, Montesquieu, Rousseau and Voltaire and seem to have been inspired by their work. Such writers had argued that the duty of individuals to obey the sovereign of a State was conditional on the respect that the sovereign demonstrated towards its citizens' rights, their 'natural' rights, which prevailed over the State's own positive law.

Thus, the year 1789 was a momentous year in the annals of the evolution of human rights, witnessing the adoption of two major declarations of rights and freedoms in both France and the United Sates. Both countries appear to have been inspired by the developments taking place in each other's jurisdiction and benefited from the exchange of ideas that would usher the world into a new territory characterised by fundamental rights and freedoms for their citizens. However, there were some subtle differences in the American and French approaches to the articulation of such rights and freedoms. While the Americans sought to articulate three cardinal rights, viz, life, liberty, and the pursuit of happiness, the French chose liberty, prosperity, and security as the defining characteristics of their respective declarations of rights.

2.5.6 Contribution of the inter-war period to the evolution of human rights

The main contribution of the inter-war period was the recognition of the collective right of self-determination of peoples and nations and workers' rights. Some advances were made in articulating and promoting these rights during the inter-war period.[28] The concept of human rights was already making its entry into various political forums during this period at the onset of the First

28 The period falling between the First World War and the Second World War saw numerous strikes by workers and led to the formation of the 'triple alliance' between trade unions representing miners, rail workers and other transport workers. During this time the suffragette movement gained significant momentum and success, whilst on the international stage there were (ultimately doomed) attempts at world peace via the League of Nations, see for example, Peter J. Yearwood, *Guarantee of Peace: The League of Nations in British Policy 1914–1925* (Oxford University Press, 2009); Ken Coates, *The Making of the Labour Movement: The Formation of the Transport and General Workers' Union, 1870–1922* (Spokesman Books, 1994).

World War. For instance, President Woodrow Wilson had said the following in his address at Independence Hall in Philadelphia on 4 July 1914:

> My dream is that as the years go on and the world knows more and more of America it will also drink at these fountains of youth and renewal; that it also will turn to America for those moral inspirations which lie at the basis of all freedom; that the world will never fear America unless it feels that it is engaged in some enterprise which is inconsistent with the rights of humanity; and that America will come into the full light of the day when all shall know that she puts human rights above all other rights and that her flag is the flag not only of America but of humanity.[29]

The humanitarian disaster during the First World War contributed to the advancement of social rights such as workers rights, the rights of women and minorities, as well as the right of the national self-determination of the colonies against imperialism. In his speech to a joint session of the US Congress on 8 January 1918, Woodrow Wilson set out his vision for world peace in 'Fourteen Points' and included a call for the application of the principle of self-determination as a way forward in reaching a territorial settlement in post-First World War Europe.[30] His 'Fourteen Points' calling for the creation of 'a world dedicated to justice and fair dealing' constituted the basis of the Treaty of Versailles of 1919 which established the League of Nations. The Covenant of the League of Nations made reference to the promotion of worker's rights and the rights of minorities was very much a preoccupation around the time of the establishment of the League. The objectives of the Covenant of the League of Nations found their expression more pertinently in the constituent documents of the International Labour Organisation (ILO).[31]

Some delegates had proposed at the Paris Peace Conference in 1919 to include respect for equality (and related rights) in the Covenant of the League of Nations. What they had in mind was to oppose religious intolerance and discrimination based on race or nationality. For instance, the delegate of Japan had proposed that a sentence be included in the Covenant of the League of Nations designed to accord just treatment to alien nationals of League member States without distinction based on nationality or race. However, proposals of

29 President W. Wilson's Address at Independence Hall. 'The Meaning of Liberty' July 4, 1914; available at http://www.presidency.ucsb.edu/ws/?pid=65381 (accessed 16 December 2014).

30 Woodrow Wilson: The Fourteen Points Address', 299–304, in Micheline R. Ishay (ed.), *The Human Rights Reader: Political Essays, Speeches and Documents from the Bible to the Present* (Routledge, 1997).

31 See Constitution of the International Labour Organization, as amended. http://www.ilo.org/public/english/bureau/leg/download/constitution.pdf (accessed 3 July 2014).

this nature did not find their place in the final draft of the Covenant.[32] This is because Western powers were not prepared to accept the principle of non-discrimination at the time as it would have meant changing fundamentally the manner in which they governed their colonial territories, or in the case of the US how the blacks were treated within the country.[33]

Although such proposals were rejected at an inter-governmental level, private initiatives continued in different learned assemblies and on an individual basis to develop the rights of citizens, including the right to equality. For instance, the *Institut de Droit International* adopted a declaration in its session in New York in 1929 proclaiming rights to life, liberty and property of all individuals (as opposed to only citizens) and on a non-discriminatory basis.[34] The British author, H. G. Wells, developed his own version of rights through the World Declaration of the Rights of Man during the Second World War outlining basic rights available to all with a view to garner popular support for the war endeavours.[35] He proclaimed that certain basic rights were available to all individuals of the world whoever they were, wherever they were residing, and whatever their origin. His message resonated with those fighting in the Second World War. It seems to have had a measure of influence around the globe and contributed to a certain extent to the adoption of the Universal Declaration of Human Rights soon after the establishment of the UN.

The ideas such as those promoted by H. G. Wells were given impetus by the US President Franklin Roosevelt in his annual State of the Union address to Congress in 1941 in which he called for four essential human freedoms: freedom of speech, freedom of worship, freedom from want, and freedom from fear. He stated that 'Freedom means the supremacy of human rights everywhere.'[36] During the same year the US President and the British Prime Minister, Winston Churchill, signed a joint declaration, known later as the Atlantic Charter, assuring people that 'all the men in all the lands may live out their lives in freedom from fear and want.'[37] Echoing the calls such as those made by H. G. Wells to galvanise the people into fighting against fascism, the US President had argued for extending the Charter globally stating that if the world were to achieve a stable peace 'it must involve the development of backward countries . . . I can't believe that we can fight a war against fascist slavery, and at the same time not work to free people all over the world from a backward colonial policy'.[38]

32 Andrew Clapham, *Human Rights: A Very Short Introduction* (Oxford University Press, 2007) 26–27.

33 For an insight into the progress of negotiations in relation to the Paris Peace Conference in 1919 and its outcomes, see Margaret Macmillan, *Peacemakers: Six Months that Changed the World* (John Murray Limited, 2001).

34 Clapham (n 32), 28.

35 H. G. Wells, *The Rights of Man; or, What are we Fighting For?* (Penguin,1940).

36 Clapham (n 32), citing President Franklin Roosevelt.

37 Ibid., 32.

38 Micheline R. Ishay, *The History of Human Rights: From Ancient Times to the Globalization Era* (University of California Press, 2004), 180.

The spirit of the Atlantic Charter was endorsed by 26 Allied nations in a Declaration by the United Nations on 1 January 1942 proclaiming that victory over the enemies was 'essential to defend life, liberty, independence and religious freedom, and to preserve human rights and justice in their own lands as well as in other lands'.[39] These 26 States were later joined by 21 other States in signing the Declaration which constituted the foundation of the human rights provisions that were eventually included in the Charter of the UN. The idea was to enshrine these commitments into a legally binding bill of rights. However, as stated by Clapham, 'efforts to include a legally binding bill of rights at the time came to nothing. Instead, the immediate focus was on the prosecution of international crimes.'[40] When the Nuremberg trials were concluded the focus was once again on the preparation of an international bill of rights which culminated in the Universal Declaration of Human Rights on 10 December 1948. The recognition by the Nuremberg trials of the impact of war crimes and crimes against humanity on the individual was influential in elaborating an international legal instrument recognising the rights of individuals.

2.6 Foundations for international human rights law

The devastating impact that the Second World War had on human dignity galvanised the international community into action to establish a new international order based on peace, collective security, economic development, and protection and promotion of human rights in order to address 'the scourge of war, which twice in our lifetime has brought untold sorrow to mankind'.[41] Accordingly, when the Charter of the United Nations was adopted, the protection and the promotion of human rights became a core objective of this new international organisation. The Preamble and several articles of the UN Charter have provisions relating to human rights. The Preamble reads as follows:

> We the peoples of the United Nations, determined . . . to reaffirm faith in fundamental human rights, in the dignity and worth of the human person, in the equal rights of men and women and of nations large and small . . . have resolved to combine our efforts to accomplish these aims.

In stipulating the purposes of the UN, Article 1 commits the organisation:

> To achieve international cooperation in solving international problems of an economic, social, cultural, or humanitarian character, and in promoting and encouraging respect for human rights and for fundamental freedoms for all without distinction as to race, sex, language, or religion.

39 Clapham (n 32), p.32.
40 Ibid., 32.
41 Charter of the United Nations, 1945, preamble.

The UN Charter goes on, in Article 55, to spell out in more concrete terms its resolve to promote and protect human rights in the following words:

> With a view to the creation of conditions of stability and well-being which are necessary for peaceful and friendly relations among nations based on respect for the principle of equal rights and self-determination of peoples, the United Nations shall promote:
> a. higher standards of living, full employment, and conditions of economic and social progress and development;
> b. solutions of international economic, social, health, and related problems; and international cultural and educational cooperation; and
> c. universal respect for, and observance of, human rights and fundamental freedoms for all without distinction as to race, sex, language, or religion.

Through Article 56 all Members of the UN have pledged themselves 'to take joint and separate action in cooperation with the Organization for the achievement of the purposes set forth in Article 55.' References to human rights can also be found in Articles 13, 62, 68 and 76 of the UN Charter. While Article 13 authorises the General Assembly to make studies and recommendations about human rights, Article 62 similarly does so in relation to the Economic and Social Council (ECOSOC) whilst Article 68 requires ECOSOC to set up commissions in the economic and social fields and for the promotion of human rights.

Although the notion of human rights had already found expression in the Covenant of the League of Nations[42] which led *inter alia* to the establishment of the International Labour Organisation in 1919, it was the Tentative Proposals for a General International Organization submitted by the United States to the Dumbarton Oaks Conference (1944) that referred to 'basic human rights' for the first time in any international document of significance. A proposal was put forward to embody a 'Declaration on the Essential Rights of Man' at the San Francisco Conference held in 1945 to draft the UN Charter.[43] However, the proposal was not examined because it required more detailed consideration than was possible during the San Francisco Conference. Therefore, the major international legal instrument that introduced the term 'human rights' to the lexicon of international law was the Charter of the United

42 Articles 22 and 23 of the Covenant of the League of Nations, 28 April 1919, available at: http://www.unhcr.org/refworld/docid/3dd8b9854.html accessed 4 July 2014

43 It was also in 1945 that Hersch Lauterpacht, a preeminent Cambridge academic, published his book *An International Bill of Rights of Man*, drawing on a range of natural rights ideas and constitutionally protected rights, see Hersch Lauterpacht, *An International Bill of the Rights of Man* (Oxford University Press, reprinted 2013).

Nations itself. Even then, in stating the aims and objective of the UN, the Charter makes reference to universal respect for 'fundamental human rights', 'equal rights of men and women', but does not create any specific organs with a mandate to this effect.[44]

Since the Charter itself only spoke of 'fundamental freedoms and human rights' and did not go on to spell out the precise nature of the rights and freedoms to be enjoyed by the peoples of the world, there was an agreement reached in San Francisco to draft an International Bill of Rights, following on from the models of English Magna Carta and American Bills of Rights and the French and American Declarations of Rights, to give flesh to the provisions of the Charter and pronounce the rights and freedoms to be enjoyed by all. Therefore, soon after the UN Charter was adopted in June 1945, the Preparatory Commission recommended that ECOSOC should immediately establish a Commission on Human Rights and direct it to prepare an International Bill of Rights. Accordingly, the General Assembly approved this recommendation in February 1946 and ECOSOC acted immediately to establish the Commission on Human Rights, consisting of representatives of governments rather than electing experts in human rights from a list of nominees submitted by governments.

2.7 Work of the UN Commission on Human Rights

When the Commission met for its inaugural regular session in January 1947, its first task was the drafting of an International Bill of Rights. When the Commission began its work it planned to have three parts in the International Bill of Rights: (1) a Declaration; (2) a Convention containing legal obligations; and (3) 'measures of implementation' containing a system of international monitoring and supervision. The task of drafting the Declaration was entrusted to a committee of eight members consisting of representatives of Australia, Chile, China, France, Lebanon, the UK, the US, and the former Soviet Union. The chairperson of both the Commission on Human Rights and the drafting committee was Mrs Eleanor Roosevelt, former First Lady of America. Upon receiving the draft of the Universal Declaration of Human Rights from the drafting committee, the full Commission adopted it with some revision and presented it to the General Assembly of the UN. The Third Committee of the Assembly examined the draft declaration and submitted a revised version of it to the General Assembly which adopted it on 10 December 1948, with 48 voted in favour, none against and 8 abstentions,[45] through Resolution 217 (III).

44 See UN Charter, Article 1(3) on the purposes of the organisation and Article 55 in Chapter IX, International Economic and Social Cooperation.

45 The abstaining States were from the Soviet bloc, South Africa, and Saudi Arabia.

2.8 The Universal Declaration of Human Rights

Over 150 years after the adoption of the American and French declaration of rights, the American and French tradition was a driving force behind the adoption of the Universal Declaration of Human Rights adopted by the UN General Assembly in 1948 following the horrors of the Second World War. It is noteworthy here that the Chairman of the UN Commission on Human Rights which drafted the Universal Declaration was an American, Mrs Eleanor Roosevelt, and one of the principal authors of it was a Frenchman, M. Rene Cassin. The Universal Declaration built on the French and American Declarations and the liberal traditions of Western democracies such as Magna Carta and the English Bill of Rights, became the catalyst for the internationalisation of the human rights agenda. It was a source of momentous development in the area of human rights within the UN and the foundation of the work of the UN human rights institutions.

This is not to say that the other members of the Human Rights Commission did not contribute to the drafting of the Universal Declaration. The members of the Commission from non-western countries appear to have made a significant contribution.

There is also no denying that certain elements of human rights values existed in other non-Western civilisations such as within Hindu, Buddhist, and Islamic traditions. Indeed, the origin of Western philosophy is the work of Greek thinkers of ancient times and they themselves 'became aware of moral practices and political institutions radically different from their own' in other parts of the world when the Greeks who inhabited the Greek city-States in antiquity ventured out to sea, first for food, and then trade.[46]

Indeed, Upendra Baxi rightly states that 'To say that the "non-Western" societies and cultures did not possess notions of human rights is patently untrue; they did.'[47] Of course, many non-Western societies encompassed some conception of human rights in their legal traditions.[48] However, these traditions had not found their expression in well articulated instruments such as Magna Carta or the English Bill of Rights or the French or American Declarations of Rights.

In sum therefore, it was mainly the British, American and French Revolutions that advanced progressive ideas and contributed significantly to the evolution of human rights, the rule of law and democracy. However, they remained incomplete revolutions since the rights proclaimed in the declarations and other

46 Anthony Quinton, 'Political Philosophy' in Anthony Kenny (ed.), *The Oxford Illustrated History of Western Philosophy* (Oxford University Press, 1994) 279.

47 Upendra Baxi, *The Future of Human Rights* (3rd edn, Oxford University Press, 2006) 42.

48 See generally, H. Patrick Glenn, *Legal Traditions of the World: Sustainable Diversity in Law* (2nd edn, Oxford University Press, 2004); Onuma Yasuaki, *A Transcivilizational Perspective on International Law* (Martinus Nijhoff 2010), especially Chapter V.

legal instruments adopted on the heels of the revolutions left behind many individuals in society, including women, property-less men, ethnic minorities, and homosexuals. In other words, rights were denied to 'passive' or 'secondary' citizens or people of perceived 'inferior' status. As Lord Bingham has noted, it was not until 1928 that women achieved full voting rights in Britain and this country was not alone in tolerating inequality:

> The revolutionary French Declaration of the Rights of Man and the Citizen, universal in its scope, was amended to deny rights to certain categories of people. The Bill of Rights adopted by the United States, while progressive and ground-breaking, in many ways, did not disturb the peculiar institution of slavery cherished in the South, which endured for ninety years after Somerset's case. No one needs to be reminded of the discrimination sanctioned by law against Jews, homosexuals and Gypsies in some European countries during the twentieth century.[49]

Thus, the world had to wait until the establishment of the UN and the adoption of the Universal Declaration of Human Rights to embrace the principle of equality in terms of equal treatment and the equal enjoyment of human rights.

2.8.1 The Universal Declaration as a standard-setting instrument

The Universal Declaration was regarded to be a standard-setting document for the world rather than a legally binding document. The operative part of the Declaration itself makes this clear in the following words:

> Now, therefore, the General Assembly proclaims this Universal Declaration of Human Rights as a common standard of achievement for all peoples and all nations, to the end that every individual and every organ of society, keeping this Declaration constantly in mind, shall strive by teaching and education to promote respect for these rights and freedoms and by progressive measures, national and international, to secure their universal and effective recognition and observance, both among the peoples of Member States themselves and among the peoples of territories under their jurisdiction.

Highlighting the significance of the Declaration, Mrs Roosevelt stated that it was 'first and foremost a declaration of the basic principles to serve as a common standard for all nations.' She went on to add that 'It might well

49 Tom Bingham, *The Rule of Law* (Allen Lane, 2010) 57.

become the Magna Carta of all mankind.'[50] Indeed, the importance of the Universal Declaration was equal to, if not greater than, the English and American Bills of Rights and the American and French Declarations of Rights. Unlike the other declarations, the Universal Declaration speaks of 'human rights' rather than the 'rights of man' and does not invoke the laws of nature or religious foundations, Christian or otherwise, of the rights and freedoms proclaimed. It is a secular and largely gender neutral document both in content and spirit. However, similar to all previous declarations, the Universal Declaration too regards human rights as rights that are inherent in, and inalienable, to all human beings.

2.8.2 Significance of the Universal Declaration of Human Rights

The Universal Declaration did indeed herald a new chapter in the evolution of the international law of human rights and has been the foundation of subsequent international human rights treaties adopted both within and outside of the UN system and has inspired the drafting of the chapters on fundamental rights and freedoms in the constitutions of numerous countries around the globe. One of the main drafters of the Universal Declaration, Rene Cassin of France, said that the Declaration was founded on four principle pillars: dignity, liberty, equality and brotherhood.[51] Indeed, as pointed out by Ishay, 'The twenty-seven articles of the declaration were divided among these four pillars.'[52] These articles include certain fundamental civil and political rights as well as some economic, social and cultural rights.[53]

50 As quoted in L. B. Sohn, 'A short history of United Nations documents on human rights', in *The United National and Human Rights*, Eighteenth Report of the Commission to Study the Organisation of Peace, New York, 1968, p.70. See, for an account of the legislative history of the Universal Declaration, William Schabas (ed.), *The Universal Declaration of Human Rights: The Travaux Preparatoires* (Cambridge University Press, 2013).

51 As cited in Micheline R. Ishay, *The History of Human Rights: From Ancient Times to the Globalization Era* (University of California Press, 2004) 3.

52 Ibid., 3.

53 They include the following civil and political rights: Right to life, liberty and security of person; Freedom from slavery or servitude; Freedom from torture or cruel, inhuman or degrading treatment or punishment; Right to equality; Right to an effective remedy by the competent national tribunals; Freedom from arbitrary arrest, detention or exile; Right to a fair trial; Right to be presumed innocent until proved guilty according to law in a public trial; Freedom from arbitrary interference with one's privacy, family, home or correspondence and from attacks upon one's honour and reputation; Right to marry and to found a family; Equal rights as to marriage, during marriage and at its dissolution; Right to own property alone as well as in association with others; Freedom from arbitrary deprival of one's property; Freedom of thought, conscience and religion; Freedom of opinion and expression; Freedom of peaceful assembly and association; Right to take part in the government of his or her country, directly or through freely chosen representatives; and Right of equal access to public service in his or her country.

The Universal Declaration was the first international instrument to grant and guarantee equal rights to all men and women regardless of their colour, creed, social and economic status, origin, nationality, etc. From this perspective the Universal Declaration was a remarkable and radical document. This is because most of the other previous human rights instruments, from Magna Carta to the American Declaration, did not extend the rights stipulated in them to all men and women on an equal footing. The rights enunciated in these instruments were not available to people below a certain threshold of property ownership, servants (or slaves), women, and homosexuals etc. For instance, the English Puritan Revolution (1642–48) ended up empowering the propertied class by granting sovereignty to Parliament rather than promoting egalitarianism and equality. This was one reason why the 'poor, oppressed' people of England issued their own declaration in 1649 calling for the establishment of communal property and arguing that land should be available for the poor to cultivate.[54]

Even in revolutionary France, voting rights were restricted to owners of property when the euphoria of the French Declaration of the Rights of Man and of the Citizen had started to fade and social divisions began to resurface; voting rights and public office holding were denied to passive citizens, including domestic servants, women, and those who did not pay taxes equivalent to 3 days of labour.[55] Dissatisfied with the exclusion of women as the beneficiaries of certain political rights in the French Declaration, the French pamphleteer and playwright Olympe de Gouges wrote a Declaration of the Rights of Women in 1790 in which she called for respect for women's rights on a footing equal to that of men.[56]

This was echoed by the English writer Mary Wollstonecraft in her *Vindication of the Rights of Women* (1792) for social and political equality for women in England. She was joined just under 100 years later by John Stuart Mill who advocated women's equality in his book, *On the Subjection of Women* (1869). Although the social condition of Englishwomen was better than that of their counterparts in continental Europe, their legal status remained inferior to that of men. Even though French women had contributed to the French Revolution

The Universal Declaration goes on to proclaim a number of economic, social and cultural rights such as: Right to social security; Right to work, to free choice of employment, to just and favourable conditions of work and to protection against unemployment; Right to equal pay for equal work; Right to form and to join trade unions; and Right to a standard of living adequate for the health and well-being, including food, clothing, housing and medical care.

54 See Gerrard Winstanley, 'A Declaration from the Poor Oppressed People of England,' 1649 in Micheline R. Ishay, *The History of Human Rights: From Ancient Times to the Globalization Era* (University of California Press, 2004) 93.

55 It was argued that voting rights should be available only to active citizens who were taxpayers and property owners because they contributed to the public establishment and were true shareholders in the great social enterprise. See in Ishay (n. 54) 97.

56 Ishay (n. 54) 110.

they were not rewarded with equal rights in the French Declaration. Ultimately, the call for equal rights for women was defeated in the French National Assembly and Olympe de Gouges was guillotined in 1793.

Of course, the French declaration had gone further than other instruments in carrying the torch of freedom but it failed to travel the full mile. After gaining independence from England, Americans were similarly limited in the scope of protection and did not go far enough to embrace equality, at least in terms of voting rights in the 1788 Constitution – they continued to favour wealthy property owners, and maintained the existence of slavery.[57] In other words, it was largely a propertied white man's constitution. Ishay sums up the situation as follows, 'while emphasizing a universal moral embrace, all great civilisations have thus tended to rationalise unequal entitlements for the weak or the "inferior".'[58] She goes on to state that 'throughout the European dominated world . . . women had failed to achieve equal rights with men, property-less men were denied the right to vote and other political rights, children's rights continued to be usurped, and the right to sexual preference was not even considered.'[59]

In the words of Zakaria 'in 1900 not a single country had what we would today consider a democracy: a government created by elections in which every adult citizen could vote.'[60] He goes on to state that: 'In 1830 Great Britain, one of the most democratic European countries, allowed barely 2 percent of its population to vote for one house of Parliament. Only in the late 1940s did most Western countries become full-fledged democracies, with universal adult suffrage.'[61] It was an incremental widening process in voting rights – through the Reform Act of 1832 and other programmes – that led to universal adult suffrage in Great Britain in 1930.[62]

57 Having initially embraced the idea of universal male suffrage, the Constitutional Convention adopted a restriction as proposed by Samuel Adams according to which the voting rights were restricted to a white man if he owned real estate worth £3 a year or real and personal property with a value of £60. As a result, according to Ishay, 'the voting constituency was far less than half of the adult male population.' Ishay, ibid., 96. It also excluded women and blacks. The threshold for property ownership to qualify for voting rights varied from one State to another within the United States.

58 Ibid., 7.

59 Ibid., 8.

60 Fareed Zakaria, *The Future of Freedom: Illiberal Democracy at Home and Abroad* (W. W. Norton & Company, 2007) 13.

61 Ibid., 20. See for a good account of the electoral politics in Great Britain during the time of William Wilberforce who led the campaign for the abolition of slavery: William Hague, *William Wilberforce: The Life of the Great Anti-Slave Trade Campaigner* (Harper Perennial, 2008). See also William Hague, *William Pitt the Younger* (Harper Press, 2004).

62 For a potted history of universal adult suffrage in the UK, see Neil Johnston, 'The History of the Parliamentary Franchise', Research Paper 13/14, House of Commons Library, 1 March 2013, www.parliament.uk/briefing-papers/RP13-14.pdf accessed 10 October 2014.

Breaking away from this tradition of inequality in rights, not only in the Christian world but also in the Hindu, Islamic and Buddhist worlds where similar discriminatory practices existed against women and people belonging to lower castes (in the latter case, mainly in Hinduism), the Universal Declaration declared that all human beings were equal and were entitled to the same rights. This was the first major victory for women and other weak and 'inferior' classes in societies. Why the Universal Declaration can be said to be truly universal (which is discussed further below) is also due to the fact that a group of philosophers, diplomats and legal scholars representing different countries and civilisations came together and agreed on its content. This group included a Chinese philosopher and diplomat, Chang, a Lebanese philosopher and rapporteur, Malik, who had worked as a spokesperson for the Arab League and a French legal scholar Cassin, a Jew who had lost many relatives in the Holocaust.

2.9 Implementation of the Universal Declaration of Human Rights

What was missing in the work of the UN Commission on Human Rights was the element of protection of the rights enshrined in the Universal Declaration. This is one reason why some eminent scholars of international law, such as Hersch Lauterpacht, had criticised the Universal Declaration at the time – it was legally non-binding and provided no system of enforcement.[63] Clapham observes that: 'The Western powers, while keen to trumpet their own political model as superior, were at the same time careful to ensure the Declaration had no immediate legal effect.'[64] Ramcharan adds that even at the San Francisco conference itself, States were not willing to create a human rights protection organ within the institutional structure of the UN.[65] He argues that it was newly independent countries that acted through the General Assembly in the mid-1960s to convince the UN Commission on Human Rights, 'to consider human

63 H. Lauterpacht, *International Law and Human Rights* (F. A. Praeger, 1950) 575, as cited in Martti Koskenniemi, *The Politics of International Law* (Hart Publishing, 2011) 155. See also Hersch Lauterpacht, *An International Bill of the Rights of Man* (First published in 1945 and republished in 2013 by Oxford University Press).

64 Andrew Clapham, *Human Rights: A Very Short Introduction* (Oxford University Press, 2007) 44.

65 Ramcharan states that: 'At the San Francisco conference, the world's great powers – including the United States, the Soviet Union, France, and the United Kingdom – opposed giving the United Nations the competence to protect human rights. The United States was a racially segregated country, the Soviet Union a totalitarian State with gulags, and France and the United Kingdom colonial powers that exploited subject populations. Clearly a UN empowered with the capacity to protect human rights was not in their interests.' Bertrand Ramcharan, *The UN Human Rights Council* (Routledge, 2011), 20–21.

rights violations in any part of the world, particularly in apartheid South Africa and in colonised and dependent countries. NGOs and similar experts used this opening to press the case for protection.'[66]

The situation is not that much different today than it was in 1948 as still there is no international court of human rights, nor a powerful ombudsman to rebuke States for their failures to uphold human rights. Although the position of the UN High Commissioner for Human Rights was created in 1993, it was not accorded any real powers. What is more, the process of appointing to this position itself is rather opaque and does not meet the highest international standards of fairness, transparency and democracy. However, the irony is that since this opaque process appears to suit Western countries in securing their preferred appointment this process may continue. Therefore, in spite of there being a myriad of international legal instruments to pronounce and declare on rights, the UN has made little progress in terms of the measures of implementation or enforcement of such rights. Of course, the Universal Declaration is one of the main instruments for the Universal Periodic Review mechanism of the UN Human Rights Council under which compliance by all States Members of the UN with its provisions become a matter for international concern and scrutiny. However, this review mechanism itself is a political mechanism subject to manipulation by States.

2.10 The first UN human rights treaty with a mechanism for implementation

A major step in the evolution of international human rights was the International Convention on the Elimination of All Forms of Racial Discrimination of 1965 with a provision for individual complaints to a committee created by the Convention.[67] This was the first international treaty which incorporated the capacity for individual complaints against State violations of the treaty provisions. What is more, this Convention also included a provision for inter-State complaints, a provision to allow States to refer the disputes relating to the Convention to the International Court of Justice and to take preventative action. Further, the protections contained within the Convention applied not only to the activities of public institutions but also the activities of private actors conducted in public: Article 2(1)(d) of the Convention obliges States parties

66 Ibid., 21.

67 See for text of this Convention: 660 UNTS 195. As of 30 September 2014 a total of 177 had ratified this Convention. To find out which countries have ratified the international human rights treaties: http://indicators.ohchr.org/; For information on the status of ratification and signature by States of UN human rights treaties, as well as reservations and declarations: http://treaties.un.org/Pages/Treaties.aspx?id=4&subid=A&lang=en. An overview of the ratification status is also available at: http://tbinternet.ohchr.org/_layouts/TreatyBodyExternal/Treaty.aspx

to 'prohibit and bring to an end, by all appropriate means, including legislation as required by circumstances, racial discrimination by any persons, group or organization.' In his analysis of this Convention, Meron states that this provision 'appears to mean that racially discriminatory action which occurs in public life is prohibited even if it is taken by any person, group or organization.'[68] Thus, this Convention is broader in its scope than many other human rights treaties. This Convention was followed by many other human rights treaties with their own mechanism for monitoring compliance by States parties to such treaties.

2.11 The International Bill of Rights

The major push to complete the unfinished business of writing an International Bill of Rights took place with the adoption of the Covenants on Civil and Political Rights and Economic, Social and Cultural Rights in 1966 under the auspices of the UN.[69] The intention at the time of drafting the Universal Declaration had been to create a legally binding document containing core rights and freedoms as part of an International Bill of Rights. Indeed, a proposed covenant had been prepared by the committee that drafted the Universal Declaration. However, the General Assembly had decided to consider only the draft Universal Declaration at its third session held in Paris in the autumn of 1948. Nevertheless, the General Assembly decided through its Resolution 217 (III) of 10 December 1948 that work should proceed on the development of a legally binding covenant containing a guarantee of human rights and freedoms and on measures of implementation (it is interesting to note that this work was completed only after the International Convention on the Elimination of All Forms of Racial Discrimination had been agreed).

Accordingly, negotiations began in 1948 on the content of the Covenant and on measures for implementation and after nearly 18 years of negotiations two covenants – the first dealing with classic civil and political rights and the other with economic and social and cultural rights – were adopted by the General Assembly in 1966. Of course, the onset of the Cold War, the escalation in political tension between NATO and the Warsaw Pact countries, and the increase in the number of developing countries with a strong emphasis on social, economic and cultural rights had an impact on these negotiations, which resulted in two Covenants dealing with two different sets of rights (though naturally with some overlap). Nonetheless, the unanimous adoption of these two land-mark international human rights instruments together with the Optional Protocol to the Covenant on Civil and Political Rights by the UN

68 Theodor Meron, *Human Rights Law-Making in the United Nations* (Clarendon Press, 1986) 18.

69 One other landmark contribution of the UN was the adoption of the Declaration on the Granting of Independence to Colonial Countries and peoples of 1960 which endorsed the right to self-determination of the peoples or national groups under colonial rule.

General Assembly marked the commitment of the international community to protect and uphold people's rights.[70]

2.12 Other human rights treaties and declarations

Although with the adoption of the Universal Declaration of Human Rights and the conclusion of the 1966 Covenants there was now an International Bill of Rights in operation, there were a number of human rights issues, either gender, race or age specific, that needed focused treaties to protect the rights of individuals belonging to groups vulnerable to issues relating to these grounds. Therefore, the human rights treaty-making agenda remained active within the UN throughout the 1960s, 1970s and the 1980s, and has continued apace into the twenty-first century. Examples include the Convention on the Rights of the Child of 1989, the Convention on the Elimination of All Forms of Discrimination against Women of 1979 and the International Convention on the Protection of the Rights of All Migrant Workers and Their Families, 1990.[71]

In addition, the UN General Assembly has adopted a number of declarations pronouncing certain rights and notable among them are the Declaration on the Granting of Independence to Colonial Countries and Peoples of 1960, the Declaration on Protection from Torture of 1975, Declaration on the Rights of Disabled Persons of 1975, the Declaration on the Elimination of All Forms of Intolerance and of Discrimination Based on Religion or Belief of 1981, the Right to Development of 1986, the Declaration on the Rights of Persons belonging to National or Ethnic, Religious and Linguistic Minorities of 1992, the Declaration on the Rights of Indigenous Peoples of 2007 and the Declaration on Decriminalization of Homosexuality of 2008.[72]

The 1990s witnessed a major international conference in Vienna in 1993 and the creation of the Office of the High Commissioner for Human Rights – a body with the task of monitoring the situation of human rights in individual countries and providing technical assistance to States that need and want such assistance.[73] The latest major development within the UN human rights system

70 For more on the two covenants, the ICCPR and the ICESCR, see for example, Dominic McGoldrick, *The Human Rights Committee: Its Role in the Development of the International Covenant on Civil and Political Rights* (Clarendon Press, 1994), Menno T. Kamminga and Martin Scheinin, *The Impact of Human Rights Law on General International Law* (Oxford University Press, 2009).

71 For a full list of UN core international human rights treaties,see http://www.ohchr.org/EN/HRBodies/Pages/TreatyBodies.aspx (accessed 4 July 2014).

72 For details of the declarations and conventions contain in UN General Assembly, see http://www.un.org/documents/instruments/docs_en.asp?type=declarat (accessed 11 October 2014).

73 Vienna Declaration and programme of Action, adopted by the world programme on human rights, 25 June 1993, http://www.ohchr.org/en/professionalinterest/pages/vienna.aspx (accessed 11 October 2014).

was the establishment of the Human Rights Council in 2006 to replace the old Commission on Human Rights.[74]

2.13 Momentum towards the universality of human rights

Great strides have been made to make human rights universally accepted, to expand their scope and to make them a reality for all human beings since the adoption of the Universal Declaration of Human Rights. The principal international instruments which constitute the foundation of human rights are the Universal Declaration itself and the 1966 Covenants referred to above, combined with the Optional Protocols to the ICCPR. Together they are known as the International Bill of Rights.[75] There has been near universal ratification of the International Bill of Rights,[76] universal acceptance of the Universal Declaration of Human Rights and of the Convention on the Rights of the Child.[77] The 2005 World Summit Outcome document adopted unanimously by the UN General Assembly in 2005 regards the fulfilment of the rights embodied in the Universal Declaration as a legal obligation.[78] Although the Charter of the UN is the key international legal instrument which constitutes the foundation of the UN regime of human rights,[79] the Universal Declaration and the 1966 Covenants constitute the core of international human rights law[80] which is supplemented and complemented by provisions in other treaties, conventions, and declarations of regional and international nature.

74 'The Human Rights Council' GA Resolution 60/251, 3 April 2006, http://www2.ohchr.org/english/bodies/hrcouncil/docs/A.RES.60.251_En.pdf (accessed 11 October 2014).

75 G.A Res. 217A, U.N. GAOR 3rd Comm., at 71, U.N. Doc. A/810 (1948), G.A. Res 2200A, 21 U.N. GAOR, Supp. No. 16, at 52, U.N. Doc. A/6316 (1966), 999 U.N.T.S. 171 (1976), G.A. Res. 2200A (XXI) 21 U.N. GAOR, Supp., No. 16 at 49, 993 U.N.T.S. 3 (1966) respectively.

76 As of 30 September 2014 the International Covenant on Civil and Political Rights had been ratified by 177 States and the International Covenant on Economic, Social and Cultural Rights by 162 States. To find out which countries have ratified the international human rights treaties: http://indicators.ohchr.org/. For information on the status of ratification and signature by States of UN human rights treaties, as well as reservations and declarations: http://treaties.un.org/Pages/Treaties.aspx?id=4&subid=A&lang=en. An overview of the ratification status is also available at: http://tbinternet.ohchr.org/_layouts/TreatyBodyExternal/Treaty.aspx

77 This Convention has been ratified by all 193 members of the UN.

78 A/RES/60/1 of 24 October 2005.

79 The text of the Charter of the United Nations can be accessed online, http://www.un.org/en/documents/charter/intro.shtml accessed 10 October 2014.

80 The term 'international human rights law' encompasses the various human rights treaties, declarations of the UN and other international conferences which are capable of carrying some legal weight, procedures and principles of customary international law and case-law. In defining this term reference could be made to Article 38 of the Statute of the International Court of Justice, part of the UN Charter, which has generally been

Although the Universal Declaration of Human Rights was not a legally binding document when it was adopted, it has since then been widely acknowledged that most of its provisions, especially those relating to civil and political rights, have gained the status of customary international law through State practice coupled with *opinio juris*. It has been accepted by a vast majority of States, as well as by judiciaries and publicists around the globe, that the Universal Declaration is a document that embodies the core and classic human rights developed through State practice over the centuries.

This is supported by the fact that the International Bill of Rights derives much of its meaning and substance from national bills of rights of countries such as England, US and France, as discussed above. State practice spanning centuries supports the majority of the rights of the Universal Declaration as having the status of customary rules of international law. Most of the provisions of the Universal Declaration meet the tests of consistency, uniformity and generality required for a State practice to become a rule of customary international law, binding on all States. Accordingly, it can be submitted that the rights and freedoms enshrined in the Universal Declaration of Human Rights are the rights forming part of international law which are available to all human beings and are binding on all States.

The Covenants on Civil and Political Rights and on Economic, Social and Cultural Rights (1966) are, as we have seen, the two legal instruments that came to develop the rights enshrined in the prima facie non-legally binding Universal Declaration. They were the first major and comprehensive international legal instruments that expressly guaranteed in law the rights and freedoms listed, and both were adopted unanimously in the UN General Assembly. Of course, the standards of realisation of some of the economic, social and cultural rights may vary from one country to another depending on the state of their economic development, but nonetheless, a vast majority of States have accepted these rights as human rights and have endeavoured their utmost to make these rights a reality for their citizens.[81]

The 1966 Covenants include provisions designed to create a mechanism to monitor and ensure compliance of the rights enunciated in them. Further, departing from the practice of stating the rights as the rights of man and expressing the rights in the masculine gender, the 1966 Covenants adopt

regarded as the most authoritative definition of the sources of international law. It reads as follows: The Court, whose function is to decide in accordance with international law such disputes as are submitted to it, shall apply: a. international conventions, whether general or particular, establishing rules expressly recognized by the contesting States; b. international custom, as evidence of a general practice accepted as law; c. the general principles of law recognized by civilized nations; d. subject to the provisions of Article 59, judicial decisions and the teachings of the most highly qualified publicists of the various nations, as subsidiary means for the determination of rules of law.

81 For details of ratification, see https://treaties.un.org/Pages/Treaties.aspx?id=4&subid=A&lang=en (accessed 11 October 2014).

gender-neutral expressions and places emphasis on the notion of equality of men and women (and transgender people too surely) in providing for rights and freedoms. While the Covenants built on the rights and freedoms contained in the Universal Declaration, they also included some new rights such as:

1. The right of self-determination[82]
2. The rights of the child
3. The rights of minorities
4. The right of detained persons to be treated with humanity
5. Freedom from imprisonment for debt
6. Prohibition of propaganda for war and of incitement to hatred

What was omitted, however, in the 1966 Covenants was the right to property, a fundamental right and an idea deeply rooted in Western civilisation and supported by European philosophers and other thinkers and writers such as Adam Smith, who championed the idea of individualism based on, among other things, the right to property and free trade which later became known as laissez-faire capitalism.[83] As stated by John Locke in 1689, 'everyman has a property in his person; this nobody has a right to but himself. The labour of his body and the work of his hand, we may say, are properly his.'[84] This was echoed in the French Declaration of the Rights of Man and of the Citizen in Article 17 which stated that 'Since property is an inviolable and sacred right, no one shall be deprived thereof except where public necessity, legally determined, shall clearly demand it, and then only on condition that the owner shall have been previously and equitably indemnified.' Although this right was included in the Universal Declaration, there was disagreement about its inclusion in legally binding Covenants on the part of the Communist countries led by the former Soviet Union.

The former Soviet Union rejected the idea of including the right to property in the 1966 Covenant, arguing that large units of property should be in the hands of the State. Interestingly, during the negotiations it was agreed that the right of self-determination of peoples would be included in both of the

82 The right of self-determination of peoples or national groups had, of course, been endorsed earlier by the UN General Assembly in its Declaration on the Granting of Independence to Colonial Countries and Peoples, Adopted by General Assembly resolution 1514 (XV) of 14 December 1960.

83 Adam Smith, in the eighteenth century, promoted the idea that the pursuit of individual self-interest would ultimately promote development of the common good through his publications such as *The Theory of Moral Sentiments* (Knud Haakonssen (ed.), Oxford University Press, 2002) and *An Inquiry into the Causes and the Nature of the Wealth of Nations* (Printed for Messrs. Whitestone, Chamberlain, Dublin, 1776).

84 John Locke, 'On Property', The Second Treatise, as quoted in Micheline R. Ishay, *The History of Human Rights: From Ancient Times to the Globalization Era* (University of California Press, 2004) 93.

Covenants and this right appears in common Article 1. With regard to the implementation of the rights enshrined in the 1966 Covenants, the Covenant on Civil and Political Rights does not speak of 'progressive realisation' of the rights included in the Covenant, but the Covenant on Economic, Social and Cultural Rights states in Article 2 (1) that:

> Each State Party to the present Covenant undertakes to take steps, individually and through international assistance and cooperation, especially economic and technical, to the maximum of its available resources, with a view to *achieving progressively the full realization of the rights recognized* in the present Covenant by all appropriate means, including particularly the adoption of legislative measures. (emphasis added)

When these two Covenants were adopted, an Optional Protocol to the Covenant on Civil and Political Rights to allow for individual petition against the violations of rights enshrined in this Covenant was also adopted. However, this was not the case with the Covenant on Economic, Social and Cultural Rights since the rights enshrined therein were to be 'progressively achieved' rather than implemented immediately (in this respect the latter have been referred to as 'second generation' rights). What is more, the same Covenant also admits, in the field of human rights, a political or economic distinction between developed and developing countries in the realisation of human rights. Article 2 (3) reads as follows:

> *Developing countries*, with due regard to human rights and their national economy, may determine to what extent they would guarantee the economic rights recognized in the present Covenant to non-nationals. (emphasis added)

The above two provisions indicate that the States which concluded these two Covenants had in mind a different approach to the full realisation of the rights embodied in them. In addition, it is worth noting that both Covenants, especially the Covenant on Economic, Social and Cultural Rights, include certain rights which are arguably too general and imprecise for them to be implemented or enforced by a court of law.

In addition to the International Bill of Rights, there are a number of other international human rights treaties[85] that provide for equality, gender, age, sector or other issue specific rights. Principal treaties among them are as follows:[86]

85 See for a list and text of such core international human rights treaties, Office of the United Nations High Commissioner for Human Rights, *The Core International Human Rights Treaties* (United Nations, 2006).

86 The UN refers to 10 core international human rights instruments, being ICCPR, ICESCR, CAT, CERD, CEDAW, CRC, CRPD, CED, the Convention on the

1. Convention against Torture and Other Cruel, Inhuman or Degrading Treatment or Punishment, 1984 (CAT)[87]
2. Convention on the Prevention and the Punishment of the Crime of Genocide, 1948[88]
3. Convention Relating to the Status of Refugees, 1951
4. Convention on the Political Rights of Women, 1953
5. International Convention on the Elimination of All Forms of Racial Discrimination, 1966 (CERD)[89]
6. Convention on the Elimination of All Forms of Discrimination against Women, 1979 (CEDAW)[90]
7. Convention on the Rights of the Child, 1989 (CRC)
8. International Convention on the Protection of the Rights of All Migrant Workers and Their Families, 1990
9. The International Convention on the Rights of Persons with Disabilities (2006) (CRPD), and
10. The International Convention for the Protection of All Persons from Enforced Disappearance (2006) (CED).

There are, of course, other international treaties dating from the time of the League of Nations providing for certain labour rights adopted under the auspices of the International Labour Organisation (ILO) such as the Convention Concerning Forced or Compulsory Labour of 1930, Right to Organise and Collective Bargaining of 1949, Equal Remuneration Convention of 1951, and Discrimination (Employment and Occupation) Convention, 1958. Likewise, the Convention against Discrimination in Education of 1960 was adopted by UNESCO.

2.14 Measures for implementation of rights

The need to secure effective measures for the implementation of rights was a major consideration, even at the time of the drafting of the Universal Declaration by the Commission on Human Rights in 1947. It was realised at that time that the proclamation or declaration of rights alone was not enough to ensure protection. Accordingly, and as noted above, the International Bill

Protection of Rights of Migrant Workers and their Families, and the optional protocol to CAT: http://www.ohchr.org/EN/ProfessionalInterest/Pages/CoreInstruments.aspx accessed 11 October 2014.

87 G.A. Res. 39/46/Annex of Dec. 10, 1984, U.N. GAOR, 39 Sess., Supp. No. 51, U.N. Doc A/39/51 (1984).

88 78 U.N.T.S. 277 (1948).

89 660 U.N.T.S. 195 (1969).

90 G.A. Res. 34/180, 34 U.N. GAOR Supp. (No. 46) at 193, U.N. Doc. A/RES/34/180 (1981).

of Rights proposed by the UN Commission on Human Rights in 1947 had three parts: a Declaration; a Convention; and 'measures of implementation'. However, the General Assembly decided in 1948 to consider only the draft Universal Declaration and asked the Human Rights Commission to continue its deliberations on the remaining two parts. Again, it was the opposition from the former Soviet Union and its Communist allies that frustrated the attempt to develop a mechanism designed to enforce human rights enshrined in the Declaration. They had invoked the principle of national sovereignty and independence and the provision in Article 2(7) of the UN Charter which prevents States from interfering in the internal affairs of other States.

While Article 1 of the UN Charter speaks of promoting and encouraging respect for human rights and fundamental freedoms on the part of all members of the UN, albeit without spelling out what these rights and freedoms were, the Charter goes on to provide for the principle of non-interference in the internal affairs of States in Article 2(7), although without stating what would and would not constitute an interference 'in matters which are essentially within the domestic jurisdiction of any State.' Although a quick glance at these two provisions may give the impression that they contradict each other, a logical interpretation of the provision in Article 2(7) would be that UN interference in the affairs of a State in respect of human rights and fundamental freedoms would not be construed as interference in the *internal* affairs of a State.

If a State decides to join the UN it is accepting international obligations arising out of that membership and thereby accepts corresponding exceptions to the principle of non-interference in the internal affairs that may arise accordingly. Therefore, by accepting the internationalisation of human rights and fundamental freedoms through the UN Charter, a Member State acknowledges that human rights matters are not limited to domestic jurisdiction, but are matters of international concern. When joining the UN, under its Charter a State also enters into a contractual relationship with other members of the UN; this entitles those other members to an interest in the fulfilment of the obligations arising out of UN membership by all member States. Therefore, a State cannot invoke national sovereignty or the principle of non-interference to prevent international scrutiny of the situation of human rights within its territory, or to escape from its duty to respect the rights of its citizens since the very purpose of the government is supposed to be to secure people's rights and facilitate their enjoyment by all.

Nevertheless, when the Commission on Human Rights and the Third Committee of the General Assembly considered the draft of the 1966 Covenants and their measures of implementation, the idea of a Human Rights Committee rather than an international court of human rights capable of handing down binding decisions was accepted as a compromise mechanism for implementation of the rights contained in the Covenant on Civil and Political Rights. There were other proposals of far-reaching changes that could be made to make the system of implementation more rigorous. For instance, Australia had suggested the creation of an International Court of Human Rights, France had suggested an International Investigation Commission, and Uruguay had proposed the establishment of an office of the UN High Commissioner for Human Rights. India had proposed that the Security Council itself should be involved in the implementation of the provisions of the Covenants stating that the Council should be appraised of alleged violations, investigate them and enforce redress.[91]

However, when the 1966 Covenants were adopted they contained a double system of implementation consisting of (1) a compulsory system of reporting to the Human Rights Committee, and (2) an optional system of fact-finding and conciliation in the case of States which had expressly agreed to this procedure. A third mechanism of implementation of the provisions of the Covenant on Civil and Political Rights in the form of individual petitions was agreed through a separate international legal instrument, an Optional Protocol to the Covenant, whereby those States that chose to ratify this separate Protocol would allow individuals to make petitions to the Human Rights Committee, alleging violations of human rights by the government of the country concerned.

Nevertheless, regarding the implementation of the Covenant on Economic, Social and Cultural Rights, implementation was limited to reporting to the Economic and Social Council of the UN, which in turn could make recommendations 'of a general nature', meaning that the recommendations would not refer to particular situations of particular States. Thus, the vision in 1947 by the Human Rights Commission of an International Bill of Rights consisting of three parts, i.e. a Declaration, a Covenant, and 'measures of implementation', was accomplished to a certain extent nearly 20 years later in 1966, and whilst this heralded a new era in the evolution and protection of human rights, the 'measure of implementation' absent in 1948 remained weak in 1966.

In addition to the general measures of implementation of the main rights contained in the International Bill of Rights, treaty bodies created pursuant to other international human rights treaties contain provisions to monitor and promote compliance with the provisions of the relevant treaty. Along with the Human Rights Committee, there are a total of ten human rights treaty bodies, comprising committees of independent experts. Nine of such treaty bodies monitor implementation of the core international human rights treaties while the tenth treaty body, the Subcommittee on Prevention of Torture, established under the Optional Protocol to the Convention against Torture, monitors all places of detention in States parties to the Optional Protocol and submits its reports to the Committee Against Torture. One of the more recent treaty bodies is that on enforced disappearance, which was created pursuant to the International Convention for the Protection of All Persons from Enforced Disappearance adopted in 2006 and came into force on 23 December 2010.

91 See in A. H. Robertson and J. G. Merrills, *Human Rights in the World* (Manchester University Press, 3rd edn, 1994) 28.

These treaty bodies exercise a sort of quasi-judicial function to monitor and ensure compliance of the relevant treaties and assist States parties to them to strengthen their domestic legal, judicial, administrative and other systems so that they attain the international threshold required to fulfil the obligations of States under such treaties. In addition to the treaty body monitoring and reporting mechanisms there are charter-based mechanisms that are similarly tasked with taking a cooperative and aspirational approach to the promotion and protection of human rights. Such mechanisms include Special Procedures and Universal Periodic Review, which are discussed in further detail in the chapters that follow in this study.

Existing outside of the measures of implementation of the 1966 Covenants and other treaty bodies are other UN political, diplomatic and quasi-judicial bodies which are entrusted with the overall task of promoting and protecting human rights worldwide. They are as follows: the UN General Assembly itself and its Third Committee, the Human Rights Council, the Office of the High Commissioner for Human Rights, the Special Procedures, the UN Economic and Social Council, and various other *ad hoc* human rights monitoring and fact-finding commissions.

While presenting an analysis of the current framework of international human rights law, mention should also be made here of the role of various *ad hoc* international criminal tribunals and the permanent International Criminal Court in protecting human rights through prosecuting and punishing those who commit war crimes and crimes against humanity whose definition includes violation of certain human rights. As will be seen later,[92] the International Court of Justice and the Secretary General of the UN have also played a role in the promotion and protection of human rights.

In addition to the treaty bodies and charter-based bodies, there have been three major world conferences held to strengthen the UN system of human rights and achieve greater international cooperation in the implementation of the provisions of the International Bill of Rights and other human rights treaties. The first major international conference that focused on human rights and their meaningful implementation was the World Conference on Human Rights in June 1993 in Vienna. Although it did not adopt any new international human rights instrument (it was not intended to do so), it adopted the Vienna Declaration on Human Rights, a document of wide ranging significance, and a Programme of Action to strengthen the regime of human rights which led to the creation of the Office of the High Commissioner for Human Rights in December 1993.[93] The Declaration sought, *inter alia*, to flesh out the principles and provisions contained in various international instruments and accord

92 Discussed below in other chapters of this study.

93 Vienna Declaration and programme of Action, adopted by the world programme on human rights, 25 June 1993, http://www.ohchr.org/en/professionalinterest/pages/vienna.aspx accessed 11 October 2014.

concrete meaning to some of the general principles of human rights. The next major conference to focus on human rights and associated matters was the World Conference against Racism which was held in August and September 2001 in Durban, South Africa with the Durban Review Conference taking place in April 2009 in Geneva.

Neither the Durban Conference of 2001 nor the Durban Review Conference of 2009 adopted any new international legal instrument against racism. However, both of these conferences highlighted the issues of racism, racial discrimination, xenophobia and related intolerance and adopted a series of recommendations to strengthen national legal and administrative regimes and policies, as well as to enhance international cooperation for the speedy and comprehensive elimination of all forms of racism, racial discrimination, xenophobia and related intolerance. In the annals of international conferences dealing with human rights matters, mention should also be made of the UN Millennium Conference and its Declaration and the 2005 World Summit Conference and its Outcome document which sought to strengthen the international commitment to human rights. Indeed, it was the World Summit Conference of 2005 which decided to create a new Human Rights Council within the UN human rights system to enhance the international regime for the protection and promotion of human rights thereby opening a new chapter within the UN system in the promotion and protection of human rights.

While all of these mechanisms do make a contribution to the promotion and protection of human rights, there is as yet no judicial body to enforce human rights nor a powerful ombudsman. The Office of the High Commissioner for Human Rights comes close to being an ombudsman for human rights, but it is largely a political position operating under the overall supervision of the Secretary General of the UN. Since it is regarded as a political appointment, political considerations have inevitably played a role in the appointment process, thereby undermining the standing of this position.

2.15 Conclusions

The analysis throughout this chapter demonstrates why human rights are universal and how they came to be universally accepted. That is not to say that all human rights meet the test of universality. There is little doubt that the rights embodied in the Universal Declaration of Human Rights and the 1966 Covenants on Civil and Political Rights and on Economic, Social and Cultural Rights meet the test of universality, and yet there remains the question of justiciability of certain economic, social and cultural rights. Some rights may not be justiciable, but this factor does not prevent them from being characterised as universally accepted rights. Other human rights are in the process of gaining universal acceptance and are rights in the States which recognise such rights. The foregoing analysis has shown that certain core human rights are universal because they were drawn from the values of humanity from all over the world.

Within the word universality is the notion of the legally binding character of these rights. Indeed, the Universal Declaration of Human Rights which was adopted without any dissent in the first place in 1948 received a strong endorsement in the 2005 World Summit Outcome document which regards the fulfilment of the rights embodied in the Universal Declaration as a legal obligation.[94] Further, there is near universal acceptance of many core human rights instruments by States, including the 1966 Covenants on Civil and Political Rights and on Economic, Social and Cultural Rights.

However, human rights remain to this day universal in terms of aspiration but not in terms of realisation. Not only do authoritarian States deny citizens their rights, but also both authoritarian and less authoritarian States deny these rights to migrant workers in their countries. The universal character of human rights requires that they be respected by all and for all. The preceding analysis evinces that UN endeavours have remained weak in terms of creating mechanisms for the protection or enforcement of human rights. The score card of the UN human rights mechanisms appears impressive in terms of promoting human rights, spreading the education of human rights and engaging States in a dialogue to promote human rights, but when it comes to holding governments to account for violations of human rights the picture is rather dismal.

The members of the UN have come to accept that human rights are one of the three major pillars of the UN edifice along with security and development, but the Charter of the UN does not reflect this as there are no human rights institutions commensurate to this idea incorporated into the Charter of the UN. None of the principal organs of the UN is an organ with a primary task of promoting and protecting human rights. The Human Rights Council, the main UN human rights body, is only a subsidiary body of the General Assembly. Whatever agencies that have been established for the promotion and protection of human rights since the establishment of the UN have been subsidiary bodies of the principal organs with a soft mandate. These are the mechanisms and the human rights treaty bodies that will form the subject of analysis in the chapters that follow.

94 A/RES/60/1 of 24 October 2005.

3 Effectiveness of the UN human rights treaty bodies

3.1 Introduction

Treaty bodies are the main mechanisms that exist to monitor implementation of the core human rights treaties by States and to consider individual petitions from those claiming human rights violations. They are expert-led mechanisms of a non-political and quasi-judicial character. Unlike the courts or commissions established under regional human rights treaties, such as the European Convention on Human Rights or the Inter-American Convention on Human Rights, they are not formal international institutions. Nor are the UN treaty bodies subsidiaries of other organisations. They are independent in their function and receive secretarial and/or technical support from the Office of the UN High Commissioner for Human Rights. They can apply not only the specific treaties which created them but also the 1948 Universal Declaration of Human Rights to define their mandate and to the cases and situation under their consideration. They offer constructive recommendations to States parties to the treaty concerning how to enhance compliance with the treaty, be that by the executive, legislative or judicial branches of the State.

The general perception is that it is only the executive branch of the State, with the military and police at its disposal, that is capable of violating human rights, but in reality even the activities of judicial and legislative branches may undermine international human rights standards and violate human rights whether it is to do with the principles of fair trial or parliamentary immunity of the members of parliament belonging to the opposition political parties.[1] It

1 For instance, about 182 supporters of the Muslim Brotherhood reportedly had their death sentences confirmed by the Southern Minya Criminal Court in Egypt. The trials have been criticised for failing to meet required standards with many being tried in absentia, see David Rankin, 'Egypt Court confirms Death sentences for over 180', *The Times* Middle East, 21 June 2014, http://www.thetimes.co.uk/tto/news/world/middleeast/article4126365.ece; 'Egypt Court confirms Death sentences for over 180' Reuters, 21 June 2014, http://economictimes.indiatimes.com/news/international/world-news/egypt-court-confirms-death-sentences-for-over-180/articleshow/36952436.cms; 'Egypt Court confirms Death sentences for over 180', Mamdouh Thabit Associated Press, http://www.elpasotimes.com/nationworld/ci_26007871/egypt-

is against all such human rights violations or lack of conformity to international human rights standards that these treaty bodies may determine individual communications. According to the UN Office of the High Commissioner for Human Rights, the development of the individual communications procedure 'is one of the major advances in the human rights protection of individuals over the last two decades.'[2] Indeed, 20 years ago there were only three treaty bodies in total, each operating under the Convention on the Elimination of Racial Discrimination, the Optional Protocol to the International Covenant on Civil and Political Rights and the Convention against Torture. Today, all core international human rights treaties contain a provision for individual complaints to be made against treaty violations by the States parties. However, there are questions as to how effective the treaty bodies have been in ensuring compliance by States of their treaty obligations. What are the strengths and weaknesses of the system of treaty bodies and what needs to be done to address the weaknesses? This chapter aims to analyse the origins and the current workings of these treaty bodies as well as their effectiveness and the challenges that they face in carrying out the functions they are mandated to perform.

3.2 The rationale for treaty bodies

When the process of standard setting of human rights reached a certain stage, the focus of the international community was on creating mechanisms to ensure compliance with those standards, with the human rights treaty bodies forming one of such mechanisms. There are a number of human rights treaty bodies created by the core international human rights treaties adopted under

confirms-180-islamist-death-sentences, all accessed 07 July 2014. Another example is the case initiated by the Supreme Court of the Maldives against five members of the Human Rights Commission of the country. When these five members submitted a written contribution to the UN Human Rights Council as part of the country's UPR they had to face criminal charges, which were initiated suo motu by the Supreme Court itself through a summons issued on 22 September 2014. See OHCHR' Briefing Notes, 17 October 2014, Geneva. Yet another example is the removal repeatedly of parliamentary immunity of the members of parliament belonging to the opposition political party by the members of parliament belonging to the ruling party in Cambodia. See the decision of the Governing Council of the Inter-Parliamentary Union, the international organisation of the Parliaments of 162 sovereign States in two cases concerning freedom of expression and parliamentary immunity: (1) Case No. CMBD/47 - Mu Sochua - Cambodia, and (2) Case No. CMBD/01 - Sam Rainsy - Cambodia. Both of these cases were decided in Bern on 19 October 2011.

2 A background paper on 'Strengthening the Rule of Law: The right to an effective remedy for victims of human rights violations' presented by the OHCHR to the Vienna + 20 Conference in Vienna, 27–28 June 2013. A copy of the paper is on file with the present author. See also Olivier De Frouville, 'Strengthening the Rule of Law: The right to an effective remedy for victims of human rights violations', http://www.frouville.org/Publications_files/de%20Frouville%20125-136.pdf

the auspices of the United Nations.[3] Although, strictly speaking, such treaty bodies are not part of the UN system of human rights as such, since they are self-standing mechanisms they constitute the cornerstone of the UN human rights programme. Since these treaties were negotiated and concluded under the auspices of the UN and the treaty bodies created by such treaties are supported by the UN mainly through the Office of the High Commissioner for Human Rights, they are treated as part of the UN human rights system. Such treaty bodies are relatively recent creations,[4] but have played an important role in protecting human rights guaranteed under their respective treaties.

A central element of the treaty body system is the reporting by States parties to the treaty concerned, and the creation of a constructive dialogue between the representatives of the State and independent experts in human rights. Another element, albeit used rarely, is a mechanism for inter-State complaints. However, more important is the individual complaints mechanism under which complaints can be lodged by aggrieved individuals against the State at the international level, a novelty in international law.

Furthermore, in some cases, such as genocide, torture and enforced disappearance, the treaties establish a legal framework for prosecution of individuals under universal jurisdiction. It was the jurisprudence of the Nuremberg trials that recognised that there could be criminal liability under international law for certain crimes, such as war crimes and crimes against humanity.[5] The Pinochet[6] and Kumar Lama[7] cases in the UK are some examples of an attempt

3 See for a list and text of such core international human rights treaties, http://www.ohchr.org/EN/HRBodies/Pages/TreatyBodies.aspx accessed 04 July 2014.

4 At the time of the 1968 World Conference on Human Rights held in Tehran, Iran, not a single human rights treaty body was functioning.

5 Ann Tusa and John Tusa, *The Nuremberg Trial* (Atheneum, 1986). On 11 December 1946, the UN General Assembly unanimously adopted a resolution affirming the principles of international law recognised by the Charter of the Nuremberg Tribunal and the judgement of the Tribunal, G.A. Res. 95 (I), U.N. GAOR, 1st Sess., pt. 2, at 1144, U.N. Doc. A/236 (1946). One of the lasting effects of the Nuremberg trials was the adoption of the Genocide Convention of 1948 by the UN.

6 *R v Bow Street Metropolitan Stipendiary Magistrate, Ex Parte Pinochet Ugarte* 3 [2000] 1 A.C. 147; [1999] 2 W.L.R. 827 (H.L. 1998), see the final Opinion of the House of Lords delivered on 24 March 1999.

7 A Nepalese army officer, Colonel Kumar Lama, was arrested and charged in January 2013 in the UK with two counts of torture during his country's civil war in 2005 under a law that allows prosecution of alleged war criminals. He was charged with intentionally 'inflicting severe pain or suffering' as a public official on two separate individuals. He was employed as a UN peace keeper in Sudan, but was visiting the UK when he was arrested. He was arrested under Section 134 of the Criminal Justice Act, a law that defines torture as a 'universal jurisdiction' crime in line with the provisions of the 1984 UN convention on torture. This showed that suspects can face trial before a British court even if their alleged offences had nothing to do with the UK. His arrest in the UK while on holiday led to the Nepalese government summoning the UK ambassador in Kathmandu to protest. Nepal said that Britain had breached Nepal's

by States to exercise universal jurisdiction for alleged torture committed in another country. It is not only the UN Convention on Torture that is invoked in such situations, but also Article 5 of the Universal Declaration of Human Rights and Article 7 of the International Covenant on Civil and Political Rights which outlaw torture.

A resolution of the UN General Assembly of 1973 proclaimed the need for international cooperation in the detection, arrest, extradition and punishment of persons guilty of war crimes and crimes against humanity.[8] A further resolution of the General Assembly in 1975 proclaimed the desire to make the prohibition on torture more effective throughout the world.[9] Prior to the adoption of the UN Convention against Torture, although States were entitled to exercise jurisdiction in respect of the offence wherever it was committed, they were not obliged to do so. Under the Torture Convention there is an obligation on States parties to the convention to exercise jurisdiction when there is a case for it.

The treaty bodies came into existence partly due to the ineffectiveness of the periodic comprehensive reporting system that was in existence within the framework of the Commission on Human Rights dating back to 1956.[10] The idea of reporting was conceived in view of the responsibilities of States under Articles 55 and 56 of the Charter of the UN. However, in the absence of a specific treaty requirement, the general reporting requirement did not work well. It was with a view to creating a more robust system of reporting that treaty bodies were devised.

Of all the UN human rights mechanisms, the treaty bodies are in effect quasi-judicial non-political entities. They are made up of independent experts tasked with the monitoring of the implementation of the core treaty relevant to the particular body. A State's commitment to a treaty is a legal commitment;

sovereignty by carrying out the arrest. Narayan Kaji Shrestha, the country's foreign minister, was reported to have said: 'The arrest of Lama, who has been serving in the United Nations mission in Sudan, without informing the concerned government and without any evidence, is against the general principle of international law and jurisdiction of a sovereign country. We express strong objection to this mistake and urge that it be corrected . . . and Lama be released.' BBC News: UK of 5 January 2013: http://www.bbc.co.uk/news/world-asia-20914282, accessed 7 July 2014.

8 UN General Assembly 3073, 1973 proclaimed the need for international cooperation in the detection, arrest, extradition and punishment of persons guilty of war crimes and crimes against humanity, A/RES/3073(XXVIII).

9 See General Assembly resolution 3452, 1975 proclaimed the desire to make the prohibition on torture more effective throughout the world, see 'Torture and Other Cruel, Inhuman or Degrading Treatment or Punishment', and GA declaration, and 3453, 1975, 'Declaration on the Protection of All Persons from Being Subjected to Torture and Other Cruel, Inhuman or Degrading Treatment or Punishment', A/RES/3452(XXX).

10 Resolution 1 (XII) of the Commission on Human Rights.

however, strictly speaking, treaty bodies in fulfilling their functions do not operate as judicial bodies or dispute settlement mechanisms in the traditional sense of the term. While the number of such treaty bodies has increased over the years, there have been concerns expressed about the effectiveness of treaty bodies, the duplicity of work by various UN human rights agencies and the lack of capacity on the part of many States, especially developing ones, in submitting their country reports in compliance with the requirements of the core human rights treaties concerned.

Commentators such as Clapham have stated that: 'Relying on these treaties to better human rights protection remains unsatisfactory. The monitoring of governments' compliance with their treaty obligations largely depends on self-reporting and "shadow reporting" by civil society.'[11] As will be seen later, while many States do not even comply with their self-reporting requirement, others do so in a half-hearted manner and treat it as a matter of mere formality.

A debate has taken place since the 1980s as to how to streamline the work of the treaty bodies and how to make them more effective and efficient. Indeed, ways to enhance the UN treaty body system 'have been discussed since the establishment of the first treaty body, the Committee on the Elimination of Racial Discrimination.'[12] It was partly against this backdrop that various proposals had been made within the UN, such as creating a unified treaty body instead of having so many[13] or a unified reporting mechanism rather than several. However, for a number of practical and legal reasons these proposals have not been accepted and the work of the treaty bodies has continued under various resource and capacity constraints, although recent commitment to increase the resources available has been made.[14]

3.3 The origins of treaty bodies

When the idea of promoting human rights through the UN was conceived, the leading nations had in mind the promotion of human rights through a soft approach and in an incremental manner. The emphasis was on promotion, rather than on protection, and this was perhaps a rather pragmatic approach for the world of that time. For instance, Ramcharan states that:

11 Andrew Clapham, *Human Rights: A Very Short Introduction* (Oxford University Press, 2007) 53.

12 'Concept paper on the High Commissioner's proposal for a unified standing treaty body', UN Doc HRI/MC/2006/2 of 22 March 2006, para 5.

13 It was in her Plan of Action of 2005 that the then High Commissioner for Human Rights, Louise Arbour, proposed a unified standing treaty body and invited States party to the seven core human rights treaties to an intergovernmental meeting in 2006 to consider her options. UN Doc. A/59/2005/Add.3, para. 147.

14 General Assembly Resolution 'Strengthening and enhancing the effective functioning of the human rights treaty body system' 68/268 21 April 2014, http://www.ohchr.org/Documents/HRBodies/TB/HRTD/A-RES-68-268_E.pdf (accessed 13 October 2014).

> At the San Francisco conference, the world's great powers – including the United States, the Soviet Union, France, and the United Kingdom – opposed giving the United Nations the competence to protect human rights. The United States was a racially segregated country, the Soviet Union a totalitarian State with gulags, and France and the United Kingdom colonial powers that exploited subject populations. Clearly a UN empowered with the capacity to protect human rights was not in their interests.[15]

It was only later that the idea of creating mechanisms to protect human rights became acceptable, and the notion of treaty bodies to this effect was conceived. Even then the idea was a piecemeal and incremental one. Rather than creating a global mechanism with comprehensive powers to protect human rights, a treaty-by-treaty mechanism – and even such a mechanism being a soft one – was developed for protection. The treaty bodies were created originally at the behest primarily of newly independent developing countries that acted through the General Assembly and the first of such treaty bodies was the one created under the Convention on the Elimination of All Forms of Racial Discrimination – not a natural top priority agenda for Western countries. Since this initial breakthrough, a number of other treaty bodies created at the behest of either Western or non-Western countries have come into existence.

Currently, there are nine human rights treaty bodies created to monitor implementation of the rights enshrined in core international human rights treaties.[16] The main task of the treaty bodies is to review the reports submitted by States. The treaty body proceeds to provide authoritative guidance to the

15 Bertrand Ramcharan, *The UN Human Rights Council* (Routledge, 2011) 20–21.

16 The following are the core international human rights treaties: International Covenant on Civil and Political Rights; International Covenant on Economic, Social and Cultural Rights; International Convention on the Elimination of All Forms of Racial Discrimination; Convention on the Elimination of All Forms of Discrimination against Women; Convention against Torture and Other Cruel, Inhuman or Degrading Treatment or Punishment; Convention on the Rights of the Child; International Convention on the Protection of the Rights of All Migrant Workers and Members of Their Families; Convention on the Rights of Persons with Disabilities; International Convention for the Protection of All Persons from Enforced Disappearance. In addition, there is a treaty body established under the optional protocol to the Convention Against Torture (OPCAT) (2007) mandated with visiting places of detention to prevent torture or other cruel, inhuman or degrading treatment or punishment. For a full list of UN core international human rights treaties, see http://www.ohchr.org/EN/HRBodies/Pages/TreatyBodies.aspx (accessed 04 July 2014). To find out which countries have ratified the international human rights treaties: http://indicators.ohchr.org/. For information on the status of ratification and signature by States of UN human rights treaties, as well as reservations and declarations: http://treaties.un.org/Pages/Treaties.aspx?id=4&subid=A&lang=en/. An overview of the ratification status is also available at: http://tbinternet.ohchr.org/_layouts/TreatyBodyExternal/Treaty.aspx

State concerned on human rights standards and recommends what States must do to ensure that all people within its territory enjoy the rights guaranteed in the treaties concerned. Many of them also sit in a quasi-judicial capacity to offer findings on cases brought before them by an individual against a State which has accepted the competence of such treaty bodies to entertain individual petitions. One of the strengths of such treaty bodies is that they are not just another UN political body which can be criticised for applying selectivity and double standards by targeting a group of countries for scrutiny. In the words of the UN High Commissioner for Human Rights, 'Treaty bodies are custodians of the legal norms established by the human rights treaties.'[17]

At the time of writing there are nine core international human rights treaties, each with its own corresponding treaty body, and the most recent one concerns enforced disappearance, which entered into force in December 2010.[18] There is a tenth body – the Subcommittee on Prevention of Torture – established under the Optional Protocol to the Convention against Torture, to monitor places of detention in States parties to the Optional Protocol. These treaty bodies are not formally part of the UN system of human rights as such, given that they are committees of independent experts elected by States parties to the treaty concerned. Furthermore, some of these experts might be experts in a certain area of human rights but not necessarily experts in law.

The Committee on Economic, Social and Cultural Rights, the Committee against Torture and the Committee on the Rights of the Child have an inter-disciplinary composition. The inter-disciplinary character of these committees has its own merits, but it is not necessarily an advantage when it comes to examining individual petitions since experts without a legal background would not find such applications easy to deal with and the recommendations made by a committee that consists of non-lawyers would not necessarily carry the same legal weight. Further, the Committee on Economic, Social and Cultural

17 Navi Pillay, 'Strengthening the United Nations Human Rights Treaty Body System: A Report by the United Nations High Commissioner for Human Rights', United Nations Office of the High Commissioner for Human Rights, Geneva, June 2012, 8.

18 As of 30 September 2014, the number of ratifications of the following treaties was as follows: the Elimination of All Forms of Racial Discrimination: 177 States (which is the joint-third highest number of ratifications); International Covenant on Economic, Social and Cultural Rights: 162 States; International Covenant on Civil and Political Rights: 177 States; Convention on the Elimination of All Forms of Discrimination against Women: 188 States (this is the second highest number of ratifications); Convention against Torture and Other Cruel, Inhuman or Degrading Treatment or Punishment: 156 States; Convention on the Rights of the Child: 193 States (this is the highest number of ratifications making it an almost universally accepted human rights treaty); International Convention on the Protection of the Rights of All Migrant Workers and Members of Their Families: 47 States; Convention of the Rights of Persons with Disabilities: 151 States; and International Convention for the Protection of All Persons from Enforced Disappearance: 43 States. Source: OHCHR, Human Rights Treaties Division, Newsletter, No. 24, July–September, 2014.

Rights is assigned the task of not only monitoring implementation of the rights enshrined in the Covenant on the Economic, Social and Cultural Rights but also assisting in the realisation of these rights as well as the decisions of the Economic and Social Council of the UN.

3.4 The working method of treaty bodies

Highlighting the significance of the work of these treaty bodies, the Secretary General of the UN, Ban Ki-moon, stated that: 'The United Nations human rights treaty body system, which combines noble ideals with practical measures to realize them, is one of the greatest achievements in the history of the global struggle for human rights.' He went on to add that, 'The treaty bodies stand at the heart of the international human rights protection system as engines translating universal norms into social justice and individual well being.'[19] Since the Office of the High Commissioner for Human Rights provides secretarial support to these bodies and the cost of their activities is covered by the UN's regular budget, it can be said that all State members of the UN, regardless of whether they have ratified a particular human rights treaty or a protocol, contribute financially to the activities of these treaty bodies.

Treaty bodies, or committees as they are commonly referred to, perform a number of functions in accordance with the provisions of their respective treaty. These include:

- consideration of the periodic reports by States parties to the treaty;
- consideration of individual complaints or communications and inter-State complaints; and
- publication of general comments or general recommendations.[20]

19 Ban Ki-moon, 'Foreword', to the Report of the UN High Commissioner for Human Rights on the Strengthening of the Human Rights Treaty Bodies, UN Doc. A/66/860 of 26 June 2012, p.7.

20 See generally, Christof H. Heyns and Frans Viljoen, *The Impact of the United Nations Human Rights Treaties on the Domestic Level* (Martinus Nijhoff Publishers 2002); Laura Theytaz-Bergman 'What Happened? A Study on the Impact of the Convention on the Rights of the Child in Five Countries: Estonia, Nepal, Peru, Uganda and Yemen', Save the Children, 2009 http://resourcecentre.savethechildren.se/sites/default/files/documents/2910.pdf; 'The UN Convention on the Rights of the Child: A Study of Implementation in 12 countries' (UNICEF 2012) http://www.unicef.org.uk/Documents/Publications/UNICEFUK_2012CRCimplementationreport%20FINAL%20PDF%20version.pdf; Report of the Study on the Impact of the UN Convention on the Rights of the Child (UNICEF Innocenti Research Centre 2004); Committee on International Human Rights Law and Practice of the International Law Association, Final report on the impact of findings of the United Nations human rights treaty bodies (2004); From Judgment to Justice: Implementing International and Regional Human Rights Decisions (Open Society Justice Initiative — Open Society Foundation, 2010), http://www.opensocietyfoundations.org/sites/default/files/from-judgment-to-justice-20101122.pdf all accessed 14 October 2014.

In making their general comments or general recommendations, the treaty bodies go on to expound the provisions of the treaty concerned. Thus, these comments become of value and interest not only to the individual States concerned but also other States, national and international judiciaries as well as international organisations, human rights defenders, academics, students and scholars.

3.4.1 Consideration of the periodic reports by States parties to the Convention

When a State decides to ratify a human rights treaty, it accepts a legal obligation to implement the rights recognised in that treaty. To ensure that States adhere to the treaty provisions in practice, many treaties require the States parties to the treaty to submit periodic reports to the monitoring committee set up under that treaty, such reports detailing how the State is implementing promotion of the rights concerned. States are required to submit their initial report usually 1 year after ratifying the treaty (2 years in the case of the Convention on the Rights of the Child) and then periodically as stipulated in the treaty concerned, the period being usually every 4 or 5 years. The Committees concerned may also receive information on a country's human rights situation from other sources, including non-governmental organisations, UN agencies such as the Office of the High Commissioner for Human Rights, other intergovernmental organisations, academic institutions and the press. The Committee then examines the report together with government representatives and subsequently publishes its concerns and recommendations in the form of 'concluding observations'.

The objective behind this reporting mechanism is to ensure that a comprehensive review is undertaken by the State concerned with respect to legislative, administrative and other measures taken to fulfil the obligations arising under the human rights treaty concerned and that the State party monitors the actual situation with respect to each of the rights guaranteed in the treaty on a regular basis and the extent to which everyone is able to enjoy such rights. The reporting procedure provides an opportunity to the Government to demonstrate to the national and international audience that principled policy-making has been undertaken to give priority to complying with the requirements of the treaty. It is also designed to facilitate public scrutiny of government policies within the State concerned.

The reporting mechanism provides an opportunity for the State, as well the relevant treaty body, to evaluate the extent to which progress has been made towards the realisation of the obligations arising out of the treaty and which challenges remain to be addressed. This process enables the State concerned to benefit from good practice by other States and to develop a better understanding of the problems and shortcomings encountered in efforts to realize progressively the full range of rights guaranteed in the treaty concerned. The essence of the treaty body system is a constructive dialogue between the representatives of the State and the independent experts of the committee to achieve the desired objectives.

3.4.2 Consideration of individual complaints or communications

Examining the periodic reports by States is not the only function of these committees. Some committees perform additional monitoring functions through three other mechanisms: the inquiry procedure, the examination of inter-State complaints and the examination of individual complaints. Six of the Conventions or the Optional Protocols to these Conventions – that is, the Covenant on Civil and Political Rights, the Convention on the Elimination of Racial Discrimination, the Convention against Torture and Other Cruel, Inhuman or Degrading Treatment, the Convention on the Elimination of All Forms of Discrimination against Women (1979) and its optional protocol (1999) and the Convention on Migrant Workers – allow individuals to make petitions to the committees established under the treaties concerned alleging violations of the rights contained in the treaties.[21] Such petitions can only be made once all domestic remedies have been exhausted or are deemed futile. The right to bring complaints extends not just to victims but also to others acting on their behalf such as human rights organisations. Having considered the individual complaints made, the committees established then make their recommendations to the governments concerned.

The recommendations vary significantly, and include *inter alia* financial compensation, release from imprisonment, retrial, commutation of death sentence, non-refoulement of persons in danger of torture or persecution if returned, reinstatement in public service and change of legislation and/or governmental policy. For instance, in three cases brought before the Human Rights Committee alleging disappearance of three individuals during the Maoist insurgency in Nepal (1996–2005), the Committee concluded that Nepal as a party to the 1966 Covenant on Civil and Political Rights and its Optional Protocol was under an obligation to provide the applicants with an effective remedy, including: (1) conducting a thorough and effective investigation into the disappearance of the individuals mentioned in the applications; (2) locating

21 Competence to consider individual communications have been conferred on treaty bodies by States either by means of ratification of the relevant optional protocols (this is the case for the Committee on Economic, Social and Cultural Rights, the Human Rights Committee, the Committee on the Elimination of Discrimination against Women, the Committee on Migrant Workers and the Committee on the Rights of Persons with Disabilities), or by a declaration under the relevant provision of the treaty in question (Article 14 of the International Convention on the Elimination of All Forms of Racial Discrimination; Article 22 of the Convention against Torture; Article 77 of the International Convention on the Protection of the Rights of All Migrant Workers and Members of Their Families; and Article 31 of the International Convention for the Protection of All Persons from Enforced Disappearance).

their remains and handing them over to their families; (3) prosecuting, trying and punishing those responsible for the violations committed; (4) providing adequate compensation to the applicants for the violations suffered, and (5) ensuring that the necessary and adequate psychological rehabilitation and medical treatment is provided to the applicants.[22]

In the absence of any other follow-up mechanism of such recommendations or views of the Committee, it is up to the Committee itself to follow up on its views. Therefore, in the above-mentioned case the Committee itself asked the State concerned, i.e. Nepal, to furnish information to the Committee within 180 days concerning the measures taken to give effect to its views. Although the recommendations of treaty bodies lack legally binding force, according to the OHCHR, many States implement the recommendations at least partly. 'In cases where treaty bodies have recommended that a person should not be deported, compliance rate is close to full. Evidence suggests that the more concrete the remedies proposed by the treaty bodies, the better chances they have to be implemented.'[23] There are other procedures for individual complaints within the UN human rights system but they fall outside of the treaty body system. They are through the complaints procedure of the Human Rights Council, through the special procedures mechanism, and through the Commission on the Status of Women.

3.4.3 Inter-State complaints

There is a provision for inter-State complaints in many of these treaties. However, this mechanism has never been used. It is quite ironic that in spite of complaining publicly that countries such as China, North Korea, Iran, Syria and a number of gulf countries have violated human rights, no country has as yet lodged a complaint to the treaty bodies. States do not seem to regard violations of human rights as violations of international law. For instance, if North Korea has ratified the 1966 Covenant on Civil and Political Rights, and there are nonetheless credible reports produced by the Special Rapporteurs for the country (as well as a UN commission of inquiry led by a distinguished jurist from Australia, Justice Michael Kirby) documenting the systematic, widespread

22 The Views of the Human Rights Committee: UN Doc. CCPR/C/112/D/2031/2011 of 10 November 2014; UN Doc. CCPR/C/112/D/20111/2011 of 10 November 2014; and UN Doc. CCPR/C/112/D/2051/2011 of 11 November 2014. See also an op-ed piece by one of the applicants to the UNHRC commenting on its findings in these cases: Ram Bhandari, 'Truth and consequences', *The Kathmandu Post*, 18 December 2014; available at http://www.ekantipur.com/2014/12/18/opinion/truth-and-consequences/399169.html.

23 A background paper on 'Strengthening the Rule of Law: The right to an effective remedy for victims of human rights violations' presented by the OHCHR to the Vienna + 20 Conference in Vienna, 27–28 June 2013. A copy of the paper is on file with the present author.

and grave violations of human rights in the country[24] then other contracting parties should be able to lodge a complaint to the Human Rights Committee if they regard human rights obligations as legally binding obligations.

3.4.4 General comments or general recommendations

In addition to the recommendations made after consideration of individual or inter-State complaints, the treaty bodies also publish their interpretation of the content of human rights provisions, known as general comments or general recommendations, on thematic issues or methods of work. Some of these general comments or general recommendations have far-reaching implications and receive much wider interest. An example of such a general comment is the one on the nature and scope of the freedoms of opinion and expression issued by the Human Rights Committee operating under the Covenant on Civil and Political Rights on freedom of speech.[25] Another example is the General Comment issued by the Committee clarifying limits on detention in relation to the application and interpretation of Article 9 of the International Covenant on Civil and Political Rights which covers liberty and security of person.[26]

3.5 Difference in the nature and mandate of individual treaty bodies

3.5.1 The Human Rights Committee

The Human Rights Committee is a body of 18 independent experts elected by the States parties to the International Covenant on Civil and Political Rights which monitors implementation of the Covenant by its States parties.[27] This is perhaps the most powerful of all treaty bodies as it deals with non-compliance with the 1966 Covenant on Civil and Political Rights. The members of the Committee are intended to be persons of high moral character and recognised

24 See the report of the Commission of Inquiry led by Justice Michael Kirby A/HRC/25/63 of February 2014.

25 General Comment No. 34, Article 19: Freedoms of Opinion and Expression, Human Rights Committee, 102nd session, CCPR/C/GC/43, 12 September 2011, http://www2.ohchr.org/english/bodies/hrc/docs/GC34.pdf (accessed 14 October 2014).

26 General Comment No.35 – Article 9: Liberty and Security of Person of 30 October 2014.

27 See generally for an analysis of the election, composition, powers and functions of the Human Rights Committee: Theodor Meron, *Human Rights Law-Making in the United Nations: A Critique of Instruments and Process* (Clarendon Press, 1986); Dominic McGoldrick, *The Human Rights Committee: Its Role in the Development of the International Covenant on Civil And Political Rights* (Clarendon Press, 1991); Yogesh Tyagi, *The UN Human Rights Committee: Practice and Procedure* (Cambridge University Press, 2011).

competence in the field of human rights and are elected for a term of 4 years. They serve in their personal capacity and may be re-elected if nominated. There are five major functions of this Committee and they are as follows:

First, the examination of periodic reports submitted by States. All States that have ratified the Covenant are obliged to submit regular reports (usually every 4 years) to the Committee on how the rights are being implemented. The Committee examines each of the reports submitted by States and addresses its concerns and recommendations to the State in the form of "concluding observations". As mentioned by Higgins, a member of the Committee, the Committee does call for special reports on certain critical issues in exceptional cases:

> There have occurred such horrific events that it would be inappropriate for the Committee simply to wait for however many years until the next Report was due. So, in exceptional cases, "special calls" have supplemented the regular cycle. And often, in these "special calls", the Committee has asked for truncated reports, addressing the perceived critical issues.[28]

Judge Higgins has noted that during her time on the Committee such "special reports" were asked of – and received from – Burundi, Rwanda, Haiti, Bosnia, Croatia and Serbia-Montenegro, and Iraq.

Second, the examination of inter-State complaints by the Committee, though this has not been used at all. Under Article 41 of the Covenant, the Committee is entrusted with the task of considering inter-State complaints concerning allegations of violations of the provisions of the Covenant by a State party to it. The role of the Committee in this regard is more conciliatory rather than adjudicatory.

Third, it is the examination of individual petitions. This is a very important vehicle for victims of human rights violations and the Committee is credited for its worthwhile work in this regard. The First Optional Protocol to the Covenant, adopted together with the Covenant in 1966, gives the Committee competence to examine individual complaints with regard to alleged violations of the rights guaranteed in the Covenant by States parties to the Protocol. The Committee has competence to entertain such individual petitions if the individual concerned is from the State that has ratified the Protocol, has exhausted all available domestic remedies, and is a victim of the violation of a right enumerated in the Covenant. The petition should not be anonymous and the matter should not be under consideration by any other international body or settlement mechanism.

28 Rosalyn Higgins, 'Seighart Lecture', delivered at the British Institute of Human Rights, London, on 22 May 1996, London, 5. A copy of the lecture was kindly sent to the present author by Judge Higgins and is on file.

Fourth, it is the examination of complaints relating to the abolition of the death penalty. The UN General Assembly adopted a resolution containing the Second Optional Protocol to the International Covenant on Civil and Political Rights, aimed at the abolition of the death penalty in December 1989.[29] Under Article 3 of the Protocol the States parties to the Protocol are required to submit to the Human Rights Committee information on the measures that they have taken to give effect to the present Protocol. Therefore, the Committee has competence to examine inter-State and individual complaints regarding non-fulfilment of its obligations by a contracting party.

Fifth, it is the issuance of general comments or general recommendations. The Committee also publishes every now and then its interpretation of the nature, scope and meaning of the rights provided for in the Covenant. They are known as 'general comments or general recommendations' and are mostly on thematic human rights issues. They seek to flesh out the principles enunciated in the Covenant and they are regarded as a helpful guide on the implementation and interpretation of the Covenant by various stakeholders, including the judiciary and human rights organisations.

3.5.2 Committee on Economic, Social and Cultural Rights

Similar to the Human Rights Committee described above, the Committee on Economic, Social and Cultural Rights is a body of independent experts that monitors implementation of the International Covenant on Economic, Social and Cultural Rights by its States parties.[30] However, while the Human Rights Committee was created by the International Covenant on Civil and Political Rights, the Committee on Economic, Social and Cultural Rights was established under an ECOSOC (Economic and Social Council) resolution, and delegated with the task of carrying out the monitoring functions assigned to the United Nations Economic and Social Council in Part IV of the Covenant.[31] While classic rights, i.e., civil and political rights, can be implemented relatively immediately or straightforwardly, social, economic and cultural rights can only be implemented in a gradual manner. That is why the task of realising economic, social and cultural rights was assigned to the Economic and Social Council of the UN, which could achieve these objectives as part of the UN endeavour to uplift the economic and social conditions of life in its member States.

The functions of this Committee are similar to the functions of the Human Rights Committee. All States parties are obliged to submit reports every 5 years

29 Second Optional Protocol to the International Covenant on Civil and Political Rights, aiming at the abolition of the death penalty, General Assembly resolution 44/128 of 15 December 1989.

30 Marco Odello and Francesco Seatzu, *The UN Committee on Economic, Social and Cultural Rights: The Law, Process and Practice* (Routledge, 2012).

31 Resolution 1985/17 of 28 May 1985.

to the Committee detailing how rights are being implemented. With regard to individual complaints, it was in December 2008 that the UN General Assembly unanimously adopted an Optional Protocol to the International Covenant on Economic, Social and Cultural Rights providing for a mechanism for individual petitions and entrusting the Committee with the task of examining such petitions.[32] Uruguay became the tenth country in February 2013 to ratify the Optional Protocol, triggering its coming into force in May 2013.[33] This is a relatively small number of States to ratify the Optional Protocol since the total number of States that are party to the International Covenant on Economic, Social and Cultural Rights is over 160.[34] In addition to individual complaints, a State can also agree to be bound by an inquiry mechanism under the Protocol allowing the Committee to initiate and conduct investigations into grave and systematic violations of economic, social and cultural rights. This mechanism, which is not available under the Optional Protocol to the International Covenant on Civil and Political Rights, will allow the committee to respond quickly to serious violations taking place within a State party to the Covenant instead of waiting up to 5 years until the next periodic report is due.

3.5.3 Committee on the Elimination of Racial Discrimination

Similar to other human rights treaty bodies, the Committee on the Elimination of Racial Discrimination is a body of independent experts established to monitor implementation of the Convention on the Elimination of All Forms of Racial Discrimination by its States parties. States parties are obliged to submit regular reports every 2 years. In addition to the reporting procedure and the examination of interstate and individual complaints, the Convention has a provision for an early-warning procedure under which it can consider preventive measures aimed at stopping existing situations escalating into conflicts and providing for urgent procedures to respond to problems requiring immediate attention to prevent or limit the scale or number of serious violations of the Convention.

Criteria for early warning measures could include factors such as the lack of an adequate legislative basis for defining and prohibiting racial discrimination, inadequate implementation of enforcement mechanisms, the presence of a pattern of escalating racial hatred and violence, racist propaganda or appeals

32 GA Resolution A/RES/63/117. This took note of the adoption by the Human Rights Council by its resolution 8/2 of 18 June 2008 of the Optional Protocol.

33 The first nine countries to ratify this Optional Protocol were as follows: Argentina, Bolivia, Bosnia and Herzegovina, Ecuador, El Salvador, Mongolia, Portugal, Slovakia, and Spain.

34 162 States were party to his Convention as at 7 July 2014, see https://treaties.un.org/Pages/ViewDetails.aspx?src=TREATY&mtdsg_no=IV-3&chapter=4&lang=en accessed 07 July 2014.

to racial intolerance by persons, groups or organisations, a significant pattern of racial discrimination evidenced in social and economic indicators, significant flows of refugees or displaced persons resulting from a pattern of racial discrimination, or encroachment on the lands of minority communities.

Unlike many other committees, this Committee has preventative powers. It can initiate urgent procedures in order to respond to problems requiring immediate attention to prevent or limit the scale or number of serious violations of the Convention. Criteria for initiating an urgent procedure could include situations such as the presence of a serious, massive or persistent pattern of racial discrimination or a situation that is serious where there is a risk of further racial discrimination. This is a rather distinctive function of this Committee compared to other human rights treaty bodies.

3.5.4 Committee on the Elimination of Discrimination against Women

The Committee on the Elimination of Discrimination against Women is a body of 23 independent experts, the largest of all treaty bodies, and monitors implementation of the Convention on the Elimination of All Forms of Discrimination against Women. Similar to other human rights treaty bodies, it has the competence to examine periodic reports from States parties to the Convention. Under the Optional Protocol to the Convention, the Committee also has the competence to receive communications from individuals or groups of individuals submitting claims of violations of rights protected under the Convention. Although the Committee has been in existence for some time, it adopted its first decision on a communication submitted under Article 2 of the Optional Protocol in July 2004. Since then, it has adopted a number of such decisions relating to women's rights in different countries.

However, unlike some other human rights treaty bodies, it has the competence to initiate inquiries into situations of grave or systematic violations of women's rights even though these procedures are optional and are only available where the State concerned has accepted them. This inquiry procedure enables the Committee to conduct inquiries into serious and systematic abuses of women's human rights in States that have ratified the Optional Protocol. It is modelled on an existing human rights inquiry procedure under the International Convention against Torture and Other Cruel, Inhuman or Degrading Treatment or Punishment. The inquiry procedure is designed to enable the Committee to carry out investigation of substantial abuses of women's human rights and is useful where individual communications fail to reflect the systematic nature of widespread violations. This procedure allows a group of international experts to conduct investigations of widespread violations where individuals or groups may be unable to make communications for practical reasons or because of fear of reprisals.

3.5.5 Committee against Torture

The Committee against Torture is the body of independent experts established to monitor implementation of the Convention against Torture and Other Cruel, Inhuman or Degrading Treatment or Punishment by its States parties. Its functions are similar to the functions of other human rights treaty bodies discussed in the preceding paragraphs. In addition to the examination of periodic reports submitted by States, the Convention establishes three other mechanisms – individual petitions, inter-State complaints and inquiries procedure – to monitor implementation. The Optional Protocol to the Convention, which entered into force in June 2006, established a separate body – the Subcommittee on Prevention of Torture – with a mandate to visit places where persons are deprived of their liberty in the States parties to the Protocol. The latter body presents a public annual report on its activities to the Committee against Torture.

3.5.6 Committee on the Rights of the Child

The Committee on the Rights of the Child is a body similar to other human rights treaty bodies and monitors implementation of the Convention on the Rights of the Child by its States parties. It is also mandated to monitor implementation of two optional protocols to the Convention – one on involvement of children in armed conflict and another one on the sale of children, child prostitution and child pornography. Thus, unlike other human rights treaty bodies which monitor implementation of one international instrument, this Committee has been entrusted with the task of monitoring three international instruments. However, until December 2011, this Committee did not have the competence to examine individual complaints. It was the third Protocol on a Communications Procedure to the Convention adopted by the UN General Assembly on 19 December 2011 that allowed individual children to submit complaints regarding specific violations of their rights under the Convention and its first two optional protocols. Costa Rica became, on 14 January 2014, the tenth country to ratify this Optional Protocol. This meant that the Protocol took effect in April 2014 and children whose rights have been violated are now able to complain to the Committee after they have exhausted domestic remedies.

3.5.7 Committee on Migrant Workers

The Committee on the Protection of the Rights of All Migrant Workers and Members of their Families is a body of 14 independent experts established to monitor implementation of the corresponding Convention by its States parties. Similar to other human rights treaty bodies, this Committee too has the competence to examine periodic country reports and consider, under certain circumstances, individual complaints or communications from individuals claiming that their rights under the Convention have been violated.

3.5.8 Committee on the Rights of Persons with Disabilities

The Committee on the Rights of Persons with Disabilities is one of the newest of the human rights treaty bodies of independent experts established to monitor implementation of the International Convention on the Rights of Persons with Disabilities (2006) by the States parties. All States parties are under an obligation to submit periodic reports every 4 years to the Committee on how the rights are being implemented. States must report initially within 2 years of accepting the Convention and thereafter every 4 years. The Optional Protocol to the Convention provides for individual petition with regard to alleged violations of the Convention by States parties to the Protocol and the Committee has the competence to examine such petitions.

3.5.9 Committee on Enforced Disappearances

Similar to the Committee on the Rights of Persons with Disabilities, the Committee on Enforced Disappearances is a relatively new human rights treaty body of independent experts established to monitor implementation of the International Convention for the Protection of All Persons from Enforced Disappearance (2006) by the States parties. It too has the competence to examine the periodic reports by States parties to the Convention and receive and consider communications from or on behalf of individuals subject to its jurisdiction claiming to be victims of a violation by the State party of provisions of the Convention if the State concerned has declared at the time of ratification of the Convention or at any time afterwards that it recognizes the competence of the Committee to do so, in accordance with Article 31 of the Convention.

3.6 An assessment of the effectiveness of the human rights treaty bodies

The analysis of the workings of the human rights treaty bodies in the preceding paragraphs demonstrates that the approach adopted in various international human rights treaties for implementation of the provisions therein is three-fold: periodic reporting by States and examination of such reports by the committee concerned, inter-State complaints and individual complaints. Although an individual complaints procedure was a novelty at the time of the adoption of the first Optional Protocol to the 1966 Covenant on Civil and Political Rights, and many States were reluctant to accept this notion, it now has become a norm as most human rights treaties, especially the latest ones, include such a provision. Of these three mechanisms, the interstate mechanism is the least useful as no

State has yet sought to lodge a complaint against another State before any of these human rights committees. This strongly suggests that the action, or lack of, taken by States in relation to international human rights is all too often politically motivated (or politically deterred).

With regard to periodic reporting, as can be seen from the foregoing analysis, what is lacking is a mechanism for enforcement of the recommendations of the treaty bodies concerned. What is more, a survey of the work of these committees demonstrates that while many States have fallen behind in their reporting obligations, others have failed to implement the recommendations of various committees. According to a report on the work of treaty bodies published by the Office of the High Commissioner for Human Rights, only 16 per cent of States parties to various treaties report on time.[35] The report goes on to say that 'even with this low compliance rate, four out of nine treaty bodies with a reporting procedure are facing significant and increasing backlogs of reports awaiting consideration.'[36]

The following is the stark comment of the High Commissioner. 'The treaty body system is surviving because of the dedication of the experts, who are unpaid volunteers, the support of staff in OHCHR and [ironically] States' non-compliance with reporting obligations.'[37] Presenting his report to the 67th Session (2012) of the UN General Assembly, the Chairperson of the UN Committee against Torture, Claudio Grossman, stated that although 153 out of the 193 UN Member States had ratified or acceded to the UN convention against torture, 29 of these had never submitted a report to the Committee. He also highlighted the resource constraints experienced by the Committee and stated that there was a backlog of more than 115 cases pending before the Committee – 'this severely weakens the system as justice cannot be provided to States and individuals within a reasonable time.'[38]

With regard to individual petitions, in spite of having such a provision in so many core human rights treaties there were 750 or so individual petitions submitted to these bodies by the end of the 2011–12 biennium. Out of this number only 250 complaints had been reviewed by the treaty bodies and 500 were pending review.[39] The main reason that these individual complaints were pending review is that these treaty bodies did not have adequate resources and

35 Report of the UN High Commissioner for Human Rights on the Strengthening of the Human Rights Treaty Bodies, UN Doc. A/66/860 of 26 June 2012, p.9.

36 Ibid.

37 Ibid.

38 'States must translate commitment to eradicate torture into action, with adequate resources – UN expert committee on torture', News Release of the OHCHR of 23 October 2012, http://www.ohchr.org/EN/NewsEvents/Pages/DisplayNews.aspx?NewsID=12689&LangID=E (accessed 7 July 2014).

39 Report of the UN High Commissioner for Human Rights on the Strengthening of the Human Rights Treaty Bodies, UN Doc. A/66/860 of 26 June 2012, p.19.

time required to review them.[40] As at June 2012, there were 172 independent experts working for these treaty bodies, all working on a voluntary basis.[41] Even then these treaty bodies do not have sufficient resources to support their activities and the OHCHR actively seeks voluntary contributions to support and sustain the work of the treaty bodies.

Although there are nine treaty bodies which have the competence to receive individual complaints,[42] the vast majority of complaints have been submitted to the Human Rights Committee and to the Committee against Torture. According to a report by the Secretary General of the UN, as of August 2011, there were 378 acceptances by States of the competence of treaty bodies to receive individual communications. The Secretary General reported that the total number of cases submitted under the communications procedures and pending decision by the respective treaty body was 459 (of which 333 cases are for the Human Rights Committee and 103 for the Committee against Torture).[43]

Although States parties to these human rights Conventions are under a legal obligation to submit periodic reports in a timely fashion to the treaty bodies concerned, in the absence of sanctions the committees have no powers to require the States to do so, nor do they have the powers to require States to implement the recommendations made by the committees. While the human rights treaties are legally binding instruments, the various human rights treaty bodies established to monitor implementation of such treaties operate as quasi-judicial bodies rather than as judicial bodies and the conclusions that they reach on individual petitions submitted to them are not judgments, decisions or verdicts, but recommendations or views of the committees.

It is ironic that the approach taken for implementation of the legally binding various human rights treaties is to rely on moral and ethical pressure and public embarrassment, rather than meaningful and systematic sanctions. The system of treaty bodies is served by an army of nearly 175 independent experts, most of whom are highly qualified to discharge high level judicial functions. Crucially,

40 Various NGOs have also expressed their concern about the level of support available to treaty bodies to carry out their activities in an effective manner and expressed their views on the strengthening of the UN treaty body system. See 'The Dublin Statement of the Strengthening of the United Nations Human Rights Treaty Body System' of 2010. A copy of this was made available to the author by a Geneva based human rights organisation, International Service for Human Rights, in December 2010 and is on file with the present author.

41 Ibid., 17.

42 The procedure for individual complaints for two treaty bodies, namely, the Committee on Migrant Workers and the Committee on the Rights of the Child had not entered into force at the time of writing http://www.ohchr.org/EN/HRBodies/TBPetitions/Pages/HRTBPetitions.aspx accessed 14 October 2014.

43 'Measures to improve further the effectiveness, harmonization and reform of the treaty body system', report of the Secretary General: A/66/344 of 7 September 2011, 6, http://daccess-dds-ny.un.org/doc/UNDOC/GEN/N11/488/85/PDF/N1148885.pdf?OpenElement (accessed 7 July 2014).

however, they lack judicial powers while working for these treaty bodies. The final outcome of the monitoring activities of these treaty bodies is their 'views' (not 'decisions' or 'determinations'), to be forwarded to the State concerned for consideration and to the author of the individual communications in the case of individual complaints.

Furthermore, with regard to the outcome of the review of the reports from States under the Covenant on Civil and Political Rights by the Human Rights Committee what it does is to send its reports and 'general comments or general recommendations' to States after studying the reports. As mentioned by Meron, this process has been interpreted to mean that the study of country reports by the Committee did not include any element of assessment or evaluation since the primary function of the Committee is understood to assist States in the promotion of human rights rather than to pronounce whether a State party concerned had succeeded or not in implementing its undertaking under the Covenant.[44] Although some treaties, including the Convention against Torture, include more empowering provisions for the committees established under the treaties, the comments of these committees remain simply comments and suggestions rather than requirements for governments to comply with.[45]

Thus, the work of the treaty bodies remains in the realms of a 'soft' law approach based on persuasion, cajoling, and diplomatic pressure rather than a hard approach to shortcomings on the part of States in the implementation of the various human rights treaties. Implementation of human rights standards has been seen as a programmatic activity to be achieved progressively and with the help of the UN agencies and other States. Therefore, capacity building to achieve compliance rather than straightforward compliance has been part of the objectives of the UN human rights system. For this reason, many of the activities of human rights treaty bodies are seen as advisory rather than requiring strict compliance with the provisions of the treaties concerned. For instance, the Optional Protocol to the Convention against Torture which established the Subcommittee on the Prevention of Torture itself states that the function of the Subcommittee is advisory – a function which consists in providing assistance to States to achieve the objectives of the Convention.[46] Of course,

44 Theodor Meron, *Human Rights Law-Making in the United Nations: A Critique of Instruments and Process* (Clarendon Press, 1986), 124.

45 However, Meron's view is that in the case of the Optional Protocol to the International Covenant on Civil and Political Rights the acceptance of the Protocol in good faith by States 'implies the duty to comply with the 'views' of the [Human Rights] Committee', ibid., 126.

46 See OHCHR Brief on the SPT: "The SPT has an operational function which consists in visiting all places of detention in States parties, and an advisory function which consists in providing assistance and advice to both States parties and National Preventive Mechanisms ("NPM")." OHCHR, Geneva, 'The United Nations Subcommittee on Prevention of Torture and Other Cruel, Inhuman or Degrading Treatment or Punishment (The SPT)' (Geneva, 2012); see also http://www.ohchr.org/EN/HRBodies/OPCAT/Pages/Brief.aspx

there is no denying that the important work the treaty bodies carry out in developing international jurisprudence through general comments or general recommendations has been helpful in advancing and protecting human rights. From this standpoint at least, the work of these various human rights treaty bodies can be regarded as effective.

However, from a purely legal perspective, the various treaty bodies are not as effective and rigorous as they could be. As discussed above, the approach of the UN human rights system on the whole is more of a diplomatic and political one rather than legal, despite the fact that when a State ratifies or accepts a treaty it is entering a binding legal agreement. For instance, the General Assembly resolution 48/141 of 20 December 1993 creating the OHCHR states that one of the purposes of the United Nations is 'to *achieve international cooperation* in promoting and encouraging respect for human rights' and that the approach taken to achieve international cooperation is largely a political and diplomatic one (emphasis added).

It should be acknowledged that a central element of the current treaty body system is the monitoring mechanism which is designed to provide an opportunity for an individual State party to conduct a comprehensive review of the legal, administrative and other measures that it has taken to bring its national law and policy into line with the provisions of the treaty ratified by the country. The hope is that the process of preparing such reports would provide a platform for national dialogue on human rights amongst the various stakeholders in the country concerned. It is also hoped that consideration of such reports by the treaty bodies concerned, through constructive dialogue with States parties, would allow individual States, and other States parties to the treaty as a whole, to exchange experience on the problems faced in implementation of the treaty concerned, and good practices that facilitate enhanced implementation.

It is submitted that a central element of the treaty body system is the complaints procedure which provides an opportunity for treaty bodies to receive complaints either from other States parties to the treaty or from individuals within a State that has ratified the treaty, in order to identify steps that States or the individual State concerned should take to comply with their treaty obligations. Therefore, the UN treaty body system is not designed, and never was designed, to provide legal redress or remedy to individuals aggrieved by the violations of the rights enshrined in the treaty, but to progressively secure compliance by the State concerned by that State either enacting new laws, amending existing laws or by taking other administrative measures. The objective is to enable the domestic legal system, via the legislature, and the judiciary, via domestic courts, to provide effective redress or legal remedy to the individuals concerned, rather than relying on the treaty bodies. Therefore, the whole treaty body system is based on cooperation on a constructive basis amongst the States parties to the treaty, rather than coercion.

However, when that cooperation is absent there is very little that the treaty bodies can do. A UN agency cannot require a State to ratify a human rights treaty. In the absence of ratification of a treaty by an individual State, no treaty body can scrutinise the situation of human rights in that country or offer constructive recommendations.[47] Even many of those States that are party to the treaty concerned do not seem to take their reporting obligation seriously. Many of the State reports have been found to be repetitive, presenting information provided in other documents, and insufficient or selective data. States all too often get away with such inadequate reports since there is no comprehensive, effective mechanism for follow-up.

The UN human rights treaty process is fundamentally flawed because it is based on the 'gentlemanly' conduct of State cooperation. However, when a State refuses to cooperate, the only power at the disposal of these bodies is the public naming and shaming of the government concerned – as has been seen to be the case in relation to Iran, Syria or North Korea. Yet, publicity of the shortcomings of the government in question may not be an effective tool to require States to comply with their human rights obligations. The track record of compliance with the 'views' or recommendations of the treaty bodies, especially the Human Rights Committee, has been poor. This may be one reason why another scholar, Oona Hathaway, concludes that 'the major engines of compliance that exist in other areas of international law are for the most part absent in the area of human rights' and that there is 'little incentive [for States] to police non-compliance with treaties'.[48]

Having said this, it should be acknowledged that the treaty bodies have done an admirable job, under the circumstances, of analysing the human rights situations in various countries and recommending to the government the steps needed to comply with the requirements of the treaty. The human rights treaties and the work of the treaty bodies have been regarded as providing the framework against which the international community as well as the domestic population can legitimately judge the performance of governments. The jurisprudence developed by these treaty bodies has helped clarify the nature and scope of the rights contained in the relevant conventions. The OHCHR had the following to say about the significance of the jurisprudence resulting from the work of the treaty bodies:

> Jurisprudence generated by treaty bodies gives life to law. There is a face, a name, a victim, a situation and a concrete recommendation how to remedy it. Moreover, jurisprudence is not just a post-hoc procedure that provides a remedy after a violation; it is also a form of education for public officials, so that when in the future a similar situation arises, States know what the implications are and can act accordingly. Accordingly, it is not

47 Although this does not preclude action from the wider international community or charter mechanisms from being employed where there is cause for concern.

48 Oona Hathaway, 'Do Human Rights Treaties Make a Difference?' (2001-2002), 111 *Yale L.J.* 1935, 1938.

> only corrective, but in a very real sense preventive of violations of human rights.[49]

As stated by Clapham, even where States ignore or dismiss the recommendations of the treaty bodies 'it is clear that the process of putting governments on notice that UN's watchdogs have been alerted has led to releases [of detainees] and changes in policy.'[50] After all, as the cliché goes, making a small difference is better than making no difference at all; because one is not able to make a big difference does not mean that all effort in making small differences should cease. A small difference for one person could amount to a big difference for another. This has been the approach of the UN treaty bodies; they could have a more significant impact if the treaty body system was reformed to better equip them and resource them to rise to the challenge. As with other UN human rights bodies, one of the main difficulties for the treaty bodies has been securing effective compliance with their decisions, known as 'views' or recommendations. As explored in this chapter, the treaty bodies possess little in the way of powers to ensure compliance. They should have the powers to bring massive violations of human rights to the attention of the Security Council with recommendations for possible action, forcible and non-forcible, by the Council. Ultimately, however, the treaty bodies lack any such powers other than moral, and at best political, pressure on non-compliant governments.

3.7 Problems and prospects for reform of the human rights treaty body system

Since the treaty bodies have to rely on soft power to discharge their mandate, whether this still is the correct approach and is suitable for the contemporary world, or whether the time has come to move on to a different method, has remained debatable. It has long been recognised that the treaty bodies suffer from chronic underfunding and under-resourcing. While there is a huge backlog of cases and reports pending before many of these committees, it has also been widely acknowledged that with the growth in the number of treaty bodies States are struggling to submit their periodic reports to so many bodies and respond to their queries. Many States do not seem to have the capacity required to cope with these obligations.

What is more, the overlapping competence of different treaty bodies can result in a situation in which a State may be required to report on virtually the same

49 A background paper on 'Strengthening the Rule of Law: The right to an effective remedy for victims of human rights violations' presented by the OHCHR to the Vienna + 20 Conference in Vienna, 27–28 June 2013. A copy of the paper is on file with the present author.

50 Andrew Clapham, *Human Rights: A Very Short Introduction* (Oxford University Press, 2007), 74–75.

issue to several treaty bodies. Instead, the number of such treaty bodies has grown over the years and with that the number of reporting requirements has multiplied, with the Universal Periodic Review, a new charter based reporting and monitoring mechanism of the Human Rights Council that considers progress made by States against the human rights commitments made, adding yet another layer of reporting requirement for States. Therefore, the ways and means of enhancing the UN treaty body system has been on the UN agenda since the establishment of the first treaty body, the Committee on the Elimination of Racial Discrimination.

The previous UN Secretary General, Kofi Annan, himself had re-emphasised the need to streamline and strengthen the treaty body system in his report 'In Larger Freedom', submitted to the UN General Assembly in 2005.[51] Perhaps the most ambitious of such proposals was the one made by the then High Commissioner for Human Rights, Louise Arbour, to establish a unified standing treaty body to replace all human rights treaty bodies.[52] Prior to this, several reports were commissioned by the Secretary General of the UN on the effectiveness of the treaty bodies.[53]

However, not much progress has been made to enhance the capacity and effectiveness of these bodies or to streamline their activities. As far back as 1997 a proposal was under discussion to eliminate the reporting requirement under various treaties and replace it with detailed questions to which answers must be given.[54] It was in a UN report of 1993 that the human rights treaty regime was said to have 'reached a critical crossroads'.[55] But some 25 years have passed since then in which the treaty body system has continued to limp on. It also was proposed way back in 1989 that States should be required to prepare a single consolidated report to satisfy several different requirements and there should be consolidation of treaty bodies into 'one or perhaps two new treaty bodies'.[56]

It also was in the same report that the UN independent expert, Philip Alston, stated that 'The current level of overdue reports (in excess of 1,000) is chronic and entirely unacceptable.'[57] However, the situation has become worse over

51 The then Secretary General of the UN, Kofi Annan, 'In larger freedom: towards development, human rights and security for all', 21 March 2005, UN GA A/59/2005, http://www.un.org/en/ga/search/view_doc.asp?symbol=A/59/2005 accessed 08 October 2014.

52 UN Doc. A/59/2005/Add.3, para. 147.

53 See for example a series of reports by Philip Alston on the subject in U.N.doc. E/CN.4/1997/74 of 27 March 1997; A/CONF.157/PC/62/Axdd.11/Rev.1 of 22 April 1993 and A/44/668 of 1989, see http://www2.ohchr.org/english/bodies/icm-mc/documents-system.htm accessed 07 July 2014.

54 U.N.doc. E/CN.4/1997/74 of 27 March 1997, para 45.

55 A/CONF.157/PC/62/Axdd.11/Rev.1 of 22 April 1993, para 3.

56 A/44/668 (of 8 November 1989), paras 179 and 182.

57 Ibid, para 13.

the years and nothing of any substance has been done about it. Whatever reform has been carried out has been timid and cosmetic in nature. Whilst treaty bodies are now being encouraged to take a more streamlined approach to the reporting procedure and seek to establish consistency across the different bodies, in recognition of the fact that 'the current allocation of resources has not allowed the human rights treaty body system to work in an effective and sustainable manner',[58] such procedural changes are of a relatively minor nature and are unlikely to go far enough.

After years of endeavour to strengthen the UN treaty bodies, in spring 2014 the Third Committee of the General Assembly adopted a resolution on 'Strengthening and Enhancing the Effective Functioning of the Human Rights Treaty Body System'.[59] However, the resolution did not contain any significant measures to strengthen the treaty bodies, let alone overhaul the treaty body system. Most of the provisions of the resolution are limited to either 'encouraging' States to adopt a more efficient system of reporting and streamlining the content of such reports, or 'encouraging' the treaty bodies to simplify their processes and procedures so that the making of recommendations is more effective. For instance, through paragraphs 1 to 6 the Third Committee of the UN General Assembly,

1. Encourages the human rights treaty bodies to offer to States Parties for consideration the simplified reporting procedure and to set a limit on the number of the questions included;
2. Encourages States parties to consider the possibility of using the simplified reporting procedure when offered to facilitate the preparation of their reports and the interactive dialogue on the implementation of their treaty obligations;
3. Encourages States parties to consider submitting a common core document and to update it as appropriate, through a comprehensive document or in the form of an addendum to the original document, bearing in mind the most recent developments in the respective State party, and in this regard encourages the human rights treaty bodies to further elaborate their existing guidelines on the common core document in a clear and consistent manner;
4. Decides, without prejudice to the formulation of the annual report of each treaty body as laid out in the respective treaty, that the annual reports of treaty bodies are not to reproduce documents published separately and referenced therein;

58 Navi Pillay, 'Strengthening the United Nations Human Rights Treaty Body System: A Report by the United Nations High Commissioner for Human Rights', United Nations Office of the High Commissioner for Human Rights, Geneva, June 2012.

59 General Assembly Resolution 'Strengthening and enhancing the effective functioning of the human rights treaty body system' 68/268 21 April 2014, http://www.ohchr.org/Documents/HRBodies/TB/HRTD/A-RES-68-268_E.pdf (accessed 13 October 2014).

5. Encourages the treaty bodies to collaborate towards the elaboration of an aligned methodology for their constructive dialogue with the States parties, bearing in mind the views of States parties as well as the specificity of the respective committees and their specific mandates, with the aim of making the dialogue more effective, maximizing the use of the time available and allowing for a more interactive and productive dialogue with States parties;
6. Also encourages the treaty bodies to adopt short, focused and concrete concluding observations, including recommendations therein, which would reflect the dialogue with the relevant State Party, and, to this end, further encourages them to develop common guidelines for the elaboration of such concluding observations, bearing in mind the specificity of the respective committees and their specific mandates, as well as the views of States parties.[60]

As can be seen from the above provisions, there is little that is new or mandatory in these recommendations to States or to the treaty bodies themselves. All of these recommendations encouraging States and treaty bodies are in the right direction, but since they are limited to mere recommendations, this resolution, similar to so many other resolutions, runs the risk of being ignored, overlooked or forgotten in due course. These are measures that essentially seek to tinker with the system with the hope of making a marginal difference, trying to make an inefficient system a little more efficient. They are mundane, technical, timid and cosmetic when what the UN treaty system really needs is a major overhaul.

3.8 Conclusions

The human rights treaty body system has made as much contribution as possible under the circumstances (such as lack of resources and effective follow-up mechanism as well as the powers needed to ensure compliance) to the promotion and protection of human rights globally, but the time has come to overhaul and streamline the system to make the system effective and efficient. One approach would be to create a robust unified standing treaty body of full-time appropriately paid experts that replaces the existing poorly resourced ten treaty bodies working on a part-time basis and consisting of unpaid experts. Owing to the proliferation of requests for information and reports from States there are legitimate grounds upon which States can claim lack of capacity and resources themselves. It is not only the treaty bodies but also UN charter-based bodies such as the Human Rights Council, the Special Rapporteurs and

60 Ibid. See also C. Broecker, 'The Reform of the United Nations' Human Rights Treaty Bodies', *ASIL Insight*, Vol. 18, Issue 16 of 8 August 2014: http://www.asil.org/insights/volume/18/issue/16/reform-united-nations%E2%80%99-human-rights-treaty-bodies (accessed on 17 December 2014).

other policy making bodies, as well as UN specialised agencies such as the ILO and UNESCO in addition to regional human rights and policy-making bodies, that request information regarding the situation of human rights in a given country.

The nature of requests made to States for human rights information is multifaceted and ranges from requests based on treaty obligations, requests from thematic Special Rapporteurs (and country-specific Special Rapporteurs where they exist), implementation of non-treaty based standards such as the Millennium Development Goals, requests relating to studies and surveys, as well as requests emanating from non-UN sources – to name but a few. It can often be beyond the capacity of a State to furnish information to such a wide range of institutions and the information requested could be repetitive or duplicative to the irritation of the officials of the State concerned. Therefore, to preserve the integrity, value and utility of the reporting system it is imperative to carry out an overhaul of the system as a whole to avoid duplicity and multiplicity and to make it fit for the purposes that the reporting system was designed for in the first place.

Although the discussion is on-going within the UN on strengthening the treaty body system, the proposals at the table are not as ambitious as they might be or should be. The current proposals are more about the accessibility and visibility of the treaty bodies to all stakeholders, the nomination and election of treaty body experts, and measures to increase the effectiveness of the reporting processes. The UN should face up to the larger issues and challenges faced by the treaty body system and overhaul it; a new single global comprehensive reporting system should be introduced to replace the reporting requirements under various human rights treaties with a single permanent body staffed by full-time experts to consider the State reports submitted. In the absence of judicialisation of the mechanisms for protection of human rights and proper sanctions for non-compliance of State obligations under the human rights treaties, there is very little the treaty bodies can do. This is one reason why Clapham states that: 'To place our faith in treaties and declarations seems rather foolish.'[61] Indeed, countries like North Korea have got away thus far with systematic, widespread and grave violations of human rights in spite of being a party to many human rights treaties including the 1966 Covenant on Civil and Political Rights.

To conclude, treaty bodies have over the decades contributed not only to the development of international law but also to the implementation of international law in general and international human rights law in particular. It has been recognised that the treaty body system has made a significant contribution to the promotion of human rights through its monitoring of the situation in those States parties to a treaty and through issuance of authoritative guidance included in observations or recommendations with regard to the

61 Andrew Clapham, *Human Rights: A Very Short Introduction* (Oxford University Press, 2007), 56.

meaning and scope of the provisions of such treaties and the steps that the States should take to ensure compliance with the provisions of the treaty.

The treaty body system has grown in an *ad hoc* manner, with a considerable degree of overlap of provisions and competencies, often resulting in duplication. The treaty body system is much better, more comprehensive and more equipped today than it was 20 years ago when the Vienna World Conference adopted the Vienna Declaration and Programme of Action, but the problems and challenges it faces have also multiplied during the intervening period. The system is chronically under-funded and is at a breaking point due to the backlog of cases and lack of resources. Therefore, there is a need to streamline the treaty body system and create a single, integrated and standing body.

4 Effectiveness of the UN Human Rights Council and its challenges

4.1 Introduction

The Human Rights Council, or the Council,[1] is the UN's human rights flagship body with a broad mandate to protect and promote human rights by addressing specifically 'situations of violations of human rights, including gross and systematic violations', as stated in the General Assembly resolution creating the Council in 2005. It is a UN Charter-based political body and is required to be guided by the principles of 'universality, impartiality, objectivity and non-selectivity'. Although the Council is required to protect individuals from abuse, its resolutions on substantive human rights issues are not binding on States. Hence, the Council is often referred to as 'a tiger without teeth'. It was established to replace the former UN Commission on Human Rights and address the 'credibility deficit' that existed in the workings of the Commission. The aim was to create an organ that would be 'better placed to meet the expectations of men and women everywhere'.

In addition to assuming mandates and responsibilities previously entrusted to the Commission, the Council, reporting directly to the General Assembly, has mandates which include making recommendations to the Assembly for further developing international law in the field of human rights, and undertaking a Universal Periodic Review (UPR) of the fulfillment by each of the UN member States' human rights obligations and commitments. The Human Rights Council is an inter-governmental body and has the ability to discuss all thematic human rights issues and situations that require its attention. Its UPR mechanism is unique since it brings the human rights record of each and every member of the UN within its radar.

The hope expressed by Kofi Annan, proposer of the idea of establishing a Human Rights Council to replace the Commission on Human Rights, was that the creation of the new Council 'would accord human rights a more

1 Both the 'Human Rights Council' and 'the Council' are used interchangeably throughout this chapter and the book as a whole for ease of reference.

authoritative position'.[2] However, the question is whether this has indeed been the case. Critics are of the view that history is repeating itself within the new Council with the election of undeserving States as members and the use of the Council for political purposes. Has the Council been able to live up to the expectations of those that devised it? What have been its strengths and weaknesses, and what reform is needed to address the weaknesses? Is the new Council a mere rebranding of the old Human Rights Commission or is there more in it than critics are prepared to accept? Accordingly, this chapter aims to examine the Council's powers, functions, composition, and election and critically assess its workings. In doing so, this chapter will focus on the Council's flagship mechanism – the Universal Periodic Review – and its effectiveness in ensuring compliance by States with their human rights obligations.

4.2 Background to the creation of the Human Rights Council

The Human Rights Council was established by the UN General Assembly on 15 March 2006 through resolution 60/1 and 60/251 to replace the former Commission on Human Rights as part of the process to reform the UN that had begun in the early 2000s when Kofi Annan was the Secretary General of the UN.[3] The Commission on Human Rights was becoming increasingly ineffective primarily due to the politicisation of its activities and the perception of double standards in the selection of States for criticism of their shortcomings in the implementation of international human rights standards. This does not imply that the Commission did not have a glorious past. Established in 1946, the Commission was instrumental in drafting the 1948 Universal Declaration of Human Rights, the 1966 International Covenants on Civil and Political Rights and on Economic, Social and Cultural Rights and a number of other international human rights instruments.

The Commission was not established as a body to respond to human rights violations, but to develop an international framework for the promotion and protection of human rights and did this job rather well. Although it refrained from directly responding to human rights violations in UN member States for

2 Kofi Annan, 'In larger freedom: towards development, security and human rights for all', UN Doc.A/59/2005 of 21 March 2005, para.183, http://www.un.org/en/ga/search/view_doc.asp?symbol=A/59/2005 (accessed 7 July 2014). This report drew heavily on an earlier report of the UN Secretary General's High level Panel on Threats, Challenges and Change, *A more secure world: our shared responsibility* (2 December 2004): UN Doc. A/59/565, http://www1.umn.edu/humanrts/instree/report.pdf (accessed on 7 July 2014).

3 The idea of establishing a Human Rights Council as such in a slightly different context and to replace the Trusteeship Council had been mooted as long ago as 1975 by a high-level group on reforms in the economic and social sectors of the UN; Bertrand Ramcharan, *The UN Human Rights Council* (Routledge, 2011), 29.

the first two decades of its existence partly due to the heightened political environment during the Cold War, the Commission did come up with some innovative mechanisms, such as the special procedures, to respond to human rights violations in individual countries – not necessarily with a view to providing a remedy but at least primarily providing investigative mechanisms. Gradually, the special procedures became the backbone of the activities of the Commission. In the words of Oberleitner: 'It seems remarkable that an accumulation of such *ad hoc* mandates, carried out by a handful of part-time, unpaid academics, constituted the core of the Commission's protective and promotional activities and continues to do so in the Human Rights Council.'[4]

However, due to some inherent and structural problems, the Commission began to lose its credibility in the 1980s and 1990s. While States like Libya and Syria, with a poor human rights record, had managed to have their representatives elected to the Commission's membership, and Libya had been elected to chair the Commission's session in 2003, the US did not win the vote in ECOSOC in that year and was denied a seat in the Commission. It was against this background that Jeanne Kirkpatrick, head of the US delegation to the Commission in 2003, called these developments 'a scandal in Geneva'. Consequently, when the then Secretary General of the UN, Kofi Annan, was leading the efforts to reform the UN in the early 2000s he proposed the creation of the Human Rights Council to replace the Commission, highlighting its weaknesses. Reform of the UN, including human rights machinery, had been on his agenda when he began his tenure as Secretary General in 1997. When he was appointed for a second term of office he sped up the process by appointing an independent High Level Panel charged with reviewing new global security threats in the twenty-first century and the challenges that they presented to the UN. This was also against the backdrop of the 9/11 attacks on America by Al-Qaeda, a non-State terrorist organisation, which invited an assessment of the existing international legal and political order premised on, and governing, relations between States. With the 9/11 attacks the world had entered a new era and the UN had to respond to this new challenge.[5]

Although the report of the High Level Panel rejected the right of pre-emptive use of force claimed by the then American President George Bush and stated that the rules on the use of force enshrined in the Charter of the UN did not require revision, it did seek to establish a connection between different sources

4 Gerd Oberleitner, *Global Human Rights Institutions: Between Remedy and Ritual* (Polity Press, 2007), 60.

5 See on the efforts made within the UN to adopt a new comprehensive convention on terrorism in the aftermath of the 9/11 attacks on America: Surya P. Subedi, 'The War on Terror and U.N. Attempts to Adopt a Comprehensive Convention on International Terrorism', in Paul Eden and Therese O'Donnell (eds), *September 11, 2001: A Turning Point in International and Domestic Law?* (Transnational Publishers, Inc. 2005) 207–25.

of threat and insecurity affecting the human rights of hundreds of millions of people around the globe, such as poverty, food insecurity, civil wars and internal conflicts, environmental degradation, and climate change. Accordingly, the High Level Panel stated that these threats and their interconnectedness had to be recognised and appropriate measures be taken to address them.[6]

The UN Secretary General proposed in his Report, *In Larger Freedom*,[7] submitted to the General Assembly in 2005 and designed to implement many of the proposals and ideas behind the report of the High Level Panel, to elevate the new Human Rights Council to become a principal organ of the UN, thereby putting the new Council on the same level as the Security Council or the Economic and Social Council. The idea was to recognize human rights as a major pillar of the UN and accord this pillar a status similar to that accorded to peace and security and development. As Boyle observes, the *In Larger Freedom* report was built on the 'theme of interconnectedness through restating the goals of the United Nations as global security, development and human rights and insisting on their interdependence.'[8] The alternative offered was to make the new Human Rights Council a subsidiary body of the General Assembly.

The proposal of Kofi Annan to establish a Human Rights Council seems to have been inspired by the idea developed and proposed in a report commissioned by the Swiss Ministry of Foreign Affairs in March 2003.[9] This report along with a further report by Professor Walter Kaelin to further develop the idea of a Human Rights Council, also commissioned by the Swiss Ministry of Foreign Affairs, was submitted to the High Level Panel. Although the report of the High Level Panel was focused on the reform of the Commission such as making its membership universal rather than creating a new body altogether to replace it, it did accept, as a 'longer term' vision, the idea of 'upgrading the Commission' to become a 'Human Rights Council' that was no longer subsidiary to the ECOSOC but a Charter body standing alongside it and the Security Council.[10] Thus, the idea of a Human Rights Council to replace

6 Report of the High Level Panel on 'Threats, Challenges and Change, A More Secure World: Our Shared Responsibility', U.N.Doc A/59/565/ (2004), http://www1.umn.edu/humanrts/instree/report.pdf (accessed 7 July 2014).

7 Report of the Secretary General, 'In larger freedom: towards development, security, and human rights for all', U.N. doc. A/59/565 of 21 March 2005.

8 Kevin Boyle, in Kevin Boyle (ed.), *New Institutions for Human Rights Protection* (Oxford University Press, 2009) 20.

9 W. Kaelin and C. Jimenez, *Reform of the UN Commission on Human Rights, Study Commissioned by the Swiss Ministry of Foreign Affairs* (Institute of Public Law, University of Bern, 2003). According to Boyle, the idea of a Human Rights Council was further developed by Professor Kaelin and submitted to the Swiss Government in 2004. Boyle (n. 8) 29.

10 The UN Secretary General's High level Panel on Threats, Challenges and Change, *A more secure world: our shared responsibility* (2 December 2004): UN Doc. A/59/565, http://www1.umn.edu/humanrts/instree/report.pdf (accessed 7 July 2014), para 291.

the Commission of Human Rights was conceived in Switzerland, accepted, in principle, by the High Level Panel, concretised by the UN Secretary General, endorsed by the World Summit Conference in 2005 and implemented by the UN General Assembly in 2006.

Kofi Annan's proposal for a new Human Rights Council had the following characteristics: (1) the Council would be a standing body; (2) it would be smaller than the former Commission on Human Rights; (3) it would be elected directly by a two-thirds majority of the General Assembly; (4) it would be based in Geneva in order to permit ease of communications and cooperation with the Office of the High Commissioner for Human Rights (OHCHR) and (5) it would act as a chamber for peer review and a forum for universal scrutiny of human rights records.[11] Annan's proposals had not supported the idea of universal membership of this new body proposed by the High Level Panel. Instead, he had proposed a body smaller than the Commission on Human Rights. He had also not taken forward the recommendation of the High Level Panel that UN members designate as heads of delegation to the Council prominent human rights experts, rather than diplomats seeking to advance narrow national interests.

At the sixtieth session of the UN General Assembly which began in September 2005 and was regarded as the 'World Summit' or the Millennium +5 Summit, a resolution adopted in the form of the 'Summit Outcome' document resolved to create a new Human Rights Council as a subsidiary body of the General Assembly.[12] However, it was a decision largely in principle and a new resolution had to be adopted by the General Assembly spelling out the details required formally to establish such a Council. The General Assembly did so through a resolution adopted in March 2006[13] and the Human Rights Council began its work in June 2006.[14] This resolution was in pursuance of the mandate given to the Assembly by the world leaders at the 2005 World Summit, which had considered the proposals for reform of the UN and resolved, *inter alia*, to strengthen the UN human rights machinery. The world leaders had acknowledged in September 2005 that the three pillars of the United Nations – development, peace and security, and human rights – were interlinked and mutually reinforcing, thereby linking the achievement of the Millennium Development Goals with the strengthening of the UN system of protection and promotion of human rights.

11 Report of the Secretary General, 'In larger freedom: towards development, security, and human rights for all', U.N. doc. A/59/565 of 21 March 2005, U.N. doc. A/59/565 of 21 March 2005, paras 181–83 and Addendum 1: 'Human Rights Council, Explanatory note by the Secretary General – the Secretary General's Proposal' of 14 April 2005.

12 '2005 World Summit Outcome', U.N. doc. A/RES/60/1, 24 October 2005, para 157.

13 A/RES/60/251, adopted 15 March 2006.

14 See Rosa Freedman, *The United Nations Human Rights Council: A Critique and Early Assessment* (Routledge, 2013).

Resolution 60/251 was adopted by an overwhelming majority of States: 170 States in favour, four against (Israel, Marshall Islands, Palau, United States), and three abstentions (Belarus, Iran, Venezuela). A further group of six States were absent in the voting.[15] The main objection of the United States to the text of this resolution was that it did not go far enough to exclude some of the world's worst human rights abusers from membership in the new body. The US had preferred the requirement of a two-thirds majority of States in the General Assembly to get elected to the Human Rights Council, which would have made it harder for countries with a poor record of human rights to win seats on the new body. The US had also proposed exclusive criteria to keep gross human rights abusers off the Council. Despite some weaknesses such as those pointed out by the US delegation at the time of voting, resolution 60/251 was adopted establishing the Council. Regarding its mandate, this was outlined in the 2005 World Summit Outcome document adopted by world leaders:

> 158. The Council will be responsible for promoting universal respect for the protection of all human rights and fundamental freedoms for all, without distinction of any kind and in a fair and equal manner.
>
> 159. The Council should address situations of violations of human rights, including gross and systematic violations, and make recommendations thereon. It should also promote effective coordination and the mainstreaming of human rights within the United Nations system.

Thus, after nearly 60 years since the adoption of the Universal Declaration of Human Rights, the UN established a Human Rights Council with a mechanism for universal periodic review of *all* members of the organisation.

4.3 The powers and functions of the Council

The main purpose of the Council is to address situations of human rights violations within all member States of the UN and make recommendations on them. It is expected to address situations of on-going violations within States and especially gross and systemic violations. According to General Assembly resolution 60/251,[16] the following are said to be the main functions and powers of the Council:

15 They are as follows: Central African Republic, Democratic People's Republic of Korea, Equatorial Guinea, Georgia, Kiribati, Liberia, Nauru, although Nauru and Georgia subsequently informed the General Assembly that they had intended to vote in favour, GA sixtieth session, A/60/PV.72, 15 March 2006, http://www.un.org/en/ga/search/view_doc.asp?symbol=A/60/PV.72 (accessed 7 July 2014).

16 A/RES/60/251, adopted 15 March 2006.

1. Be responsible for promoting universal respect for the protection of all human rights and fundamental freedoms for all, without distinction of any kind and in a fair and equal manner;
2. Address situations of violations of human rights, including gross and systematic violations, and make recommendations on them.
3. Serve as a forum for dialogue on thematic issues on all human rights;
4. Promote the full implementation of human rights obligations undertaken by States and follow-up to the goals and commitments related to the promotion and protection of human rights emanating from United Nations conferences and summits;
5. Undertake a universal periodic review, based on objective and reliable information, of the fulfillment by each State of its human rights obligations and commitments in a manner which ensures universality of coverage and equal treatment with respect to all States; and
6. Make recommendations to the General Assembly for the further development of international law in the field of human rights.

The Council was required to assume, review and, where necessary, improve and rationalize all mandates, mechanisms, functions and responsibilities of the Commission on Human Rights in order to maintain a system of special procedures, expert advice and a complaints procedure within 1 year after the holding of its first session. It also was required to develop the modalities and necessary time allocation for the universal periodic review mechanism within 1 year after the holding of its first session. Accordingly, 1 year after starting its work the Council adopted an 'Institution-Building Package' through resolution 5/1 of 18 June 2007 in which it outlined the basic framework for its future work. Accordingly, the Council proposed to implement its mandate through the following mechanisms:

1. Universal Periodic Review system of the human rights situations in all UN Member States.
2. A new Advisory Committee to serve as the Council's 'think tank' providing it with expertise and advice on thematic human rights issues.
3. The revised Complaints Procedure mechanism allowing individuals and organisations to bring complaints about human rights violations to the attention of the Council.
4. Continued close cooperation with the UN Special Procedures established by the former Commission on Human Rights and assumed by the Council.

The Council went on to elaborate upon these mechanisms and outlined the basic features of each of them. In doing so, it provided the rationale behind these mechanisms and their legal bases.

4.4 New features of the Council

The Human Rights Council has a number of new features compared to its predecessor, the Commission on Human Rights. First, while the former Human Rights Commission was a subsidiary organ of the Economic and Social Council of the UN, the new Council was created as a subsidiary organ of the General Assembly, elevating the institutional standing of the Human Rights Council – albeit not elevating it to the status of the Security Council, which would have required amending the Charter of the UN, a much more difficult undertaking.

Second, there is a provision spelling out membership standards, that is, the qualification for membership of the Council. Perhaps for the first time in the history of international diplomatic relations, the resolution of the General Assembly establishing the Council sets out the qualifications required of States seeking to get elected to any international institution. Although the membership of the Council remains open to all UN member States, the General Assembly is required to take into account 'the contribution of candidates to the promotion and protection of human rights and their voluntary pledges and commitments made thereto'.[17] In addition, the General Assembly resolution stipulates that members elected to the Council shall uphold the highest standards in the promotion and protection of human rights, be subject to review under the UPR mechanism and fully cooperate with the Council. In summing up these new elements and highlighting the practical difficulties in ensuring their compliance Oberleitner states that:

> These five new elements – members' contribution to human rights, voluntary pledges, the obligation to cooperate, the duty to uphold the highest standards of human rights and the universal periodic review procedures for members – are certainly not the qualitative criteria some States and observers wanted introduced. There are no sanctions for failing to comply with the requirements.[18]

He goes on to add that: 'The proactive elements (the General Assembly's responsibility to choose candidates carefully, their pledges, their anticipated cooperation and their responsibility to uphold the highest human rights standards) lack binding force and any non-fulfillment will remain without consequences.'[19] However, he concludes that 'the attempts to introduce criteria for States' participation in inter-governmental bodies which are no longer in line with traditional legal requirements based on sovereignty as an absolute right

17 Ibid., para 8.

18 Oberleitner, *Global Human Rights Institutions – Remedy or Ritual?* (Polity Press 2007) 64–65.

19 Ibid 65.

must be viewed as an inspiring innovation and a possible example for other institutions to follow.'[20]

Even though the General Assembly has laid out no criteria for assessing the pledges made by the candidate States, some civil society organisations have taken the task upon themselves to scrutinize such pledges. For instance, in anticipation of the Human Rights Council's elections on 12 November 2012, the Geneva-based International Service for Human Rights and Amnesty International held an event to provide the candidate States an opportunity to present their vision for membership of the Council and respond to the question as to how they would realize their pledges and commitments, if elected. Although only 8 of the 18 candidate States chose to participate in the event, it was an interesting exercise in the sense that those eight, including the US, chose to outline their agenda to the public and open themselves to questioning by civil society representatives.[21] Developments like these are somewhat unprecedented and are welcome in that they can lead to a standard practice in future, thereby increasing public accountability and transparency in electing members of the Human Rights Council.

Third, the General Assembly has introduced a universal periodic review mechanism. Under this mechanism *every* member State of the UN, whether they voted in favour of the resolution establishing the Council or not, regardless of the State's size, whether the State has a more established system of democracy or not, would be reviewed by the Council in a 4-yearly cycle. This was quite a notable development in the sense that the resolution subjects States to human rights scrutiny even if they had not consented to it in the first place. The review would be based on objective and reliable information of the fulfillment by each State of its human rights obligations and commitments, and be conducted in a manner that ensures universality of coverage and equal treatment with respect to all States.

Fourth, another novelty in this resolution was that if any member of the Council failed to uphold high human rights standards, it could be suspended by a two-thirds majority vote by Assembly members present at the meeting. As will be seen later, Syria was suspended from its membership of the Council in 2011.

Fifth, a further note-worthy development was that no permanent seat was reserved in the Council for any permanent members of the UN Security Council. Although no provision as such exists with regard to the election to other UN bodies such as the International Law Commission, the five permanent members have secured in practice their representation within that

20 Ibid 66.

21 International Service for Human Rights (ISHR) press release: 'States and NGOs welcome discussion of pledges by Human Rights Council Candidates', 27 October 2012. A copy of this press release is on file with the present author.

Commission.[22] However, by making it clear that no State, whether big or small, can be reelected to the Council's membership immediately after serving for a period of two 3-year terms, the resolution does not allow any permanent member of the Security Council or any other major power to maintain its representation in the Human Rights Council on a continuous basis. This is a notable departure from the practice of electing members of many UN and other international bodies and is arguably liable to make the Human Rights Council more democratic than the Security Council.

Sixth, the Universal Periodic Review is the first UN mechanism which covers *all States* and *all human rights issues*. It is a comprehensive and global mechanism and no State which is a member of the UN is automatically exempted from scrutiny of its human rights record. It must be borne in mind, however, that the process is voluntary and therefore States can choose to not engage with it and there would, arguably, be little in the way of sanction. Even those States which voted against the General Assembly resolution creating the Human Rights and those which abstained or were absent have participated in the review (indeed all UN member States partook in the first UPR cycle). Interestingly, none of the States that did not vote in favour of the Council, or did not vote, has sought to shield itself from public scrutiny by invoking either the principle of State sovereignty or the principle of non-interference in the internal affairs of States under Article 2(7) of the Charter of the UN.

Seventh, the role of non-State actors or civil society organisations has become more prominent within the UN human rights system and certainly more so than in other areas of international activity such as international trade or the environment. International organisations and conferences concerned with international trade and the environment such as the WTO dispute settlement body (DSB) do accept *amicus curiae* briefs from civil society organisations, but little more than this. Further, the *amicus curiae* briefs can to all intents be ignored by institutions such as the DSB in reaching their decisions. But in the UPR within the Human Rights Council, the views of civil society organisation have an important role to play and are part of a formal structure. The reports of civil society organisations on the situation of human rights in the country under review, along with national reports and the compilation of treaty body reports and recommendations prepared by the OHCHR, form the core of the documentation considered during review and their representatives can have their voices heard in the deliberations within the Human Rights Council itself.

4.5 From standard setting to implementation

In establishing the Council, emphasis was placed on implementation of the human rights standards by the Council as opposed to mainly the standard-

22 See International Law Commission membership during the quinquennium 2012–2016, http://legal.un.org/ilc/ilcmembe.htm accessed 14 October 2014.

setting work carried out by its predecessor, the Human Rights Commission. The establishment of the Council heralded a new attempt within the UN system to have a more comprehensive system of implementation of the existing human rights standards through cooperation and a constructive approach and in a non-selective, objective and universal manner designed to ensure that there was equal treatment with respect to all States. This was done against the backdrop of the alleged politicisation of human rights issues by the targeting of a select group of countries for closer scrutiny during the existence of the Human Rights Commission. The establishment of the Council was also an attempt at mainstreaming human rights in the UN system and to provide a more high-profile focal point for discussion of human rights issues of the day.

4.6 Membership of the Council

The Council consists of 47 member States responsible for strengthening the promotion and protection of human rights worldwide. These members would be individually elected by an absolute majority in the General Assembly. The membership in the new Council would be based on equitable geographic representation, and seats would be distributed as follows among regional groups: African Group, 13; Asian Group, 13; Eastern European Group, 6; Latin American and Caribbean Group, 8; and Western European and Others Group, 7. Thus, the distribution of seats in the Council makes it a body tilted towards developing countries and dominated by Asian and African States.

The members of the Council would serve for a period of 3 years and would not be eligible for immediate re-election after two consecutive terms. When electing members of the Council, Member States would take into account the candidate States' contribution to the promotion and protection of human rights and their voluntary pledges and commitments made to this effect and members elected to the Council would be expected to uphold the highest standards in the promotion and protection of human rights, fully cooperate with the Council and be reviewed under the newly introduced universal periodic review mechanism during their term of membership.

4.7 The working methods of the Council

In order to fulfil its human rights protection mandate, the Council has created the following mechanisms, and most innovative of all is its UPR mechanism. It is proposed to examine the effectiveness of these mechanisms and especially the UPR.

4.7.1 Advisory Committee

A new Advisory Committee to assist the Human Rights Council was created as part of the 'institution-building' package of 2007 contained in Resolution

5/1. The Human Rights Council Advisory Committee, often described as the 'think- tank' of the Council, is composed of 18 experts serving in their personal capacity whose function is to provide expertise to the Council in the manner and form requested by it, focusing mainly on studies and research-based advice. The Advisory Committee has no powers to adopt its own resolutions or decisions. In many respects, the Advisory Committee can be regarded as a successor to the former Sub-commission on the Promotion and Protection of Human Rights.

Although the Committee itself is a body consisting of independent experts, its mandate, which comes from the Human Rights Council, could be a political one. For instance, resolution 16/3 of March 2011 of the Council which mandated the Committee to conduct a study on the issue of traditional values of humankind was a divisive resolution led by the Russian Federation; it was adopted with 24 votes in favour, 21 against and 7 abstentions.[23] The Advisory Committee has widely been regarded as an additional bureaucratic layer in the UN system of human rights without any meaningful powers and functions and could thus be abolished altogether without having much detrimental impact on the work of the Human Rights Council itself.

4.7.2 Complaint procedures

An improved mechanism to deal with the complaints of human rights violations was included in the 'institution-building' package of 2007 contained in Resolution 5/1. The improved complaints procedures were built on the old mechanism known as the '1503 Procedures' that existed under the Council's predecessor, the Human Rights Commission.[24] The improved procedure retains the confidential nature of the 1503 procedures with a view to enhancing cooperation with the State concerned. Resolution 5/1 establishes two distinct working groups to examine the communications and to bring to the attention of the Council consistent patterns of gross and reliably attested violations of human rights and fundamental freedoms.

The first working group is on communications and the second is on the situation of human rights. The first examines the communications received, including dealing with admissibility issues, and decides on the transmission of the content of such complaints to the individual member of the UN concerned for comments. On the basis of the information and recommendations provided by the first working group, the second working group is entrusted with the

23 'Promoting Human Rights and Fundamental Freedoms through a better understanding of traditional values of Humankind', A/HRC/RES/16/3, 8 April, 2011, http://daccess-dds-ny.un.org/doc/RESOLUTION/GEN/G11/124/92/PDF/G1112492.pdf?Open Element (accessed 20 October 2014).

24 Economic and Social Council resolution 1503 (XLVIII) of 27 May 1970 as revised by resolution 2000/3 of 19 June 2000.

task of presenting to the Council a report on consistent patterns of gross and reliably attested violations of human rights and fundamental freedoms and making recommendations to the Council on the course of action to take, normally in the form of a draft resolution or decision with respect to the situations concerned. Since there are 10 other human rights treaty bodies entitled to entertain individual petitions, this mechanism of the Human Rights Council could be utilised in cases of violations of human rights not covered by the treaty bodies or in the case of States which have not ratified such treaties. However, since the Council itself has no real legal powers there is not much that a victim of human rights violations can expect by way of effective remedy from the Council.

4.7.3 Special procedures

The new Human Rights Council retained the special procedures mechanism with a pledge to review, rationalize and improve the existing mandates, as well as create new ones, on the basis of the principles of universality, impartiality, objectivity, non-selectivity, constructive international dialogue and cooperation, and with a view to enhancing the promotion and protection of all human rights – including civil, political, economic, social and cultural rights, and the right to development. Accordingly, the existing mandates were renewed until the date on which they were to be considered by the Council according to its programme of work. Mandate-holders were asked to continue serving, provided they had not exceeded the 6-year term limit. Through its resolution 5/2 of 18 June 2007 and as part of the 'Institution-Building Package of 2007',[25] the Human Rights Council adopted a Code of Conduct for Special Procedures Mandate-holders on 18 June 2007.

4.7.4 Commissions of inquiry

The Human Rights Council has established a number of commissions of inquiry to investigate violations of human rights and humanitarian law which have helped to document violations of human rights and bring them to the attention of the international community. The content of such reports would help the International Criminal Court or other *ad hoc* international criminal courts in their own investigation and prosecution which can lead to conviction. For instance, the Human Rights Council appointed an Independent International Commission of Inquiry on Syria which concluded in its report of 15 August 2012 that the Syrian Government and the opposition forces had

25 Code of Conduct for Special Procedures Mandate-holders of the Human Rights Council, contained in Resolution 5/2; available at http://www.ohchr.org/Documents/HRBodies/SP/CodeofConduct_EN.pdf

perpetrated war crimes and crimes against humanity in Syria. It stated that the evidence showed a State policy to commit war crimes and gross violations of international human rights. In the view of the Commission, the intensity and duration of the conflict, combined with the increased organisational capabilities of anti-Government armed groups, had met the legal threshold for a non-international armed conflict.[26]

A similar report was submitted to the Council by a commission of inquiry into the situation of human rights in North Korea. The Council acted upon the recommendations of the commission and recommended to the General Assembly to take appropriate action, including referring the matter to the International Criminal Court. In turn, the General Assembly itself adopted a resolution, recommending to the Security Council to take appropriate action, including referring the matter to the International Criminal Court. However, since two of the permanent members of the Security Council, China and Russia, did not support the resolution in the General Assembly the likelihood of the Security Council acting on the recommendations of the General Assembly remained slim.

The Human Rights Council may set up fact-finding missions or commissions of inquiry into cases of alleged violations of human rights, but it has no powers to act in any meaningful manner on the findings or recommendations of such missions or commissions. What the Human Rights Council can do is recommend that the Security Council act on such reports including referring the matter to the prosecutor of the International Criminal Court. However, since the Security Council is handicapped by the veto power of the permanent five, there is no guarantee that action will be taken subsequent to the Commission of Inquiry's findings and recommendations. For instance, the UN High Commissioner,[27] as well as a large number of States in the debate in the Human Rights Council's special session on the situation in Syria following the El-Houleh massacre on 25 May 2012, did recommend that the Security Council refer the matter to the International Criminal Court.[28] Yet, the problem was that the Human Rights Council itself failed to make such a call when it concluded its 21st Session on 28 September 2012 (this is in spite of holding four special sessions on Syria – a highly unusual event), and the Security

26 UN Doc. A/HRC/21/50. It was submitted pursuant to Council resolution A/HRC/RES/19/22 of 23 March 2012, which extended the mandate of the Commission established by resolution A/HRC/RES/S-17/1 of 22 August 2011.

27 The High Commissioner did so through a media statement of 7 June 2012 delivered in New York and a statement to the 19th Special Session of the Human Rights Council on 1 June 2012. This was also echoed in a letter of 28 September sent to the President of the Human Rights Council by a group of prominent human rights organisations, including the International Commission of Jurists and Human Rights Watch. A copy of this letter is on file with the present author.

28 'Council continues its engagement with the situation in Syria', News release of the International Service for Human Rights, Geneva, 3 July 2012.

Council, another UN political body, was unable to act because of the veto power of the permanent five.

It is all the more striking that the Human Rights Council itself failed to make such a call in spite of the report of the Independent International Commission of Inquiry on Syria, a Commission appointed by the Council, which concluded that the Syrian Government and opposition forces had perpetrated war crimes and crimes against humanity in Syria. The Commission determined that 'the intensity and duration of the conflict, combined with the increased organisational capabilities of anti-Government armed groups, had met with the legal threshold for a non-international armed conflict.'[29]

The Commission of Inquiry concluded in its report published on 22 February 2012 that the Government in Syria had 'manifestly failed in its responsibility to protect the population; its forces have committed widespread, systematic and gross human rights violations, amounting to crimes against humanity, with apparent knowledge and consent of the highest levels of the State.'[30] These are significant conclusions that should not be overlooked and ought not only to have prompted the Human Rights Council to make clear recommendations to the Security Council, but also should have triggered the Security Council to take action. However, due to power-politics within the Security Council no noteworthy or credible action was taken against the authorities in Syria nor was the matter referred to the International Criminal Court. The Human Rights Council on its part had to limit itself to adopting resolution after resolution condemning such violations of human rights.

Both the Security Council[31] and the General Assembly[32] did adopt resolutions on Syria but they merely called upon Syria to cease all violence, protect its population and guarantee the freedom of peaceful demonstrations, etc. The British Foreign Secretary, William Hague, indicated in November 2012 that it was important to document the atrocities committed in Syria for future prosecutions, including possible action at the International Criminal Court.[33] Supported by 50 other States, Switzerland wrote to the UN Security Council

29 As quoted in the *News Bulletin of the American Society of International Law*, 24 August 2012, p.1. See also for a report on the situation of human rights in Syria, U.N.Doc. A/HRC/S-17/2/Add.1 of 23 November 2011.

30 As quoted by the UN High Commissioner for Human Rights, Navi Pillay, at the urgent debate on the human rights and humanitarian situation in Syria at the Human Rights Council on 28 February 2012: Media Statement of the OHCHR of 28 February 2012.

31 U.N. Doc. S/2012/77 of 4 February 2012.

32 On 16 February 2012, the general Assembly voted overwhelmingly in favour of a resolution that strongly condemned the continued widespread and systematic human rights violations by Syrian authorities. The resolution was cosponsored by more than 70 States and was passed with 137 votes in favour, 12 against, and 17 abstentions and the content of the resolution is similar to the resolution adopted by the Security Council on 4 February 2012.

33 Press release of the FCO, London of 28 November 2012 (on file with the present author).

in January 2013 asking it to refer the situation in Syria to the International Criminal Court.[34]

Speaking at the UN General Assembly, the UN High Commissioner for Human Rights also encouraged the Security Council to refer the situation to the International Criminal Court.[35] The then High Commissioner reiterated her belief later that, on the basis of evidence gathered from various credible sources, crimes against humanity and war crimes had been, and continued to be, committed in Syria. She went on to add that, 'those who are committing them should not believe that they will escape justice. The world does not forget or forgive crimes like these.'[36]

Addressing the 21st Session of the UN Human Rights Council on 10 September 2012, the High Commissioner reminded member States of the UN that 'when a State fails to protect its population from serious international crimes, the international community is responsible to step in by taking protective action in a collective, timely and decisive manner. The international community must assume its responsibilities and act in unison to prevent further violations.'[37] She reiterated her call for the Security Council to refer the case of Syria to the International Criminal Court and stated that those responsible for human rights violations must eventually be brought to justice. However, nothing much more concrete came out of these calls.

4.7.5 Universal Periodic Review

While the Human Rights Council is the flagship human rights organ of the UN, the Universal Periodic Review (UPR) is the Council's flagship procedure, which emphasizes dialogue and cooperation rather than naming and shaming to promote human rights. It is, relatively speaking, a new and unique intergovernmental political mechanism designed to promote the improvement of human rights at country level. It brings within its public scrutiny the situation of human rights in all members of the UN in a non-selective manner. The core

34 American Society of International Law, News Bulletin, 22 January 2013. Among the States that supported the Swiss Government's letter, two were the permanent members of the Security Council: France and the UK.

35 'States must "act now" to protect Syrian population, Pillay tells the General Assembly', News Release of the OHCHR of 13 February 2012, http://www.ohchr.org/EN/NewsEvents/Pages/DisplayNews.aspx?NewsID=11819&LangID=E (accessed 14 October 2014).

36 'Pillay warns of consequences under international law as Syria conflict escalates', New Release of the OHCHR of 27 July 2012, http://www.ohchr.org/EN/NewsEvents/Pages/DisplayNews.aspx?NewsID=12393&LangID=E accessed 14 October 2014.

37 'Bearing witness: human rights and accountability in Syria', Media Statement of the OHCHR of 10 September 2012, http://www.ohchr.org/EN/NewsEvents/Pages/DisplayNews.aspx?NewsID=12491&LangID=E (accessed 14 October 2014).

of its work is aimed at strengthening State compliance with human rights obligations. It is a universal mechanism and does not replace any of the existing mechanisms, whether treaty bodies or special procedures. Rather, the hope is that the new mechanism will strengthen the existing ones.

More importantly, it gives an unprecedented voice to civil society – making their reports on the human rights record of individual States an integral part of the process. It is a periodic process requiring States to subject themselves to global public scrutiny every 4 years. As stated by Cerna and Stewart, the Universal Periodic Review 'is premised on the idea that there is intrinsic value in a non-selective examination of the human rights record and policies of every member of the United Nations.'[38] Since the UPR mechanism was a new one, the Council identified the following instruments as the basis of the review: The Charter of the United Nations; the Universal Declaration of Human Rights; Human rights instruments to which a State is party; and Voluntary pledges and commitments made by States.[39]

In addition, the Council stated that such a review would also take into account applicable international humanitarian law. However, it did not define the term 'international humanitarian law' nor did it include a list of international humanitarian law related international legal instruments. In the absence of this, one would have to refer to the sources of international law which includes customary law, treaties, general principles of law, decisions of international courts and tribunals and writings of publicists.[40] The objectives of the UPR are as follows:

1. The improvement of the human rights situation on the ground;
2. The fulfillment of the State's human rights obligations and commitments and assessment of positive developments and challenges faced by the State;
3. The enhancement of the State's capacity and of technical assistance, in consultation with, and with the consent of, the State concerned;

38 Christina M. Cerna and David P. Stewart, 'The United States before the UN Human Rights Council' (November 2010) 14 (32) *ASIL Insight*, 2.

39 'Institution-building of the United Nations Human Rights Council', Human Rights Council Resolution 5/1, 9th meeting, 18 June 2007, para 1.

40 The statement of the sources of international law contained in Article 38 of the Statute of the International Court of Justice has been widely regarded as the most authoritative statement of the sources of international law. It reads as follows:

> '1. The Court, whose function is to decide in accordance with international law such disputes as are submitted to it, shall apply: a. international conventions, whether general or particular, establishing rules expressly recognized by the contesting States; b. international custom, as evidence of a general practice accepted as law; c. the general principles of law recognized by civilized nations; d. subject to the provisions of Article 59, judicial decisions and the teachings of the most highly qualified publicists of the various nations, as subsidiary means for the determination of rules of law. 2. This provision shall not prejudice the power of the Court to decide a case *ex aequo et bono*, if the parties agree thereto.'

4. The sharing of best practice among States and other stakeholders;
5. Support for cooperation in the promotion and protection of human rights;
6. The encouragement of full cooperation and engagement with the Council, other human rights bodies and the Office of the United Nations High Commissioner for Human Rights.[41]

In other words, the objectives of the UPR mechanism are to: (i) ensure that a comprehensive review is undertaken with respect to national legislation, administrative rules, procedures and practices with a view to ensuring fullest possible compliance with the above instruments; (ii) ensure that the State concerned monitors the implementation of the provisions of the human rights treaties ratified by it; (iii) provide an opportunity to the State concerned to demonstrate that it has a policy in place to make sure that individuals, minorities and indigenous groups, etc. are able to exercise their rights enshrined in such treaties and the above-listed international legal instruments; (iv) enable the State to involve other stakeholders, in particular civil society, to make a contribution to policy formulation, implementation and review process; (v) provide an opportunity to the State concerned to evaluate the extent to which progress has been made to implement human rights obligations and what challenges it is facing in this regard; and (vi) facilitate dialogue and information sharing between different national stakeholders within the State, and between member States of the UN, so that all parties and stakeholders develop a better understanding of the issues involved and the strategy needed to address the shortcomings existing in the implementation of human rights obligations of the State concerned.[42]

These objectives are reflected in the procedure for a UPR: every State is required to submit a report of no more than 20 pages outlining the State's efforts to protect and promote human rights. Alongside this report there are two other reports prepared and submitted by the OHCHR – one is a summary of findings and recommendations of human rights treaty-bodies and special procedures and another is a summary of the views of civil society. These three reports are considered together during the review of the State concerned by

41 Resolution 5/1 of 18 June 2007 of the Human Rights Council.

42 The UPR is a cooperative mechanism rather than an adversarial one to be found in the justice systems of the common law countries. It is designed to encourage States to (i) prepare comprehensive data regarding the internal human rights situation, thereby encouraging countries to carry out their own internal audit or stock-taking of the situation of human rights, (ii) prompt and encourage a national dialogue on the situation of human rights, the challenges remaining and the ways and means of addressing the challenges, (iii) submit the national audit report to the Human Rights Council with a view to benefitting from the debate in the Council in terms of the best practice/good practice of other countries and the constructive recommendations made towards the end of the UPR process and (iv) make the whole process transparent, inclusive and participatory.

the Council. The latter two reports serve a very useful purpose in making sure that the reports prepared by States, which often include a positive spin of the situation, are balanced and an objective view of the situation is presented to the Council, and to the participating States. Thus, one of the special features of the UPR mechanism is a strong civil society input. However, civil society representatives are not permitted to contribute to the interactive dialogue – this involves only States that have registered their wish to speak in advance.

The periodicity of the review for the first cycle was 4 years. Accordingly, the first cycle was completed in 2011 and the new cycle began in 2012. A total of 48 States were included in the review each year thereby covering all 193 Members of the UN by the end of 2011. The format of the outcome of the review is a report prepared by the troika,[43] consisting of a summary of the proceedings of the review process, conclusions and/or recommendations, and the voluntary commitments of the State concerned. Regarding the follow-up to the review, the primary responsibility stated to rest in the State concerned and the subsequent review would focus, *inter alia*, on the implementation of the preceding outcome.

4.8 An assessment of the Universal Periodic Review mechanism

4.8.1 Lack of rigour

Although the UPR subjects all member States of the UN to a 4-yearly scrutiny, most States with a dubious human rights record seem to have learned how to 'play the game' within the Human Rights Council. They and their allies seem mainly concerned with 'treading water' during the review and simply with 'getting through' the 3 hours of examination of their report, so that these matters can be shelved again for another 4 years. Many countries were willing to accept most, if not all, of the UPR recommendations. This is most likely because there is no proper mechanism to follow up the extent to which those recommendations accepted are subsequently implemented by the State under review and the State has another 4 years before it will be called upon again to report the progress made. The attitude of States within the Council during the UPR of a given country seems to be divided broadly along developed Western countries and developing countries.

For Western countries, the process is all about the scrutiny of the human rights record of the developing countries. Although Western countries also

43 'Each State review is assisted by groups of three States, known as "troikas", who serve as rapporteurs. The selection of the troikas for each State is done through a drawing of lots following elections for the Council membership in the General Assembly'. 'Basic Facts about UPR', http://www.ohchr.org/en/hrbodies/upr/pages/BasicFacts.aspx accessed 14 October 2014. The role of the troika is outlined in more detail in Resolution 5/1 of 18 June 2007 of the Human Rights Council, paras 18–24.

submit their UPR reports and participate in the deliberations within the Human Rights Council, the impression is often given that the process is not really for them, because the observance of human rights is fully guaranteed in their countries. What is more, when criticism is made relating to the human rights situation in a country (often one with a poor human rights record) it is all too easy for State representatives to claim that others 'do not understand our culture'[44] in terms of that country's primary concern being its need to develop its economy and have the requisite political stability to do so.

The UPR is a global forum for the discussion of all areas of human rights. It is devised as a means to encourage States to address shortcomings, to ratify additional human rights treaties and relevant optional protocols and to take measures to introduce and implement relevant domestic legislation. However, many States have written their national report as a progress report on the overall situation in the country, including economic and social progress and political changes, rather than confining themselves to presenting a serious analysis of the human rights challenges facing the nation and measures, legal or administrative, taken to promote and protect human rights and to fulfil their obligations under various human rights treaties. In some cases the national reports give the impression of being a propaganda document designed to impress the international community. The same is too often true of the behaviour of States at the UPR working group session at which the State is subject to review by peer States; delegates from 'friendly' countries are keen to congratulate the State under review. It is common to witness in the UPR one repressive government after another queuing up to praise each other's record of improvement of the situation of human rights and manipulate the whole process. In addition, the national reports submitted by many countries for the second cycle of the UPR that began in 2012 gave the impression of the task being a mundane or tedious piece of work to be performed as a matter of routine exercise to satisfy the UPR's formality requirement, rather than being an endeavour with intrinsic value that is part of a wider programme of review.

Although the reports submitted for the second cycle by many States did provide an update on the progress made in implementing the recommendations made in the first cycle, some reports were ritualistic and technical or mechanical, rather than being taken substantively seriously to create a document produced out of a conviction to fulfil an important legal requirement. This attitude runs the risk of diluting the significance of human rights as serious legal rights as well as the work of more serious legal bodies such as the human rights treaty bodies.

44 When the present author submitted his report on the situation of human rights in Cambodia with a set of recommendations in his capacity as the UN Special Rapporteur for human rights for the country, the standard response from the Cambodian Government was that the Special Rapporteur 'does not understand our culture'.

4.8.2 Generality and vagueness of the process

Many of the recommendations of the UPR are not necessarily about human rights but about social, economic and political issues and there are simply too many recommendations to be taken seriously. Most States appear to feel like making a recommendation whether it made sense or not or whether it was something directly related to human rights or not. This has meant that some of the recommendations have been ritualistic and redundant. While most of the recommendations made by Western countries have been about civil and political rights, those made by developing countries have focused predominantly on social, economic and cultural rights. Some States appear to take the exercise seriously and send high level delegations led by a senior member of the government, while others have entrusted the task of leading the delegation to the ambassadors based in Geneva itself. Those that treat the exercise as a legal one, or at least as having importance in legal terms, have sent Ministers of Law or Justice or the Attorney General of the country to lead the delegation, and those who regard it as a political exercise have sent ministers from the Ministry of Foreign Affairs.[45]

4.8.3 Promotion rather than protection of human rights

It is evident from the powers and functions of the Human Rights Council that its focus is on the promotion of human rights through cooperation, rather than on the protection of human rights through enforcement, and this approach is reflected in the mandate and workings of the UPR mechanism.

4.8.4 A common platform for all States

The UPR enables States to say at an international level what they may not wish to say at a bilateral level regarding the situation of human rights in a given country. What is interesting about the UPR is that the human rights records of all 193 States members of the UN, including new democracies as well as well-established democracies such as the UK, US, France and Germany, have been reviewed by the Council, allowing these countries to share their best practices with other countries, and expecting and encouraging those other countries to aspire to implement the same/similar good practices. For instance, the following was the self-reflection of the UK on its second UPR:

> The UK approached its second review in a spirit of openness and welcomed the level of scrutiny it received from member States. While we believe the

45 For instance, the UK delegation to Geneva for the second round of the UPR was led by the Minister for Justice, Lord McNally, rather than a minister from the Foreign Office. This was the case with many other delegations.

> UK has a good human rights record, we have consistently made clear that there is always room for improvement and that we are open to learning from others. In the spirit of cooperation, we took care to respond in writing those member States which raised issues during our interactive dialogue which we were not able to respond during our session.[46]

This, of course, also gives an opportunity to the countries such as Iran, North Korea and Cuba, to criticize the US adding some spice to the UPR process. Some of their criticism concerned the treatment of inmates in Abu Ghraib in Iraq and Guantanamo Bay, the drone killings, and a long legacy of rights abuses within the US itself, especially against its black and ethnic minority populations.

The UPR puts the human rights record of each and every State under an international spotlight, including the record of ratification of human rights treaties by the country concerned. No matter how powerful or big the States were either in terms of their military or political or economic might or geographic or demographic size, all are subject to review and often criticism for their shortcomings. The human rights record of all of the so-called 'Big Five', or P5, the five permanent members of the Security Council has also been under international scrutiny and subject to criticism for certain failings.[47]

As with any of the UN human rights monitoring mechanisms, there is much about the UPR that is far from perfect and a full and detailed assessment of this particular mechanism is beyond the scope of this book, suffice to say that the process does succeed in bringing together into one space the voices of the State under review, the international community at large and civil society.[48] Taken together as a whole, the documentation produced as part of the UPR

46 Foreign & Commonwealth Office, 'Human Rights and Democracy: The 2012 Foreign & Commonwealth Office Report (London, April 2013), p.13.

47 For more on the criticism levied at the US, and the treatment of the other permanent five members of the Security Council, during the UPR's first cycle see Rhona Smith, '"To See Themselves as Others See Them": The Five Permanent Members of the Security Council and the Human Rights Council's Universal Periodic Review' (2013) 35 *Human Rights Quarterly*, 1.

48 For critiques of the UPR see for example, Hilary Charlesworth and Emma Larking, *Human Rights and the Universal Periodic Review: Rituals and Ritualism* (Cambridge University Press 2015); Edward McMahon, 'The Universal Periodic Review: a work in progress', *Dialogue on Globalization*, September 2012, http://library.fes.de/pdf-files/bueros/genf/09297.pdf, accessed 10 October 2014; Elvira Domínguez Redondo, 'The Universal Periodic Review of the UN Human Rights Council: An Assessment of the First Session' (2008), 7(3), *Chinese Journal of International Law*, 721; Nico Schrijver, 'The UN Human Rights Council: A New 'Society of the Committed' or Just Old Wine in New Bottles?' (2007), 20, *Leiden Journal of International Law*, 809; Purna Sen (ed.), *Universal Periodic Review: Lessons, Hopes and Expectations* (Commonwealth Secretariat 2011); Rhona Smith, '"To See Themselves as Others See Them": The Five Permanent Members of the Security Council and the Human Rights Council's Universal Periodic Review' (2013), 35, *Human Rights Quarterly*, 1.

exercise presents a snapshot of the human rights situation of the country concerned.

The UPR presents a forum for leading democracies to demonstrate their record of human rights, outline best practices and to lead the way, at least in procedural terms, by example.[49] For instance, the UK was one of the countries that took the initiative to introduce an update on the implementation of recommendations received and the commitments it made during its UPR review. Furthermore, countries such as China, Cuba and Iran which had long evaded international scrutiny of their human rights records having not ratified some of the core human rights treaties, and countries such as the US which used to assert that since its system of governance was robustly democratic it did not have to submit to the scrutiny of the international community nonetheless engaged with the UPR process and have been subjected to scrutiny by the Council and peer States. Some of the UPR recommendations made to the US asked it to ratify the many core international human rights treaties to which the US was not yet a party, to remove reservations to certain treaties to which the US is a party and to establish a moratorium on the death penalty with a view to abolition.

What was interesting was that the US delegation has been willing to acknowledge imperfections and injustices, to discuss and debate them, and to work through democratic means by which to remedy them. The US expressed its commitment to ratifying core human rights conventions such as the Convention on the Elimination of Discrimination against Women, and the International Convention on the Rights of Persons with Disabilities; combating racial discrimination and racial profiling; addressing torture and ill-treatment and exploring the possibility of setting up a national human rights institution at the federal level. This approach of the Obama administration was in contrast to the stance taken by the Republican administration during the Bush years in which the US administration had decided to boycott the UN Human Rights Council. Some Republican Party leaders were critical of the approach of the Obama administration to work with and within the Council. One of them had

49 This is not to say that no recommendations were made to the UK, US, France and Germany during the UPR. There were. For instance, some of the recommendations made to the UK during the second round of the UPR were as follows: Ratify ILO Convention 189 on domestic workers and the Convention on Migrant Workers; Ensure that migrant workers can retain their overseas worker visa as a safeguard of their rights; Withdraw reservations concerning the Optional Protocol to the Convention on the Rights of the Child on children in armed conflict; Combat prejudices and negative stereotypes leading to racial discrimination or incitement to racial hatred; Adopt legislation to further restrict the detention of terror suspects without charge and ensure that 'secret evidence' is only used in cases where there is a threat to public security; Combat racial profiling within counter-terrorism. For documents relating to the UK's second UPR, see http://www.ohchr.org/EN/HRBodies/UPR/Pages/gbsession1.aspx (accessed 16 October 2014).

the following remarks to make: 'So long as the inmates are allowed to run the asylum, the Human Rights Council will continue to stand in the way of justice, not promote it. The US should walk out of this rogues' gallery and seek to build alternative forums that will actually focus on abuses and deny membership to abusers.'[50]

4.8.5 Inclusiveness of the process

Although the UPR is primarily a political rather than legal process, the mechanism promotes inclusivity; the individual States concerned, civil society organisations, both national and international, and other States with an interest in the situation in the country under review are able to participate in the process. Although the participation of civil society is limited to the submission of a report to the OHCHR some 6–8 weeks prior to review, and presence at side events in Geneva at the time of the review, civil society representatives can be granted observer status to be present in the main auditorium and can pursue informal access to State representatives. Further, many States seem to have taken the process seriously and regarded the process more as legal rather than political. This has been demonstrated by the choice of the leader and/or composition of the delegation of various countries.[51]

4.8.6 Constructive approach

As with the UN approach to human rights in general, the approach of the UPR is cooperative and persuasive; States apply moral and political pressure on their counterparts and the UPR process places the State under review in the international spotlight regarding their record of human rights. This may be one reason why the Russian delegation to the UPR process regarded it as 'the most important instrument of international control in the field of human rights'.[52]

50 Republican political leader from Florida, Ileana Ros-Lehtinen, as quoted in Colum Lynch, 'U.S. gets earful from Human Rights Council, courtesy of Iran, North Korea and Cuba', *Turtle Bay Foreign Policy*, http://turtlebay.foreignpolicy.com, 5 November 2010 (accessed 12 November 2010).

51 See above comments in relation to UK delegation to Geneva. In addition, during the UPR 18th working group session, Afghanistan's delegation was led by Mr Mohammad Qasim Hashimzai, senior adviser to the Ministry of Justice, the New Zealand delegation was led by Ms Judith Collins, Minister for Ethnic Affairs, Ministry of Justice, and the Yemeni delegation was led by Ms Hooria Mashhoyr Ahmed, Ministry of Human Rights, to access the UPR documentation and the individual State reports providing further information regarding the delegations and the recommendations made, see http://www.ohchr.org/EN/HRBodies/UPR/Pages/Documentation.aspx (accessed 16 October 2014).

52 'Report of the Working Group on the Universal Periodic Review: Russian Federation', A/HRC/11/19 of 5 October 2009, 3, http://daccess-ods.un.org/TMP/4688 459.03873444.html (accessed 16 October 2014).

The process offers an opportunity not only to States which are critical of the record of human rights in a given country but also to States which are perceived to be friendly to give constructive and friendly advice to improve the situation of human rights. The process provides an opportunity to other States to encourage the State concerned, for example to: ratify the human rights treaties that remain un-ratified, withdraw reservations that may have been made in relation to particular human rights treaties; investigate reports of violations of human rights; adopt specific laws to address specific human rights issues; and take other legislative and administrative measures to fill the gaps where they exist. In other words, the UPR process encourages the member States to perfect their record of human rights.

As Boyle says, the intention from the very outset 'was to institute UPR as a cooperative mechanism to review practice of all States as regards their human rights obligations and commitments'.[53] The UPR process is not, however, helpful in addressing immediate matters of concern, but useful to encourage States to improve their record of human rights in the longer term. As stated by Cerna and Stewart, the UPR provides an opportunity for States to make a routine self-examination and to report to this international review its progress, and receive commendation (as well as criticism), which can motivate improvement in national performance.[54] There is criticism that beyond this, the significance and utility of UPR is limited. This is because, for some observers, the UPR process functions 'largely at a level of generality that frustrates incisive analysis and invites States to indulge in self-congratulatory superficiality',[55] and the process operates largely through a regional prism, reinforcing alliances rather than making objective and rational human rights related statements.[56]

4.8.7 Absence of a follow-up mechanism

The absence of a follow-up mechanism of the recommendations of the UPR is a major handicap for the system. First of all, too many recommendations are made, totaling more than 10,000 by the time eight of the nine UPR sessions had been completed during the first cycle. At the eighth session, an average of 128 recommendations had been issued per country.[57] A report indicated that

53 Kevin Boyle (ed.), *New Institutions for Human Rights Protection* (Oxford University Press, 2009) 5.

54 Christina M. Cerna and David P. Stewart, 'The United States before the UN Human Rights Council' (2010) 14 (32) *ASIL Insight*, 2.

55 Ibid.

56 Edward R. McMahon, 'Universal Periodic Review: a work in progress' (2012) *Dialogue on Globalization*, 24 http://library.fes.de/pdf-files/bueros/genf/09297.pdf (accessed 16 October 2014).

57 See the statement made by Dr Said Hammamoun, Senior Legal Advisor, UPR-Watch, at a conference in Geneva between 22 and 23 November 2010 on 'Improving Implementation and Follow-Up: Treaty-Bodies, Special Procedures, Universal Periodic

only 16 per cent of the recommendations made in the first cycle in 2008 were followed up by reviewing States during the second cycle of review in 2012.[58] This was one reason why the UK led a cross-regional statement at the 19th session of the Human Rights Council in which a commitment was made to make no more than two clear, focused and implementable recommendations to each UN member State when they are under review. The UK-led initiative was supported by 39 countries.[59]

States are free to accept or reject the UPR recommendations and do not have to account for the recommendations accepted either. It is left to the good faith of States to implement them. The recommendations may not be implemented even after accepting them and there is not much the Human Rights Council can do about it except wait for another 4 years for another round of UPR of the country concerned. For instance, nothing much could be done when North Korea rejected most, if not all, of the UPR recommendations made to it on 18 March 2010. Therefore, the verdict of some commentators on the effectiveness of the UPR is not an encouraging one. For instance, Ramcharan states that this process has 'mostly been without significance inside countries'.[60] However, it is too early to come to any definitive view only on the basis of the first and second cycles of UPR. As Rodley says, 'the system is sufficiently new that it may be premature to assume that it has achieved its mature shape'.[61]

The process is political if not politicised. The first round of the UPR demonstrated that States can survive the UPR process relatively unscathed if they are able to orchestrate friendly States to make complimentary remarks. A powerful and well-organised State can also make an attempt to dilute criticism in the civil society report compiled by the OHCHR by flooding the office with submissions from government-organised NGOs praising the national report, as seems to have happened with China's UPR.[62] Without a strong procedure to deal with countries which continue to commit gross violations of human rights, the UPR process runs the risk of being a meaningless paper exercise. Therefore, it remains to be seen whether the UPR process, touted as

Review', organised by the Open Society Justice Initiative, the Brookings Institution's Foreign Policy programme, and UPR-Watch. A copy of the report of proceedings of the conference is on file with the present author.

58 *Human Rights Monitor Quarterly*: Issue 3/212, p.8.

59 Foreign & Commonwealth Office, 'Human Rights and Democracy: The 2012 Foreign & Commonwealth Office Report (London, April 2013), 14.

60 Bertrand Ramcharan, *The UN Human Rights Council* (Routledge, 2011) 123.

61 Sir Nigel Rodley, 'The United Nations Human Rights Council, Its Special Procedures, and Its Relationship with the Treaty Bodies: Complementarities or Competition?' in Kevin Boyle (ed.), *New Institutions for Human Rights Protection* (Oxford University Press, 2009) 49–73 at 55.

62 Sonya Sceats with Shaun Breslin, 'China and the International Human Rights System' (Chatham House October, 2012) 14–15. http://www.chathamhouse.org/sites/files/chathamhouse/public/Research/International%20Law/r1012_sceatsbreslin.pdf (accessed 14 October 2014).

an innovative feature of the new Human Rights Council, can produce an objective, informed, and productive assessment of a given State's human rights situation.

4.8.8 Enhancing the universality of human rights

Although a plethora of UN documents declare that the core human rights are universal and almost all States sign up to such declarations, the practice of some States is not conducive to lending universal character to these rights. For instance, Article 26 of the Basic Law of Governance of Saudi Arabia states that 'The State shall protect human rights in accordance with the Islamic Shari'a.'[63] Therefore, the enjoyment of human rights by the citizens of Saudi Arabia depends on Islamic Shari'a. However, when submitting its national report to the Human Rights Council for UPR, Saudi Arabia stated that under the Basic Law 'governmental power is assigned to the judicial, executive and regulatory/legislative authorities. . . . The judiciary shall be an independent authority and, in their administration of justice, judges shall be subject to no authority than that of the Islamic Shari'a in the Kingdom'.[64] This implies that Islamic Shari'a too admits the notion of the separation of powers which constitute the bedrock of democracy.[65]

However, when it comes to actual rights, Saudi Arabia has no legal provision for certain rights, such as freedom of religion, and this country was one of those which did not support the adoption of the Universal Declaration of Human Rights in 1948. Since the report of the Working Group on the Universal Periodic Review[66] did not go beyond recording and summarising the recommendations made by individual States, it was not clear what impact the UPR made on the situation of human rights in the Kingdom and what changes in law and policy the country made in response to the UPR recommendations. The report of the Working Group concludes by stating that the recommendations 'will be examined by Saudi Arabia which will provide responses in due course'.[67] It is therefore left to the State concerned to accept or reject the recommendations made. It is notable that Saudi Arabia has not yet ratified some of the core human rights treaties such as the 1966 International Covenant on Civil and Political Rights and that the UPR did little to change that position.

63 National Report of Saudi Arabia submitted to the Human Rights Council as part of the UPR: A/HRC/WG.6/4/SAU/1 of 4 December 2008, 3.

64 Ibid.

65 It should be noted that Saudi Arabia is described as an autocracy by the Polity IV Project: Political Regime Characteristics and Transitions, 1800–2013, http://www.systemicpeace.org/polity/polity4.htm (accessed 16 October 2014).

66 A/HRC/11/23 of 4 March 2009, http://daccess-dds-ny.un.org/doc/UNDOC/GEN/G09/117/53/PDF/G0911753.pdf?OpenElement (accessed 8 July 2014).

67 Ibid.16.

Unlike the Saudi Arabian position, China on its part stated in its national report for UPR that it 'respects the principle of the universality of human rights and considers that all countries have an obligation to adopt measures continuously to promote and protect human rights in accordance with the purposes and principles of the Charter of the United Nations and the relevant provisions of international human rights instruments, and in the light of their national realities'.[68] Thus, the only qualifying notion in China's support for the universality of human rights was that when implementing human rights 'national realities' had to be taken into account. China did not explicitly invoke Communism or socialism to evade its human rights obligations.

Although China did not spell out what these 'national realities' were, the Chinese report went on to state that, 'given differences in political systems, levels of development and historical and cultural backgrounds, it is natural for countries to have different views on the question of human rights. In particular it is worthy of note that China stated that democracy and the rule of law were being improved in its country, rather than rejecting these as 'Western concepts'. Indeed, China stated that during the three decades of reform and the opening up of the country, it had enacted nearly 250 laws relating to the protection of human rights. The thrust of the Chinese message was not an arrogant one, as is often made out in the populist media, but a positive one designed to plead to the international community to be patient with the process of reform underway. By saying that China was a developing country, the Chinese report was seeking to justify slow progress in improving human rights. The report was candid enough in admitting the shortcomings in the Chinese system and outlined the difficulties and challenges facing the country.

The plea made by China was that it was a developing country and the economic growth that the country had managed to make had taken millions of people out of poverty and the international community should recognize this. Further, the claim was that even if the country had not advanced sufficiently in relation to human rights, it was the first country in the world to meet the poverty reduction target set by the UN Millennium Development Goals.[69] China had signed the 1966 International Covenant on Civil and Political Rights in 1998 and said that 'the relevant departments are carrying out necessary legislative, judiciary and administrative reforms to create the conditions for the early ratification of the ICCPR'.[70]

As with Saudi Arabia, since China had not ratified certain core human rights treaties such as the ICCPR, it could not be questioned regarding breaches of

68 National Report of China to the Human Rights Council as part of the UPR: A/HRC/WG.6/4/CHN/1 of 10 November 2008, 5. http://lib.ohchr.org/HRBodies/UPR/Documents/Session4/CN/A_HRC_WG6_4_CHN_1_E.pdf (accessed on 8 July 2014).

69 Ibid., pp. 8–9.

70 Ibid. p. 7.

that treaty's civil and political rights. Having said this, unlike the treaty bodies, whose remit is limited to monitoring implementation of the relevant treaty, the UPR mechanism enables the Human Rights Council to discuss the whole range of human rights issues in the country concerned. Accordingly, other States were able to urge China to ratify certain core human rights treaties such as the ICCPR and to investigate reports of human rights violations[71] even though China said that some of the recommendations of the UPR did not enjoy its support. Explaining the reasons for not accepting some of the recommendations the Chinese delegation stated that it 'was due to complicated factors'.[72] However, China affirmed its readiness to study them further and a key important factor here is China's apparent commitment to the UPR process.

Unlike the Chinese national report, the national report of the Russian Federation was confident and unapologetic.[73] This confidence was based mainly on the fact that Russia had ratified most of the core human rights treaties including the ICCPR, stating that they constituted an integral part of the Russian legal system, applied directly and had supremacy over its national legislation.[74] Further, the report also made it clear that Russia was a party to the European Convention for the Protection of Human Rights and Fundamental Freedoms and the rulings by the European Court of Human Rights were binding on the Russian Federation, implying that Russia was as good a democracy as any other State. Although China and Russia have often stood in the same camp on many matters of international affairs such as on Syria and opposed the 'Western agenda', regarding human rights, democracy and the rule of law, Russia is much closer to the West than China is. In fact, Russia implied in its remarks made during the UPR that it wanted to be closer and part of the European (meaning Western) and world's legal processes.[75] Therefore, Russia accepted all of the recommendations except one made to it during its UPR at the Human Rights Council.

71 'Report of the Working Group on the Universal Periodic Review: China.' A/HRC/11/25 of 5 October 2009, 27 http://daccess-dds-ny.un.org/doc/UNDOC/GEN/G13/188/55/PDF/G1318855.pdf?OpenElement (accessed 16 October 2014).

72 'Report of the Human Rights Council on its eleventh session', A/HRC/1137 of 16 October 2009, 142.

73 'National Report of the Russian federation to the Human Rights Council as part of the UPR: A/HRC/WG.6/4/RUS/1 of 10 November 2008, http://lib.ohchr.org/HRBodies/UPR/Documents/Session4/RU/A_HRC_WG6_4_RUS_1_E.PDF (accessed 16 October 2014).

74 Report of the Working Group on the Universal Periodic Review: Russian Federation', A/HRC/11/19 of 5 October 2009, 3, http://daccess-dds-ny.un.org/doc/UNDOC/GEN/G09/162/59/PDF/G0916259.pdf?OpenElement (accessed 16 October 2014).

75 'Report of the Working Group on the Universal Periodic Review: Russian Federation', A/HRC/11/19 of 5 October 2009, 4, http://daccess-dds-ny.un.org/doc/UNDOC/GEN/G09/162/59/PDF/G0916259.pdf?OpenElement accessed 16 October 2014.

To conclude, although the UPR is not a perfect mechanism, what has been witnessed thus far is encouraging in the sense that it involves a vibrant and diverse participation of States, national human rights institutions, UN agencies and civil society organisations. For instance, when the UPR of the US took place on 5 November 2010, the State delegation consisted of more than 40 persons (including three secretaries of State – for International organisations; Democracy, Human Rights and Labour; and the Legal Adviser for the State Department); more than 70 NGO representatives from the US came to Geneva to attend the review; and 15 NGO side events on the human rights situation in the US were held.

The review in the Human Rights Council itself attracted a high level of State interest with more than 80 States registering to speak. It was reported that diplomats from several countries, especially those critical of the US, had even spent the night in front of the UN building in Geneva to get on the list of speakers.[76] All in all, the UPR mechanism has acted as a comprehensive audit of the situation of human rights in all 193 members of the UN and has demonstrated that no country has a perfect record of human rights. Each and every State has more to do to live up to the expectations of the international community and the international human rights treaties.

4.9 An assessment of the Human Rights Council

4.9.1 Standard setting

Along with its agenda for implementation, the Human Rights Council has also taken a number of standard-setting measures. For instance, the Council has approved a number of new human rights treaties and guidance documents including the International Convention for the Protection of All Persons from Enforced Disappearances; the Convention on the Rights of Persons with Disabilities; the Optional Protocol to the International Covenant on Economic, Social and Cultural Rights establishing a complaints mechanism; Guiding Principles on Business and Human Rights: Implementing the United Nations 'Protect, Respect and Remedy Framework'; and the draft Declaration on the Rights of Indigenous Peoples. The latter was approved by the General Assembly despite the opposition from Australia, Canada, and the US. Further, in June 2014 the Council adopted a resolution entitled 'Elaboration of an international legally binding instrument on Transnational Corporations and other Business Enterprises with respect to Human Rights' which provided for the establishment of an open-ended intergovernmental working group that is mandated with

76 'UPR of the United States: no new commitments', News release of the International Service for Human Rights (ISHR), Geneva, 5 November 2010, http://archived2013.ishr.ch/archive-upr/942-upr-of-the-united-states-no-new-commitments (accessed 16 October 2014).

elaborating an international legally binding instrument to regulate, in international human rights law, the activities of transnational corporations and other business enterprises.[77]

The Council has also established a subsidiary expert mechanism to provide the Council with thematic expertise on the rights of indigenous peoples and two other forums – one is the Forum on Minority Issues and another one is the Social Forum – to provide a platform for promoting dialogue and co-operation on the respective issues. The breadth of the new instruments undermines the allegation that the UN in general and the Human Rights Council in particular promotes a Western agenda and has a hollow ring to it.

4.9.2 Asserting and expanding its activities

The Council has created a number of country-specific and geographic Special Rapporteurs in Iran,[78] Syria, Belarus, Eritrea, Central African Republic, and the Cote d'Ivoire, reversing the decline in the number of such rapporteurs during the last years of its predecessor – the Commission on Human Rights. There was considerable opposition to the creation of the country mandate on Belarus from countries such as Russia, China and Cuba. However, the Council succeeded in creating such a mandate. As stated by Sceats and Breslin, the Council has flexed its muscle in its approach during its later sessions.[79] Both Libya[80] and Syria have been suspended from the Council for violating the rights of their citizens, an unprecedented development in both international relations and in the practice of the UN.[81]

The Council has held special sessions to address the crisis in Libya and Syria, drawing the world's attention to the atrocities committed by the regime against its own people. The Council has itself also highlighted the urgent situation in the Cote D'Ivoire, Central African Republic, Guinea and Kyrgyzstan. It has also decided to appoint various commissions of inquiry to examine the situation of human rights in places such as Darfur, Eritrea, North Korea, Libya, Sri Lanka, Syria[82] and the Occupied Territories of Palestine.

77 A/HRC/26/L.22 of 26 June 2014.

78 Resolution 16/25 of 21 March 2011 on the situation of human rights in the Islamic Republic of Iran, A/HRC/16/L.33.

79 Sonya Sceats with Shaun Breslin, *China and the International Human Rights System* (Chatham House, 2012) 14–15.

80 The decision to ask the General Assembly to suspend Libya's membership of the Human Rights Council was taken by the Council at a special session on Libya on 25 February 2011.

81 Adopting a consensus resolution on 1 March 2011, the General Assembly acted on the 25 February 2011 recommendation by the Human Rights Council, which had urged the suspension of Libya in its own resolution.

82 For instance, the 17th Special Session of the Human Rights Council held on 22–23 August 2011 passed a resolution setting up an independent commission of inquiry into the situation of human rights in Syria, A/HRC/RES/S-17/1, http://daccess-dds-

The resolution of the Council adopted on 26 March 2014 on Sri Lanka asked the UN High Commissioner for Human Rights to undertake a comprehensive investigation into alleged serious violations and abuses of human rights and related crimes by both parties in the country during the ethnic conflict.[83] It should also be noted here that the report of some of such commissions have been marred by political controversy during the appointment of members of the commissions, in the submission of their reports, or in their consideration by the Human Rights Council thus exposing the weaknesses caused by the politicisation that is inherent in the Council being a political body. A case in point is the Goldstone report on the Gaza conflict of 2008–2009. Three of the members of the UN fact finding mission wrote a public letter distancing themselves from the remarks of its chairman, Justice Goldstone, in a newspaper article.[84]

In another case relating to the report of the Panel of Inquiry on the flotilla incident of 31 May 2011, a number of UN Special Rapporteurs issued a statement criticising the conclusion of the report (known as the Palmer Report) that Israel's naval blockade of the Gaza Strip was legal. Commenting on the report, Professor Richard Falk, the UN Special Rapporteur for Human Rights in the Occupied Palestinian Territories had the following remarks to make: 'The Palmer Report was aimed at political reconciliation between Israel and Turkey. It is unfortunate that in the report politics should trump the law.'[85]

4.9.3 Politicisation of the Council

The Council is not immune to politicisation of its work and it thereby invites inevitable criticism of bias, ineffectiveness, and pursuing a selective agenda. As Ramcharan asks: 'Can one expect the Human Rights Council to be other than what it is, namely a body in which government members are represented by

ny.un.org/doc/UNDOC/GEN/G11/169/88/PDF/G1116988.pdf?OpenElement (accessed 9 July 2014). The commission was an upgrade on an earlier fact-finding mission of the OHCHR to investigate all alleged violations of human rights in the country in accordance with a resolution of the Council adopted at its 16th Special Session. See pp. 112–115 in this chapter for comment on the outcome of the Syrian Commission of Inquiry and comment made by the then Commissioner for Human Rights, Navi Pillay.

83 'Promoting reconciliation, accountability and human rights in Sri Lanka', 26 March 2014, A/HRC/25/L.1/Rev.1

84 See on the controversy surrounding the Goldstone report on the Gaza conflict of 2008–2009, 'Goldstone report: Statement issued by members of the UN fact-finding mission to Gaza, May–September 2009, *Guardian*, London, 14 April 2011, http://www.theguardian.com/commentisfree/2011/apr/14/goldstone-report-statement-un-gaza (accessed 9 July 2014).

85 'How can Israel's blockade of Gaza be legal? – UN independent experts on the "Palmer Report"', News Release of the OHCHR, Geneva, 13 September 2011, http://www.ohchr.org/EN/NewsEvents/Pages/DisplayNews.aspx?LangID=E&NewsID=11363 (accessed 9 July 2014).

their ambassadors in Geneva whose mission is to protect the interests of their respective governments?'[86] Indeed, not. What is more, many such ambassadors, especially those from countries which are not democracies, represent the interests of the dictators and autocratic rulers of their countries rather than of the people. For instance, the ambassadors of Egypt during the time of Hosni Mubarak or Libya during Colonel Gaddafi's rule represented the interests of these ruling dictators as opposed to the concerns of the people.

In addition, the majority of the State members elected to the Council are from the Asian and African regional groups and many of them belong to cross regional blocs such as the Organisation of the Islamic Co-operation (OIC) and the Non-Aligned Movement (NAM). Although the NAM has lost much of its utility and relevance after the end of the Cold War and the OIC is not necessarily a homogeneous bloc, they do often work to oppose or block initiatives within the Council designed to hold States to account for violations of human rights. The resolution on Sri Lanka in 2009 is indicative here – the Council ended up effectively congratulating the country for ending the internal conflict on the strength of the support it was able to garner mainly from the Asian and African States, rather than holding the government to account for gross human rights violations during the country's internal armed conflict with the Tamils. As Boyle says, such political groupings of States played their role in the work of the former Commission on Human Rights too, 'but in the somewhat reduced size of the Council their dominance is more pronounced'.[87]

The elections to the Council in many cases are becoming a mere formality in which the candidates selected by the party leaders get elected. Regional groups of States have started to run 'closed lists' where the number of candidate States matches the number of seats available for the region concerned, therefore guaranteeing membership of the candidates proposed. There were occasions, especially during the formative years of the Council, when States with a poor record of human rights were rightly defeated in the elections to the Council. Examples were Venezuela (2006), Iran (2006), Belarus (2007), Sri Lanka (2008) and Azerbaijan (2009). In the face of mounting concern, Iran withdrew its candidacy in 2010 and Sudan in 2012.

In the elections to the Council in November 2012, except for Western Europe and Others (in which there were five candidates for three seats) all other regions ran a closed list, not giving any choice for the General Assembly. This practice undermines the credibility of the process, opens the Council's door to 'abuser' States, and frustrates the spirit and the letter of the UN resolution that established the Council. Further, the State members of regional organisations, such as the ASEAN group, seem to support in bloc the candidature of a member within the organisation for election to the Council regardless of its record of

86 Bertrand Ramcharan, *The UN Human Rights Council* (Routledge, 2011), 10.

87 Kevin Boyle in Kevin Boyle (ed.), *New Institutions for Human Rights Protection* (Oxford University Press, 2009) 4.

human rights. An example was the support pledged in October 2012 by other ASEAN members for Vietnam's candidature for election to the Human Rights Council in 2013.[88]

Eventually, in the elections to the Human Rights Council in November 2013 the following Asian countries, with a poor record of human rights of their own, were elected: China, Maldives, Saudi Arabia, and Vietnam. This was the reason that various international human rights organisations expressed their concern at their election as well as the election of Algeria, Cuba and Russia.[89] Although the UN General Assembly resolution establishing the Human Rights Council is replete with references to objectivity, transparency, non-selectivity, and genuine dialogue which is designed to convey the message that the work of the Council should be free of politicisation, the Human Rights Council has become a forum for governments and (inevitably) politics is creeping into the work of the Council just as it did during the time of the Commission on Human Rights.

4.10 The 2011 review of the Council

The resolution of the General Assembly establishing the Human Rights Council (60/251 of 2006) provides in operative paragraph 1 that the Assembly will review the status of the Council within 5 years of the establishment of the same. In addition, in operative paragraph 16 of the resolution, the Assembly also decided that the Human Rights Council will itself review its work and functioning 5 years after its establishment and report to the Assembly. Accordingly, reviews of the work and functioning of the Human Rights Council took place in 2011, culminating in the adoption of resolution 16/21 of 23 March 2011 to the General Assembly in which the Council outlined proposals for reform of some of the human rights protection and promotion mechanisms, which were in turn endorsed by the General Assembly through a resolution of 17 June 2011. Adopting the 'Outcome of the review of the work and functioning of the United Nations Human Rights Council' submitted to the General Assembly, the Human Rights Council had stated that this document would be a supplement to the Institution-Building Package contained in Council resolutions 5/1 and 5/2 of 18 June 2007.[90]

88 'ASEAN back Vietnam's candidacy for Human Rights Council', *Voice of Vietnam*, 30 September 2012, as reported in the *Newsletter of the Asian Society of International Law*, 2012/10 of 17 October 2012 (a copy of this *Newsletter* is on file with the present author).

89 BBC News: Europe, 'Concerns over new UN Human Rights Council members', 13 November 2013. http://www.bbc.co.uk/news/world-24922058?print=true (accessed on 19 November 2013).

90 'Review of the work and functioning of the Human Rights Council', A/HRC/16/L.39, 23 March 2011, http://daccess-dds-ny.un.org/doc/UNDOC/LTD/G11/122/69/PDF/G1112269.pdf?OpenElement (accessed 20 October 2014).

The outcome document did not propose any substantial or significant changes as the majority of developing countries led by Egypt on behalf of the Non-Aligned Movement, China, Pakistan, Philippines and India were not in favour of making major changes to the institutional framework, composition, powers and functions of the Council. The view held by these countries was that the process that they were engaged in was not a reform of the Council but only a review. Thus, the review process was focused on fine-tuning the work and functioning of the Human Rights Council. The Council stated in the outcome document that the second and subsequent cycles of the review should focus on, *inter alia*, the implementation of the accepted recommendations and the developments of the human rights situation in the State under review.

By a recorded vote of 154 in favour, four against (Canada, Israel, Palau, and United States), and no abstentions, the UN General Assembly adopted a resolution endorsing the proposal of the Human Rights Council. Under the terms of the text adopted on 17 June 2011, the Assembly decided to maintain the status of the Council as a subsidiary body of the Assembly.[91] The resolution also stated that the Assembly would consider again the question of whether to maintain the Council's status at an appropriate moment and at a time no sooner than 10 years and no later than 15 years.

Outlining the reasons why the United States had voted against the resolution, the US delegate stated that the review process did not carry out a comprehensive review of the Council to improve its ability to meet its core mission and the process had failed to yield even 'minimally positive' results. According to the US delegate, the Council diminished itself when the worst human rights violators had a seat at its table. The proposals made by the US during the review process included a provision calling on regional groups to run competitive slates and for an interactive dialogue between candidates for Council membership and civil society groups, but none of them had found expression in the final resolution.

A group of prominent human rights organisations such as Amnesty International and Human Rights Watch criticised the outcome document of the Human Rights Council stating that it was disappointing and urged members of the General Assembly to:

1. support the establishment of a public-pledge review mechanism to improve Council members' accountability to their pledges;
2. endorse an annual 'cooperation audit' as a central element of the procedure, where the general Assembly reviews and assesses the state of cooperation with the Council and the special procedures of candidate countries and members of the Council;

91 See Draft Resolution presented by the President of the Human Rights Council 'Review of the work and functioning of the Human Rights Council' http://daccess-dds-ny.un.org/doc/UNDOC/LTD/G11/122/69/PDF/G1112269.pdf?OpenElement (accessed 9 July 2014).

3. define and elaborate the meaning of cooperation, and to set guidelines on how to measure if members are abiding by pledges and commitments; and
4. support measures to guarantee that elections are genuinely competitive and contested, such as prohibiting 'clean slates' with only as many candidates as vacancies.[92]

However, the General Assembly did not act on these suggestions and endorsed the review resolution as submitted by the Council. After the adoption of the Outcome Document on the review of the Human Rights Council by the General Assembly the same international human rights organisations wrote a letter stating that the resolution adopted by the Assembly contained only 'a few technical and bureaucratic changes' and the result overall was 'extremely inadequate and sorely lacking in substance'.[93] Expressing his disappointment at the missed opportunity to reform the Council, Peter Splinter of Amnesty International, compared the review process to an 'elephant giving birth to a cockroach'.[94]

4.11 Conclusions

The Human Rights Council is basically a talking shop on human rights. It does not have much real world impact on human rights. That is what it was designed for and that is the role it has played thus far. Diplomats in Geneva expend a great deal of time and resources conceiving, drafting and negotiating texts, and human rights NGOs expend significant levels of energy and resources lobbying for or against the adoption of such resolutions that have little impact on the ground where human rights violations take place. A large number of resolutions, many of which are repetitive and bloated, are passed in Geneva at every session of the Council with marginal impact outside of the Geneva-based diplomatic-cum-human rights community. One of the reasons for this is that the Council is a body without powers to impose sanctions or to have its decisions implemented. According to Schaefer, the Council has over the past 10 years 'focused increasingly on human rights issues not directly related to gross and systematic violations of human rights. Instead, it has spent the majority of its time, resources, and attention on a growing number of "thematic" human rights topics of political, esoteric or specialized character.'[95] At the same time, it is a more democratic body than the Security Council since no State has a permanent seat or a veto power in the Human Rights Council. However, since it is a

92 A letter of 31 March 2011. A copy of this is on file with the present author.
93 A letter of 21 June 2011. A copy of this is on file with the present author.
94 *The Economist* (London), 5 March 2011, 65.
95 Brett D. Schaefer, 'The Human Rights Council's Failings should Lead to Reassessment', *Bulletin of the Universal Rights Group*, Geneva, August 2015.

political body, the expectations of it and its performance should be measured accordingly. The present author has himself observed the proceedings of the Human Rights Council for several years, during which States would argue for or against a particular resolution for hours not necessarily on the basis of their commitment to human rights but on the basis of their political affiliations and alliances.

The test of the effectiveness of the Council depends upon how real the debate is within the Council. There is a tendency on the part of States with a poor human rights record of their own to crowd the agenda of the Council with broad, vague and general thematic issues rather than on more concrete country-specific situations. According to a study, since the Council's creation 69 per cent of the resolutions it has adopted were on such thematic issues, while only 24 per cent dealt with on-the-ground situations in particular countries.[96]

Having said that it must be noted that such talking shops have their own merits: they maintain dialogue, keep States engaged in the process, promote some degree of cooperation, and bring about some positive changes, however marginal or nominal they may be. For instance, Saudi Arabia is not a party to many international human rights treaties. The treaty bodies created under these treaties cannot require Saudi Arabia to account for its activities to promote human rights in the country. The country has no Special Rapporteur. Thus, in the absence of the UPR there was no venue for the international community to enquire into the progress the country was making to promote and protect human rights. With the introduction of the UPR mechanism, Saudi Arabia has to submit a 4-yearly periodic report on the progress made on the situation of a whole range of human rights issues in the country, including equality for women and other areas covered by specific human rights treaties to which the country is not a party.

The Saudi government promised to implement a large number of recommendations made during both its UPR first round in 2009 and its second in 2014, including the abolition of the notoriously strict guardian system, under which a woman must have a male relative's permission to marry or travel abroad. Even if the Saudi Government was not initially serious in implementing these recommendations it made the promise and the international community, the human rights organisations and the individuals in the country, including women, can ask the government to abide by and implement its promise. According to a report, due partly to this promise made by the Saudi Government, some progress has been made to improve the situation of women and towards granting them equal rights, including the appointment of 30 women to the 150-member Shura Council, an advisory body to the King.[97]

96 Subhas Gujadhur and Toby Lamarque, 'UN Human Rights Council: The Case for Hybrid Resolutions', *URG Insights,* Universal Rights Group, Geneva, 10 November 2014.

97 Carla Power, 'No More Broken Promises' *Time*, 7 April 2014, 33.

Ultimately, since the Human Rights Council is a political body similar to its predecessor, the Council has faced many of the challenges that its predecessor did and has thus been subjected to similar criticisms, including politicisation of human rights. For instance, Freedman states that the Council 'has failed universally to protect and promote human rights, particularly through its ignoring, or being prevented from addressing, many grave human rights situations'.[98] Politics has undermined and discredited some of the work of the Council but it is difficult not to have politicisation in a political body. That is one reason why some commentators have stated that the replacement of the Commission on Human Rights by the Human Rights Council 'was more "make-over" than re-make'.[99]

The desire of the international human rights community was to see a Human Rights Council with fewer members, with stricter criteria for election for States with a poor record of human rights, and with a tougher electoral procedure for electing members to the Council.[100] At the end of the process of establishing the new Council none of these was achieved. One cannot expect that which its structural arrangement is not designed to deliver. Having said that, the UPR itself, the main mechanism of the Council, seems to have had a measure of impact on the situation of human rights in different countries. For instance, a UN report states that one positive side-effect of the introduction of the UPR has been 'increased ratification and, increasingly, more timely reporting by States under the international human rights treaties'.[101] The report goes on to elaborate that in 2000, there were a total of 927 ratifications of the six core international human rights treaties. By August 2011, that is, around the conclusion of the first round of the UPR, this figure had risen to 1,206 ratifications of the nine core international human rights treaties.

The existence of the Human Rights Council and its UPR mechanism become more crucial in the case of States which have not ratified any or many of the core human rights treaties. In that case, they cannot be subjected to scrutiny by the treaty bodies. There is not much the UN High Commissioner for Human Rights can do if the State in question does not accept the field presence of the OHCHR or does not cooperate at all with the office. Nor can the mechanism of special procedures do much if the country concerned has no country-specific mandate holder appointed for the country or even if a country-specific mandate

98 See Rosa Freedman, *The United Nations Human Rights Council: A Critique and Early Assessment* (Routledge, 2013) 298.

99 Lord Hannay, '2011 Review of the UN Human Rights Council: Recommendations submitted to the UK Foreign & Commonwealth Office by the United Nations Association of the UK', December 2010, 4.

100 Ibid.; what Lord Hannay has summed up in his report reflects the views of the international human rights community.

101 Report of the Secretary General, 'Measures to improve further the effectiveness, harmonization and reform of the treaty body system', U.N. Doc. A/66/344 of 7 September 2011, 5.

holder is appointed but if the country does not accept, recognize or cooperate with the mandate holder or does not extend any invitations or visa to the thematic mandate holders to visit the country.

The significance of the work of the Human Rights Council and the UPR mechanism becomes more crucial if a State decides to denounce a human rights treaty or its Optional Protocol, for example, as per the actions of Guyana, Jamaica, and Trinidad and Tobago in relation to the Optional Protocol to the ICCPR. As Venezuela did with the American Convention on Human Rights[102] in September 2012, States may denounce a human rights treaty altogether when the treaty body created under it expresses its deep concern regarding gross or systematic or egregious violations of human rights in the country. If a State decided to denounce the Charter of the UN and leave the world organisation it is a different matter, but so long as a State remains a member of the UN it should not escape the scrutiny of the Human Rights Council and will have to subject itself to the UPR mechanism.

It is conceivable that States may refuse to participate in the UPR, which is a voluntary process, and to cooperate with the Human Rights Council. For instance, Israel decided in March 2012 to cut working relations with the Council as it felt it had been singled out for targeted criticism through a series of politically motivated resolutions of the Council. The trigger for this disengagement was the decision of the Council to investigate Jewish settlements in the West Bank.[103] In January 2013, Israel decided to boycott a review of its human rights record by the Council, making it the first country to do so. However, in the first round of the UPR even countries like North Korea participated in the process despite rejecting most, if not all, of the UPR recommendations. Thus, the UPR on the whole has been regarded as a process that is universally accepted, and whilst there was some concern as to whether Israel would engage with the UPR during the second cycle in October 2013, given its boycott of the Human Rights Council, ultimately it did, albeit with strong reservations.[104]

102 See Diego German Mejia-Lemos, 'Venezuela's Denunciation of the American Convention on Human Rights' (2013) Vol.17 (1) *ASIL Insights*, and 'Pillay urges Venezuela to reconsider withdrawal from American Convention on Human Rights', News Release of the OHCHR, Geneva, 11 September 2012.

103 'Israel ends contact with the UN Human Rights Council', BBC News: Middle East, 26 March 2012, http://www.bbc.co.uk/news/world-middle-east-17510668 (accessed on 27 March 2012).

104 'Israel boycotts UN rights council in unprecedented move', BBC News: Middle East, 29 January 2013: http://www.bbc.co.uk/news/world-middle-east-21249431. A joint statement issued by eight Israeli human rights groups said that it was legitimate for Israel to express criticism of the work of the Council and its recommendations, "but Israel should do so through engagement with the Universal Periodic Review, as it has done in previous sessions". This should have been the course of action for Israel since the recommendations of the UPR or the decisions of the Council are not binding. There was no need for Israel to boycott the Human Rights Council process itself.

To conclude, since the powers and functions of the Human Rights Council are geared to the promotion of human rights through cooperation rather than to the protection of human rights through enforcement there is not much that can be expected from the Council in terms of protection and enforcement. Ultimately, what the UN, the international community, and the victims of human rights violations around the globe need in the twenty-first century is an effective international body which can provide effective remedy against violations of human rights and take effective action against States engaged in gross violations of human rights, and the Human Rights Council is not well equipped to do so.[105]

To access documentation relating to Israel and the UPR, go to http://www.ohchr.org/EN/HRBodies/UPR/Pages/Highlights29October2013pm.aspx, accessed 4 November 2014.

105 Some might argue that this function is addressed elsewhere, for example via the International Criminal Court, however, it is for States to voluntarily accept the ICC's jurisdiction. Further, similar allegations of politicisation at the ICC have been made. For example, see a report on the ICC, 'International Justice: Nice idea, now make it work', *The Economist* (London), 6 December 2014, pp.68–69. There is also the alleged bias against African States since all of the prosecutions at the ICC have been people from Africa. There is a debate taking place in many African countries to withdraw from the Rome Statute and both South Africa and Burundi have already announced their intention to do so.

5 Effectiveness of the Office of the UN High Commissioner of Human Rights

5.1 Introduction

Often over-enthusiastically referred to by some people, and with some degree of naivety, as 'the world human rights leader' or 'conscience for the world' or 'the UN ambassador for human rights', the UN High Commissioner for Human Rights[1] is a political and administrative position within the UN system who is appointed by, and works under, the overall direction of the Secretary General who can often be more of a secretary himself rather than a general. The High Commissioner has no judicial or even quasi-judicial powers. It is in reality an administrative position forming part of the UN Secretariat. It does not have even administrative autonomy or budgetary independence. It is a UN agency designed primarily to influence policy in the member States of the UN rather than to protect human rights. But it has multi-faceted roles and responsibilities.

The exercise of the powers and functions of this role are to be informed by the norms of international human rights law and humanitarian law. Therefore, the expectation has been that the person appointed to this position will be from a legal background with experience and expertise in international human rights law and possessing human rights credentials earned as a professional human rights activist or advocate or defender. However, the significance of this position is at times undermined by its treatment as a lowly bureaucratic position within the UN hierarchy and sometimes as a result of appointing political or diplomatic people rather than leading human rights experts, professionals or defenders with international standing in this area to the position.

It was with a sense of optimism after the end of the Cold War, the talk of the end of history following the triumph of Western liberal democracy, and a growing commitment to multi-party democracy around the globe that the Vienna World Conference on Human Rights was held in June 1993. During

1 This office of the UN is widely referred to as the OHCHR or the UN OHCHR in the academic literature and in official publications and is used interchangeably throughout this study.

the conference came the adoption of the Vienna Declaration and Programme of Action (VDPA). As a new commitment to human rights, and with a view to strengthening the UN system of human rights and advancing the objectives of the VDPA, the World Conference created the new position of the High Commissioner for Human Rights. This position is mandated to promote and protect the enjoyment and full realisation of the rights of individuals, groups of individuals, indigenous peoples and other peoples as stipulated in the Charter of the United Nations and in international human rights law and treaties.

The UN High Commissioner has a unique mandate to protect and promote human rights which has been in existence now for more than 20 years. It was in Vienna in June 2013 that the Vienna +20 Conference took place to review the progress made since the adoption of the VDPA and the establishment of the Office of the High Commissioner, and to celebrate the twentieth anniversary of the landmark decisions made in Vienna in 1993. It is in this context that this chapter seeks to assess the effectiveness of the Office of the High Commissioner for Human Rights over the last two decades or so in protecting and promoting human rights. It considers the contribution the High Commissioner has made to the promotion and protection of human rights, the challenges facing this role, and what reforms, if any, are needed on the basis of the experience of the last 20 years. In so doing, the chapter will cast a critical eye on the workings of the High Commissioner's role and its strengths and weaknesses.

5.2 Evolution of the Office of the High Commissioner for Human Rights

As stated in a review of the Office of the High Commissioner for Human Rights, the Office 'has a dual nature'.[2] It goes on to state that 'On the one hand, it is a part of the United Nations Secretariat, with the High Commissioner, as its head, serving as the head of a department/office of the Secretariat, and is consequently subject to the (governance) structure of the Secretariat and its policies, regulations and rules. On the other, it is an entity entrusted with supporting an independent mandate, namely, that of the post of High Commissioner, as set out in General Assembly resolution 48/141.'[3] Indeed, in resolution 48/141, the General Assembly 'bestowed independence on the High Commissioner. At the same time, the Office is part of the Secretariat, and hence subject to its accountability, governance and oversight structure and framework.'[4] Not only the Office but also the High Commissioner itself is

2 Review of Management and Administration of the Office of the United Nations High Commissioner for Human Rights, Prepared by Gopinathan Achamkulangare, JIU/REP/2014/7, Joint Inspection Unit, United Nations, Geneva 2014, para 21.
3 Ibid.
4 Ibid., para 22.

accountable to the Secretary-General, with whom he or she concludes a senior manager's compact, as other Under-Secretaries-General do.

The Office of the High Commissioner for Human Rights (OHCHR) was established as part of an attempt to strengthen the UN human rights system, especially in view of the rather rapidly evolving situation across the globe in the aftermath of the collapse of Communism in Europe and the demise of the former Soviet Union which signalled the end of the bipolar world dominated by the Cold War.[5] The end of the Cold War had a profound impact not only on Eastern European countries but also on Asian, African and Latin American countries. When the cloud of the Cold War hanging over them was lifted, freedom-loving people across the world were galvanised into action for democracy and human rights. While dramatic changes were taking place in Eastern Europe with the emergence of a number of new States as a result of the redrawing of boundaries, the ripples of the new wave of democracy reached many States in Asia, Africa and Latin America. This provided both a challenge and an opportunity for the UN in general, and the UN human rights machinery in particular, to assist people fighting for democracy and human rights and make the process smoother for those countries which had just embarked on the road to independence, democracy and human rights.

Unprecedented political and economic changes were taking place around the globe. It was in the midst of this profound change and political upheaval that the UN convened the Vienna World Conference on Human Rights in 1993. People around the globe had high expectations of this conference since the main UN agencies responsible for human rights, namely, the General Assembly, the former Commission on Human Rights, the Centre for Human Rights, the special procedures, and the treaty bodies, were in need of a significant boost to cope with the demands of the time. It was felt that these UN agencies and particularly the Commission on Human Rights were not well equipped to respond effectively to the rapidly unfolding cases of human rights violations and that the Centre for Human Rights was under-resourced, poorly equipped and lacked the powers that would have been needed for it to viably work as a major UN human rights agency.

It was against this background that various major human rights organisations, such as Amnesty International,[6] and some governments, mooted the idea of the creation of the post of the UN High Commissioner for Human Rights.[7]

5 See generally on the background to the creation of this UN position, Andrew Clapham, 'Creating the High Commissioner for Human Rights: The Outside Story' (1994) 5 *European Journal of International Law*, 556.

6 See Amnesty International, 'Facing Up to the Failures: Proposals for Improving the Protection of Human Rights by the United Nations', Amnesty Doc. IOR41/16/92, 1 December 1992, http://www.amnesty.org/en/library/info/IOR41/016/1992/en accessed 17 October 2014.

7 Leonard Doyle, 'Clinton wants UN to take on tyrannical rulers', *Independent*, 14 July 1993, 6.

Of course, the idea was not a completely new one. Similar ideas had been around for some time already. For instance, in the late 1940s France had proposed an 'Attorney-General for Human Rights', whilst with the support of some NGOs the Government of Uruguay and Costa Rica had proposed the appointment of a UN High Commissioner for Human Rights in 1950 and again in 1965 with a third attempt being made to this effect between 1977 and 1983.[8] Thus, the idea was simply subsequently revived during the Vienna World Conference on Human Rights in 1993, as opposed to being a completely new proposal.

However, the Vienna Conference itself could not agree on any specific proposal on this issue and the matter was referred to the UN General Assembly which adopted a resolution on 20 December 1993 creating this new flagship human rights position within the UN system. In July 1997, the pre-existing UN Human Rights Centre was merged with the OHCHR, which positioned the OHCHR as a member of the newly established executive committees on peace-keeping, humanitarian affairs, developmental, economic and social issues within the UN to ensure that human rights were 'mainstreamed' throughout the UN system. In the words of Mary Robinson, a former High Commissioner for Human Rights, these changes, 'enabled [the] OHCHR, from a very weak base, to become the thought leader on protection and promotion of human rights which it is today'.[9]

5.3 Functions and responsibilities of the UN High Commissioner

The General Assembly resolution that created the position of the High Commissioner for Human Rights, refers to the role as 'the United Nations official with principal responsibility for United Nations human rights activities', implying a great deal of power and significant responsibility is bestowed upon this role.[10] Even the title of the General Assembly resolution indicates the enormity of the task to be undertaken by the individual in this role, being as they are a 'High commission for the promotion and protection of *all* Human Rights'. The functions of the High Commissioner can broadly be put in the following four categories: (1) support for human rights standard-setting (2) monitoring (3) supporting implementation and (4) human rights advocacy.

8 Philip Alston, 'The United Nations High Commissioner for Human Rights', *ASIL Insight*, Sept–Oct 1995, 1.

9 See the observations made by Mary Robinson in 'Vienna Declaration and Programme of Action + 20', *Human Rights Monitor Quarterly* of the International Service for Human Rights, Geneva, Issue 1, 2013, 11.

10 'High Commissioner for the promotion and protection of all Human Rights', General Assembly Resolution GA/48/141, http://www.un.org/documents/ga/res/48/a48r141.htm, accessed 10 July 2014.

The High Commissioner is to provide substantive and technical support to the various UN human rights bodies responsible for standard-setting and monitoring work and to develop human rights knowledge and awareness. The field presence of the OHCHR via subsidiary offices in States around the globe enables it to monitor and support the implementation of human rights standards. The advocacy role of the High Commissioner is central to the fulfilment of the mandate of the OHCHR and involves, *inter alia*, speaking out on behalf of victims, developing and implementing appropriate responses, preparing learning tools and outreach to multiple stakeholders, including civil society organisations and human rights defenders.

The mandate of the High Commissioner is based on Articles 1, 13, 55 and 56 of the Charter of the UN, the Vienna Declaration and Programme of Action of 1993 and General Assembly resolution 48/141 of 20 December 1993. The High Commissioner is appointed by the Secretary General, the appointment is approved by the General Assembly and the High Commissioner is then accountable to the Secretary General. Within the UN bureaucracy, the position of the High Commissioner is only one of more than a dozen or so under-secretaries-general. The process of appointment to this position itself is rather opaque since it is not, strictly speaking, an elected position, but a bureaucratic one and the qualifications of this position are not spelt out in much detail. The resolution states that the High Commissioner for Human Rights would:

(a) Be a person of high moral standing and personal integrity and shall possess expertise, including in the field of human rights, and the general knowledge and understanding of diverse cultures necessary for impartial, objective, non-selective and effective performance of the duties of the High Commissioner;
(b) Be appointed by the Secretary-General of the United Nations and approved by the General Assembly, with due regard to geographical rotation, and have a fixed term of four years with a possibility of one renewal for another fixed term of four years.[11]

The resolution goes on to state that the High Commissioner will:

(a) Function within the framework of the Charter of the United Nations, the Universal Declaration of Human Rights, other international instruments of human rights and international law, including the obligations, within this framework, to respect the sovereignty, territorial integrity and domestic jurisdiction of States and to promote the universal respect for and

11 Paragraph 2(a) – (b), 'High Commissioner for the promotion and protection of all Human Rights', General Assembly Resolution GA/48/141, http://www.un.org/documents/ga/res/48/a48r141.htm (accessed 10 July 2014).

observance of all human rights, in the recognition that, in the framework of the purposes and principles of the Charter, the promotion and protection of all human rights is a legitimate concern of the international community;

(b) Be guided by the recognition that all human rights – civil, cultural, economic, political and social – are universal, indivisible, interdependent and interrelated and that, while the significance of national and regional particularities and various historical, cultural and religious backgrounds must be borne in mind, it is the duty of States, regardless of their political, economic and cultural systems, to promote and protect all human rights and fundamental freedoms;

(c) Recognize the importance of promoting a balanced and sustainable development for all people and of ensuring realisation of the right to development, as established in the Declaration on the Right to Development.[12]

While carrying out these functions, the High Commissioner should operate under the direction and authority of the Secretary General and within the framework of the overall competence, authority and decisions of the General Assembly, the Economic and Social Council and the Human Rights Council. The main responsibilities of the High Commissioner could be said to be as follows:

(a) To promote and protect the effective enjoyment by all of all civil, political, economic, social and cultural rights;

(b) To promote and protect the realisation of the right to development and to enhance support from relevant bodies of the United Nations system for this purpose;

(c) To play an active role in removing the current obstacles and in meeting the challenges to the full realisation of all human rights and in preventing the continuation of human rights violations throughout the world, as reflected in the Vienna Declaration and Programme of Action;

(d) To engage in a dialogue with all Governments in the implementation of his/her mandate with a view to securing respect for all human rights;

(e) To coordinate the human rights promotion and protection activities throughout the United Nations system.

Thus, the modus operandi of the High Commissioner can broadly be divided into the following five areas: (1) urgent measures, (2) prevention, (3) technical assistance, (4) coordination, and (5) cooperation. The High Commissioner is required to report annually on their activities, in accordance with their mandate,

12 Paragraph 3(a) – (c), 'High Commissioner for the promotion and protection of all Human Rights', General Assembly Resolution GA/48/141, http://www.un.org/documents/ga/res/48/a48r141.htm (accessed 10 July 2014).

to the Human Rights Council and to the General Assembly. Since the mandate of the High Commissioner includes preventing human rights violations, securing respect for all human rights, promoting international cooperation to protect human rights, coordinating related activities throughout the UN system, and strengthening and streamlining it in the field of human rights, the High Commissioner reports on these issues and situation on the ground. The High Commissioner is guided in their work by the mandate provided by:

(1) The General Assembly in resolution 48/141 of 1993,[13]
(2) The Charter of the United Nations,
(3) The Universal Declaration of Human Rights and subsequent human rights instruments,
(4) The Vienna Declaration and Programme of Action of the 1993 World Conference on Human Rights,[14] and
(5) The World Summit Outcome Document of 2005.[15]

In addition, the Secretary General of the UN, the General Assembly, the Human Rights Council and an international diplomatic conference can entrust the High Commissioner with certain tasks within the overall mandate of the role.

5.4 A snapshot of the activities of the UN High Commissioner

The position of the High Commissioner is a demanding job. One day reacting to the military coup in Thailand and another day visiting South Sudan after massacres. While the High Commissioner is expected to give early warning to the international community, including the UN Security Council, about the evolving situation in countries in crisis they have to act as a thought leader and global human rights leader at the same time. As the UN's principal human rights official, the High Commissioner must lead global human rights efforts and speak out objectively in the face of human rights violations worldwide. As stated by Koh, the High Commissioner must be the world's 'emergency human rights first-responder'.[16]

13 'High Commissioner for the promotion and protection of all Human Rights', General Assembly Resolution GA/48/141, http://www.un.org/documents/ga/res/48/a48r141.htm (accessed 10 July 2014).

14 'Vienna Declaration and Programme of Action', Adopted by the World Conference on Human Rights in Vienna on 25 June 1993, http://www.ohchr.org/en/professional interest/pages/vienna.aspx (accessed 17 October 2014).

15 '2005 World Summit Outcome', A/RES/60/1, 24 October 2005, http://www.un.org/womenwatch/ods/A-RES-60-1-E.pdf (accessed 17 October 2014).

16 Harold H. Koh, 'The UN High Commissioner for Human Rights: From the Personal to the Institutional' in Felice D. Gaer and Christen L. Broecker (ed.), *The United Nations High Commissioner for Human Rights: Conscience for the World* (Martinus Nijhoff, 2013), 45.

Indeed, the High Commissioner has not only to act, but also to be seen to act in cases of crisis or in the face of serious violations of human rights, whether in Syria, Egypt, the Central African Republic, Iran, North Korea or Sri Lanka or indeed any other hot-spot around the world. Therefore, Koh goes on to add, the High Commissioner 'must be part politician, part bureaucrat, and part human rights expert without tipping too far in any direction'.[17] He should also have added a number of other adjectives to the role's description: 'part CEO' because the High Commissioner has to manage and oversee the operation of a large office in Geneva with a large number of professionals, human rights experts and support staff as well as field offices in many countries around the globe; 'part diplomat', it being the role of the High Commissioner to perform in cases of political or humanitarian crisis or when delivering difficult messages to governments; 'part government adviser', as the High Commissioner is to assist governments in their capacity-building in promoting human rights and offering advice on areas for improvement, and 'part thought-leader in human rights', as the High Commissioner is expected to provide intellectual leadership in promoting, enhancing and championing the UN human rights agenda and in coming up with new ideas to cater for the needs of a changing world in terms of the conduct of human and State behaviour.

It is indeed a complex, demanding and challenging position relying on the use of 'smart' or 'soft' power rather than any real tangible power. The High Commissioner is expected to speak truth to power, raise the profile of human rights globally, monitor the situation of human rights globally and at the same time perform the role of a comparative evaluator of human rights abuses according to global standards, as well as report findings to the Human Rights Council and other UN bodies as appropriate.

There is no separate code of conduct as such to be observed by the High Commissioner in discharging the role's responsibilities, but it is implied that the position holder fulfils obligations under international law, makes consistent application of this body of law and observes objectivity, independence and neutrality. Further, since it is a bureaucratic position within the UN system, the High Commissioner would be subject to all the internal rules and regulations applicable to UN personnel operating under the overall supervision of the Executive Team headed by the Secretary General.

The position is designed to provide constructive criticism of governmental policy, rather than providing any redress to victims of human rights. It is expected to provide a forum for identifying, highlighting and developing responses to today's human rights challenges, and act as the principal focal point of human rights research, education, public information, and advocacy activities in the UN system. Successive High Commissioners have put in place a number of thematic strategies designed to counter discrimination, combat impunity,

17 Ibid., 49.

strengthen accountability, the rule of law, and democratic society, protect human rights in situations of conflict, violence and insecurity and strengthen international human rights mechanisms. The Office of the High Commissioner has also taken the lead in mainstreaming human rights within the UN, which means injecting a human rights perspective into all UN programmes. The Office is expected to work to offer the best expertise, and substantive and secretariat support to the different UN Charter-based and treaty bodies as they discharge their standard-setting and monitoring duties. It serves as the Secretariat of the Human Rights Council, the key UN intergovernmental body responsible for human rights, and supports the work of the special procedures mandate holders – including Special Rapporteurs, independent experts, working groups and commissions of inquiry – appointed by the Council to monitor human rights in different countries or in relation to specific issues.

Another major feature of the Office of the High Commissioner is the work carried out by the field offices located in different parts of the world, ensuring the implementation of international human rights standards on the ground. Whilst the Headquarters of the High Commissioner is in Geneva with an Office in New York, there are regional offices in places as diverse as Brussels and Bangkok and several country offices.[18] It is through these offices that the High Commissioner provides assistance to Governments, such as expertise and technical training in the areas of administration of justice, legislative reform, and electoral process, to help implement international human rights standards on the ground. These field offices and presences play an important role in identifying, highlighting, and developing responses to human rights challenges, in close collaboration with governments, the UN system, non-governmental organisations, and members of civil society. Such responses range from monitoring human rights situations on the ground to implementing projects, such as technical training and support in the areas of administration of justice, prison reform, legislative reform, human rights treaty ratification, preparation of country reports to various human rights treaty bodies and human rights education.[19]

5.5 Effectiveness of the UN High Commissioner

Measuring effectiveness of any institution or position is a subjective activity. The effectiveness of this role should be measured against the mandate and the powers accorded to it by the constituent documents. As stated earlier, while the High Commissioner has a broad remit defined in very general terms, the

18 For a list of regional offices, see http://www.ohchr.org/EN/Countries/Pages/RegionalOfficesIndex.aspx, for details of country offices, see http://www.ohchr.org/EN/Countries/Pages/CountryOfficesIndex.aspx, both accessed 17 October 2014.

19 An example is a successful prison reform programme carried out by the Government of Cambodia with the support from the Cambodia Office of the High Commissioner.

role lacks much in the way of real power. It is primarily a political agency entrusted with the task of influencing policy in the UN member States. Therefore, much of the effectiveness of the work of the Office of the High Commissioner depends upon who is appointed to this position. The High Commissioners appointed to date have come from varied backgrounds, are of different calibre and have had varying degrees of success in raising the bar and in taking forward the UN human rights agenda. The most recent appointee in July 2014 is a person with a political and diplomatic background, rather than a background with experience as a jurist or human rights professional in terms of advocacy, activism or defending.

The Office of the High Commissioner has been able to play an important role in improving the compliance of national laws, policies and institutions with international standards, increasing ratification of international human rights standards, establishing and strengthening justice and accountability mechanisms in various countries, improving access to justice and basic services, increasing participation and use of national protection mechanisms by rights holders, and increasing State and civil engagement with human rights mechanisms. The Office has also worked towards strengthening international and regional laws and institutions relating to human rights, promoting coherence among human rights mechanisms such as special procedures and treaty bodies, increasing international responsiveness to critical human rights situations and enhancing the mainstreaming of human rights within the UN system as a whole.[20]

The Office of the High Commissioner has come a long way from its humble beginnings in 1993 with a meagre budget of US$ 1,471,400 and a broad but a vague mandate, to a situation where it had a budget of US$ 142,743,800 in 2011–2012[21] and currently occupies centre-stage within the UN system, playing a key and very visible role as the flagship UN human rights agency. As of 31 July 2014, the OHCHR had staff in 58 countries and was providing support to some 74 special procedures, mandate holders, or working group members (36 thematic and 12 geographic mandates) as well as nearly 175 experts serving different treaty bodies. In addition to the 68 field offices, the OHCHR receives requests for human rights advisers, who are posted with the UN Resident Coordinators and UN country teams in different countries. The OHCHR is also mandated to support the establishment and operation of commissions of inquiry and fact-finding missions such as those on Syria or North Korea.

20 An example is the UN's new 'Human Rights Up Front' approach to require all UN agencies to make their own contribution to the promotion and protection of human rights.

21 The total 2010–2011 biennium budget of the OHCHR. Available at http://www.ohchr.org/EN/AboutUs/Pages/FundingBudget.aspx (accessed 3 September 2012).

The success of the OHCHR has depended upon the courage, vision, and strategic approach taken by successive High Commissioners from Josse Ayala-Lasso and Mary Robinson to Navi Pillay.[22] They have not hesitated to bring into the spotlight the situation of human rights in any State whether big or small, developed or developing, Western or non-Western. For instance, Navi Pillay was quite outspoken about the situation of human rights in China in general and in Tibet in particular in her remarks on 2 November 2012 in which she called upon the Chinese authorities to address the grievances of the people of Tibet.[23] Neither has she spared India from the highlighting of the situation of human rights in its country, especially in Jammu and Kashmir. At a press conference on 18 October 2012 she called on the Indian Government 'to fully investigate past killings and disappearances and bring the perpetrators to justice'.[24] Similarly, she expressed her concern about the situation of human rights in the Russian Federation on 18 July 2012.[25] It is her outspoken character that earned her the title of 'a tigress' in an article in *The Economist*.[26]

Given her background as a jurist and human rights activist, when Navi Pillay spoke, she spoke with both personal and professional authority and an aura of legitimacy. She was outspoken on matters of transitional justice in countries in transition or in a post-conflict situation. For instance, she intervened in the internal legislative process in Nepal when a draft bill on Truth and Reconciliation, tabled by the government before parliament, included provisions that did not go far enough in bringing to account those people that had committed atrocities during the 10-year long Maoist insurgency in the country. The bill was designed to bring the peace process to a logical conclusion following the conclusion of a comprehensive peace agreement between the government and the Maoists, to end the Maoist-led insurgency and to abolish the autocratic monarchy. But the bill was not robust enough in bringing to justice the perpetrators of atrocities during the conflict. Her intervention

22 Felice D. Gaer, 'The High Commissioners and the Special Procedures: Colleagues and Competitors', in Felice D. Gaer and Christen L. Broecker (ed.), *The United Nations High Commissioner for Human Rights: Conscience for the World* (Martinus Nijhoff, 2013) 133–56.

23 'Pillay: China must urgently address deep-rooted frustrations with the human rights in Tibetan areas', News Release of the OHCHR of 2 November 2012. It is on file with the present author, see http://www.ohchr.org/EN/NewsEvents/Pages/DisplayNews.aspx?NewsID=12729&LangID=E (accessed 11 July 2014).

24 Navi Pillay's Opening Statement at a press conference held in Geneva on 18 October 2012. This is on file with the present author. See also http://www.ohchr.org/en/NewsEvents/Pages/DisplayNews.aspx?NewsID=12675&LangID=E (accessed 11 July 2014).

25 'Pillay concerned about series of new laws restricting human rights in Russian Federation', News Release of the OHCHR of 18 July 2012, http://www.unog.ch/80256EDD006B9C2E/%28httpNewsByYear_en%29/48C8A35CC9F95D3DC1257A3F003361B8?OpenDocument accessed 11 July 2014.

26 'A tigress and her tormentors' *The Economist* (London), 8 October 2011, 70.

became headline news in all major media outlets and a focus for debate within the country.[27]

The Office of the High Commissioner comes under attack from States that have been singled out for criticism. For instance, the High Commissioner's description of specific human rights concerns in some States such as Canada, Syria and the Democratic Republic of Congo drew defensive and hostile responses from their delegations at the twentieth regular session of the Human Rights Council on 18 July 2012.[28] Further, countries like Cuba have made an attempt to undermine the independence of the Office of the High Commissioner by introducing a resolution on 'strengthening dialogue, collaboration and coordination' between the Office of the High Commissioner and the Human Rights Council. Under such a seemingly positive title, the resolution actually appears to be designed to reduce the effectiveness and independence of the High Commissioner.[29]

Each of the High Commissioners that served between 1994 and 2014 (the time covered in this study; since the current High Commissioner was appointed only in 2014 it is too early to assess his overall performance) has asserted a constructive and expansive role for their office, and has worked tirelessly to command the trust and respect of human rights stakeholders around the globe. This has been achieved by their having strongly argued their case within the UN system for a greater level of support, financial or otherwise, for their work; persuading international donors, both public and private, to provide financial support; concretising the rather vague mandate of the office; filling the gaps that existed in the initial mandate; and fleshing out the principles behind the creation of the office. Furthermore, these individuals have championed human rights by becoming a critic, where necessary, of those States which have violated human rights. The national and regional OHCHR offices and those around the globe are fast becoming the first port of call for victims of human rights seeking international assistance against their grievances.[30] The OHCHR was credited for its role during and after the revolutions in Egypt, Libya, and Tunisia as well as in other Arab countries in 2011–2012.

27 For instance, see 'No Amnesty for serious HR violation: Pillay', *Republica* (Kathmandu), 16 April 2014, 3.

28 'States defensive against High Commissioner's criticism', News Release, International Service of Human Rights, Geneva, 26 July 2012, http://archived2013.ishr.ch/archive-council/1324-high-commissioner-attacked-by-states-highlighted-in-her-report-to-the-councils-20th-session (accessed 17 October 2014).

29 'States attempt to undermine High Commissioner's independence', News release of International Service for Human Rights, Geneva, 27 September 2010, http://www.ishr.ch/news/states-attempt-undermine-high-commissioners-independence (accessed 11 July 2014).

30 It now employs about 850 staff based in Geneva and New York and in country regional offices around the world, including a workforce of some 250 international human rights officers serving in UN peace missions. It is funded from the United Nations regular budget and from voluntary contributions from Member States, intergovernmental organisations, foundations and individuals.

5.6 Institutional limitations of the position

The mandate of this office is limited;[31] whilst the mandate as provided by the General Assembly appears to be quite broad, it is ultimately limited in terms of the specific purpose and power bestowed upon it.[32] Further, the High Commissioner is not an independent authority as it must operate under the direction and authority of the Secretary General of the UN. Assessing the mandate of the High Commissioner and providing a background to the creation of this office, Alston sums up the situation as follows:

> The High Commissioner's mandate has always been the most contentious issue. At the end of the negotiations, the recipe that attracted consensus was a combination of vagueness and comprehensiveness. The former ensured that no specific independent fact-finding mandate was conferred, the coordination role remained limited and imprecise, responding to violations was only one part of a broad mandate, questions of staff and funding were left largely unaddressed. . . . While the generality of the mandate leaves the High Commissioner with a great deal of discretion, its key provision requires him or her to play "an active role . . . in preventing the continuation of human rights violations throughout the world".[33]

Successive High Commissioners have sought to use the generality and comprehensiveness of their mandate to strengthen the office. An open-ended mandate has enabled rather than hindered the work of the High Commissioner; each new holder of the post has developed and expanded the role of the office by interpreting their mandate to suit the needs of the day and has exercised powers as needed to address specific situations of violations of human rights, raising funds to finance such activities. This has enabled the High Commissioner to carry out its activities in each of the key areas outlined above, namely, urgent measures, prevention, technical assistance, coordination, and cooperation.

However, in terms of its place in the UN structure, the Office of the High Commissioner operates as a department of the United Nations Secretariat and has engaged mainly in capacity building and providing support to other UN human rights agencies. It is also still subject to the general budgetary cuts and constraints of the UN. Although the publications of the Office of the High Commissioner state that it is 'the leading UN entity on human

31 For an overview of the structure of the Office of the High Commissioner for Human Rights, see http://www.ohchr.org/Documents/AboutUs/OHCHR_orgchart_2014.pdf (accessed 17 October 2014).

32 'High Commissioner for the promotion and protection of all Human Rights', General Assembly Resolution GA/48/141, http://www.un.org/documents/ga/res/48/a48r141.htm (accessed 10 July 2014).

33 Philip Alston, 'The United Nations High Commissioner for Human Rights', ASIL Insight, Sept–Oct 1995, 2.

rights'[34] it is 'a' leading rather than 'the' leading entity on human rights. Whilst the Office of the High Commissioner for Human Rights might be understood as an umbrella organisation in terms of the assistance and support it provides to the many and various UN human rights institutions and the assistance provided to States in terms of capacity building, its success, and therefore its status, as 'the' leader is questionable particularly given the apparently 'deaf ears' of the international community that the concerns and warnings raised by the Office in relation to specific crises since the office's inception fall upon.

5.7 Political labelling of the position

The perception in some quarters of the developing world seems to be that the High Commissioner is appointed on the orders of the West or even of the US, acts as a political agent of the West, pays more attention to civil and political rights than social, economic and cultural rights, applies double standards, and singles out States for criticism. These criticisms may be far from true, but the rather opaque process for the appointment of the High Commissioner,[35] the lack of funding for this office and its activities in general, and for social, economic and cultural rights in particular, do not help in dispelling this perception. This has a detrimental impact on the effectiveness and stature of the High Commissioner.

Critics are also sceptical about the effectiveness of the hundreds of press statements or media advisories issued by the Office of the High Commissioner each year on certain human rights issues, and highlighting human rights violations in a given country. Many of these statements are not picked up by the media, and the States concerned pay them little attention and attach little concern or importance to them. However, it should be noted that although such statements may not bring about immediate or tangible change on the ground, they do have an impact. They create awareness, warn States, put them in the spotlight, remind them of their obligations, seek to deter future violations, inspire and support human rights defenders, boost their morale, and galvanize some people into action. These activities of the High Commissioner may not bring the perpetrators of human rights violations to justice or provide any direct remedy, but they are not in vain.

5.8 Problems of funding

One of the crucial factors for the effectiveness and independence of any institution is its funding, and the Office of the High Commissioner is no

34 OHCHR, 'OHCHR Report 2011' (OHCHR, Geneva, 2011), p. 21, http://www2.ohchr.org/english/ohchrreport2011/web_version/ohchr_report2011_web/ (accessed 11 July 2014).

35 This is considered further below.

exception. Although the Office is part of the UN system and the High Commissioner is the principal UN human rights official, it receives only about one third of its funding needs from the United Nations regular budget, which is approved by the General Assembly every 2 years. Despite the huge range of activities the Office of the High Commissioner carries out across the globe and the support it provides to numerous Charter-based and treaty bodies, the proportion of the overall UN regular budget devoted to human rights remains small, at just under 3 per cent.[36]

This is the reason why the High Commissioner for Human Rights, Navi Pillay, said that human rights are treated as the 'Cinderella' of the three pillars of the UN, those three pillars being peace and security, development and human rights.[37] The remaining two thirds of its budgetary needs are met by voluntary contributions from member States and other donors. Thus, the Office has constantly to seek funding from sources outside of the UN, and it is inevitable that those outside donors will seek to influence the work of the OHCHR. Although it is expected to provide support to all other UN human rights agencies such as the human rights treaty bodies, the Human Rights Council and the ever-growing number of Special Procedure mandate holders, the Office is simply not provided with adequate resources. When addressing the UN General Assembly after being appointed as the new High Commissioner in 2014, Zeid stated that little more than a third of the current finances came from the UN regular budget. He went on to add that as one of the three pillars of the UN, human rights receives on average 85 per cent less in UN funds than either peace and security or development.[38]

5.9 Design fault in the appointment process

As with any high profile public role, concerns will be raised if the process of appointment is somewhat unclear. Indeed, it is only relatively recently that the appointment of Special Rapporteurs, forming the key part of the Human Rights Council's special procedures, has been reviewed to provide a more structured, coherent and transparent approach.[39] The position of the High Commissioner requires a person who defends the independence of the Office from all States and of civil society actors alike to establish in words and

36 'About OHCHR Funding', http://www.ohchr.org/EN/ABOUTUS/Pages/Funding Budget.aspx (accessed 11 July 2012).

37 The High Commissioner for Human Rights, Navi Pillay's report to the 67th session of the UN General Assembly's Third Committee on 24 October 2012, http://www.ohchr.org/EN/NewsEvents/Pages/DisplayNews.aspx?NewsID=12690&LangID=E (accessed 11 July 2014).

38 http://www.ishr.ch/news/high-commissioner-calls-general-assembly-deal-message-not-messenger, http://www.ishr.ch/news , 24 October 2014.

39 See Chapter 6 for more detail on this.

in deeds the primacy of human rights and rule of law principles over power politics in the West, East, North and South – and thus, restore and maintain the credibility of the human rights agenda. This is the central objective of the mandate of the High Commissioner, and this requires courage. The expectations on the part of the victims of human rights violations and human rights defenders of the High Commissioner are high. Therefore, the position requires a high calibre CEO as well as a principled human rights leader; finding a person who successfully combines both of these qualities can be a challenge.

However, the process of appointment of the High Commissioner is opaque and is dominated more by political considerations of leading Western countries. The process is neither transparent nor based solely on merit. There are no formal selection criteria, timetables or scrutiny of candidates. The Secretary General decides, in secret, on solely one name for the rest of the UN's members to rubberstamp. Unlike in the appointment of the Secretary General himself there is no opportunity for the P5 to use their veto power either. There is no check and accountability in this decision-making process. Consequently, backroom deals are common, with States seeking promises from the Secretary General himself or from the candidates on other UN appointments. It is a public position, but not an elected one and therefore arguably lacks the gravitas and credibility of an elected position and diminishes any element of open competition.

The designated or nominated person does not have to face an American Senate or EU-style parliamentary hearing either. The process of appointment is tightly controlled by the executive team at the UN Headquarters in New York and gives the impression of being a secretive mission to recruit a CEO of a major international company, rather than a global human rights leader. There is apparently little in the way of meaningful consultation with member States during the selection process. Normally a team of senior UN bureaucrats selects the names from a pool of applications for recommendation to the Secretary General. The candidates have no opportunity to submit their own manifesto to support the consideration of their application by the UN membership. The absence of a transparent and participatory process is liable to give rise to the question of legitimacy and general acceptability, and undermine the authority of the position holder.

If there were a provision to elect the High Commissioner by the General Assembly through an open contest, the position holder would perhaps carry greater legitimacy and authority. It could be argued that if the judges of the International Court of Justice and the members of the International Law Commission can be elected by the General Assembly and be regarded as independent after their election there is no reason why the same could not be done for the position of the High Commissioner who, after all, is required to discharge some quasi-judicial functions in amongst their duties. Granted, any election process would require careful thought to strengthen the credibility of the process as opposed to further undermining it, with consideration being given to the distribution of votes, particularly to avoid politicisation and regionalism taking control.

To raise the profile of the position and to ensure that the best qualified person is able to command the respect of the majority of UN members and is appointed to this position, the power of appointment could be taken out of the hands of senior UN bureaucrats and given to a representative committee of the General Assembly. At the moment, the process of appointing the UN Special Rapporteurs is more transparent and more participatory than the process of appointing the High Commissioner. Since some of the UN Secretary Generals are regarded to have been more Secretary than General, the High Commissioner appointed by such Secretaries on the recommendation of a team of their deputies and subordinates is not conducive to enhancing the stature of the High Commissioner. Recent experience has shown that by according the power of appointment to this position to the Secretary General the UN has run the risk of bureaucratising human rights. The current process of appointment to High Commissioner is liable to political manipulation, reducing the authority and stature of the position.

5.10 Utility of the position of the UN High Commissioner

As stated by Martin, the 'greatest advance [of the OHCHR] has been the extent to which OHCHR has taken human rights protection beyond the committee rooms of Geneva and into the field'.[40] Indeed, it now has a global field presence, monitoring the situation of human rights and providing assistance to governments, civil society organisations and human rights defenders. The OHCHR was created at a time when the Commission on Human Rights was regarded as inefficient, politicised and ineffective. The High Commissioner succeeded in filling a gaping hole in the UN system of human rights. After the creation of a more powerful Human Rights Council with broad powers to replace the Commission, the Office of the High Commissioner has served as the secretariat of the Council while continuing its other traditional functions, such as taking urgent and preventive measures, providing technical assistance to States, coordinating the activities of various UN human rights agencies and mainstreaming human rights, etc. In spite of the increase in its remit, neither the General Assembly nor the Human Rights Council have accorded the High Commissioner more powers, enhanced its status or provided more funding to enable it to carry out its activities in an effective manner. It is a political body operating as part of the UN Secretariat and lacking in any meaningful legal powers for the protection of human rights.

The title 'UN High Commissioner for Human Rights' carries weight. But in reality the position is devoid of much real power. It is mainly about warning

40 See the observations made by Ian Martin in 'Vienna Declaration and Programme of Action + 20', *Human Rights Monitor Quarterly* of the International Service for Human Rights, Geneva, Issue 1, 2013, 13.

the world of the situation of human rights from the high altar of morality and assisting those governments that are willing to improve the situation of human rights in their country. The helplessness of the High Commissioner in the face of the human rights and humanitarian crisis in Syria is a telling example. Speaking at the UN General Assembly, the then UN High Commissioner for Human Rights encouraged the Security Council to refer the situation to the International Criminal Court.[41] The then High Commissioner subsequently reiterated her belief that on the basis of evidence gathered from various credible sources, crimes against humanity and war crimes had been, and continued to be, committed in Syria. She went on to add that: 'Those who are committing them should not believe that they will escape justice. The world does not forget or forgive crimes like these.'[42]

Addressing the twenty-first Session of the UN Human Rights Council on 10 September 2012, the then High Commissioner, Navi Pillay, reminded member States of the UN that 'when a State fails to protect its population from serious international crimes, the international community is responsible for stepping in by taking protective action in a collective, timely and decisive manner. The international community must assume its responsibilities and act in unison to prevent further violations.'[43] She reiterated her call for the Security Council to refer the case of Syria to the International Criminal Court and stated that those responsible for human rights violations must eventually be brought to justice.

The High Commissioner also called for the situation in North Korea to be referred to the International Criminal Court following the publication of a report by a commission of inquiry led by Justice Michael Kirby[44] documenting 'systematic, widespread and gross' human rights violations in the country.[45] But these calls were limited to mere calls and no concrete action was followed,

41 'States must "act now" to protect Syrian population, Pillay tells the General Assembly', News Release of the OHCHR of 13 February 2012, http://www.ohchr.org/EN/NewsEvents/Pages/DisplayNews.aspx?LangID=E&NewsID=11820 (accessed 11 July 2014).

42 'Pillay warns of consequences under international law as Syria conflict escalates' New Release of the OHCHR of 27 July 2012, http://www.unog.ch/80256EDD006B9C2E/%28httpNewsByYear_en%29/75E30E0DB7C00120C1257A48002CFFB6?OpenDocument (accessed 11 July 2014).

43 'Bearing witness: human rights and accountability in Syria', Media Statement of the OHCHR of 10 September 2012, http://www.ohchr.org/en/NewsEvents/Pages/DisplayNews.aspx?NewsID=12486&LangID=e (accessed 11 July 2014).

44 'Report of the commission of inquiry on human rights in the Democratic People's Republic of Korea', UN Doc. A/HRC/25/63, of 7 February 2014, http://www.ohchr.org/en/hrbodies/hrc/coidprk/pages/commissioninquiryonhrindprk.aspx accessed 11 July 2012.

45 'Pillay calls for urgent action on "historic" DPRK report', News Release, OHCHR, Geneva, 18 February 2014, http://www.ohchr.org/EN/NewsEvents/Pages/DisplayNews.aspx?NewsID=14258& (accessed 11 July 2014).

partly due to China, a permanent member of the Security Council with veto power, stating that it rejected the report, terming it 'unreasonable criticism' of North Korea.[46] Yet, all the Human Rights Council did was to ask the Office of the High Commissioner to 'follow up urgently on the recommendations made by the Commission of Inquiry' on North Korea in its resolution in March 2014.[47]

The Office of the High Commissioner has overall responsibility to coordinate the activities of UN human rights agencies as well as the human rights activities of the entire UN system. When Navi Pillay was the High Commissioner, she was credited for developing a new policy, known as 'Rights Up Front', within the UN system, meaning that every department within the UN, regardless of its respective mandate, had to be committed to advancing the protection of human rights. This was a major step in the right, and human rights, direction which should help in mainstreaming human rights within the whole of the UN agencies and making the third pillar of the UN a stronger pillar. However, the consolidation of the UN human rights activities under the umbrella of the High Commissioner has not yet taken place. For instance, the High Commissioner has little or no say in several rule of law support projects carried out by various UN bodies such as the UNDP in a number of countries. As stated by John Pace, the Office of the High Commissioner 'inserted itself alongside the rest of the agencies wherever field operations exist, thereby putting into second place the position assigned to it by the General Assembly. As a consequence its role has been diluted as has its authority in UN human rights activities.'[48] He goes on to add that:

> It was to be expected that the High Commissioner, consistent with the mandate setting up the position, would provide guidance [also by example] in regard to human rights priorities consistent with the mandate of the individual components of the UN system. This has not happened. The central role of the Office has not materialised. For example, the field activities, OHCHR acts as another UN programme, alongside the others.

However, the Office of the High Commissioner has carried out studies on the ways and means of strengthening the work of the treaty bodies and has

46 'China rejects 'unfair criticism' in North Korea report', BBC News: http://www.bbc.co.uk/news/world-asia-26242278, 18 February 2014 (accessed 9 June 2014).

47 Briefing Notes of the OHCHR, Geneva, 30 May 2014, http://www.unog.ch/80256EDD006B9C2E/%28httpNewsByYear_en%29/1FB4E2B5ECA3F87EC1257CE800351D38?OpenDocument accessed 11 July 2014.

48 John Pace, 'Strengthening the Rule of Law: the Right to an Effective Remedy for Victims of Human Rights Violations: Reflections', a paper submitted to the Vienna + 20 Conference held in Vienna, 27–28 June 2013. A copy of the paper is on file with the present author.

defended, supported and protected the special procedures. But it has done so, and continues to do so, without a specific mandate. Furthermore, the creation of the Human Rights Council has affected the role of the High Commissioner as there is a vague delineation of responsibilities between these two institutions.

5.11 Areas for reform

On the basis of the foregoing analysis it can be submitted that the High Commissioner should be accorded an independent status similar to the status enjoyed by an ombudsman in many countries rather than remain a part of the UN Secretariat. While the High Commissioner has vast authority and responsibility to protect and promote human rights, it is a rather inferior position within the UN administrative or bureaucratic structure. The position of the High Commissioner is one of several under-secretaries general within the UN system. This means that the High Commissioner is instructed, or can be, by political bodies to carry out assigned 'tasks'. The High Commissioner should be accorded a higher status within the UN system and be afforded an independent status similar to that enjoyed by the special procedures mandate holders.

In terms of function, the position of the High Commissioner is not so different to that of the Special Rapporteurs; both are expected to exercise independence, objectivity and neutrality in discharging their responsibilities. The Special Rapporteurs are also appointed by a political body – the Human Rights Council – but through a more transparent, participatory and competitive process, and once appointed they are independent of the Council in status and function. The same should be so for the High Commissioner. In terms of the process of appointment and the degree of independence, the UN Special Rapporteurs are arguably in a better position than the UN High Commissioner for Human Rights.

Of course the mandate of the Special Rapporteurs is based on a resolution of the Human Rights Council but they do not take any instructions from any political bodies and do not have to carry out assigned 'tasks'. As the present author did in implementing his mandate on Cambodia, the Special Rapporteurs can by and large define their own mandate and determine the modality to achieve the objectives stated in the relevant resolution of the Council. Political manipulation of the appointment process, especially when there is a weak Secretary General in place, brings its own challenges to the integrity of the position of the High Commissioner. Therefore, in order to maintain and enhance the stature and authority of the position the power to appoint the High Commissioner should be taken out of the hands of an individual, in this case the Secretary General, and given to an expert search and appointment body appointed by the Security Council or made an elected position similar to the judges of the International Court of Justice or the members of the International Law Commission.

If it is not elected through an open competitive process, the appointment process should incorporate the following procedures to enhance the transparency, accountability, fairness, and inclusiveness for the selection and appointment of a qualified and effective candidate with human rights credentials:

1. Formal candidate qualifications;
2. Record of contribution to the promotion and protection of human rights;
3. Official time-table and systematic reporting;
4. Procedure for assessment of candidates;
5. Mechanism to carry out meaningful consultation with the members of the UN, both developed and developing; and
6. Gender and geographic diversity considerations.

An organisation which preaches transparency, fairness and democratic principles must practice them itself and must be led by a High Commissioner appointed on merit and through open competition. The procedures for appointment or selection should include the publication of an official candidate list at the end of the nomination or application phase, distribution of candidate CVs, statements from candidates specifying how they fulfil the requirements of the post, and panel interviews and question-and-answer sessions with UN member States and, where possible, key relevant stakeholders such as Amnesty International and Human Rights Watch. Much of this is already in place regarding the appointment of UN Special Rapporteurs, but these procedures or expectations do not currently appear to apply to the appointment of the UN High Commissioner. A failure to adopt a similar approach to the future appointment of the High Commissioner for Human Rights runs the risk of a significant loss of credibility, as was suffered by the appellate body of the World Trade Organisation when ambassadors in Geneva started to get themselves 'elected'.

There was no sign of transparency in the appointment process when the present author was a candidate for the position of the High Commissioner in 2014; the candidates were not informed of the process that would follow. Consequently, it was left to the candidates to deduce developments via rumour and speculation, fed by information trickling down from the Executive Office of the Secretary General in New York. The entire process lacked transparency. Of late, the position of the High Commissioner has been treated by the Executive Secretariat, the Secretary General and many leading Western countries as a political one rather than as a professional one. There is a danger that such an approach will further erode the credibility of the position and the ability of the incumbent to speak on human rights issues with authority and an aura of impartiality and independence. The impression that the present author had when he was a government nominated candidate to this position in 2014 was that the many Western powers themselves do not wish to make the process of appointing the High Commissioner a transparent one because they wish to be able to assert some influence over the UN Secretary General as to whom to appoint to this position. Therefore, there must be some check on how the Secretary General exercises their power. At a minimum, there should be a hearing before a committee of the General Assembly, perhaps the Third Committee, in which the nominee should be able to establish their credentials to be the UN human rights leader.

There have been attempts to review the functioning of the Office of the High Commissioner. For instance, the Human Rights Council, in operative paragraph 14 of its resolution 22/2, adopted in March 2013 and taken note of by the General Assembly in resolution 68/144 of 18 December 2013, requested the Joint Inspection Unit (JIU) to undertake a comprehensive follow-up review of the management and administration of the Office of the United Nations High Commissioner for Human Rights (OHCHR), in particular regarding its impact on the recruitment policies and the composition of the staff, and to submit a report thereon containing concrete proposals for the implementation of the resolution to the Council at its twenty-seventh session.[49] However, the review was limited to providing an independent external assessment of the regulatory frameworks and related practices concerning the management and administration of OHCHR, and to identifying areas for further improvement. It was focused on governance, executive management, organisational structure, strategic planning, programming and budgeting, human resources management, general administration, knowledge management and oversight. The review was not designed to and did not assess the substantive work of OHCHR and this is what is needed to enhance the role of the High Commissioner in protecting human rights.

5.12 Conclusions

The Office of the High Commissioner is a UN agency with a progressive agenda designed not to fight against States but cajole, persuade and argue with reason to bring States on board with the human rights agenda. The successive High Commissioners have sought to apply pressure on governments that do not respect human rights and rebuke those that violate human rights. But there is more that the High Commissioner can do, should do and is expected to do. This was certainly the expectation when the position was created in 1993. As a minimum, the High Commissioner should have the powers and status similar to those accorded to ombudsmen in many democratic countries. The High Commissioner should be granted administrative autonomy and independent budgetary powers. Therefore, the time has without doubt come to

49 Review of Management and Administration of the Office of the United Nations High Commissioner for Human Rights, Prepared by Gopinathan Achamkulangare, JIU/REP/2014/7, Joint Inspection Unit, United Nations, Geneva 2014.

review in a more comprehensive manner both substantive and procedural issues including the status, powers and functions, funding arrangements and appointment or election process of this flagship UN human rights entity. The terms of reference of this Office outlined in the 1993 resolution should be revisited and amended.

6 The UN Human Rights Special Rapporteurs and their effectiveness in protecting human rights

6.1 Introduction

The UN Special Rapporteurs for human rights, operating under the scheme known as special procedures, have been in existence for nearly six decades and their number have been growing all the time. They now number around 14 country or territory specific mandates and 37 thematic mandates. This chapter considers a number of key issues and questions in relation to such Special Rapporteurs, namely, the object and purpose of their appointment, their effectiveness in protecting and promoting human rights, the impact of their work on the situation of human rights in the countries concerned, and the weaknesses and the strengths of this institution. In examining these questions this chapter will offer some suggestions to strengthen the institution of the special procedures to better equip it to deal with the challenges of the twenty-first century.

6.2 An outcome of accidental events

The institution of Special Rapporteurs for human rights known as the special procedures is one of the main mechanisms employed by the UN to protect and promote human rights worldwide. The objective of this mechanism is to monitor compliance and document human rights violations by States and recommend measures designed to prevent violations. It is a flexible preventative mechanism which has grown in an *ad hoc* and incremental manner. The Special Rapporteurs have traditionally been appointed to examine, in a country or a territory, situations of particularly serious violations of human rights that require an urgent response. Their appointment has frequently reflected the concern of the international community about the situation of human rights in a given country or territory and holds particular significance as a means of exerting international pressure on governments whose human rights practices are considered to seriously undermine international standards.

However, there was no well-thought-out plan or resolution or treaty to create this human rights mechanism. It simply grew out of practice, some accidental and some with a degree of determination on the part of developing countries.

While a more considered view played a role in the appointment of the first group of country- or territory-specific mandate holders in the 1960s and 1970s, the thematic mandates came into existence as a compromise when it was difficult to appoint a country mandate holder for a given country. The establishment of the Working Group on Enforced Disappearances in 1980 in relation to the attempt to appoint a country mandate holder for Argentina is an example.

The 1990s represented a decade of a proliferation of special procedures mechanisms covering a wide range of issues relating to both human rights and humanitarian law. Towards the end of the 1990s there were approximately 26 country mandates and 27 thematic mandates. The number of country mandate holders fell to as low as 7 around 2008, but started to rise again with appointments for Iran, Syria, Belarus and Eritrea in recent years. While the resolution on the appointment of a Special Rapporteur for Eritrea was adopted unanimously, the one for Belarus was highly politicised and was adopted with 22 votes in favour, 5 against and 20 abstentions.

As at 1 July 2016, there were 14 country mandates[1] and 38 thematic mandates,[2] bringing the total to 52 for both the country and thematic mandates. Add to this individuals working as members of a Working Group on a particular thematic issue, and there are over 75 special procedures in operation across the world.[3] A Coordination Council of the special procedures holds an annual

1 They are as follows: Myanmar (in operation since 1992), Cambodia (1993), Palestinian Occupied Territories (1993), Somalia (1993), Haiti (1995), Democratic People's Republic of Korea (2004), Sudan (2005), Iran (2010), Syria (2011), Cote d'Ivoire (2011), Eritrea (2012), Belarus (2012), Central African Republic (2013), and Mali (2013), http://www.ohchr.org/EN/HRBodies/SP/Pages/Countries.aspx (accessed 14 July 2014).

2 They include, but are not limited to, the following mandates: enforced or involuntary disappearances (established in 1980), extrajudicial, summary or arbitrary executions (1982), torture (1985), freedom of religion or belief (1986), sale of children, child prostitution and child pornography (1990), arbitrary detention (1991), freedom of opinion and expression (1993), racism, racial discrimination (1993), independence of judges and lawyers (1994), violence against women (1994), toxic wastes (1995), right to education (1998), extreme poverty (1998), migrants (1999), right to food (2000), adequate housing (2000), human rights defenders (2000), economic reform policies and foreign debt (2000), indigenous people (2001), people of African descent (2002), physical and mental health (2002), internally displaced persons (2004), trafficking in persons (2004), mercenaries (2005), minority issues (2005), international solidarity (2005), countering terrorism (2005), and human rights and transnational corporations (2005), the promotion of truth, justice, reparation and guarantees of non-recurrence (2011), the promotion of obligations relating to the enjoyment of a safe, clean, healthy and sustainable environment (2012), the enjoyment of all human rights by older persons (2013), the rights of persons with disabilities (2014), human rights and unilateral coercive measures (2014), right to privacy (2015) and the right to development (2016). See http://www.ohchr.org/EN/HRBodies/SP/Pages/Themes.aspx (accessed 14 July 2014).

3 OHCHR, Media Advisory: 'Human Rights: a media Guide to the new UN independent experts and mandates (2012)', Geneva, 14 December 2012. As of 31 December 2014,

meeting of Special Rapporteurs and interacts with the Human Rights Council and the Office of the High Commissioner for Human Rights on matters pertaining to the rapporteurs.[4] Thus, in the words of the special procedures mandate holders themselves,

> [T]his broad range of procedures constitutes a unique and crucial element in the implementation of the study of specific standards that have been adopted by universal consensus through the United Nations General Assembly. While it may have never been conceived as a 'system', the evolving collection of these procedures and mechanisms now clearly constitutes and functions as a system of human rights protection.[5]

Indeed, they are a rather unusual mechanism created by the UN system and operating in a rather distinctive and paradoxical manner being, as they are, independent of the UN system itself. However, unlike treaty bodies or the High Commissioner for Human Rights, they do not form a system or organisation as such, since the special procedures mandate holders have different mandates and discharge their responsibilities independently of each other and the UN as an organisation itself, in an objective and impartial manner. They are known as Special Rapporteurs or independent experts and their mandate can be thematic or country-specific. Special Rapporteurs can also be members of a working group constituted around a human rights theme. While the mandate of some may be primarily to promote human rights, others may have protection as their main mandate plus there will be those that have both protection and promotion of human rights within their remit, particularly thematic mandates.

The thematic mandate holders may also be required to carry out the task of clarifying the extent and nature of the relevant human rights obligations of States. Thus the main role of different mandate holders could be either receiving or acting on petitions received, or norm-setting and norm-shaping. Traditionally, the Special Rapporteurs have contributed to the progressive development of international human rights and humanitarian law, through studies, consultations and elaboration of guidelines in a variety of specific areas. For instance, the Special Rapporteur on the right to water and sanitation published a 'Handbook for Realising the Human Right to Safe Drinking Water

there were a total of 77 mandate-holder positions out of which 31 were appointed in 2014 alone. The percentage of female mandate-holders was 38 per cent and male 62 per cent. See A/HRC/28/41 of 16 January 2015.

4 The UN High Commissioner for Human Rights invites Special Rapporteurs to an annual meeting in Geneva, usually in the summer, such a meeting being held pursuant to paragraph 95, Part II of the 1993 Vienna Declaration and Programme of Action adopted by the World Conference on Human Rights.

5 Joint declaration of the independent experts responsible for the special procedures for the protection of human rights issued during the Vienna World Conference on Human Rights, U.N. doc. A/CONF.157/9, 1993.

and Sanitation' in 2014 which acts as a source of reference for all relevant actors. Similarly, the Special Rapporteur on trafficking in persons, especially women and children, issued 'Basic Principles on the Right to Effective Remedy for Victims of Trafficking in Persons' in 2014. As of January 2015, the Working Group on Arbitrary Detention was preparing a 'Draft Basic Principles and Guidelines on Remedies and Procedures on the Right of Anyone Deprived of his or her Liberty to bring Proceedings before Court'. The Special Rapporteurs are appointed by the Human Rights Council but are not accountable to it nor to any other person or entity. They are accountable only to the principles of the Charter of the UN, the rule of law, human rights instruments and the resolutions creating their positions.

The institution of the UN Special Rapporteurs has seen a proliferation of the number of UN mandate holders, especially thematic ones, in recent years. There are now about 77 such mandate holders and the number is rising. The institution has been in existence in some form since the late 1960s; various Special Rapporteurs have been appointed since then by various agencies within the UN system, mainly by the Commission on Human Rights until 2006, and since then by the Human Rights Council. Although Special Rapporteurs form a subsidiary body of the Council, they are independent experts who decide independently on their focus, priorities and work schedule.

There have been occasions when the Secretary General of the UN, the Economic and Social Council, the General Assembly and, in a few cases, the Security Council itself have appointed such experts or a group of experts as fact-finding missions. The term 'Special Rapporteur' for human rights is used within the UN system to signify not only the thematic and country mandate holders, but also the special representatives of the Secretary General of the UN, and other independent experts acting individually or as members of a working group to work on a particular country or theme.[6] They help both directly and

6 See generally, Philip Alston, 'Hobbling the Monitors: Should U.N. Human Rights Monitors be Accountable?' (2011) 52 (2) *Harvard International Law Journal*, 561–649; David Weissbrodt, 'The Three "Theme" Special Rapporteurs of the UN Commission on Human Rights' (1986) 80 *American Journal of International Law*, 685–699; Helena M. Cook, 'The Role of the Special Procedures in the Protection of Human Rights: The Way Forward After Vienna' (1993) 50 *Review of the International Commission of Jurists*, 31–55; Marc J. Bossuyt, 'The Development of Special Procedures of the United Nations Commission on Human Rights' (1985) 6 *Human Rights Law Journal*, 179–210; Lyal S. Sunga, 'The Special Procedures of the UN Commission on Human Rights: Should they be Scrapped?', in Gudmundur Alfredsson *et al.* (ed.), *International Human Rights Monitoring Mechanisms: Essays in Honour of Jakob Th. Moller* (Martinus Nijhoff Publishers, 2001), 233–77; Paulo S. Pinheiro, 'Musings of a UN Special Rapporteur on Human Rights' (2003) 9 *Global Governance*, 7–13; Jeroen Gutter, 'Special Procedures and the Human Rights Council: Achievements and Challenges Ahead' (2007) 7 *Human Rights Law Review*, 93–107; Ingrid Nifosi, *The UN Special Procedures in the Field of Human Rights* (Intesentia, 2005); Menno T. Kamminga, 'The Thematic Procedures of the UN Commission on Human Rights',

indirectly the victims of human rights abuses worldwide as well as assisting the Human Rights Council, the UN General Assembly, the Security Council, the Secretary General, and other UN bodies and entities in discharging their responsibilities in this area.

6.3 Current status of UN Special Rapporteurs

When the international human rights standard-setting process reached a certain height with the adoption of a number of international instruments, the UN programme of human rights began to move to the next phase of development characterised by initiatives to implement through reporting, monitoring, and enforcement – the norms enunciated in such instruments. Accordingly, despite the principle of non-interference in the internal affairs of States embodied in Article 2(7) of the Charter of the UN, the UN began a process to examine the respective internal situations of human rights in individual countries and to report publicly the findings of investigations. The appointment of Special Rapporteurs with investigative and related powers was one of the mechanisms developed for this purpose. It is a *special* UN mechanism of a quasi-judicial nature. Hence, the formal name of this institution itself is 'special procedures' within the UN system of human rights.

Indeed, the appointment of such rapporteurs represents an attempt by the UN 'to pierce the veil of the national sovereignty' of States to deal with serious cases of violations of human rights.[7] This may be one reason why Kofi Annan, the former Secretary General of the UN, described the institution of UN Special Rapporteurs for human rights as 'the crown jewel' of the UN human rights machinery[8] and Louise Arbour, the then UN High Commissioner for Human Rights, called it 'an essential element' in the efforts by the UN to protect human rights,[9] with the individual Special Rapporteurs as 'the frontline human rights troops'[10] or the 'hands of the UN

(1987) XXXIV *Netherlands International Law Review*, 299–323; Bertrand Ramcharan, *The Protection Roles of UN Human Rights Special Procedures* (Koninklijke Brill NV, 2009); Surya P. Subedi, 'Protecting Human Rights through the Mechanism of UN Special Rapporteurs', 33 *Human Rights Quarterly* 2011, pp. 201–28; Felice D. Gaer, 'The High Commissioners and the Special Procedures: Colleagues and Competitors', in Felice D. Gaer and Christen L. Broecker (ed.), *The United Nations High Commissioner for Human Rights: Conscience for the World* (Martinus Nijhoff, 2013), 133–56.

7 Remarks by Thomas Buergenthal at the session on 'New Customary Law: Taking Human Rights Seriously' made at the 87th Annual meeting of the American Society of International Law (ASIL), 1993: Proceedings of ASIL 87th Annual Meeting, 87 *Am. Soc'y Int'l L.* Proc. i (1993), 231.

8 See Annan, SG/SM/10788-HR/4909-OBV/601 of 8 December 2006.

9 'Plan of Action submitted by the United Nations High Commissioner for Human Rights.' UN Doc. A/59/2005/Add.3 of 26 May 2005, p. 23.

10 Statement by High Commissioner for Human Rights to Last Meeting of the Commission on Human Rights, 27 March 2006.

High Commissioner',[11] they thus form an essential part of the UN human rights system. The then President of the Human Rights Council, Laura Dupuy Lasserre, stated in a letter to the Chairperson of the Coordination Committee of Special Procedures that they were the 'eyes and ears' of the Council and their reports 'constitute one of the main sources of reliable information for the Council'.[12] Indeed, the Special Rapporteurs have their fingers on the pulse and can act as a warning mechanism, alerting other UN agencies such as the Security Council and the Executive Office of the Secretary General of an impending human rights and humanitarian crisis in a given country.

Special Rapporteurs come in different forms. While some are called UN Special Rapporteurs, others are referred to as UN independent experts. There are thematic and country-specific mandate holders. The country-specific Special Rapporteurs can be further divided into two kinds: mandates aimed at providing governments with technical assistance and monitoring mandates. Examples of those that provide technical assistance are those for Cambodia and Somalia, and those which carry out monitoring mandates such as the Special Rapporteurs for Myanmar, Sudan, Iran and North Korea. However, the mandate holder on Haiti is a hybrid one with elements of both providing technical assistance and monitoring.

Members of various working groups such as on arbitrary detention also form part of UN special procedures that exercise their functions collectively as a group. Many of such Special Rapporteurs or working groups have been instrumental in fleshing out, interpreting and elaborating upon the provisions of international human rights instruments or pointing to the need for the adoption of a new instrument. For instance, the UN Working Group on Arbitrary Detention has worked on developing foundations for the draft guiding principles on the right of anyone deprived of his or her liberty to challenge the legality of their detention in court.[13]

The Special Rapporteurs are essentially a disparate group of experts drawn from different backgrounds who operate mostly as autonomous lone individuals rather than as part of a system or cohesive institution. However, in the absence of a UN system to bring them together under an institutional framework, the Special Rapporteurs have formed their own committee, known as the Coordination Committee. This has operated since 2005 and is designed to facilitate cooperation amongst Special Rapporteurs to assist with rationalising and harmonising their work, sharing best practice and voicing their common

11 Editorial, *Human Rights Monitor* (International Service for Human Rights, Geneva), No. 63 (2005), p. 4.

12 A letter of 11 December 2012 (on file with the present author).

13 'The Right to challenge the legality of arbitrary detention: UN expert panel to develop new guiding principles', Media Advisory of the UN OHCHR, Geneva, 12 November 2013, http://www.ohchr.org/EN/NewsEvents/Pages/DisplayNews.aspx?NewsID=13977&LangID=E (accessed 14 July 2014).

position on procedural or operational issues within the UN system and on some overarching or urgent substantive human rights issues.

The practice of cooperating amongst themselves originated from the 1993 Vienna Declaration and Programme of Action which stated that the Special Rapporteurs should be enabled to meet periodically in order to rationalise and harmonise their work.[14] Since Vienna, special procedures have evolved dramatically. Their existence was *ad hoc* in nature until Vienna and was focused on 'problem' countries. Post-Vienna special procedures have evolved more as a 'system', serving several purposes and, as stated by Pace, acting mainly with the purpose of 'buttressing protection of human rights and complementing the treaties'.[15]

Special Rapporteurs have developed different tools to enhance their effectiveness, to protect their independence, to harmonise their working methods and to give a sense of accountability to their work. Such tools include a Manual of Operations and the Internal Advisory Procedure to Review Practices and Working Methods (IAP). The IAP is a form of self-regulation designed to ensure that Special Rapporteurs carry out their activities in accordance with the Manual of Operations and the Code of Conduct. This is not a mechanism which encompasses the substantive evaluations the experts make in relation to the situation of human rights, but is a mechanism designed to provide different human rights stakeholders, including the UN member States, with an opportunity to bring to the attention of the Coordination Committee matters associated with compliance by the mandate holders with the Manual of Operations and the Code of Conduct.

The main function of Special Rapporteurs, in the case of country mandate holders, has been to examine, monitor, advise, and report publicly to the Human Rights Council since 2006 and prior to that, to the Commission on Human Rights, on the situation of human rights or allegations of violation of such rights in a given country. In the case of thematic mandate holders, their role is the same except regarding the situation globally of a particular phenomenon or right or freedom, whether collective or individual.[16] In practice,

14 UN Doc. A/CONF.157/23, Part E, para 95, http://daccess-dds-ny.un.org/doc/UNDOC/GEN/G93/142/33/PDF/G9314233.pdf?OpenElement (accessed 14 July 2014).

15 John Pace, 'Strengthening the Rule of Law: the Right to an Effective Remedy for Victims of Human Rights Violations: Reflections', a paper submitted to the Vienna + 20 Conference held in Vienna, 27–28 June 2013. A copy of the paper is on file with the present author.

16 The Human Rights Council was established as a result of the recommendations made by the UN Secretary General High-level panel on Threats, Challenges and Change, *A more secure world: our shared responsibility* (December 2004), UN Doc. A/59/565, Part XVIII: The Commission on Human Rights and the report by Kofi Annan, the then Secretary General of the UN, to reform the UN as outlined in his report entitled, *In larger freedom: towards development, security and human rights for all*, UN Doc.A/59/2005 (21 March 2005), paras.181–83.

the Special Rapporteurs perform a supervisory, advisory, consultative, or monitoring function rather than one of enforcement. As summed up by Rodley, 'A main focus, if not the only one, of the thematic special procedures is to provide the whole UN membership with comparative and global understanding of the human rights problem in question, as well as with guidance on how to deal with it.'[17]

The institution of Special Rapporteur has its basis in the Charter of the UN and is thus regarded as a charter-based mechanism. The overall mandate of the special procedures is similar to the mandate of the Human Rights Council. As stated in the UN General Assembly resolution establishing the Human Rights Council, the work of the Council must be 'guided by the principles of universality, impartiality, objectivity and non-selectivity, constructive international dialogue and cooperation, with a view to enhancing the promotion and protection of all human rights'.[18] Thus, the work of the Special Rapporteurs should also be carried out in accordance with the same ethos. The work of the Special Rapporteurs is guided by two major instruments: firstly, the Code of Conduct adopted by the Human Rights Council on 18 June 2007[19] and secondly, the Manual of Operations of the Special Procedures of the Human Rights Council adopted by the meeting of Special Rapporteurs under the auspices of the Coordination Council of special procedures in June 2008. The Special Rapporteurs are accountable to the Council for their work, and to such other UN bodies that appointed them if relevant, such as the General Assembly.

6.4 The UN approach to protecting human rights through UN Special Rapporteurs

6.4.1 Initial approach – no power to act

Although an inter-governmental body, the UN is supposed to be a people-centred international organisation. Indeed, the Charter of the UN begins with the words 'we the people of the United Nations' and speaks of promoting and protecting human rights as one of its main objectives. Hence, since its creation the UN has received petitions and complaints from people seeking the help of

17 Sir Nigel Rodley, 'The United Nations Human Rights Council, Its Special Procedures, and Its Relationship with the Treaty Bodies: Complementarity or Competition?' in Kevin Boyle (ed.), *New Institutions for Human Rights Protection* (Oxford University Press, 2009), 49–73 at 72.

18 UN GA Resolution 60/251 of 3 April 2006: UN Doc. A/RES/60251, preamble paragraph 4.

19 See for an analysis of the Code of Conduct: Meghna Abraham, *Building the New Human Rights Council: Outcome and Analysis of the Institution Building Year* (Friedrich Ebert Stiftung, Occasional Papers, No 33, August 2007), 29–32.

the UN and alleging violation of their human rights by their governments. An early response of the UN to such communications was to establish the Commission on Human Rights in 1946 by the Economic and Social Council,[20] under Article 68 of the Charter which had given the UN the powers to set up commissions for, *inter alia*, the promotion of human rights.[21]

In 1947 a resolution of ECOSOC recognised the capacity of the Commission to receive communications submitted by individuals, and stated at the same time that the Commission had no power to take any action regarding such communications.[22] Another resolution of ECOSOC adopted in 1959 put in place new procedures authorising the Commission to compile and consult communications received, and to request the governments concerned to reply, but it too reiterated the position that the Commission had no power to take any action in regard to any complaint made to it concerning human rights.[23]

6.4.2 *Shift in approach towards taking action*

A precursor of the special procedures mechanism was a visit to Vietnam in October 1963 by a delegation of the representatives of seven States led by the Chairman of the Commission to look into the human rights situation of the Buddhist community. However, a coup d'état in Vietnam the following month removed the government in power, rendering the matter moot and warranting no further action in this regard.[24] While seeking to address the situation resulting from apartheid in South Africa at the time, the Economic and Social Council of the UN adopted a landmark resolution (Resolution 1235 (XLII)) in June 1967 under which the Commission on Human Rights could hold an annual public debate on violations of human rights in any of the member States of the UN. This resolution paved the way to the appointment of Special Rapporteurs by the Commission to examine the situation of human rights in a country. The first example was a concrete set of special procedures developed by the Commission relating to the situation of human rights violations by the

20 Resolution 5 (1) of 16 February 1946 of the ECOSOC.

21 Article 68 reads as follows: 'The Economic and Social Council shall set up commissions in economic and social fields and for the promotion of human rights, and such other commissions as may be required for the performance of its functions.'

22 Resolution 75 (V) of 5 August 1947 of the ECOSOC, http://daccess-dds-ny.un.org/doc/UNDOC/GEN/NR0/752/61/IMG/NR075261.pdf?OpenElement (accessed 14 July 2014).

23 Resolution 728 (F) of 30 July 1959: U.N. Doc. E/3290 (1959), http://daccess-dds-ny.un.org/doc/UNDOC/GEN/NR0/758/03/IMG/NR075803.pdf?OpenElement (accessed 14 July 2014).

24 See Lyal S. Sunga, 'The Special Procedures of the UN Commission on Human Rights: Should they be Scrapped?' in Gudmundur Alfredsson *et al.* (ed.), *International Human Rights Monitoring Mechanisms: Essays in honour of Jakob Th. Moller* (Martinus Nijhoff Publishers, 2001), 233–77, at 237–38.

apartheid government of South Africa, when it created a 'Special Working Group of Experts on Southern Africa' in 1967.[25]

Another set of special procedures was adopted in 1968, this time by the General Assembly, in relation to the situation of human rights in territories under Israeli occupation, when it created a 'Special Committee to Investigate Israeli Practices Affecting the Human Rights of the Population of the Occupied Territories', composed of the representatives of three Member States.[26] The first individual Special Rapporteur with a country mandate in the form that it exists today was appointed in 1979 and was concerned with the situation in Chile after the overthrow, by Augusto Pinochet, of the democratically elected Allende Government in 1974. Subsequent appointments were in relation to the human rights situation in El Salvador, Equatorial Guinea, Bolivia, and Guatemala in the early 1980s and slightly later, in 1984, in Afghanistan and Iran.

6.4.3 Taking a thematic approach

It was also in the early 1980s that the Commission on Human Rights created the Working Group on Enforced or Involuntary Disappearances, marking the beginning of a number of thematic special procedures to deal with human rights violations committed anywhere in the world. The first thematic individual Special Rapporteur, appointed in May 1982, was a Special Rapporteur on Extrajudicial, Summary and Arbitrary Executions. In 1985 the Special Rapporteur on Torture, and Other Cruel, Inhumane or Degrading Treatment was appointed. The trend to appoint thematic or country special procedure mechanisms continued throughout the 1980s and 1990s, as virtually every annual session of the Commission resulted in the creation of one or another type of this mechanism.

This was so much so that in 1998 the Commission decided to appoint five new Special Rapporteurs or experts dealing with various aspects of economic, social, and cultural rights. Since then, not only the Commission but also the General Assembly and the Security Council have appointed such experts. An example of the creation of special procedures by the Security Council was a Commission of Experts on Rwanda in July 1994[27] under Chapter VII of the Charter of the UN. Such commissions of experts appointed by the Security Council have been assembled to address severe cases of human rights abuse, and have been asked to look into the question of criminal responsibility under international law for alleged violations of international human rights and humanitarian law; the Commission of Experts for the Former Yugoslavia is one

25 Resolution 2 (XXIII) of 6 March 1967 of the Commission on Human Rights.
26 Resolution 2443 of 19 December 1968 of the General Assembly.
27 Security Council Resolution 935 (1994) of 1 July 1994.

such example. Similarly, the special procedure mechanism is not limited to examining the activities of governments; it also investigates those of insurgency organisations. For instance, the appointment of an investigative mission to the Democratic Republic of Congo was to look into reports of massacres allegedly perpetrated by forces of the insurgent organisation led by Laurent Kabila in the 1990s.

6.4.4 Special Rapporteurs as the public face of the UN human rights system

Along with other UN human rights institutions such as the UN High Commissioner for Human Rights,[28] the UN Special Rapporteurs are regarded as the public face of the UN human rights system and enjoy a high degree of autonomy in their work. Since they are not part of an intergovernmental body as such they have greater freedom of action, greater flexibility, and fewer political constraints on speaking their mind. Their authority does not derive directly from the consent of States parties to an international human rights treaty.

Special Rapporteurs have been appointed primarily to react to a particular situation of violations of human rights or humanitarian law, or patterns of human rights violations, in order to highlight the problem and seek constructive solutions with the government(s) concerned. The consultative status of Special Rapporteurs enables them to work with a government willing to cooperate with them to find a way forward. Even in situations where the government concerned is not willing to cooperate with the Special Rapporteurs, their appointment has functioned as a way of putting the international spotlight on human rights' practice of the government concerned. Such adverse international attention and the subsequent national and international public opinion against the government's practice has sometimes helped move the government towards adopting a policy more closely in keeping with international human rights norms.

6.4.5 The scope of activities of the Special Rapporteurs

In discharging their responsibilities special procedures receive information on specific allegations of human rights violations and send urgent appeals or letters of allegation to governments asking for clarification. In simple terms the Special

28 Other main reporting and monitoring mechanisms are as follows: The Human Rights Council, the Universal Periodic Review, the Office of the High Commissioner for Human Rights, human rights treaty bodies, the 1503 Procedure, programme of technical cooperation in the field of human rights, and support funds (victims of torture, indigenous populations, slavery, racism, etc). There are, of course, other treaty-bodies established under various human rights treaties such as the 1966 International Covenant on Civil and Political Rights that have mainly reporting and supervisory roles in ensuring compliance with the provisions of the human rights treaty concerned.

Rapporteurs receive, share and analyse information on human rights situations; respond to individual complaints; conduct studies; send urgent appeals or letters of allegation to Governments; undertake country visits at the invitation of Governments and produce findings and recommendations based on these visits; provide advice on technical cooperation at the country level; and engage in general promotion of human rights. More formally speaking, the following six different functions are combined into one package of functions of Special Rapporteurs:

(a) To analyse the relevant thematic issue or country specific situation on behalf of the international community;
(b) To advise on the measures which should be taken by the Government(s) concerned and other relevant actors;
(c) To alert UN organs and agencies and the international community in general to the need to address specific situations and issues. In this regard rapporteurs have a role in providing an 'early warning' and encouraging preventive measures;
(d) To advocate on behalf of the victims of violations, through measures such as requesting urgent action by relevant States and calling upon Governments to respond to specific allegations of human rights violations and to provide redress to the victims;
(e) To activate and mobilise the international and national communities to address particular human rights issues and to encourage cooperation among Governments, civil society and inter-governmental organisations; and
(f) To follow up on the recommendations they make to governments.[29]

Thus, a Special Rapporteur is expected simultaneously to be a human rights activist, a rallying point for human rights, an international diplomat, a human rights advocate, a human rights academic, and a government adviser. The mandate holders themselves have described their role as follows:

> Our task is clear: what we do is render the international norms that have been developed more operative. We do not merely deal with theoretical questions, but strive to enter into constructive dialogues with governments and to seek their cooperation as regards concrete situations, incidents and cases. The core of our work is to study and investigate in an objective manner with a view to understanding the situations and recommending to governments solutions to overcome the problem of securing respect for human rights.[30]

29 Manual of Operations of the Special Procedures of the Human Rights Council, Office of the UN High Commissioner of Human Rights, Geneva, August 2008.
30 'Joint declaration of the independent experts responsible for the special procedures for the protection of human rights', issued during the Vienna World Conference on Human Rights, U.N. doc. A/CONF.157/9, 1993.

As stated by Lempinen, the Special Rapporteurs, especially the country mandate holders, seek to establish and continue a dialogue between the various UN agencies and governments concerned, promote acceptance of human rights norms and standards and generally engage governments in a multilateral environment.[31]

Special Rapporteurs are selected on the basis of their expertise and experience in the area of the mandate, personal integrity, independence, impartiality, and objectivity. The key to their ability to perform their duties effectively is their independent status and their ability to command respect from different stakeholders in a given society. Private individuals, civil society organisations or any other governmental, non-governmental and intergovernmental institutions, including UN agencies, and governments can nominate the names of individuals for consideration of possible appointment as Special Rapporteurs.

The pool of resources available to Special Rapporteurs is large. In discharging their responsibilities, they can take into account all available sources of information that they consider to be credible and relevant. They can act on credible information by sending a communication to the relevant government(s) in relation to any actual or anticipated human rights violations that fall within the scope of their mandate. Communications from Special Rapporteurs are not intended as a substitute for judicial or other proceedings at national level; the purpose of such communication should be to obtain clarification in response to allegations of violations and to promote measures designed to protect the rights in question. However, a communication may be sent by the Special Rapporteur even if local remedies in the country concerned have not been exhausted.

Special Rapporteurs can send urgent appeals in cases where the alleged violations are time-sensitive in terms of involving loss of life, life-threatening situations or either imminent or on-going damage of a very grave nature to victims that cannot wait to be addressed in a timely manner. The purpose of appeals is to ensure that the appropriate State authorities are informed as quickly as possible of the circumstances so that they can take necessary measures to end or prevent future or current human rights violations. Special Rapporteurs can also send letters of allegation to communicate information to governments about violations alleged already to have occurred and in situations where urgent appeals do not apply. In such letters the government concerned is usually requested to provide a substantive response within 2 months. Thus, the Special Rapporteurs do play the role of protective and preventive 'humanitarian' agents.

A distinct and popular feature for the mandate and for the country concerned is the country visit of a Special Rapporteur. Such visits are an essential means of obtaining direct and first-hand information because they allow for direct observation of the human rights situation. Country visits allow Special

31 Miko Lempinen, *Challenges Facing the System of Special Procedures of the United Nations Commission on Human Rights* (Institute for Human Rights, Abo Akademi University, 2001), 27–30.

Rapporteurs to facilitate a dialogue with all relevant State authorities; they also allow contact with and information gathering from victims, witnesses, international and local NGOs, other members of civil society, the academic community, and officials of international agencies present in the country concerned. Raising awareness among the general population of the situation of human rights in the country concerned also forms part of the purpose of a country visit.

Special Rapporteurs report on their activities to the relevant UN bodies, and particularly to the Human Rights Council and the General Assembly, depending on the nature of their mandate. When they have presented their report to the Council or the Assembly it is followed by an interactive dialogue during which the country concerned is given the opportunity to respond to the contents of the report, in addition, other countries have an opportunity to pose questions to the mandate holders. The reports include factual summaries, conclusions, and recommendations arrived at on the basis of observations of the reality on the ground during country visits, and information received from various sources such as academic studies and the reports of research institutions and civil society organisations.

In sum, as stated by Oberleitner, the special procedures are 'the most autonomous [of] bodies' amongst all of the international human rights institutions and have 'overturned the perception of the Commission [now the Council] as a mere instrument of governments', going on to say that Special Rapporteurs are[32]:

> Indeed, unlike other UN human rights institutions, they move around, go to places where human rights are violated and talk to victims. They link the domestic with the international and the global with the local. They have given operation capacity to the Commission [now the Council] and remain perhaps the most successful devices the UN has yet developed to protect and promote human rights, assist victims, suggest solutions, give visibility to human rights, expose States which routinely violate human rights, and bring human rights from the conference room to the field and to the public domain.[33]

These reasons contribute to why Special Rapporteurs are regarded by international human rights organisations such as Amnesty International as the 'most innovative, responsive, and flexible tools of the human rights machinery'.[34] Similarly, the International Commission of Jurists stated in a report in 2005 that the special procedures mandate holders

32 Gerd Oberleitner, *Global Human Rights Institutions: Between Remedy and Ritual* (Polity Press, 2007) 60–61.

33 Ibid.

34 As quoted in Oberleitner, ibid., 60.

> have provided valuable conceptual analysis on key human rights themes; have served as a mechanism of last resort for victims; have sometimes prevented serious abuses, and even saved lives, through urgent appeals; have served as an early-warning mechanism to draw attention to human rights crises; and have frequently provided high-quality diagnosis of individual country situations, including by carrying out country missions.[35]

The country visits of Special Rapporteurs can often galvanise both the government and other stakeholders into action. For instance, there have been a number of examples of States ratifying certain human rights instruments prior to or in the aftermath of the visit to a country by a Special Rapporteur. Further, the reports of Special Rapporteurs and Working Groups are used by other UN agencies such as the OHCHR and the UN Development Programme (UNDP), etc. to legitimise the concerns that they themselves have been expressing in relation to various countries.

6.5 Effectiveness of Special Rapporteurs in protecting human rights

6.5.1 Independent actors

The picture of effectiveness of the work of the Special Rapporteurs has varied according to the nature of the mandate and the mandate holder. The mechanism allows the mandate holder immense flexibility and they can be creative, innovative and bold in implementing their mandate. The mandate holders can define their own mandate and their modus operandi. The Special Rapporteurs in general and the country-specific mandate holders in particular are arguably more powerful than other UN human rights bodies. This is because the country-specific mandate holders can look at any human rights issues any time and take up the matter with the government directly and often at the highest level possible. They are largely free to define their mandate and the scope of their activities. Because they are able to carry out follow up missions, governments are more sensitive to the reports and recommendations of the country-specific mandate holders. This certainly was the approach and experience of the present author while serving as the UN Special Rapporteur for Human Rights in Cambodia between 2009 and 2015.

Although Special Rapporteurs are not necessarily part of the political system of the UN, they are a product of it. They are there not only to criticise governments for their failings but also to offer a helping hand to a receptive

35 International Commission of Jurists, *Reforming the United Nations Human Rights System: A Chance for the United Nations to Fulfil its Promise* (International Commission of Jurists, Geneva, 2005) 4, http://www.icjcanada.org/ICJenglish/documents/doc_2005-06-27.pdf (accessed 14 July 2014).

government. Since the enforcement of public international law itself is, by and large, based on persuasion, cajoling, and reasoned argumentation, little difference can be expected in terms of the implementation of international human rights law, a member of the family of public international law. It is here the Special Rapporteurs can offer their expertise as UN experts and a helping hand to a willing government in realising the obligations undertaken by the State concerned under international human rights instruments.

6.5.2 Flexibility

The flexibility offered by the *ad hoc* nature of this institution allows the UN system to respond to human rights situations more easily, diplomatically, and speedily than would be the case either under a treaty-based system, which would have its own conference of parties to endorse any new decision, or under the present system within the Security Council, where nothing much or meaningful can be implemented without the support (or at least silence) of its five permanent members.[36] Each member has its own power politics to protect. Thankfully, the Human Rights Council is a standing body; it is free of the shackles of the veto power of any State. Therefore, the Human Rights Council is better equipped than its predecessor or certain other UN agencies to make the best use of the institution of Special Rapporteurs to promote and protect human rights worldwide.

6.5.3 Utility of the interactive dialogues in the Human Rights Council

Special Rapporteurs present their reports to the Council and participate in an interactive dialogue with member States of the UN and civil society representatives. However, while the Council may listen to them, this process has no consequences in terms of the follow up of their recommendations. Many of the recommendations of the Special Rapporteurs remain unimplemented and their communications to governments left without response. That is why critics say that there is 'a lot of bark but not much bite' in the reports of the Special Rapporteurs. This weakness existed during the time of the Commission on Human Rights and improved little even after the establishment of the Human Rights Council.

Since the Charter of the UN itself gave the ECOSOC no enforcement powers, it could not give enforcement powers to the Commission on Human

36 Whilst each of the permanent five members of the Security Council has the power to block a resolution by exercising their right of veto, they can choose to abstain, in which case the vote may be passed. This was the approach of both China and the Russian Federation in relation to the UN Security Council resolution 1973/2011 regarding the implementation of a no-fly zone over Libya.

Rights. Although the Human Rights Council was established as a subsidiary organ of the General Assembly, this too made little difference since the Assembly itself is lacking in enforcement powers. States may make political commitments to implement the recommendations of either the Special Rapporteurs or the Council itself yet without putting into place an effective mechanism or policy to perform this there would be no effective follow up.

6.5.4 Lack of access to countries

Another major problem is the lack of access to the countries of concern by the special procedures. To visit a country the Special Rapporteurs must secure an invitation, which is not always forthcoming. This can be very frustrating for any Special Rapporteur. UN members like North Korea and Iran have not allowed the country mandate holders into the country, and countries such as Zimbabwe have every now and then denied entry to the country to some Special Rapporteurs.[37] The group of States putting in place standing invitations to Special Rapporteurs amounts to just over half of the UN's membership; as of 1 January 2014, this amounted to 108 out of the total 193 members of the UN.[38]

6.5.5 Allegation of selectivity and the challenge of achieving balance

Certain developing countries argue that the way forward for the institution of Special Rapporteurs should be to move from a confrontational approach to a constructive one; from naming and shaming to guiding and offering concrete advice towards improving a situation. The argument for a constructive approach claims it would go some way to dispelling the perception of 'us' *versus* 'them'; it would also promote the notion of working together to achieve the standards required not by Western countries, but by international human rights treaties ratified by the country concerned. There is a perception amongst the developing countries that they are targeted for criticism by the Special Rapporteurs, especially those holding mandates relating to civil and political rights.

However, it should be noted that the Special Rapporteurs have not spared the leading developed or Western countries any criticism for their failings. For instance, the Special Rapporteur on extrajudicial, summary or arbitrary executions, Christof Heyns, issued a statement on 6 May 2011 urging the US to disclose supporting facts in respect of the use of deadly force against Osama bin Laden to allow an assessment in terms of international human rights law standards. Heyns stated that it would be particularly important to know if the

37 See 'UN expert "denied Zimbabwe entry"', BBC News, http://news.bbc.co.uk/1/hi/world/africa/8329984.stm (accessed 29 October 2009).

38 See information provided by the OHCHR http://www.ohchr.org/EN/HRBodies/SP/Pages/Invitations.aspx (accessed 14 July 2014).

planning of the US mission to attack Osama bin Laden allowed an effort to capture him.[39]

Similarly, the then Special Rapporteur on extrajudicial, summary or arbitrary executions, Philip Alston, criticised the US in June 2010 over drone attacks stating that the US practice was doing damage to rules designed to protect the right to life. He stated that drone killings carried a significant risk of becoming war crimes because intelligence agencies 'do not generally operate within a framework which places appropriate emphasis upon ensuring compliance with international humanitarian law'.[40] Likewise, the UN Special Rapporteur on Torture, Juan E. Mendez, has called on the US to end the practice of holding people in long and indefinite solitary confinement, adding that such indefinite and long solitary confinement can amount to torture.[41]

The UN Special Rapporteur on human rights and counter-terrorism, Ben Emmerson, has urged the governments of the UK and the US to release findings of confidential inquiries into the George W. Bush administration's secret CIA detention and interrogation practices.[42] The Special Rapporteur on the human rights of migrants, Jorge Bustamante, and the Working Group on the use of mercenaries expressed their concern over the treatment of migrants in the UK on 21 October 2010.[43] In another case involving plans to evict people living illegally at England's largest traveller site, Dale Farm, in Essex in August 2011, the UN Special Rapporteur for Adequate Housing, Raquel Rolnik, and the UN Independent Expert on minority issues, Rita Izsak, called on the UK government to find a peaceful solution to the matter stating that planned forced eviction could breach human rights of the travellers.[44]

39 'Osama bin Laden: statement by the UN Special Rapporteurs on summary executions and on human rights and counter-terrorism' 6 May 2011, http://www.ohchr.org/EN/NewsEvents/Pages/DisplayNews.aspx?NewsID=10987&LangID=E (accessed 14 July 2014).

40 'UN official criticises US over drone attacks', BBC News, 2 June 2010: http://news.bbc.co.uk/i/hi/world/us_and_canada/10219962.stm (accessed 3 June 2010).

41 'US: "Four decades in solitary confinement can only be described as torture" – UN rights expert', News Release of the OHCHR, 7 October 2013, http://www.ohchr.org/EN/NewsEvents/Pages/DisplayNews.aspx?NewsID=13832 (accessed 14 July 2014).

42 'CIA rendition programme: UN expert on human rights and counter-terrorism asks for truth and accountability', News Release of the OHCHR, 6 March 2013, http://www.ohchr.org/en/NewsEvents/Pages/DisplayNews.aspx?NewsID=13080&LangID=E (accessed 14 July 2014).

43 'UN experts criticize treatment of migrants after deportee dies while in custody of a UK private security company', New Release of the OHCHR, 21 October 2010, http://www.ohchr.org/SP/NewsEvents/Pages/DisplayNews.aspx?NewsID=10463&LangID=E (accessed 14 July 2014.

44 'UK urged to find negotiated settlement to eviction stand-off with 86 Irish Traveller families – UN experts', News Release of the OHCHR of 5 August 2011. See also 'Dale Farm traveller evictions "may breach human rights"', BBC News: Essex, 6 August 2011, http://www.bbc.co.uk/news/uk-england-essex-14431494 (accessed 7 August 2011) and Josie Ensor, 'Eviction of 400 travellers defies human rights, says UN official', *The Daily Telegraph* (UK), 8 August 2011, p.11.

6.5.6 Changing roles of the Special Rapporteurs

While the Special Rapporteurs are perceived in some quarters as 'investigating judges', they lack real powers. However, they are judges in the sense of objectively assessing facts presented to them and coming to their own conclusion as to whether and how to act on the information received. In reality they are human rights advocates representing the UN system and they can be, and many of them have been, effective advocates. Over the years their role has changed gradually from a naming and shaming institution to a constructive mechanism which can be expected to assist in capacity building.

The institution of special procedures accords individual mandate holders a high degree of independence and flexibility in discharging their responsibilities. They can, essentially, define their own mandate and select the approach best suited to them personally and to their mandate. For instance, the present author made the scope of his mandate on Cambodia much wider, embracing political issues such as parliamentary and electoral reform that had a bearing on the enjoyment of human rights by the people in the country. The institution of special procedures is a flexible mechanism that can be utilised to prevent human rights violations rather than merely deal with the aftermath of the violations. The special procedures' use of urgent appeals can be an effective mechanism designed to prevent human rights violations and has no counterpart in the current treaty bodies' methods or in the working method of the Human Rights Council.

6.5.7 Wider utility of the reports of Special Rapporteurs

Their reports are considered by various human rights monitoring and reporting mechanisms both charter based, for example the Universal Periodic Review, and treaty bodies. In addition, the International Law Commission takes into account the work of Special Rapporteurs when writing its own reports.[45] Generally speaking, the Special Rapporteurs look at the situation in the country concerned, identify what the problems are and make recommendations, including changes in law or governmental policy, on the basis of international standards, including the legal obligations under the human rights treaties ratified by the country. Many States go on to adopt a plan of action to implement such recommendations since many such recommendations may have actually originated from within the country. This is because the Special Rapporteurs work with civil society in the country concerned to advance the cause and/or to influence and apply pressure on governments. That may be one reason why commentators such as Ramcharan have stated that Special Rapporteurs are 'the strongest protection actors in the UN'.[46] Others have

45 See for example, the most recent annual report of the International Law Commission, http://www.un.org/law/ilc/ (accessed 23 October 2014).

46 Bertrand Ramcharan, *The UN Human Rights Council* (Routledge, 2011), p.7.

described the mechanism of Special Rapporteurs or procedures as 'the most directly accessible mechanism of the international human rights machinery'[47] and have been regarded by some as the 'crown jewel' of the UN human rights system.[48]

The reports of many Special Rapporteurs have led to the raising of international standards for human rights, according concrete meaning to existing human rights principles, expanding their scope, guiding their implementation and interpretation and the conclusion or adoption of a new international human rights instrument.[49] For instance, on the basis of the proposals made by the Special Representative of the UN Secretary General on business and human rights, John Ruggie, the UN Human Rights Council passed a resolution on 16 June 2011 endorsing the 'Guiding Principles on Business and Human Rights: Implementing the UN "Protect, Respect and Remedy" Framework'.[50]

The reports of Special Rapporteurs are consulted for a wide range of purposes by foreign governments, donor agencies, international development institutions, civil society representatives, and academic and research institutions. The reports of the Special Rapporteurs have an educational value too since they generate knowledge and inform the world of the situation of human rights in a given country and recommend measures whether legal, administrative or policy orientated. In the case of the country mandate holders they also often perform an inherently diplomatic role involving a conciliatory function between different stakeholders in the society and the use of 'good offices' to facilitate an outcome. To some extent they also perform a prosecutorial role by 'accusing' the government for their failure to protect certain rights, and make legal and policy-orientated suggestions to address the situation of human rights in the country concerned.

6.5.8 Lack of meaningful powers to entertain individual petitions

One of the frustrations the present author had while working as the UN Special Rapporteur for Cambodia was not being able to entertain in a meaningful manner the hundreds of individual petitions submitted to him by the victims

47 Navi Pillay, the then UN High Commissioner for Human Rights, in OHCHR, 'United Nations Special Procedures: Facts and Figures, 2012' (Geneva, February 2013), Introduction, p.1.

48 See 'Annan calls on Human Rights Council to strive for unity, avoid familiar fault lines', a report of the UN News Centre of 29 November 2006: http://www.un.org/apps/news/story.asp?NewsID=20770 (accessed 10 July 2014).

49 See Surya P. Subedi *et al.*, 'Introduction: The Role of the Special Rapporteurs of the United Nations Human Rights Council in the Development and Promotion of International Human Rights Norms', 15 (2) *The International Journal of Human Rights* (Taylor & Francis, London), 2011, pp.155–61.

50 A/HRC/17/31 of 21 March 2011, http://www.ohchr.org/Documents/Issues/Business/A-HRC-17-31_AEV.pdf (accessed 14 July 2012).

or potential victims of human rights violations in the country. The UN Special Rapporteurs are basically a one-person band who have no real powers and no adequate resources to practically deal with human rights violations. The mechanism of special procedures is not designed for such practical effect either. It is more of a monitoring and advisory mechanism designed to bring about change in policy. However, the ordinary citizens in the country are not fully aware of the limitations of the UN Special Rapporteurs and have high expectations of the mandate holders. During each of his country visits the present author received a large number of delegations consisting of women, children and elderly, the most vulnerable groups in society, who would come from far flung rural areas of the country travelling for long hours with a petition asking for help when their homes and livelihood were under threat from forcible eviction from their land. Their very survival and their dignity was under direct attack from land grabbers, whether the government, companies or the rich and powerful people in the society. They would have knocked on the door of the representatives of the executive, legislative and judicial branches of the government to no avail and would come to the UN Special Rapporteur as a last resort.

Their grievances were not always necessarily about the violations of rather elitist human rights such as freedom of speech or of peaceful assembly, but often about violations of their basic land rights, their very survival in dignity as individuals or as family units. Many of the victims of human rights violations would also send their petitions directly to the university office of the Special Rapporteur in Leeds in England hoping that the rapporteur would be able to do something for them. Of course, the rapporteur would use all means at his disposal, such as writing directly to the people in the government bringing the matter to their attention in the forms of urgent appeals or allegation letters, and sometimes the violation would stop or the threat of eviction would not be carried out. But if the government ignored the communication and the eviction proceeded resulting often in the burning down of the dwellings of the villagers and forcible eviction of families there was little the Special Rapporteur or any of the other UN human rights mechanisms could do about it.

6.6 Implementation of the recommendations of Special Rapporteurs

One of the major weaknesses of the institution of Special Rapporteurs is the absence of an effective follow-up procedure to the reports submitted and to communications sent to governments alleging violations of human rights or even to urgent appeals made as a preventative measure. Many of the recommendations of the Special Rapporteurs remain unimplemented and their communications to governments have not been responded to. This weakness existed during the time of the Commission on Human Rights and improved little after the establishment of the Human Rights Council. As noted above, since the Charter of the UN did not provide ECOSOC with enforcement powers, powers of enforcement could not be bestowed upon the Commission on Human Rights.

Although the Human Rights Council was established as a subsidiary organ of the General Assembly, this made little difference since the Assembly itself is lacking in enforcement powers. States may make political commitments to implement the recommendations of either the Special Rapporteurs or the Council, yet without an effective enforcement mechanism or policy there is an absence of any truly effective follow up. Whilst Special Rapporteurs are UN Charter-based human rights experts, States are under no obligation to implement the recommendations they make. Many States view Special Rapporteurs as UN human rights volunteers and regard them as advisors. Consequently, the view is that such advisors should not expect to have all (or on occasion, any) of their advice accepted or implemented. It is up to the State to decide whether to accept the recommendations and when and how to implement those recommendations that are accepted. Therefore, there are no direct sanctions available to ensure compliance with the recommendations of the special procedures.

However, in practice there is some political and economic leverage and/or ability to use 'soft power' that could be employed to induce the government concerned into action towards compliance. The influence and success of special procedures as pursued by Special Rapporteurs is evident from the present author's first-hand experience as the UN Special Rapporteur on the situation of Human Rights in Cambodia when he witnessed the employment of soft economic leverage on Cambodia by the EU on the basis of his reports on the situation of human rights in the country.[51] A resolution adopted by the European Parliament called for the suspension of the concession enjoyed by Cambodia under the Everything But Arms (EBA) trade scheme (pursuant to which all least developed countries are granted unhindered access for all of their exports, except arms to the EU countries) where the companies benefitting from such a scheme were found to be engaged in human rights violations.[52]

The World Bank also weighed in by stopping loans to Cambodia when the Cambodian authorities wanted to go ahead with the decision to allow a property developer to fill in a large lake in the middle of Phnom Penh in order to build luxury flats and upmarket shops which would have entailed evicting

51 Resolution 2012/2844 (RSP) of the European Parliament adopted on 26 October 2012, also see generally, Surya P. Subedi, 'The UN Human Rights Mandate in Cambodia: The Challenges of a Country in Transition and the Experience of the UN Special Rapporteur for the Country' (2011) 15 (2) *The International Journal of Human Rights*, 247–61.

52 See Regulation (EU) No. 978/2012 of the European Parliament and the Council of 25 October 2012 on applying a scheme of generalised tariff preferences and repealing Council Regulation (EC) no 732/2008. *Official Journal of the European Union*, 303/1, 31 October, 2012.

some 700 families from the area. The World Bank stated that it would not resume lending until the government settled the dispute with the local residents.[53] When both national and international pressure was applied to the Government it entered into a negotiated deal with most of the families. The Inspection Panel of the World Bank had also been involved in investigating a complaint lodged by a housing NGO, the Centre for Housing Rights and Evictions (COHRE), on behalf of the residents of the Beoung Kak lake area and the World Bank had offered an action plan offering the Government financing and technical advice to aid practical solutions.[54]

Similarly, the Senates of both Australia (a major donor country to Cambodia) and the Philippines (a fellow ASEAN State) as well as the Inter-Parliamentary Union (IPU),[55] an inter-governmental organisation of sovereign parliaments, and the European Parliament, passed resolutions in October 2012 calling upon the Government of Cambodia to implement the recommendations on electoral reform made in the July 2012 report of the present author in his capacity as the UN Special Rapporteur on the situation of human rights in Cambodia. Similarly, a group of prominent US congressmen, including high profile Senators such as John McCain (a former Republican presidential candidate) wrote a letter[56] on 31 October 2012 to President Obama urging him to insist on democracy, electoral reform and human rights when visiting Cambodia in November 2013. It was subsequently revealed that President Obama did do so during his visit to the country.[57] Employment of such 'soft-power' did succeed in putting some pressure on the Government of Cambodia to implement recommendations made by the present author in his Special Rapporteur capacity.

6.7 Impact of the work of Special Rapporteurs

It is difficult to measure the impact of the work of the Special Rapporteurs as it varies from one mandate to another and from one mandate holder to

53 'World Bank blocks Cambodia loans amid Boeung Kak row', BBC News: Asia-Pacific, 9 August 2011: http://www.bbc.co.uk/news.world-asia-pacific-14457573, accessed 14 July 2014.

54 'Cambodia: Land Management and Administration Project' in *The Update* (Inspection Panel Newsletter) Issue 4 June 2011, 2–3.

55 See for full text of the Resolution of the IPU in English: http://www.ipu.org/pdf/hrres191_en.pdf (accessed 3 November 2012).

56 David Boyle, 'U.S. lawmakers slam PM', *The Phnom Penh Post*, 12 November 2012, 1, http://www.phnompenhpost.com/national/us-lawmakers-slam-cambodias-prime-minister (accessed 14 July 2014).

57 See Matthew Reisz, 'Obama: you must listen to this man', *The Times Higher Education* (London), 7 February 2013, 13 and 'Rapporteur backed: rights or a rough ride, warns US', *The Phnom Penh Post* of 14 December 2012, 3, as reported by Nepal News see http://www.timeshighereducation.co.uk/news/obama-you-must-listen-to-this-man/2001368.article and http://www.nepalnews.com/archive/2012/dec/dec18/news20.php respectively, both accessed 14 July 2014.

another.[58] Nonetheless, there have been various suggestions of indicators of impact that range from (a) the number of references to the work of the Special Rapporteurs in UN publications or major UN reports on human rights, (b) the number of civil society organisations making use of the reports of the Special Rapporteurs, (c) the number of references made to the reports of Special Rapporteurs by the UN treaty bodies, General Assembly, the Security Council and other international organisations, to (d) the release of prisoners, (e) change in law and policy by governments, or (f) change in other activities of States resulting from the work of the Special Rapporteurs.

However, measuring success on the basis of the first three criteria is not necessarily a measure of success as such – it relates more to the profile of the work of a particular Rapporteur, although of course that profile could have a positive impact upon the attention given to the matter and subsequent action made. The real test should be on the basis of impact on the lives of people. The difficulty is that there will be a number of actors or stakeholders that would have contributed to bringing about specific positive change in a country that can all legitimately claim some credit for any success story whether it is to do with the release of a prisoner, enactment of a new law, or amendment of an existing law or change in government policy. What is certain is that the Special Rapporteurs, especially country-specific mandate holders, act as a focal point for human rights activity in the country concerned or on the human rights theme they are responsible for.

The work of many mandate holders has resulted in human rights standard setting on the subject matter concerned whether through the adoption of a resolution or declaration by the UN General Assembly or in a few cases conclusion of a new treaty. When the recommendations made by Special Rapporteurs are implemented by States this can be evidence of *opinio juris* giving rise in due course to the crystallisation of the norms recommended by the Special Rapporteurs into rules of customary international law. Thus, while the actual role of Special Rapporteurs is to do no more than monitor human rights situations, the impact of their work could be the development of international law through the elaboration of their recommendations, through an international instrument or through their development as a rule of customary international law.

The country visits of Special Rapporteurs succeed in having a considerable impact on the situation of human rights in the country concerned. As stated in a study prepared by the Brookings Institute, 'the very fact that a mission is taking place tends to have a salutary impact on the human rights situation in a given country . . . such visits tend to elevate human rights on the national agenda, bring public attention and debate through the media, validate

58 See generally, Surya P. Subedi, 'Human Rights Experts in the United Nations: A Review of the Role of the United Nations Special Procedures', in Monika Ambrus *et al.* (ed.), *The Role of 'Experts' in International and European Decision-making Process* (Cambridge University Press, 2014), 241–62.

allegations of human rights violations in a credible way, and allow human rights concerns to be raised and discussed at the highest level of government'.[59]

Even if the work of Special Rapporteurs has no visible direct or tangible impact the educational value of their reports is huge. Their reports are cited by national and international courts and tribunals, civil society organisations, development partners or donor agencies, academics, researchers, human rights defenders and governments. Their reports can be and have been used by prosecutors in international criminal courts. Thus, the impact of the work of Special Rapporteurs can be both direct and indirect, immediate as well as longer term. For instance, the present author was credited for a number of changes in Cambodia. When he began his work as the UN Special Rapporteur for human rights in the country, he took a macro rather than a micro approach to tackling human rights problems in Cambodia and gave constructive recommendations in this regard.

The present author began his work by assessing the whole political structure of the country and produced four substantive and substantial reports focusing on judicial, parliamentary, and electoral reform and on the impact of economic and other land concessions on people's lives. Collectively, these four reports provided an analytical picture of democracy, human rights and the rule of law in the country and quickly became a primary source of reference for human rights defenders, UN agencies, donor agencies and ordinary citizens.[60]

As with other previous Special Rapporteurs, the Government has been hostile to the present author in his capacity as the Special Rapporteur for the country. Prime Minister Hun Sen, the longest serving autocratic prime minister of any Asian country, even made attacks descending to a personal level in September 2012 to destabilise the Special Rapporteur. Undeterred from his mission he weathered the storm and responded to the criticisms from the Prime Minister in a diplomatic and professional manner.[61] The international community came to the defence of the Special Rapporteur and his reports and recommendations for reform of the Cambodian judiciary, parliament and the electoral system.[62]

59 March Limon and Ted Piccone, *Human Rights Special Procedures: Determinants of Influence* (Policy Report of the Brookings Institute and Universal Rights Group, March 2014), 23.

60 This included support from the US president Barack Obama, as noted above, who called upon the Prime Minister of Cambodia to implement the recommendations made by the current author. To access the various reports of the present author in his capacity as UN Special Rapporteur on the situation of human rights in Cambodia, see http://www.ohchr.org/EN/countries/AsiaRegion/Pages/KHIndex.aspx (accessed 14 July 2014).

61 Surya P. Subedi, 'Mutual respect can bridge differences of opinion', *The Phnom Penh Post*, 5 October 2012. See also 'Subedi objects to Cambodian PM's remarks', *Republica*, Kathmandu, 7 October 2012.

62 See, for example, above reference to support provided by President Barack Obama and the support of the Senates of Australia and the Philippines, the IPU and the European parliament.

The rare display of international support for the Special Rapporteur's work prompted the government to reconsider its position. Gradually, the Special Rapporteur's sustained efforts brought about tangible results for the people of Cambodia. They included the release from prison of a prominent journalist and human rights defender, Mr Mam Sonando in March 2013 and the return of the leader of the opposition, Mr Sam Rainsy, in July 2013 to the country from his long exile in Paris. Both of them wrote letters thanking the Special Rapporteur for his assistance.[63]

The Special Rapporteur has also been credited for dissuading the Government of Cambodia from enacting a restrictive law against NGOs, for persuading the Government to impose a moratorium on economic land concessions that have a detrimental impact on human rights, and encouraging the Government to enact a law on expropriation to provide compensation to people affected by land evictions. Taking the above into account, it can be said that the impact of the UN Special Rapporteur's work on Cambodian political discourse has been deep and far reaching, so much so that the Government, which had initially rejected his recommendations for electoral reform and subjected him to harassment and intimidation, came around to accepting the logic of the recommendations made.

Parliament enacted three fundamental laws designed to enhance the independence and capacity of the judiciary in May 2014 as recommended by the Special Rapporteur in his report of 2010, which had a focus on judicial reform.[64] The Government and the Opposition Party decided to set up a high-level committee to consider implementing his recommendations for electoral reform, making them part of the national agenda. It resulted in an amendment to the constitution of the country itself in September 2014 to accord constitutional status to the National Election Committee and change the composition and method of appointment of the election commissioners.

6.8 Challenges ahead

There has been a division in views in the Human Rights Council between the developed and developing countries in the use and utility of Special Rapporteurs. Both groups of States have tried to use the mechanism of special procedures to advance their political agenda. While the developed countries have sought to promote the work of the UN mandate holders whose focus is on civil and political rights, the developing countries on the other hand have

63 The thank you letters to Professor Subedi from Mr Mam Sonando for his release and from Mr Sam Rainsy for his return from exile are on file with the present author.

64 Surya P. Subedi, 'Report of the Special Rapporteur on the situation of human rights in Cambodia', 16 September 2010, A/HRC/15/46, http://daccess-dds-ny.un.org/doc/UNDOC/GEN/G10/161/45/PDF/G1016145.pdf?OpenElement (accessed 14 July 2014).

sought to do the same with regard to the mandate holders whose work is focused on economic, social, cultural rights and the like.

The allegations on the part of developing countries, which are often on the receiving end of the reports and recommendations of the Special Rapporteurs dealing with civil and political rights, is often that such Special Rapporteurs have not carried out their work strictly within the code of conduct stipulated in Human Rights Council Resolution 5/2. When it comes to making such allegations even democratic developing countries such as India and South Africa often join the club of other developing countries with a poorer record of human rights such as Algeria, Belarus, China, Cuba, North Korea, Egypt, Myanmar, Russia, Saudi Arabia, Sudan and Venezuela. An example is a statement made to this effect by the Indian delegation to the Human Rights Council in June 2014.[65]

While the Western and developed countries place a great deal of emphasis on the mandates concerning civil and political rights, the developing countries prefer to focus upon economic, social, cultural rights and third or even fourth generation 'rights' or issues. Thus, there is growing politicisation of the institution of Special Rapporteurs which undermines its effectiveness and utility. Likewise, while countries such as China and Russia see the role of the Special Rapporteurs as promoting human rights through cooperation and mutuality of respect rather than condemning and criticising governments, they maintain that the Special Rapporteurs are basically UN human rights volunteers and mere advisers who should not expect to have all their recommendations implemented by the countries concerned. The governments can pick and choose such recommendations for implementation according to their own agenda and priority for reform within the country.[66]

The country or territorially specific mandates are more controversial than the thematic mandates. Many countries with a Special Rapporteur regard the appointment as a stigma attached to their record of human rights. Therefore, States go out of their way to garner support within the Human Rights Council to abolish the mandate. Israel has long complained of and opposed the appointment of a Special Rapporteur for the Occupied Territory of Palestine with a mandate for an indefinite period. It says this is an example of selectivity on the part of the Human Rights Council. The appointment to the mandate on Palestine after the expiry of the 6-year term of Professor Richard Falk, a professor of international law at Princeton University, became so controversial that the Human Rights Council was unable to make a new appointment in March 2014. Consequently, the appointment of all other vacant positions could

65 A copy of the statement by a delegate from India is on file with the present author.

66 Based on the statement of these countries in the informal annual interaction between the UN Special Rapporteurs and UN member States in Geneva in September 2014.

not be made either.[67] This demonstrates how highly politicised the appointment of Special Rapporteurs has become.

Political lobbying has reached such a level that often ministers from different countries are dispatched to Geneva or New York to lobby for and against mandates or mandate holders. This increasing level of politicisation of the institution of Special Rapporteurs is bound to undermine the integrity, effectiveness and utility of the institution itself. Lobbying for votes for elected positions within the UN is not a new phenomenon. However, lobbying intensely for appointments that should supposedly be made on expertise and merit alone is quite another.

Also of concern is that some thematic mandates created at the behest of some developing countries are based upon rather vague, general and politically motivated topics.[68] It would be difficult for any serious mandate holder to make a meaningful contribution to such an area and produce a report that is succinct and to the point and capable of advancing the agenda. Examples are the mandates on the promotion of a democratic and equitable international order, international solidarity, the promotion of truth, justice, reparation and guarantees of non-recurrence, and the enjoyment of all human rights by older persons. Those very countries that contribute least to the budget of the UN in general and the human rights mechanism in particular, i.e. the developing countries, seem to be the ones in support of such mandates since the expenses for their maintenance is picked up by other States, i.e. the developed countries.

With an increase in the number of mandates, the Special Rapporteurs seem to produce a large number of recommendations. This sheer number of recommendations seems to provide States with an excuse not to have regard for any of the recommendations made. Further, when there are so many recommendations, States have started to play the game themselves by picking and choosing recommendations that suit their domestic political agenda. Since there are so many special procedures mandate holders requesting a visit, States have the choice to invite only those mandate holders whose visit will help the government domestically and internationally or advance the political ideology embraced by that government.

6.9 Attempts to reform the system

Certain improvements were made to the institution of Special Rapporteurs during the review of the Human Rights Council in 2011 through a resolution of the UN General Assembly 62/281 of 20 July 2011. In addition to the existing entities, it was stated that national human rights institutions in

67 A communication of 28 March 2014 to all UN mandate holders from the Special Procedures Branch (on file with the present author).

68 Fernando Falcón y Tella, *Challenges for Human Rights* (Martinous Nijhoff, 2007) 5–68.

compliance with the Paris Principles may also nominate candidates as special procedure mandate holders. Unlike in the past when no application as such was required from candidates themselves to the position of Special Rapporteur, the 2011 review outcome document stated that they will have to from then onwards submit an application for each specific mandate, together with personal data and a motivation letter no longer than 600 words. Similarly, in the past there was no provision or mechanism to interview candidates for such positions.

The 2011 review stated that the consultative group, consisting of five ambassadors based in Geneva from five geographical regions of the world, had to consider the applications in a transparent manner and more importantly it had to interview shortlisted candidates to ensure equal treatment of all. The Consultative Group is entrusted with the task of proposing to the President of the Human Rights Council a list of candidates who possess the highest qualifications for the mandates in question and meet the general criteria and particular requirements. When the Consultative Group makes its recommendations to the President of the Council it gives its reasoning for its recommendation. Those that are shortlisted are interviewed, often by telephone, and the details of the candidates shortlisted, those who applied or were eligible for consideration are publicised. This new procedure has brought about more transparency and increased the chances of appointing the right people for the right mandates.[69]

With regard to working methods, the review outcome provided that States should cooperate with and assist special procedures mandate holders in the performance of their tasks and respond in a timely manner to requests for information and visits. It also stated that it was incumbent on mandate holders to exercise their functions in accordance with their mandates and in compliance with the code of conduct and that they must continue to foster a constructive dialogue with States.

The General Assembly resolution called on the special procedures mandates to endeavour to formulate their recommendations in a concrete, comprehensive and action-orientated way and to pay attention to the technical assistance and capacity-building needs of States in their thematic and country mission reports. No provisions were included for a follow-up mechanism of the recommendations of the Special Rapporteurs. Nor were States required to extend invitations to Special Rapporteurs. Although the review process did bring about some changes to the institution of Special Rapporteurs, it was by no means a significant improvement of the system. This is because the changes, which are more about the process of appointing Special Rapporteurs than empowering them or better equipping them, have not made much difference to the ability of the Special Rapporteurs to deal with human rights violations.

69 The progress made in this respect provides a good example upon which the appointment of the High Commissioner for Human Rights could be based.

However, most of the reforms included in the review did not go far enough to make the institution of Special Rapporteurs more robust and proactive in protecting and preventing human rights violations. For instance, the outcome document did not give a specific role to special procedures in early warning, and did not specifically mandate follow-up by States to the recommendations of Special Rapporteurs. Even when a group of UN Special Rapporteurs collectively call for some concrete measures in relation to the situation of human rights in a given country, the Human Rights Council may be handicapped by a lack of support for such measures amongst its membership, which is often driven by political considerations rather than human rights considerations. Although in its landmark decision in March 2013 the Human Rights Council did heed such a call made collectively by UN Special Rapporteurs for an international inquiry into North Korean human rights abuses[70] in February 2013 by agreeing unanimously to establish a commission of inquiry, such unanimity within the Human Rights Council is relatively rare.

6.10 Human Rights treaty bodies and Special Rapporteurs

While the Human Rights Council has a global mandate to examine the situation of human rights across a whole range of cross-cutting issues with a view to protecting and promoting human rights, the core function of the treaty bodies is to review periodic reports of States to promote enhanced respect for the human rights embodied in the individual treaty concerned together with guidance in the form of general comments providing States with guidance as to how to fulfil their obligations under the treaty. The institution of special procedures is a flexible mechanism which can be utilised to promote human rights and to prevent human rights violations rather than merely to deal with the aftermath of the violations. For instance, the special procedures' use of urgent appeals can be an effective mechanism to prevent human rights violations and has no counterpart in the current treaty bodies' methods or in the working method of the Human Rights Council.

As Rodley states, 'the special procedures, with one exception (the Working Group on Arbitrary Detention) do not pursue individual cases to a formal conclusion on whether or not there has been a violation, whereas the treaty bodies do just that.'[71] He goes on to say that, 'By contrast, the special

70 News Release of the OHCHR of 27 February 2013: 'UN experts call for an international inquiry into North Korea human rights abuses.' After holding several 'public hearings' in different countries, conducting interviews and other fact-finding activities, the commission, headed by Justice Michael Kirby of Australia, submitted its report to the Human Rights Council in February 2013. A/HRC/25/63 of 7 February 2014.

71 Sir Nigel Rodley, 'The United Nations Human Rights Council, Its Special Procedures, and Its Relationship with the Treaty Bodies: Complementarity or Competition?' in Kevin Boyle (ed.), *New Institutions for Human Rights Protection* (Oxford University Press, 2009), 49–73, 72.

procedures' use of urgent appeals has no real counterpart in the current treaty bodies' methods. . . . The purpose of the special procedures' urgent appeals is to prevent, inhibit, or stop any feared violations.' Another noteworthy difference between the complaints procedure of human rights treaty bodies and the Special Rapporteurs' handling of communications is that while authors of complaints submitted to treaty bodies must exhaust domestic remedies before lodging their complaint, those complaining to the Special Rapporteurs do not have to fulfil this requirement, and may send their communication to the Special Rapporteurs at any stage.

While Special Rapporteurs are more about fact-finding, the treaty bodies are more about assessing the reports received from States. However, some synergy takes place between the activities of both these UN human rights institutions. For instance, some of the General Comments adopted by various treaty bodies as well as the decisions adopted in cases considered by them have been cited frequently by Special Rapporteurs as a guide to the interpretation and possible application of international standards in a particular country. Conversely, the treaty bodies have benefitted from the specialist knowledge of the Special Rapporteurs on the situation of human rights in a given country. There has, therefore, often been an exchange of views between Special Rapporteurs and treaty bodies on the situation of human rights in a country concerned.

However, unlike human rights treaty bodies, which derive their authority from hard law instruments, one of the major weaknesses of the institution of Special Rapporteurs is its soft law nature and at best quasi-judicial nature. The Special Rapporteurs do not provide legal remedies, are not designed to, nor do they possess any powers of enforcement. Of course, they do receive individual or collective petitions and take action on these petitions by way of asking the State concerned to provide details of steps taken or being taken to address violations that have allegedly already occurred, or in the case of on-going violations, to put an immediate end to them.

Unlike treaty bodies, which can take a long time to reach a conclusion on an individual petition, Special Rapporteurs can take swift action that may result in some degree of redress for the victims of human rights violations. The general perception amongst the human rights NGOs and victims of human rights violations is that the Special Rapporteurs can provide a speedy international remedy to their situation. This was the experience of the present author during his work on Cambodia. This is especially true when Special Rapporteurs are on a fact-finding mission to the country concerned during which victims of human rights violations or those facing the threat of violation can and do routinely petition the Special Rapporteur. Instantaneous intervention by the Special Rapporteur on cases with valid *prima facie* grounds, or the mere fact that the matter has been brought to the attention of the Special Rapporteur, may deter public officials from violating people's rights or put an end to activity which violates human rights.

6.11 Conclusions

The mechanism of Special Rapporteurs grew initially in response to massive violations of human rights, be it in Apartheid South Africa or during the military rule in Argentina. It was then gradually utilised in response to specific cases of human rights violations. It is largely a cooperative mechanism in which the mandate holder is expected to bring something new to the table in the dialogue with the States concerned in order to improve the situation of human rights. While treaty bodies are there for monitoring compliance with specific treaty obligations, Special Rapporteurs are designed more to cooperate with States to promote all human rights, including those enshrined in the Universal Declaration of Human Rights.

The institution of Special Rapporteurs is designed primarily to influence change in policy in the country concerned. As an institution it may be subject to criticism for being a 'weak' mechanism, but it is designed to act as a mechanism that assists both the States concerned and the international community, to be instructive and constructive. Special Rapporteurs are expected to go beyond 'naming and shaming' and offer constructive recommendations. It is largely a preventative mechanism rather than a remedial one. Despite the weakness inherent in the institution of Special Rapporteurs as a soft law institution without enforcement powers, it has played an important role in the promotion and protection of human rights. The deployment of Special Rapporteurs is about mobilising the moral potential of the UN. It is about an attempt at engagement rather than isolation of the States of concern with regard to the situation of human rights in those States.

However, the mechanism has witnessed an organic growth in such a manner that it now seems to be spiralling out of control. A proliferation of Special Rapporteurs runs the risk of not only diluting the work of the UN mandate holders, but also undermining the gravitas and quality attached to the institution of Special Rapporteurs, and is a significant strain on the already limited financial resources available to the OHCHR to support these mandates. While the so-called 'crown jewel' of the UN human rights system receives less than half a per cent of the UN regular budget, the mechanism as a whole is suffering from uncontrolled and unregulated development.

One possible way of addressing the allegations of selectivity and the problems of politicisation of the institution of Special Rapporteurs would be to abolish all thematic mandates and create one Special Rapporteur for every country in a non-selective manner. In this case, the position of the Special Rapporteurs could be made full-time and be remunerated to a level commensurate with their responsibility; the voluntary nature of their posts means that individuals from many developing countries or those without any independent means of support are unlikely to volunteer for such a position.[72] In the absence of reforming other

72 For instance, one Special Rapporteur had to step down from their academic position due to a lack of support from their institution. Ilias Bantekas and Lutz Oette, *International*

UN human rights institutions, this approach is at the disposal of the Human Rights Council without the need to amend any treaty or an international instrument. In such a situation allegations of selectivity and double standards in the appointment would be silenced.

Since the UN has moved from Universal Declaration to Universal Periodic Review it would be a natural progression to appoint a country-specific mandate holder universally to monitor compliance with not only the provisions of the Universal Declaration and treaty provisions but also with the recommendations of the UPR.[73] If every State had a UN Special Rapporteur there would be no need for other human rights monitoring mechanisms.

Working on a full-time basis and remunerated accordingly, the country mandate holder would cover the whole range of human rights and report back to the Human Rights Council on the compliance with treaty obligations, implementation of the UPR recommendations and the recommendations of the Special Rapporteurs. Since the number of special procedures mandate holders is already over 70, and there are 172 or so other UN human rights experts working for the 10 human rights treaty bodies, it should not be much of an additional problem to add another 85 mandate holders to streamline the monitoring work and achieve uniformity, consistency and universality in their work and enhance the effectiveness and impact of their work as part of a package of reform of the UN system of human rights.

Human Rights Law and Practice (Cambridge University Press, 2013) 163, interview with Cephas Lumina, UN Special Rapporteur on the effects of debt on the enjoyment of human rights (2008–2014).

73 I suggest above that a Special Rapporteur should be appointed to each country. At first glance, the concerns I raise about the recent number of appointments might appear to contradict my proposal, however, the implementation of the appointment to each country of a Special Rapporteur would be part of a larger scale programme of reform that would necessitate strategic funding and be part of an overall and coherent programme.

7 Effectiveness of other UN Charter-based bodies and agencies associated with the UN

7.1 Introduction

In addition to the main human rights bodies within the UN system, namely, treaty bodies and the Charter-based bodies such as the Human Rights Council, the High Commissioner for Human Rights and the Special Rapporteurs, there is a plethora of other UN agencies that have a direct and indirect mandate for the protection and promotion of human rights. Since the Charter of the UN makes the protection and promotion of human rights one of the main objectives, purposes and principles of this world organisation, the principal organs of the UN, namely, the General Assembly (also referred to as the Assembly in this chapter), the Security Council, the Economic and Social Council, the International Court of Justice, and the Secretary General as the head of the UN Secretariat all have a certain role to play in the protection and promotion of human rights. It is in this context that this chapter aims to evaluate the work of these principal organs of the UN and other UN charter-based bodies in the promotion and protection of human rights. In doing so, this chapter examines the role that these bodies are mandated to play for the protection and promotion of human rights, how effective they have been in discharging their mandate, and their limitations, strengths and weaknesses.

7.2 The General Assembly

Under Article 10 of the Charter of the United Nations (the Charter), the General Assembly has a very broad mandate to discuss any questions or any matters within the scope of the Charter or relating to the powers and functions of any organs provided for in the Charter. Except for those matters under consideration by the Security Council as provided in Article 12, the General Assembly may make recommendations to the Members of the United Nations or to the Security Council or to both on any such questions or matters. No other organs of the UN have as broad a mandate as the General Assembly. However, since the powers of the Assembly are limited to making recommendations, any decisions, save for those relating to administrative and budgetary matters, are not binding on States or other organs of the UN. Having said this, as the most representative organ of the UN (all members of the UN are represented and all States, small or big, rich or poor, have one vote at the General Assembly), the decisions or recommendations of the Assembly carry a great deal of authority and legitimacy. The provisions and principles contained within General Assembly declarations, especially those adopted with the support of a vast majority of States, are liable to become rules of customary international law in due course, and thus binding on all States except for those which are persistent and subsequent objectors, provided that what States do and what their delegates say in the General Assembly constitutes evidence of State practice.

The contribution of the General Assembly to the promotion and protection of human rights has been a profound one. It was the Assembly which adopted the 1948 Universal Declaration of Human Rights and the 1966 Covenants on Civil and Political Rights and on Economic, Social and Cultural Rights, to name a few. A number of other ground breaking resolutions and declarations such as the 1986 Declaration on the Right to Development have been adopted by the Assembly. The Human Rights Council itself, the principal UN human rights organisation, is a subsidiary organ of the Assembly. A number of other *ad hoc* human rights committees, sub-committees and agencies such as the Special Rapporteurs for human rights have been appointed by the Assembly.

The Social, Humanitarian and Cultural Committee, otherwise known as the Third Committee, of the General Assembly acts as a major forum for debate and decision on human rights issues within the UN system, including examination of the special procedures reports of the Human Rights Council. In addition, Article 13 of the Charter specifically mandates the Assembly to initiate studies and make recommendations for the purpose of, *inter alia*, promoting international cooperation in the economic, social, cultural, educational, and health fields, and '*assisting in the realization of human rights and fundamental freedoms for all* without distinction as to race, sex, language, or religion' (emphasis added).[1]

The Assembly also derives its authority under Chapter IX of the Charter. Article 55 of that Chapter requires the UN to promote 'universal respect for, and observance of, human rights and fundamental freedoms for all without distinction as to race, sex, language, or religion' and Article 60 makes it clear that 'Responsibility for the discharge of the functions of the Organization set forth in this Chapter *shall be vested in the General Assembly* and, under the authority of the General Assembly, in the Economic and Social Council, which shall have for this purpose the powers set forth in Chapter X' (emphasis added). In other words, it can be submitted that the Assembly is the lead UN organ

1 The Charter of the United Nations was signed on 26 June 1945, in San Francisco, at the conclusion of the United Nations Conference on International Organization, and came into force on 24 October 1945. It has been ratified by 193 States, available at http://www.un.org/en/documents/charter/ (accessed on 18 December 2014).

for the promotion and protection of human rights. Even the Security Council is required to submit annual and, when necessary, special reports to the General Assembly for its consideration.

Indeed, through the 2005 World Summit Outcome document the Heads of State and Government of the members of the UN reaffirmed the central position of the Assembly in the following words: 'We reaffirm the central position of the General Assembly as the chief deliberative, policymaking and representative organ of the United Nations, as well as the role of the Assembly in the process of standard-setting and the codification of international law.'[2] Article 22 of the Charter authorizes the Assembly to establish such subsidiary organs as it deems necessary for the performance of its functions, which includes protection and promotion of human rights, the creation of the Human Rights Council as a subsidiary organ of the Assembly in 2006 to replace the Human Rights Commission being one such example.

7.3 The Third Committee of the General Assembly

The Social, Humanitarian and Cultural Affairs Committee (commonly referred to as the Third Committee) covers a range of social, humanitarian affairs and human rights issues that affect people all over the world.[3] An important part of the work of the Third Committee involves the examination of human rights questions, including reports of the special procedures mandate holders, the Human Rights Council, and the High Commissioner for Human Rights. The Committee also takes up matters concerning the advancement of women, the protection of minorities, children, and indigenous peoples, the protection of refugees, the promotion of fundamental freedoms through the elimination of racism and racial discrimination, and the right to self-determination. It also addresses important social development issues that have a direct bearing on human rights such as issues related to youth, family, ageing, persons with disabilities, crime prevention, criminal justice, and international drug control. The Third Committee also adopts country-specific resolutions on human rights situations.

Membership of the Third Committee is universal, however, unlike within the Human Rights Council, civil society organisations have no opportunity to participate in the work of this Committee. With the creation of the Human Rights Council the significance of the Third Committee has somewhat diminished. The following is the verdict of Oberleitner on the relevance of this Committee:

> With few significant governmental initiatives in the Committee, scarce availability of human rights expertise in New York (as compared to Geneva),

2 'World Summit Outcome', A/RES/60/1 of 24 October 2005, para 149.
3 See http://www.un.org/en/ga/third/ (accessed 15 July 2014).

> the absence of any NGO involvement, and little media attention, the Third Committee has been reduced to a mere additional bureaucratic layer, occasionally tinkering with the resolutions of subsidiary bodies.[4]

Nevertheless, this Committee still has a role of coordinating the resolutions of the General Assembly concerning human rights (which is roughly one-third of all the resolutions passed by the Assembly). For instance during the 67th session (2012) of the General Assembly, the Third Committee adopted a number of resolutions dealing with a wide range of issues from extrajudicial executions and violence against women, including the ban on female genital mutilation, to freedom of religion and belief and the moratorium on the use of the death penalty.[5] It also adopted a number of country resolutions concerning Myanmar, Iran, North Korea, and Syria. During the 67th session the country resolutions on Myanmar and North Korea were adopted by consensus which was a significant positive development within the UN.[6]

7.4 The Sixth Committee of the General Assembly

Although the Sixth (Legal) Committee of the UN General Assembly does not play as significant a role as the Third Committee in human rights related matters, the Sixth Committee may be involved in the process of the adoption of a human rights-related treaty on the basis of a referral to it. Since many of the international treaties, especially those which are law-making or belonging to the realm of public international law negotiated under the auspices of the UN, do pass through the Sixth Committee before they are presented to the Assembly, the Sixth Committee can play a role in the conclusion of a human rights treaty or a treaty containing some human rights element or impact on human rights. It is also possible to have a joint committee of members drawn from both the Third and Sixth Committees to consider a matter, including human rights related matters that would be placed for consideration by the General Assembly.

4 Gerd Oberleitner, *Global Human Rights Institutions: Between Remedy and Ritual* (Polity Press, 2007) 86–87.

5 See for a summary of the activities of the Third Committee in 2012: 'General Assembly Third Committee: Third Committee holds the course on the death penalty, and makes historic gains on SOGI [sexual orientation and gender identity] rights' (2013) Issue 1, *Human Rights Monitor Quarterly* of the International Service for Human Rights, Geneva, 20–26.

6 'Third Committee holds course on death penalty, makes gains on SOGI rights', International Service for Human Rights, Geneva, 30 January 2013, http://www.ishr.ch/news/human-rights-monitor-quarterly-general-assembly-third-committee (accessed 23 October 2014).

7.5 The Economic and Social Council

In the absence of a principal organ of the UN devoted to the protection and promotion of human rights, the main UN organ entrusted with this task is the Economic and Social Council (ECOSOC). However, its role in the protection and promotion of human rights has somewhat diminished after the abolition of the UN Commission on Human Rights, which had been one of its subsidiary bodies. The Human Rights Council, which was established to succeed the Commission on Human Rights, is a subsidiary body of the General Assembly rather than ECOSOC, nonetheless, the historical role played by ECOSOC in relation to human rights has been a profound and far reaching one. ECOSOC consists of 54 members of the UN elected by the General Assembly. Its functions and responsibilities concerning the protection and promotion of human rights are based on the provisions in paragraph 2 of Article 60 of the Charter which states that it 'may make recommendations for the purpose of promoting respect for, and observance of, human rights and fundamental freedoms for all'.

Paragraphs 3 and 4 of Article 60 go on to provide more specific indications as to the nature of the work that ECOSOC may carry out: the Council 'may prepare draft conventions for submission to the General Assembly, with respect to matters falling within its competence' (which includes human rights matters) and it 'may call, in accordance with the rules prescribed by the United Nations, international conferences on matters falling within its competence'. Utilising these powers, the Council has prepared draft conventions relating to a number of human rights issues and convened a number of human rights related conferences.

Working under the auspices of ECOSOC are a number of other UN human rights agencies such as the UN Commission on the Status of Women, which is a functional commission and a principal global policy-making body dedicated exclusively to gender equality and the advancement of women. It meets every year and representatives of Member States gather in New York to evaluate progress on gender equality, identify challenges, set global standards and formulate concrete policies to promote gender equality and women's empowerment worldwide. It was established by ECOSOC through resolution 11 (II) of 21 June 1946 with the aim of preparing recommendations and reports to ECOSOC on promoting women's rights in political, economic, civil, social and educational fields.

The mandate of this Commission was expanded in 1987 by ECOSOC to include the functions of promoting the objectives of equality, development and peace, monitoring the implementation of measures for the advancement of women, and reviewing and appraising progress made at the national, sub-regional, regional and global levels. Following the 1995 Fourth World Conference on Women held in Beijing, the General Assembly mandated the Commission to integrate into its programme a follow-up process to the Conference. There are 45 member States of the United Nations which serve as members of the Commission at any one time and are elected by the Economic and Social Council for a period of 4 years on the basis of equitable geographical distribution: 13 members from Africa; 11 from Asia; 9 from Latin America and the Caribbean; 8 from Western Europe and other States and 4 from Eastern Europe.

7.6 The role of the Security Council

As the name itself suggests, the Security Council was established as a principal organ of the UN to deal primarily with matters of international peace and security. However, since the Charter itself has established a link between the enjoyment of human rights by all persons without any discrimination of any kind and international security, the Security Council has had a role, direct and indirect, to play in the promotion and protection of human rights. It is not only the Charter of the UN but also other treaties that grant some powers to the Council; the Rome Statute establishing the International Criminal Court is an example. Under the Rome Statute it is the Security Council that has the powers to refer matters concerning crimes against humanity to the International Criminal Court if the State in which such crimes have been committed is not a party to the Rome Statute. Having said this, the measures taken by the Security Council have largely been preventive.

What makes the Security Council more powerful than the General Assembly though is that under Article 24 of the Charter, UN Members have conferred on the Security Council primary responsibility for the maintenance of international peace and security, and agree that in carrying out its duties under this responsibility the Security Council acts on their behalf. Furthermore, under Article 25 the members of the organisation have agreed to accept and carry out the decisions of the Security Council in accordance with the Charter.[7] Since the Security Council has to carry out the task ascribed to it in Article 24 'in accordance with the Purposes and Principles of the United Nations', the Security Council is required to pay attention to human rights principles embodied in the principles and purposes of the organisation.

What is interesting is that in the absence of a definition in the Charter of the term 'international peace and security' it is for the Security Council to decide what is meant by the 'maintenance of international peace and security' and what constitutes 'a breach or threat' to international peace and security which will then enable it to take Chapter VII measures, including enforcement measures or the use of force. Under Article 39 of the UN Charter, the Security Council has the right to determine the existence of any threat to the peace, breach of

7 See generally about the competence of the Security Council, Surya P. Subedi, 'The Doctrine of Objective Regimes in International Law and the Competence of the UN Security Council to Impose Territorial or Peace Settlements on States' (1994) Vol. 37, *German Yearbook of International Law*, 162–205.

the peace, or act of aggression and to make recommendations, or decide what measures should be taken in accordance with Article 41 (which provides for non-forcible measures such as economic or diplomatic sanctions) and Article 42 (which provides for forcible measure or the use of force), to maintain or restore international peace and security.

Accordingly, the role of the Security Council is in preventing human rights violations of a bigger scale which pose a threat to the maintenance of international peace and security. Therefore, a gross and systemic pattern of violation of human rights of the individuals or groups of individuals, including minority groups or indigenous communities, in a State by the government of that State or by the government of another State may entitle the Security Council to take measures including the Chapter VII measures. For instance, the Security Council authorised the NATO countries on 17 March 2011 to use force in Libya under Resolution 1973 (S/RES/1973 (2011)) in the face of mounting humanitarian disaster and massive violation of human rights. The Council also adopted a resolution on 22 February 2014 (S/RES/2139 (2014)) on Syria condemning violations of human rights and international humanitarian law committed by the Syrian Government and non-State actors such as Al-Qaida.

This is because a gross and systemic pattern of violation of human rights may be interpreted as constituting a threat to or breach of international peace and security because of the wider impact of such violations on the international community. Human rights violations are often the root causes of armed conflict and internal uprising and the cross-border flow of refugees resulting from internal strife and international armed conflict lead to instability. Thus, the measures that the Security Council can take are the ultimate sanctions available against certain violations of human rights, albeit the threshold that has to be reached to trigger such a measure by the Security Council is normally a very high one. An example of this is the UN Security Council measures against the oppressive regime of Colonel Gaddafi in Libya in 2011.[8] Another example of Security Council intervention to protect a population is the adoption of resolution 688 of 1991 which allowed for the creation of 'safe havens' in Iraq to protect the Kurdish population from the repression of Saddam Hussein's regime in the aftermath of the first Gulf War.[9]

8 UN Security Council Resolution 1973 (2011), 17 March 2011 which expressed 'grave concern at the deteriorating situation, the escalation of violence, and the heavy civilian casualties', and reiterated 'the responsibility of the Libyan authorities to protect the Libyan Population' as stated in earlier resolutions, ultimately provided for the establishment of a no-fly zone, thereby banning all flights in the Libyan airspace save for those with a solely humanitarian purpose. This included authorising member states 'to take all necessary measures to enforce compliance with the ban on flights'.

9 See generally, Surya P. Subedi, 'The Legal Competence of the International Community to Create "Safe Havens" in "Zones of Turmoil"' (1999) Vol. 12 (1), *Journal of Refugee Studies*, March, 23–35.

As summarised by Oberleitner, the Security Council is today prepared to act in favour of human rights in at least the following five important areas: where it considers human rights violations to pose a threat to international peace and security; in integrating human rights components in peace operations; using human rights language to support democratisation; denouncing violations of international humanitarian law and protecting civilian victims of armed conflict, and holding perpetrators of human rights violations accountable by setting up international tribunals.[10]

Indeed, in exercise of its powers, functions and responsibilities under the Charter of and especially Chapter VII, the Security Council has established or facilitated the establishment of a number of international criminal tribunals and courts to bring to justice those accused of committing atrocities. They are as follows:

- International Criminal Tribunal for the former Yugoslavia (ICTY)
- International Criminal Tribunal for Rwanda (ICTR)
- Special Court for Sierra Leone
- Extraordinary Chambers in the Court of Cambodia (ECCC), and
- Special Tribunal for Lebanon[11]

Although these tribunals have been established in response to violations of international humanitarian law, war crimes and crimes against humanity, the allegations of violations of international humanitarian law have included gross or systematic violations of international human rights law. In essence, international humanitarian law is one branch of the international law of human rights. Although the former is older than the latter, the latter provides the basis for the former. Some of these tribunals were preceded by the United Nations commissions of inquiry or fact-finding missions, or commissions of experts appointed by the Security Council itself or by other UN organs or agencies, in response to the violations of international human rights law and humanitarian law. For instance, reports about the massacre of thousands of civilians, rape and torture in detention camps within the troubled former Yugoslavia moved the UN in late 1992 to establish a Commission of Experts to examine the situation on the ground.

In its report, that Commission documented horrific crimes and provided the UN with evidence of grave breaches of the Geneva Conventions and other violations of international humanitarian law. These findings eventually led the Security Council to decide, acting under Chapter VII, that it would establish

10 Gerd Oberleitner, *Global Human Rights Institutions: Between Remedy and Ritual* (Polity Press, 2007) 141.

11 See http://www.icty.org/, http://www.unictr.org/, http://www.haguejusticeportal.net/index.php?id=6413, http://www.eccc.gov.kh/en, and http://www.stl-tsl.org/ respectively (accessed 15 July 2014).

an international tribunal to bring to justice persons responsible for these crimes in order to stop the violence and safeguard international peace and security. Thus, by establishing a link between the maintenance of 'international peace and security' and violations of international humanitarian law the Security Council established the International Criminal Tribunal for the former Yugoslavia (the ICTY), on 25 May 1993.[12]

There have been other occasions during which the Security Council has received reports from the UN Special Rapporteurs for human rights or from the Special Representatives of the Secretary General on certain human rights issues and interacted with them. The Security Council has also appointed on a few occasions commissions of experts to investigate violations of human rights in a given State where the situation has been grave and warranting action from the Security Council itself. Exercising the powers given to it under the Rome Statute establishing the International Criminal Court (ICC), the Security Council has decided on occasion to refer matters to the ICC. An example of such an occurrence is the decision of 26 February 2011, asking the prosecutor of the International Criminal Court to probe the Libyan crisis. Prior to referring such a matter to the Prosecutor of the Court, the Security Council would be expected to base its recommendation either on a commission of inquiry, a commission of experts or a fact-finding mission appointed by the Security Council itself to examine the situation, or on the recommendations of the Human Rights Council or the High Commissioner for Human Rights or various human rights treaty bodies.

However, since the Security Council is a political body it lacks the powers to protect and enforce human rights of individuals. It can prevent mass scale human rights violations, but cannot provide any remedy to victims of such violations. The main weakness of the Security Council is the veto power held by its five permanent members, China, France, Russia, United Kingdom and the United States. It is mainly due to this veto power that the Council has been rendered helpless even in the face of mounting credible mass scale violations of human rights and humanitarian law in countries such as Syria and North Korea.

In spite of the call of the UN High Commissioner for Human Rights and the Human Rights Council itself that the matters relating to Syria and North Korea be referred to the International Criminal Court, the Security Council has not done this. For instance, speaking at the UN General Assembly, the then UN High Commissioner for Human Rights encouraged the Security Council to refer the situation to the International Criminal Court.[13] The then High Commissioner subsequently reiterated her belief that on the basis of evidence

12 Security Council Resolution 827, 25 May 1993, S/RES/827 (1993).

13 'States must "act now" to protect Syrian population, Pillay tells the General Assembly', News Release of the OHCHR of 13 February 2012, http://www.ohchr.org/EN/NewsEvents/Pages/DisplayNews.aspx?LangID=E&NewsID=11820 (accessed 11 July 2014).

gathered from various credible sources, crimes against humanity and war crimes had been, and continued to be, committed in Syria. She went on to add that: 'Those who are committing them should not believe that they will escape justice. The world does not forget or forgive crimes like these.'[14]

The High Commissioner also called for the situation in North Korea to be referred to the International Criminal Court following the publication of a report by a commission of inquiry led by Justice Michael Kirby[15] documenting 'systematic, widespread and gross' human rights violations in the country.[16] But these calls were limited to mere calls and no concrete action was followed partly due to China, a permanent member of the Security Council with veto power, stating that it rejected the report terming it 'unreasonable criticism' of North Korea.[17] However, the General Assembly took up the matter and passed a resolution in December 2014 calling on the Security Council to refer the matter to the International Criminal Court, putting more pressure on China and other reluctant states such as Russia.[18]

Finally, the Security Council also receives reports from Special Representatives of the Secretary General for countries going through a difficult period. Many such Special Representatives are heads of UN political, peace-making or peace-keeping missions in the country concerned and their reports cover not only

14 'Pillay warns of consequences under international law as Syria conflict escalates' New Release of the OHCHR of 27 July 2012, http://www.unog.ch/80256EDD006B9C2E/%28httpNewsByYear_en%29/75E30E0DB7C00120C1257A48002CFFB6?OpenDocument (accessed 11 July 2014).

15 'Report of the commission of inquiry on human rights in the Democratic People's Republic of Korea', UN Doc. A/HRC/25/63, of 7 February 2014, http://www.ohchr.org/en/hrbodies/hrc/coidprk/pages/commissioninquiryonhrindprk.aspx (accessed 11 July 2012).

16 'Pillay calls for urgent action on "historic" DPRK report', News Release, OHCHR, Geneva, 18 February 2014, http://www.ohchr.org/EN/NewsEvents/Pages/DisplayNews.aspx?NewsID=14258& (accessed 11 July 2014).

17 'China rejects "unfair criticism" in North Korea report', BBC News: http://www.bbc.co.uk/news/world-asia-26242278, 18 February 2014 (accessed on 9 June 2014).

18 The resolution was passed by 116 votes to 20, with more than 50 abstentions. This resolution was adopted upon the recommendation of the Third Committee of 14 November 2014. A/C.3/69/L.28/Rev.1 of 14 November 2014. Following a report by a commission of inquiry led by Justice Michael Kirby (A/HRC/25/63) documenting the systematic, widespread and grave violations of human rights in North Korea, the General Assembly decided to 'submit the report of the commission of inquiry to the Security Council, and encourages the Council to consider the relevant conclusions and recommendations of the commission and take appropriate action to ensure accountability, including through consideration of referral of the situation in the Democratic People's Republic of Korea to the International Criminal Court and consideration of the scope for effective targeted sanctions against those who appear to be most responsible for acts that the commission has said may constitute crimes against humanity'. See also 'UN General Assembly seeks North Korea ICC charges' BBC News: Asia, http://www.bbc.co.uk/news/world-asia-30540379 (accessed on 19 December 2014).

political and security matters but also the situation of both human rights and humanitarian law on the basis of which the Security Council may take appropriate measures, including those under either Chapter VI or VII of the Charter. Thus, the Security Council has played and can play an important role, direct or indirect, in the protection of human rights.

7.7 The role of the Secretary General

As the chief administrative officer (or CEO in common parlance) of the UN Secretariat, which is a principal organ of the UN, the Secretary General performs a number of functions designed to protect and promote human rights. As the CEO of the UN, the Secretary General can do a great deal to promote and protect human rights internationally and especially when it comes to arresting a situation of an urgent nature. How effective the Secretary General is depends heavily on their leadership qualities, intellectual ability, the ability to command respect from different stakeholders and their own personal inclination. Two of the former Secretaries General, Dr Boutros Boutros-Ghali and Mr Kofi Annan, have been particularly effective and proactive and their achievements have been far reaching. In addition to the personal initiatives the Secretary General may take, they have a number of functions, powers and responsibilities for the protection and promotion of human rights under the UN Charter and other resolutions of the principal organs of the UN and other subsidiary bodies.

To begin with, it is the Secretary General who appoints the UN High Commissioner for Human Rights as the principal human rights official within the UN system.[19] In addition, in response to a variety of UN organs such as the General Assembly, human rights treaty bodies, and other UN human rights agencies the Secretary General has appointed a number of Special Representatives over a long period of time either to carry out in-depth studies of a human rights theme or issue, or of the situation of human rights in a given State concerned. For instance, when the General Assembly requested the Secretary General to conduct an in-depth study on the question of violence against children, following a recommendation of the Committee on the Rights of the Child in 2001, the Secretary General appointed an independent expert to lead the study.[20] Following the report of this independent expert, in which it was recommended that there should be an appointment of a Special Representative of the Secretary General on Violence against Children, the Secretary General appointed his Special Representative as a global independent advocate in favour of the prevention and elimination of all forms of violence against children.[21]

19 For a discussion of the appointment procedure in relation to the position of High Commissioner for Human Rights, see Chapter 5.
20 General Assembly Resolution 56/138, 19 December 2001.
21 See http://srsg.violenceagainstchildren.org/ (accessed 15 July 2014).

There have been a number of other Special Representatives of the Secretary General appointed over the years. Examples include the Special Representatives for: Children and Armed Conflict; on the Issue of Human Rights and Transnational Corporations and other Business Enterprises; on the Human Rights for Internally Displaced Persons; on the Human Rights for Internally Displaced Persons; and on Domestic Violence against Women. In addition, the Secretary General has appointed his Special Representatives for countries experiencing significant challenges relating to internal conflict, rule of law, internal stability, and so on. Such countries include, for example, Afghanistan, Cambodia, Sierra Leone, Sudan, East Timor, and even a whole region such as West Africa.[22]

While the appointment of many of such Special Representatives for a country concerned has been purely political to head UN political, peace-making or peace-keeping missions in the country concerned, some others, including those for specific countries, have been appointed for monitoring human rights situations or human rights fact-finding activities. The Special Representatives for human rights, who act as bridge builders and catalysts for action in the area concerned, report directly to the Secretary General. Many of them also report annually to the Human Rights Council, the General Assembly and occasionally to the Security Council and issue thematic reports on key areas of concern which contribute to standard setting in the area concerned. The Special Representatives therefore often communicate across a number of UN institutions as part of their role.

Working within the framework of the UN Secretariat and assisting the Secretary General and other UN agencies on legal matters, including human rights matters, is the Office of Legal Affairs headed by an Under-Secretary General for Legal Affairs and the Legal Counsel. Its activities include providing a unified central legal service for the Secretariat and the principal and other organs of the United Nations, and contributing to the progressive development and codification of international public law.

Mention should also be made of the United Nations Development Programme (UNDP) with offices in some 177 countries and territories 'offering global perspective and local insight to help empower lives and build resilient nations'.[23] Its activities include helping countries build and share solutions to the challenges of democratic governance by engaging in the promotion of human rights, rule of law, and good governance. It is the UNDP Resident Representative who normally also functions as the Resident Coordinator of development activities for all UN agencies present in the country concerned, including any offices of the UN High Commissioner for Human Rights. The

22 For a full list of the UN Secretary General's special and personal representatives, envoys and advisers, see http://www.un.org/sg/srsg/africa.shtml (accessed 23 October 2014).

23 See http://www.undp.org/content/undp/en/home/operations/about_us.html (accessed 15 July 2014)

national UNDP office also provides support to the UN special procedure mandate holders and field visits by members of the UN human rights treaty bodies to the countries concerned.

7.8 UN High Commissioner for Refugees

The Office of the United Nations High Commissioner for Refugees (UNHCR) has a vital role to play in the protection of refugees. Through its resolution 319 (IV), of 3 December 1949, the UN General Assembly decided to establish a High Commissioner's Office for Refugees as of 1 January 1951 with a 3-year mandate to complete its work and then disband. The Statute of this agency was adopted by the General Assembly on 14 December 1950.[24] The following year, the United Nations Convention Relating to the Status of Refugees – the legal foundation of helping refugees and the basic statute guiding UNHCR's work – was adopted.

The UNHCR is mandated to lead and coordinate international action to protect refugees and resolve refugee problems worldwide. The primary purpose of this UN body is to safeguard the rights and well-being of refugees and to ensure that everyone in need can exercise the right to seek asylum and find safe refuge in another State, with the option to return home voluntarily, integrate locally or to resettle in a third country. It is governed by the General Assembly and ECOSOC and its mandate is defined by the 1950 UNHCR Statute. By a resolution of 2003 the General Assembly extended the organisation's mandate 'until the refugee problem is solved.' The High Commissioner reports annually to ECOSOC and the General Assembly on the work of UNHCR.

The work of UNHCR consists of providing assistance to refugees, internally displaced persons and asylum seekers by intervening in situations of emergency to provide relief. Using the 1951 Geneva Refugee Convention as its major tool, the UNHCR strives to ensure the international protection of 31.7 million uprooted people worldwide. According to the latest figures, the UNHCR now deals with 33.9 million people of concern: 14.7 million internally displaced people, 10.5 million refugees, 3.1 million returnees, 3.5 million stateless people, more than 837,000 asylum seekers and more than 1.3 other persons of concern.[25]

Advocacy is a key element in its activities, seeking to influence governments and other decision-makers, non-governmental partners and the public at large to adopt practices ensuring the protection of those of concern to the UNHCR. Although it is not a treaty-body, it promotes refugee protection by monitoring the asylum practice of States and seeks to advise and assist them to achieve

24 'Statute of the Office of the United Nations High Commissioner for Refugees', General Assembly Resolution 428(V) 1950, annex.

25 History of UNHCR: http://www.unhcr.org/pages/49c3646cbc.html (accessed 10 August 2012).

conformity with international standards under its supervisory responsibility.[26] It also promotes refugee protection by encouraging and providing support for accession to relevant conventions, such as the 1951 Convention relating to the Status of Refugees and its 1967 Protocol, the 1954 Convention relating to the Status of Stateless Persons, and the 1961 Convention on the Reduction of Statelessness. In addition, the UNHCR has produced a Handbook for Determining Refugee Status and Guidelines on International Protection containing a number of guidelines and procedural standards.[27]

The High Commissioner for Refugees does provide immediate relief and interim protection to refugees, but is not designed to protect their rights as victims of human rights violations as such in the country of their origin or the country where they reside since this UN agency has no adjudicatory power or the power to provide effective legal remedy. It is more of a humanitarian organisation designed to provide humanitarian relief rather than a human rights organisation.

7.9 The role of the International Court of Justice

Although the International Court of Justice (the Court), the principal judicial organ of the UN, is not an international human rights court and individuals have no *locus standi* before this Court, it has on occasion delivered judgments touching upon or relating to human rights and humanitarian law matters designed to bring violators of such laws to justice. It would be well within its jurisdiction to hear a matter relating to human rights and/or humanitarian law if two or more States decided to refer a dispute to this world Court. Article 36 of the Statute of the Court states that the jurisdiction of the Court 'comprises all cases which the parties refer to it and all matters specifically provided for in the Charter of the United Nations or in treaties and conventions in force'.

Since the respect of fundamental rights and freedoms are the matters specifically provided in the Charter of the UN and several human rights treaties,

26 This is as provided in paragraph 8 of the UNHCR's Statute, and in conjunction with Article 35 of the 1951 Convention relating to the status of refugees and Article II of its 1967 Protocol.

27 A list of such documents is available at: http://www.unhcr.org/pages/49c3646cce.html (accessed 10 August 2012), and includes Guidelines on International Protection No. 7: The Application of Article 1A(2) of the 1951 Convention and/or 1967 Protocol Relating to the Status of Refugees to Victims of Trafficking and Persons at Risk of Being Trafficked; Procedural Standards for Refugee Status Determination under UNHCR's Mandate; Guidelines on International Protection No. 6: Religion-Based Refugee Claims under Article 1A(2) of the 1951 Convention and/or the 1967 Protocol relating to the Status of Refugees; Guidelines on International Protection No. 5: Application of the Exclusion Clauses: Article 1F of the 1951 Convention relating to the Status of Refugees; and Guidelines on International Protection No. 4: 'Internal Flight or Relocation Alternative' within the context of Article 1A(2) of the 1951 Convention and/or 1967 Protocol relating to the Status of Refugees.

the Court has competence to adjudicate upon human rights matters if they become a point of dispute between States or the States themselves refer the matter to the Court. Since, for example, the human rights treaty bodies do not have, strictly speaking, the competence to interpret the relevant treaties (although it is within their practice to issue General Comments providing general guidance), matters relating to the legal interpretation of such treaties can always be referred to the International Court of Justice.

Similarly, under Article 36(2) of the Statute of the International Court of Justice, States parties to the Statute may at any time declare they recognize as compulsory *ipso facto* and without special agreement, in relation to any other State accepting the same obligation, the jurisdiction of the Court in all legal disputes concerning, *inter alia*, the interpretation of a treaty or any question of international law. Thus, since human rights law related questions fall under both of the above categories (interpretation of a treaty/question of international law), disputes between states relating to such matters can be referred to the Court by States making such a declaration. It is also possible for any of the UN organs or other UN specialised agencies, with authorisation from the General Assembly, to ask the Court to render its advisory opinion on a human rights matter.

The Court has made a number of pronouncements relating to property rights and the right to the fair and equitable treatment of aliens in international law in relation to cases of protection of foreign investors brought on behalf of foreign investors to the Court by States of their nationality.[28] For instance, in the *Barcelona Traction* case the Court suggested that 'basic rights of the human person' create obligations *erga omnes*:

> 33. When a State admits into its territory foreign investments or foreign nationals, whether natural or juristic persons, it is bound to extend to them the protection of the law and assumes obligations concerning the treatment to be afforded them. These obligations, however, are neither absolute nor unqualified. In particular, an essential distinction should be drawn between the obligations of a State towards the international community as a whole, and those arising vis-à-vis another State in the field of diplomatic protection. By their very nature the former are the concern of all States. In view of the importance of the rights involved, all States can be held to have a legal interest in their protection; they are obligations *erga omnes*.

28 See generally, R. Dolzer and C. Schreuer, *Principles of International Investment Law* (Oxford University Press, 2012); C. McLachlan *et al.*, *International Investment Arbitration: Substantive Principles* (Oxford University Press, 2007); S. Montt, *State Liability in Investment Treaty Arbitration: Global Constitutional and Administrative Law in the BIT Generation* (Hart Publishing, 2011), P. Muchlinski *et al.*, *The Oxford Handbook of International Investment Law* (Oxford University Press, 2008); Surya P. Subedi, *International Investment Law: Reconciling Policy and Principle* (Hart Publishing, 3rd edition, 2016).

> 34. Such obligations derive, for example, in contemporary international law, from the outlawing of acts of aggression, and of genocide, as also from the principles and rules concerning the basic rights of the human person, including protection from slavery and racial discrimination. Some of the corresponding rights of protection have entered into the body of general international law . . . ; others are conferred by international instruments of a universal or quasi-universal character.[29]

These are statements that carry far-reaching implications. The characterisation of the 'basic rights of the human person' as obligations *erga omnes* by the Court has led, as articulated by Meron, to 'a growing acceptance that . . . all States have a legitimate interest in and the right to protest against significant human rights violations wherever they may occur, regardless of the nationality of the victims'.[30] The above cited statements of the Court can also be relied upon to argue that the right of other States to express their concern about the violations of basic human rights which are of *erga omnes* character can no longer be included in the definition of the terms 'matters which are essentially within the domestic jurisdiction of any State' in Article 2(7) of the Charter which forbids a State from intervening in the internal affairs of another State.

A case more to the point (and not related to the protection of foreign investment) that was brought before the Court was a dispute between the Republic of Georgia and the Russian Federation in which Georgia alleged that the Russian Federation had violated its obligations under the 1965 International Convention on the Elimination of All Forms of Racial Discrimination (CERD) and sought to ensure that the individual rights under CERD of all persons on the territory of Georgia were fully respected and protected.[31] Indeed, Article 22 of CERD confers jurisdiction, under narrowly defined conditions, on the International Court of Justice to resolve disputes between the States parties. However, the ICJ held in its judgment on preliminary objections of 1 April 2011 that it had no jurisdiction to adjudicate on this case and it reached this conclusion after evaluation that the conditions under which the Court could entertain the application under Article 22 of CERD had not been fulfilled.[32]

In another case, Belgium brought before the Court a dispute with Senegal alleging the latter's failure to act on its obligation to punish crimes under

29 Barcelona Traction, Light and Power Company, Limited (Belgium v. Spain), 1970 ICJ Reports 3.

30 Theodor Meron, 'On a Hierarchy of International Human Rights' 80 *AJIL* (1986), 1, at p.11.

31 Case Concerning Application of the International Convention on the Elimination of All Forms of Racial Discrimination (Georgia v. Russian Federation) Preliminary Objections, Judgment, 1 April 2011, see: http://www.icj-cij.org/docket/files/140/16398.pdf (accessed 15 July 2014).

32 For more on this matter, see Phoebe Okowa, 'The International Court of Justice and the Georgia/Russia Dispute', *Human Rights Law Review* 11:4(2011), 739–57.

international humanitarian law as alleged against the former President of Chad, Mr. H. Habré, living in Dakar, Senegal.[33] Belgium took the view that, under international law which bound the two States, Senegal was obliged to prosecute Mr. H. Habré for the acts alleged against him, failing his extradition to Belgium. The Court agreed with Belgium in its judgment delivered on 22 July 2012. The Court held unanimously that it had jurisdiction to entertain the dispute between the Parties concerning the interpretation and application of Article 6, paragraph 2, and Article 7, paragraph 1, of the United Nations Convention against Torture and Other Cruel, Inhuman or Degrading Treatment or Punishment of 10 December 1984 and that the Republic of Senegal must, without further delay, submit the case of Mr. H. Habré to its competent authorities for the purpose of prosecution, if it does not extradite him.

In another case between the Republic of Guinea and the Democratic Republic of the Congo (DRC) referred to the Court in December 1998, Guinea alleged that the DRC had violated certain major principles of international law in respect of a Guinean national, Mr. Diallo Ahmadou Sadio.[34] These were, namely, the principle that foreign nationals should be treated in accordance with a minimum standard of civilisation, the obligation to respect the freedom and property of foreign nationals, and the right of foreign nationals accused of an offence to a fair trial on adversarial principles by an impartial court. In its judgment of 30 November 2010 the Court held unanimously that 'in respect of the circumstances in which Mr. Diallo was expelled from Congolese territory on 31 January 1996, the Democratic Republic of the Congo (DRC) violated Article 13 of the International Covenant on Civil and Political Rights and Article 12, paragraph 4, of the African Charter on Human and Peoples' Rights'.

The Court also unanimously held that 'in respect of the circumstances in which Mr. Diallo was arrested and detained in 1995–1996 with a view to his expulsion, the Democratic Republic of the Congo violated Article 9, paragraphs 1 and 2, of the International Covenant on Civil and Political Rights and Article 6 of the African Charter on Human and Peoples' Rights'. What is interesting is that for the first time since the Corfu Channel case of 1949 and for the first time ever in a case concerning diplomatic protection the ICJ had awarded damages for violation of a rule of international law.[35]

33 For documents relating to this case, see http://www.icj-cij.org/docket/index.php?p1=3&p2=3&case=144 (accessed 15 July 2014).

34 For documents relating to this case, see http://www.icj-cij.org/docket/index.php?p1=3&p2=3&k=7a&case=103&code=gc&p3=4 (accessed 15 July 2014).

35 See Republic of Guinea v. Democratic Republic of the Congo, Compensation owed by the Democratic Republic of the Congo to the Republic of Guinea, http://www.icj-cij.org/docket/files/103/17044.pdf accessed 15 July 2014, see also See Mads Andenas, 'International Decisions: Ahmadou Sadio Diallo', *American Journal of International Law*, Vol. 107, No. 1(January 2013), pp.178–83.

The predecessor of the ICJ, the Permanent Court of International Justice (PCIJ) had also made some important pronouncements which were helpful in establishing the obligations of States with respect to human rights. In its Advisory Opinion in a case concerning *Exchange of Greek and Turkish Populations* the PCIJ held that 'a State which has contracted valid international obligations is bound to make in its legislation such modifications as may be necessary to ensure the fulfilment of the obligations undertaken'.[36] Here the PCIJ was stating that the rule of law principle requires compliance by the State with its obligations in international law as in national law. Thus, by implication the court was of the view that international human rights treaties must be adhered to by the States parties to them.

7.10 The role of the International Criminal Court and other tribunals

The International Criminal Court (ICC) has an important role in bringing to justice violators of international humanitarian law and, in some of the more serious cases, human rights law. There are some who argue that the threat of prosecution before such courts has frustrated the attempts to bring about a negotiated settlement to many problems around the globe and instilled determination in dictators to fight out to the end rather than meet the fate met by people like Slobodan Milosevic or Charles Taylor.[37] Although the ICC is not part of the UN system as such (nor indeed is it a court created to entertain or adjudicate on human rights matters) it was the United Nations Diplomatic Conference of Plenipotentiaries on the Establishment of an International Criminal Court that adopted the Rome Statute establishing the ICC. In addition, following the adoption of the Rome Statute, it was the UN that convened the Preparatory Commission for the International Criminal Court. Therefore, the Court is the result of the endeavours of the UN system.

Unlike other *ad hoc* international criminal courts and tribunals such as the International Criminal Tribunal for the former Yugoslavia (ICTY), the International Criminal Tribunal for Rwanda (ICTR), the Special Court for Sierra Leone or the Special Tribunal for Lebanon, the ICC is a permanent court. It is governed by the Rome Statute which was adopted by 120 States on 17 July 1998 to help end impunity for the perpetrators of the most serious crimes

36 Exchange of Greek and Turkish Populations, PCIJ, 21 February 1925, 20, http://www.icj-cij.org/pcij/serie_B/B_10/01_Echange_des_populations_grecques_et_turques_Avis_consultatif.pdf (accessed 23 October 2014).

37 Douglas Murray, 'Dictating terms: What has this era of "international justice" done to deter genocide?' *The Spectator* (London), 25 August 2012, 12, http://www.spectator.co.uk/features/123489/dictating-terms/ (accessed 23 October 2014).

of concern to the international community.[38] The International Criminal Court tries persons accused of the most serious crimes of international concern, namely genocide, crimes against humanity and war crimes. However, it is a court of last resort. This is because it will not act if a case is investigated or prosecuted by a national judicial institution unless the national proceedings are not genuine. It has jurisdiction over individuals accused of the gravest of the crimes defined in the Rome Statute. Article 5 of the Statute provides that:

> The jurisdiction of the Court shall be limited to the most serious crimes of concern to the international community as a whole. The Court has jurisdiction in accordance with this Statute with respect to the following crimes:
> (a) The crime of genocide;
> (b) Crimes against humanity;
> (c) War crimes;
> (d) The crime of aggression.

However, this is a court with limited powers. It can entertain cases only if the State in question has ratified the Rome Statute, and States such as Syria, Iran, North Korea, Sudan, and Saudi Arabia have not. Nor have bigger countries such as China, India, Russia and the US. The Security Council has the powers to refer any matter relating to the crimes included in Article 5, above, but the Security Council is inherently politicised and as a result is often prevented from referring the matters to the ICC due to the exercise of veto power by one of the permanent five.[39] It is ironic that with the exception of Great Britain and France, the very other three countries which have a permanent seat in the Security Council and have the powers to refer to the Court have not ratified the Rome Statute. They thus lack the legitimacy required to exercise such power. Further, the Court has been criticised for being biased against Africa since all the cases tried by the Court have been against African individuals for violating human rights and humanitarian law when in a position of authority.[40] Although cases in Afghanistan, Colombia, Georgia, Honduras and Iraq seem to be under investigation by the prosecutors of the Court, no non-African has appeared before the Court facing charges of crimes against humanity.

38 The Rome Statute entered into force on 1 July 2002 after ratification by 60 countries and the International Criminal Court celebrated its 10th anniversary in the first week of July 2012. As of 23 October 2014, a total of 122 States had become a party to the Rome Statute, http://www.icc-cpi.int/en_menus/asp/states%20parties/Pages/the%20states%20parties%20to%20the%20rome%20statute.aspx (accessed 23 October 2014).

39 The five permanent members of the Security Council are China, France, the Russian Federation, the United Kingdom and the United States.

40 'International Justice: Nice idea, now make it work', *The Economist* (London), 6 December 2014, pp. 68–69.

The architecture of the ICC itself is not satisfactory enough to deal with the challenges of the multi-polar world of the twenty-first century. It is largely a state-centric or state-driven court. Individuals have no direct access to the Court. No matter how credible the evidence may be, ordinary people cannot sue the individuals in government or in other positions of public authority for committing crimes against humanity before the ICC. All ordinary people can do is to appeal to the prosecutor of the ICC to investigate such crimes and such appeals can often fall on deaf ears for a number of reasons including political considerations. It is not a satisfactory state of affairs for victims of gross and systemic violations of human rights and humanitarian law in States which are not a party to the Rome Statute to have to rely on the cooperation of States to have their rights protected and enforced, or to rely on political bodies such as the Security Council of the UN to have legal proceedings commenced against the perpetrators of gross violations of human rights. When states do not cooperate with the ICC, cases before it can collapse any time as exemplified by the collapse of a case against the President of Kenya[41] and suspension of investigation against the President of Sudan[42] in December 2014.

In essence, international humanitarian law is a branch of the international law of human rights. As noted above, although the former is older than the latter, the latter provides the basis for the former. For instance, the crimes included in Article 7(1) of the Rome Statute are those prohibited or regulated

41 Prosecutors at the International Criminal Court withdrew charges of crimes against humanity against Kenya's President Uhuru Kenyatta in December 2014. Kenyatta had been indicted in connection with post-election ethnic violence in 2007–08 resulting in the death of 1,200 people. The prosecutor's office said the government of Kenya had not cooperated with the prosecutors and refused to hand over evidence vital to the case. It said the evidence had 'not improved to such an extent that Mr Kenyatta's alleged criminal responsibility can be proven beyond reasonable doubt'. 'ICC drops Uhuru Kenyatta charges for Kenya ethnic violence', BBC News, 5 December 2014: http://www.bbc.co.uk/news/world-africa-30347019 (accessed 15 December 2014). Earlier in the week, the ICC had rejected a request from the prosecution for further adjournment of the trial in the case. See a Press Release of 3 December 2014 of the ICC: Kenyatta case: 'ICC Trial Chamber rejects request for further adjournment and directs the Prosecution to indicate either its withdrawal of charges or readiness to proceed to trial'; ICC-CPI-20141203-PR1071 Case: The Prosecutor v. Uhuru Muigai Kenyatta. http://www.icc-cpi.int/en_menus/icc/press%20and%20media/press%20releases/Pages/PR1071.aspx (accessed on 15 December 2014).

42 The prosecutors of the ICC decided to end their probe into allegations of war crimes in Darfur, Sudan also in December 2014. The ICC had charged Omar al-Bashir, the President of Sudan, in 2009 for crimes in the region dating back to 2003. Announcing the suspension on investigations, ICC chief prosecutor Fatou Bensouda blamed it on lack of action by the UN. She called for a 'dramatic shift' in the UN Security Council's approach, stating that inaction on the part of the Council was emboldening the perpetrators of war crimes in Darfur. See 'Sudan President Bashir hails "victory" over ICC charges', BBC News: Africa, 13 December 2014: http://www.bbc.co.uk/news/world-africa-30467167 (accessed 15 December 2014).

by both international humanitarian law and international law of human rights. They are as follows:

> 1. For the purpose of this Statute, 'crime against humanity' means any of the following acts when committed as part of a widespread or systematic attack directed against any civilian population, with knowledge of the attack:
> (a) Murder;
> (b) Extermination;
> (c) Enslavement;
> (d) Deportation or forcible transfer of population;
> (e) Imprisonment or other severe deprivation of physical liberty in violation of fundamental rules of international law;
> (f) Torture;
> (g) Rape, sexual slavery, enforced prostitution, forced pregnancy, enforced sterilization, or any other form of sexual violence of comparable gravity;
> (h) Persecution against any identifiable group or collectivity on political, racial, national, ethnic, cultural, religious, gender as defined in paragraph 3, or other grounds that are universally recognized as impermissible under international law, in connection with any act referred to in this paragraph or any crime within the jurisdiction of the Court;
> (i) Enforced disappearance of persons;
> (j) The crime of apartheid;
> (k) Other inhumane acts of a similar character intentionally causing great suffering, or serious injury to body or to mental or physical health.

Those who can be brought to justice before the ICC include those directly responsible for committing the crimes as well as others who may be liable for the crimes, for example by aiding, abetting or otherwise assisting in their commission. This can include military commanders or other superiors whose responsibility is defined in the Rome Statute. It should also be noted that the Court: (1) does not have universal jurisdiction, (2) its jurisdiction is limited to events taking place since 1 July 2002, when the Court was established, (3) if a State ratifies the Rome Statute after 1 July 2002, the Court only has jurisdiction after the Statute has entered into force for that State, and (4) the jurisdiction of the Court is limited by the principle of 'complementarity', according to which certain cases will be inadmissible even though the Court has jurisdiction if the matter has been, or is being, investigated or prosecuted by a State with jurisdiction. Any State party to the Rome Statute or the UN Security Council may refer situations of crimes within the jurisdiction of the Court to the Prosecutor. In addition, the Prosecutor may also begin an investigation on his or her own initiative on the basis of information received from a variety of sources.

As of 1 July 2012, the Court had 20 warrants of arrest issued, 16 cases were in its docket, and there were 7 ongoing investigations. By this date, three States Parties to the Rome Statute – Uganda, the Democratic Republic of the Congo and the Central African Republic – had referred situations occurring within their territories to the ICC, the Security Council had referred the situation in Darfur, Sudan, and the situation in Libya – both non-States Parties – to the ICC and the Office of the Prosecutor was conducting preliminary examinations in a number of situations including Afghanistan, Georgia, Guinea, Colombia, Honduras, Korea and Nigeria.

The *ad hoc* international criminal tribunals, the ICTY, ICTR, the Special Court for Sierra Leone, and the ECCC, known also as the Khmer Rouge Tribunal, have given a voice to victims by prosecuting those accused of grave human rights abuses during conflict in the countries concerned. Along with the ICC, these tribunals have played a role in holding violators responsible for war crimes, crimes against humanity and genocide, etc.

7.11 The role of the UN International Law Commission

Mention should also be made of the role of the UN International Law Commission in human rights law-making. The UN as an organisation, or the General Assembly as the most representative body, has no law-making powers as such. It is the member States of the organisation that make laws by adopting, signing, ratifying or acceding treaties and adopting declarations. Article 13(1) of the UN Charter confers on the General Assembly the more limited powers of study and recommendation in the following words: 'The General Assembly shall initiate studies and make recommendations for the purpose of: . . . encouraging the progressive development of international law and its codification.'

The General Assembly adopted resolution 94(I) during its very first session in December 1946 establishing the Committee on the Progressive Development of International Law and its Codification, which in turn adopted a report recommending the establishment of an international law commission setting forth provisions designed to serve as the basis for its statute. Accordingly, on 21 November 1947, the General Assembly adopted resolution 174(II), establishing the International Law Commission and approving its Statute. Article 1, paragraph 1, of the Statute provides that the 'Commission shall have for its object the promotion of the progressive development of international law and its codification'.

The International Law Commission meets in plenary session normally once a year for a number of weeks in Geneva primarily to consider the reports of Special Rapporteurs, working groups, the Drafting Committee, and the Planning Group, as well as any other matters that may require consideration by the International Law Commission as a whole. The role of the Special Rappporteur is crucial in the work of the International Law Commission since it is the Special Rapporteur who marks out and develops the topic, explains the state of the law and makes proposals for draft articles in the reports on the topic.[43]

The International Law Commission has a well-developed and systematic approach to law-making. Once the International Law Commission has completed its work on draft international treaties the General Assembly decides whether to adopt the draft treaty through a resolution or convene a separate diplomatic conference for this purpose.

The International Law Commission has not been regarded as a primary body for the making of recommendations relating to human rights treaties. Most of the international human rights treaties in existence today did not originate from this Commission, mainly because there was a separate specialist body for these purposes – the Commission on Human Rights working under the aegis of ECOSOC. Nonetheless the International Law Commission has performed an important role in the development of the law relating to a number of areas such as nationality, including statelessness; treatment of aliens; and right of asylum.

7.12 The role of the International Labour Organization

The International Labour Organization (ILO) is responsible for drawing up and overseeing international labour standards. It operates to formulate policies, develop international standards through international treaties and implement them with a view to promoting rights at work, encourage decent employment opportunities, enhance social protection and strengthen dialogue on work-related issues. It was established in 1919 as part of the Treaty of Versailles that ended World War I with a view to promoting the belief that universal and lasting peace can be accomplished only if it is based on social justice by setting international labour standards.

The constitution of the organisation was drafted in 1919 by the Labour Commission set up by the Peace Conference which resulted in the only tripartite organisation of its kind that brought together representatives of governments, employers and workers in its executive body. As stated in the Preamble to the ILO's Constitution, the High Contracting Parties were 'moved by sentiments of justice and humanity as well as by the desire to secure the permanent peace of the world'. The Preamble states:

1. Whereas universal and lasting peace can be established only if it is based upon social justice;
2. And whereas conditions of labour exist involving such injustice hardship and privation to large numbers of people as to produce unrest so great that

43 See for example, the most recent annual report of the International Law Commission, http://www.un.org/law/ilc/ (accessed 23 October 2014).

the peace and harmony of the world are imperilled; and an improvement of those conditions is urgently required;

3. Whereas also the failure of any nation to adopt humane conditions of labour is an obstacle in the way of other nations which desire to improve the conditions in their own countries.

The following are some of the areas in the preamble listed for improvement to achieve social justice.

1. Regulation of the hours of work including the establishment of a maximum working day and week;
2. Regulation of labour supply, prevention of unemployment and provision of an adequate living wage;
3. Protection of the worker against sickness, disease and injury arising out of his employment;
4. Protection of children, young persons and women;
5. Provision for old age and injury, protection of the interests of workers when employed in countries other than their own;
6. Recognition of the principle of equal remuneration for work of equal value;
7. Recognition of the principle of freedom of association;
8. Organization of vocational and technical education, and other measures.

Since its establishment the ILO has made an important contribution to the world of work. The ILO provides a brief account of some of its work; the first International Labour Conference held in Washington in October 1919 adopted six International Labour Conventions covering areas such as hours of work in industry, unemployment, maternity protection, night work for women, minimum age and night work for young persons in industry. Since then, a number of International Labour Conventions and Recommendations have been adopted and international labour standards have grown into a comprehensive system of instruments on work and social policy, supported by a supervisory system designed to address problems in their application at the national level.[44]

The organisation regularly examines the application of standards at the national level in its member States and points out areas where they could be better applied. In doing so, the organisation seeks to assist its members through social dialogue and technical assistance if there are any problems in the application of standards. The organisation has developed a number of mechanisms for supervising the application of Conventions and Recommendations in law and practice.

44 For further information relating to the ILO, its origins and history, see http://www.ilo.org/global/about-the-ilo/history/lang-en/index.htm (accessed 15 July 2014).

The ILO has it own system of supervision which involves, under Article 22 of the ILO's Constitution, an examination of periodic reports submitted by Member States on the measures that have been taken to implement the provisions of the ratified Conventions. Article 22 provides that:

> Each of the Members agrees to make an annual report to the International Labour Office on the measures which it has taken to give effect to the provisions of Conventions to which it is a party. These reports shall be made in such form and shall contain such particulars as the Governing Body may request.

Accordingly, this mechanism is based on examination by (1) The Committee of Experts on the Application of Conventions and Recommendations; (2) The International Labour Conference's Tripartite Committee on the Application of Conventions, and (3) Recommendations of reports on the application in law and practice of relevant ILO conventions sent by member States and on observations in this regard sent by workers' organisations and employers' organisations.

The ILO also has a special procedures mechanism which involves a representations procedure and a complaints procedure of general application, together with a special procedure for freedom of association, under Articles 24 and 25 of the ILO's Constitution. The Constitution of the ILO grants an industrial association of employers or of workers the right to present to the ILO Governing Body a representation against any member state which, in its view, 'has failed to secure in any respect the effective observance within its jurisdiction of any Convention to which it is a party'. This mechanism consists of the following three procedures concerning the submission of a representation or a complaint: (1) Procedure for representations on the application of ratified Conventions; (2) Procedure for complaints over the application of ratified Conventions; and (3) Special procedure for complaints regarding freedom of association. This ILO mechanism predates the UN mechanisms and is therefore one of the oldest international mechanisms designed to protect certain rights of workers and has largely been regarded as a mechanism which is more effective than many other treaty mechanisms.

7.13 The role of the World Health Organization

Although the World Health Organization (WHO) is not a human rights agency, it plays an important role in promoting health as a human right.[45] A rights based approach to health has now become an integral part of the

45 For further information on this aspect of the organization's work, see http://www.who.int/topics/human_rights/en/ (accessed 15 July 2014).

endeavours of many health and developmental organisations around the globe and the WHO is making its own contribution to realising this approach. The preamble of the constitution of the WHO conveys the message that the enjoyment of the highest attainable standard of health is one of the fundamental rights of every human being. This is one reason why the WHO has moved, especially in recent years, towards promoting and protecting the right to health. As summed up by Oberleitner, the WHO has identified 'three ways to do so: to apply a human rights-based approach in its own activities; to support governments in adopting and implementing a human rights-based approach to health development; and to advocate the right to health in international law development processes.'[46]

7.14 Conclusions

As seen in the preceding paragraphs, the role of these various Charter-based and associated UN bodies is limited in scope in protecting human rights. The main purpose of these bodies is not the protection of human rights. While their role is important in promoting human rights when it comes to the protection of human rights, their role is auxiliary or ancillary. It is ironic that none of the principal organs of the UN is devoted to the third pillar of the organisation, that is, human rights. The Security Council does have the power to take measures under Chapter VII of the Charter to prevent serious cases of human rights violations and protect people from atrocities; it has proven ineffective in most of the cases due to its political nature, politicisation of its work and the exercise of the veto power by one or two of the P5.

Whilst the ICC has jurisdiction in cases relating to human rights and humanitarian law, this is limited and applicable only to some of the most serious crimes. Additionally, many of the States where such crimes have taken place have not ratified the Rome Statute, in the absence of which the Court cannot exercise its jurisdiction over the people in those States. The role of the International Court of Justice too is limited since it is accessible only by States and can exercise jurisdiction only when States concerned have made a declaration accepting the jurisdiction of the Court. Thus, in spite of having a plethora of Charter-based and associated bodies, in the face of on-going human rights violations and increasing humanitarian disaster, many such mechanisms remain ineffective and/or are paralysed by political wrangling and disagreement. Many of these bodies such as the General Assembly and the ECOSOC adopt a large number of reports and resolutions of recommendatory character generating a mountain of paper work, but in reality none of them is well equipped to protect human rights on the ground.

46 Gerd Oberleitner, *Global Human Rights Institutions: Between Remedy and Ritual* (Polity Press, 2007) 126, citing a working paper published by the WHO in 2005: 'Working Paper on Health and Human Rights Activities within WHO', 2005.

8 Reform of the UN human rights system and the judicialisation of human rights at the international level

8.1 Introduction

Having carried out an analysis of the effectiveness of the UN human rights institutions in the preceding chapters and coming to the conclusion that most of these mechanisms have been *effective in promoting* human rights but *not effective in protecting* human rights, this chapter seeks to argue the case for the judicialisation of human rights at the international level. In doing so, it pulls together some of the key themes and issues that have arisen throughout this book and puts them in a wider context. As seen in the preceding chapters, the UN human rights system was designed initially as a norm-setting system. It gradually embraced the idea of implementing the norms set and raised high the expectations of the people around the globe whose rights were violated.

Indeed, pursuant to the Charter of the UN generally, and in particular Articles 1, 24, 25, 55 and 56, this world organisation has an obligation to promote, protect and fulfil the rights of the people worldwide. However, the current UN system has not been able to meet these obligations because it suffers from a number of institutional, conceptual, procedural and resource-related weaknesses. Since there is as yet no consensus on the meaning, definition and scope of human rights, making human rights universally respected has been a challenge. There is now a plethora of international political and legal bodies, which are either UN Charter-based or treaty-based, with powers ranging from quasi-judicial to political and/or diplomatic mandated to promote compliance with human rights obligations of States. The powers of these bodies may extend into every aspect of State activity and every corner of domestic jurisdiction. However, now the question under consideration is the effectiveness of these various bodies in protecting human rights and promoting compliance by States of the provisions of international legal instruments. The analysis of the workings of these institutions has demonstrated in the preceding chapters that much of the UN system of implementation of human rights is a political and diplomatic one rather than judicial.

Of course, human rights are political, but the mechanisms to protect human rights do not have to be political. Law-making is political in any country, but law-enforcement mechanisms such as the judiciary are not, or at least should not be, political. The same should be true of the international human rights system. Therefore, the time has come to treat human rights obligations of States as legal requirements and to establish judicial mechanisms and procedures to ensure compliance with such obligations.

The making of international human rights law is political, but when the law has been enacted through a treaty, human rights provisions embodied in such treaties should be treated as legally binding and enforced through a judicial mechanism. International human rights obligations should be treated on a par with national human rights standards when it comes to enforcement. Far too much reliance has been placed on cooperative mechanisms to ensure compliance with human rights standards, but such mechanisms can work only when States cooperate and take their obligations seriously. Examples from around the globe have demonstrated that many States are not willing to cooperate with the UN human rights institutions and/or often ignore the recommendations made by such institutions. A basic principle of law is that rights must be accompanied by remedies. But this is not necessarily the case with regard to the rights enshrined in many human rights treaties. It is in this context that this chapter seeks to analyse the major weaknesses of the UN system of human rights and offer some proposals for reform of the UN human rights mechanisms and the judicialisation of human rights at the international level.

8.2 Major weaknesses of the UN human rights system

As seen in the preceding chapters, the bulk of the responsibility of promoting and protecting human rights falls on the shoulders of the following three kinds of institutions: treaty bodies (currently there are 10 such bodies in operation and they are quasi-judicial in nature and lack enforcement powers), charter-based bodies (which include the Human Rights Council and the Special Procedures, both of which are largely political bodies) and the Office of the High Commissioner for Human Rights (OHCHR which is a political-cum-administrative body). These institutions have certain inherent constitutional and conceptual limitations in protecting human rights against totalitarian, dictatorial and autocratic regimes around the globe and some of these limitations are as follows:

1. There is a design fault in many of the UN human rights mechanisms.
2. Violation of human rights is still not regarded as a violation of international law. For instance, North Korea is party to the 1966 Covenant on Civil and Political Rights which has a provision for inter-State complaints. However, no other contracting parties to the Covenant have availed themselves of this opportunity to bring North Korea into the spotlight for the systematic, widespread and grave violations of human rights in the country.

3. Far too many States are still getting away far too easily with failing to fulfil their reporting and other obligations under international human rights law.
4. Despite expecting members of the Human Rights Council to have maintained a high threshold of upholding human rights, States with a poor record of human rights are able to get themselves elected to the Human Rights Council and they often gain a dominating position in the Council.
5. Many of the meaningful or more robust implementation procedures still remain optional and far too many States evade accepting them.
6. Since the focus of UN endeavours has been on encouraging States to ratify more human rights treaties, less pressure has been applied on States to accept the competence of more rigorous mechanisms such as the competence of the Human Rights Committee to entertain individual petitions alleging violations of human rights under the first Optional Protocol to the 1966 Covenant on Civil and Political Rights.
7. In the absence of a central coordinating body for human rights mechanism within the UN system, there is duplication of work and sometimes conflicts of jurisdiction and a waste of scarce resources.
8. Many institutions which need more powers and more independence to function effectively are denied such powers and resources.
9. Even when a relatively robust or effective body such as the Human Rights Committee (treaty body) makes its recommendations, there is no effective mechanism for follow-up; no adequate resources are made available to support the work of these bodies and no effective institutional or other support is provided to implement their decisions or recommendations.
10. Much of the implementation mechanisms of the UN are still stuck in the framework adopted during the Cold War period of the bi-polar world and too much political accommodation is at work in the workings of the various UN human rights bodies.
11. Since many of the UN human rights bodies, including the flagship bodies, are political and/or political considerations have a role to play in their work, they have been perceived in many quarters as applying double standards and being selective in scrutinising the human rights records of States. This was especially the case with the former UN Commission on Human Rights and is now the case with the new Human Rights Council and it has not been successful in shaking off this image.
12. Since the UN as a whole is seen as a political institution with its own bureaucratic image, many of the UN human rights bodies are also put in that jacket and their recommendations are perceived in many quarters more as moral and political rather than legally binding obligations.
13. Since many of these UN human rights bodies lack enforcement powers, many States have a tendency not to take seriously the decisions and recommendations of such bodies. The recommendations of the treaty bodies are not binding and the track record of compliance is poor.

14. The Human Rights Council may set up fact-finding missions or commissions of inquiry into cases of alleged violations of human rights, but it has no powers to act in any meaningful manner on the findings or recommendations of such missions of commissions. Nor does the UN High Commissioner for Human Rights have such powers. What both the Human Rights Council and the High Commissioner can do is recommend that the Security Council act on such reports including referring the matter to the prosecutor of the International Criminal Court. If the Security Council does not act on the recommendations the matter does not go forward.
15. Politicisation of the UN human rights machinery, with the exception of the treaty bodies, is getting as bad as it was in the times of the old Commission on Human Rights and the old East–West divide within the Human Rights Council is becoming more apparent. Therefore, people have started to comment whether we have made much progress by establishing the new Human Rights Council to replace the Commission on Human Rights.
16. Although most of the UN human rights mechanisms are political in nature, many of them attempt to assert some quasi-legal and often even quasi-judicial role in their work. But many of these efforts are largely in vain because the very architecture of these mechanisms acts as a hindrance to these endeavours and the reports of very many commissions of enquiry, whether in relation to Syria or North Korea or elsewhere.

The underlying reasons for such deficiencies are many, but at the core are the institutional and conceptual limitations of the UN human rights institutions and the whole mindset that was at work when the UN human rights agenda was conceived. Accordingly, it is proposed to examine the major limitations or weaknesses as follows.

8.2.1 Conceptual and constitutional limitations

Despite there being numerous human rights treaties and institutions within the UN system, human rights violations are taking place in very many parts of the world, as was exemplified during the Arab Spring or Arab Awakening, which in turn further exposed the fault lines within the UN system of human rights. The challenges for the UN human rights system are many and the situation generated by the Arab Spring has brought some of them to the fore. These developments have tested the effectiveness of the UN in general and its human rights system, mainly the Human Rights Council, in particular. While the killings of the people of Syria by the Assad regime have continued for years now, the international community has done little to protect them. This was the situation despite there being a plethora of international institutions created to protect the human rights of people in such a circumstance. The UN Security Council was rendered helpless by the Chinese and Russian vetoes of even a relatively mild resolution initiated by the Arab countries and supported by Western countries.[1]

Consequently, critics and supporters alike have questioned the efficacy of the UN system in general and the Human Rights Council in particular. For instance, the OHCHR has stated, in relation to Syria, that 'gross human rights violations, including torture, under the cloak of emergency legislation, have been documented since 1963 – so four decades'.[2] Then the question arises as to what the various UN human rights institutions, including the treaty bodies, have been doing over all these four decades. Syria is not alone in having such a long history of abuse. Egypt under Hosni Mubarak, Libya under Colonel Gaddafi, North Korea under Kim-Il Sung and many other dictatorial regimes around the globe have committed grave abuses for decades and some of them are still doing so.

8.2.2 Politicisation of the UN human rights agenda

Another problem with the UN human rights agenda is its politicisation. International politics has had a tremendous role to play in the pursuit of the international human rights agenda. While Western countries have used the human rights agenda to spread the values of liberal democracy, non-Western countries have tried to use the human rights agenda to promote their own political agenda. For instance, while the US has not ratified many major international human rights treaties arguing that its internal legal system took care of human rights, the former Soviet Union ratified a number of important human rights treaties yet without adopting measures to implement them, even though the ratification of some human rights by the Soviet Union became a catalyst for the eventual downfall of the Soviet Union and Communism in Europe.[3] This is because the ratification of such human rights instruments gave famous dissidents such as Andrei Sakharov a base to fight the regime at home and project their message effectively internationally. Similarly, the ratification of the main international human rights instrument by

1 See 'Security Council Fails to Adopt Draft Resolution on Syria as Russian Federation, China Veto Text Supporting Arab League's Proposed Peace Plan', Security Council 6711th meeting (a.m.), 4 February 2012, http://www.un.org/News/Press/docs/2012/sc10536.doc.htm; 'Security Council Fails to Adopt Draft Resolution on Syria That Would Have Threatened Sanctions, Due to Negative Votes of China, Russian Federation', Security Council 6810th meeting (a.m.), 19 July 2012 both accessed 17 July 2014.

2 Briefing Notes of the OHCHR on Syria of 6 March 2012, http://www.ohchr.org/en/NewsEvents/Pages/DisplayNews.aspx?NewsID=11910&LangID=E (accessed 18 July 2014).

3 See generally, Samuel Moyn, *The Last Utopia: Human Rights in History* (Harvard University Press, 2010). See also, Samuel Moyn, 'Human Rights, not so pure anymore', *The International Herald Tribune* (12 May 2012), 6.

Communist Czechoslovakia was exploited successfully by people like Vaclav Havel in support of dissident initiatives such as Charter 77.

Although the UN discharges its responsibilities along the following nine broad categories for the promotion and protection of human rights, that is, as global conscience, law-maker, monitor, nerve centre, defender, researcher, forum of appeal, fact-finder, and discreet diplomat,[4] the fact is that it is an intergovernmental body and, by definition, a political one. That is why the UN human rights agenda itself has been part of power politics and subject to use and in some cases misuse by varying groups of States to advance their own foreign policy agenda. It was mainly the Western countries that were instrumental in introducing the human rights agenda to the UN and laying the framework for human rights in the first two decades of the UN. As observed by Boyle, it was the US, the principal architect of the UN as a whole, which was the source of the idea of a Commission on Human Rights. Indeed, John Foster Dulles, the then US Secretary of State, who had worked for the establishment of the UN at the San Francisco Conference, had dubbed the Commission the 'soul' of the Charter.[5] However, it was not as powerful a commission as it could have been with investigative powers and the powers to entertain individual petitions from victims of human rights violations.

When the newly independent Asian and African States joined the UN, they wanted to make the UN system more responsive to violations of human rights enunciated in the international human rights instruments. Their initial concern was mainly with the violations of human rights in colonial territories or in countries ruled by racist regimes such as apartheid South Africa and action against intolerance, xenophobia, discrimination and racism. It was against this background that the developing countries were instrumental in introducing the mechanism of Special Rapporteurs with investigative powers to examine the situation of human rights in a given country, a complaints mechanism within the Commission on Human Rights[6] and a treaty body to monitor implementation of the provisions of an international human rights treaty as well as strengthening the right of self-determination.

Thus, it was the developing countries themselves which sought to circumvent the principle of non-interference in Article 2(7) of the Charter of the UN and make an exception to this rule in favour of human rights in the 1960s and 1970s. Not surprisingly, the first such treaty with a treaty body with powers to monitor implementation of the provisions of the treaty was the International

4 See for a summary of these activities: UN Department of Public Information, *Basic Facts About the United Nations* (United Nations, 2004), 237–38.

5 See Kevin Boyle, 'The United Nations Human Rights Council: Origins, Antecedents, and Prospects', in Kevin Boyle (ed.), *New Institutions for Human Rights Protection* (Oxford University Press, 2009), 21.

6 It was through Resolutions 1215 of 1967 and 1503 of 1970 of the Commission on Human Rights that complaints procedures were set up.

Convention on the Elimination of All Forms of Racial Discrimination of 1965 and the number of such treaty bodies has now grown to 10. As stated by Rodley, the treaty bodies were created to fill the human rights monitoring deficit that existed in the work of the Commission on Human Rights: 'had the UN from the beginning been ready to establish a human rights monitoring system analogous to that found in the current Charter-based system, it would not have then gone on to create the system of treaty bodies.'[7]

Throughout the 1970s and the 1980s both the NATO and Warsaw Pact countries tried to use the international human rights agenda to advance their own agenda through the UN Commission on Human Rights. It was the Cold War rivalry that was played out in the sessions of the Commission on Human Rights that contributed to the undermining of its standing and credibility. It was accused of being biased, selective and applying double standards in its selection of countries for criticism for violations of human rights and often appointment of Special Rapporteurs to investigate the situation of human rights in a given country. While powerful States and their political allies were able to avoid the scrutiny of the Commission, the least powerful were not, thereby inviting the accusations of selectivity and targeting soft States.

With the collapse of Communism in Europe, the fall of the Berlin Wall, and the demise of the Soviet Union, there was an attempt made to challenge the universalist UN human rights agenda by some Asian countries such as China and Singapore by advancing the idea of 'Asian values', but this soon dissipated, lacking the substance or the clout to challenge the idea of universality of human rights.[8] Consequently, the UN human rights agenda was reinvigorated through events like the Vienna World Conference on Human Rights of 1993, the establishment of the position of the UN High Commissioner for Human Rights and expansion of special procedures mandates, so much so that towards the end of the 1990s the UN Commission on Human Rights had about 26 country-specific mandate holders with powers to investigate the situation of human rights in different countries.

7 Nigel Rodley, 'The United Nations Human Rights Council, its Special Procedures, and its Relationship with the Treaty Bodies: Complementarity or Competition?' in Kevin Boyle (ed.), *New Institutions for Human Rights Protection* (Oxford University Press, 2009), 49, 71.

8 The idea of the so-called 'Asian values' sought to (1) argue that Asian history and culture rooted in family and collective wellbeing was different from Western individualist culture and thus human rights values developed in the West and promoted by Western countries were not fully applicable to the Asian situation; (2) support the model of economic development led by 'benevolent' authoritarian rulers; (3) place economic, social and cultural rights above civil and political rights; (4) support the argument that the right to development had to be given precedence over other individual rights and liberties; and (5) argue that the UN human rights norms had to take into account the theory based on regional and cultural relativism. See generally, Yash Ghai, 'Human Rights and Governance: The Asia Debate' (1994) 15 *Australian Yearbook of International Law*, 1.

However, with the rise in prosperity in the developing world and the undermining of human rights values by the Western countries themselves in the name of fighting the war on terror following the 9/11 attacks on America,[9] a new alliance was in the making within the UN in the early 2000s consisting of countries mainly with autocratic regimes to undermine the UN human rights agenda. This alliance now consists mainly of an assortment of non-democratic countries from the Organisation of Islamic Co-operation, the remnants of the former Warsaw Pact, some from the Non-Aligned Movement and other Socialist States. This alliance is supportive of a progressive agenda of the UN concerning economic, social and cultural rights but opposed to elements of the agenda concerning civil and political rights or the imposition of sanctions on States violating human rights obligations. Thus, in the absence of judicialisation of human rights, politicisation of human rights has continued within the UN.

8.2.3 Lack of democracy at the heart of the UN

The UN is an organisation designed to promote democracy through the promotion of human rights. But the decision-making process at the heart of this organisation, that is, within the executive branch of the organisation, the Security Council, is not democratic due to the veto power bestowed on the Permanent Five.[10] One of its founding principles is the sovereign equality of States, but it has a decision-making process within the Security Council which makes a mockery of this principle. Democracy is about the power of the elected majority to take decisions on matters of governance while respecting the views of the minority. But this principle does not apply within the UN Security Council. The Permanent Five (P5) are not elected and do not have to be elected. What is more, the unelected Five have a power to veto any decision within the Council. This undemocratic structure of the Security Council has often undermined the UN system as a whole, enabling a tiny minority to hold the majority hostage and to abuse the power of veto. The crisis in Syria and the lack of response of the UN to hold the Assad government to account for massive violations of human rights and humanitarian law is an example of the abuse of such power.

9 See for an account of why the people in the US are giving up their freedom, bit by bit, Jonathan Turley, 'Ten reasons we're no longer the land of the free', *The Washington Post* (Washington DC) (Outlook) of 15 January 2012, B1; see also the views of the US Attorney General, Eric Holder, on the rationale that he invoked in defence of the US administration's policy on drone attacks and other counter-terrorism measures in a speech delivered at Northwestern University School of Law, Chicago, on 5 March 2012: Justice News of the US Department of Justice, http://www.justice.gov/iso/opa/ag/speeches/2012/ag-speech-1203051.html (accessed 7 March 2012).

10 The permanent five members of the Security Council being China, France, Russia, United Kingdom and United States of America.

The UN had appointed a Special Rapporteur for Syria and independent commissions of inquiry to investigate violations of human rights and humanitarian law, and the Human Rights Council, the Security Council and the General Assembly all passed resolutions either condemning serious, gross and systematic violation of human rights or calling for cessation of violence and violation of human rights in Syria. However, both violence and violations continued in the country under the Assad regime and there was little the UN could do about it. Speaking at the UN General Assembly, the then UN High Commissioner for Human Rights reiterated her belief that on the basis of evidence gathered from various credible sources, crimes against humanity and war crimes had been, and continued to be, committed in Syria and urgent action had to be taken.[11]

However, nothing much came out of this urgent and passionate appeal by such a high ranking UN official to the international community to act in favour of human rights. This was mainly due to the veto power wielded by China and the Russian Federation which were not willing to enable the Security Council to act under Chapter VII of the UN Charter. Frustrated by the inaction on the part of the Security Council, the General Assembly itself passed a resolution on 3 August 2012 deploring the failure of the Security Council. This inaction by the Security Council on the ongoing tragedy in Syria, causing a blow to the standing of the UN,[12] has brought to the fore the fault lines that exist within the UN system as a whole. The *United* Nations became an organisation of *divided* nations.[13] This state of affairs has raised the question of relevance of the spirit of international cooperation and multilateralism upon which the UN project was founded. It also has exposed the deficiencies that exist within the UN system in general and the UN human rights machinery in particular.

Two weeks after Russia and China vetoed a Western-backed resolution threatening sanctions against Syria, the General Assembly voted overwhelmingly in favour of a resolution tabled by Saudi Arabia condemning the escalation in violence and continued widespread violation of human rights and humanitarian law by Syrian authorities.[14] It was co-sponsored by more than 60 States and

11 'States must "act now" to protect Syrian population, Pillay tells the General Assembly', News Release of the OHCHR of 13 February 2012.

12 See for instance, Mathew Parris, 'The lights are going out across Planet Earth', *The Times* (London), 4 August 2012, 25, who states that 'the UN has lost the authority to bang heads together. Rogue members, in this case Russia and China, cannot be shamed into a consensus. That the UN General Assembly is now considering censuring its own Security Council for its paralysis is a brave and honest gesture, but it breathes despair.'

13 See generally, Adam Roberts and Kingsbury Benedict (eds), *United Nations, Divided World, the UN's Roles in International Relations* (Clarendon Press, 1988).

14 The resolution was sponsored by the Arab countries neighbouring Syria with the support of Western and many other developing countries and was adopted by 133 votes in favour to 12 against, with 31 abstentions. In the resolution, the General Assembly expressed its concern about a raft of gross human rights violations being carried out by

adopted 133 votes in favour, 12 against and 31 abstentions.[15] There was not much more the General Assembly, the most representative UN body in terms of its membership, could do in the face of the veto power in the Security Council since the resolutions of the Assembly are not binding.

It is not only China and Russia, but the US as well that has abused its veto power on several occasions in the past to protect its political allies; a long list of the situations when the US exercised its veto power in relation to the resolutions on the Middle-East is an example. Not only because the US is the biggest contributor to the UN budget, the UN has its headquarters in New York, and it was under the US leadership that the UN was established and the UN Charter written, but also the use of the UN by the US for its political convenience has led many to believe that the UN is very much 'in the pocket' of the US State Department.

Indeed, the US has used the UN whenever it is convenient and expedient to do so and ignored and marginalised it when it is not needed or when the UN is not prepared to work in accordance with the wishes of Washington. From this perspective, the veto power held by the other four Permanent Five has worked as a check on the US from misusing its own position. Thanks to the veto power wielded by others, the US has every now and then been prevented from using the UN for its political purposes. In the absence of the veto power for other States the UN would be seen to be even more pro-US which would further undermine its credibility. The challenge is to introduce more objectivity and democracy into the workings of the UN and to make it difficult for a small minority or a single State to push the Security Council into inaction when there is a clear need for action.

8.2.4 Lack of enforcement powers

The whole edifice of the UN system is premised on the promotion of human rights through cooperation rather than protection of human rights through enforcement powers, although there are limited powers akin to adjudication

Syrian Government forces, systematic attacks against civilians, and the increasing use of 'heavy weapons, armour and the air force against populated areas'. It also expressed its concern about the humanitarian impact of the violence, including repression of fundamental rights, and the influx of Syrian refugees into neighbouring countries. Deploring the Security Council's failure to agree on measures to ensure the Syrian authority's compliance with its decisions, the Assembly expressed its determination to seek ways and means to provide protection for the Syrian civilian population, A/RES/66/253 B of 3 August 2012. The 12 States which voted against the resolution were the following usual suspects: Belarus, Bolivia, China, Cuba, Democratic People's Republic of Korea, Iran, Myanmar, Nicaragua, Russian Federation, Syria, Venezuela, Zimbabwe.

15 Seventeen States did not vote, http://www.un.org/News/Press/docs//2012/ga11266Rev1.doc.htm (accessed 17 July 2014).

via the complaints mechanisms of some treaty bodies. The UN human rights agenda has been perceived in many quarters as aspirational or programmatic, and something to be achieved through incremental measures rather than overnight or implemented through a judicial process. This was the mindset which was at work during the formative years of the UN and the UN human rights agenda. The world has moved on since then but that mindset entrenched in the system has not changed much.

8.3 The way forward

It was the difficulties experienced by the UN human rights agencies in implementation of human rights standards and protection of the victims of human rights violations, whether in relation to Syria or elsewhere, which encouraged the present author to think of the possible ways and means of making sure that:

(1) international power politics has no or very limited impact on the work of the UN human rights agencies when they are discharging a function under the Charter of the UN or a human rights treaty,
(2) the emergence of a multi-polar world helps rather than hinders the UN human rights agenda, and
(3) the powers and functions of the existing international human institutions within the UN system are strengthened so that they are able to deal with the current and future cases of human rights crises around the globe.

The effectiveness of the whole UN human rights system depends upon cooperation in a constructive manner among States, but when that spirit of cooperation is absent there is very little that the present UN system can do. This is where the law should come into play and coerce States into compliance with the law and bring to account those who breach it. Thus, the challenge is to create a shift in paradigm and create new institutions which can remedy the situation. Accordingly, the following are presented as some such measures.

8.3.1 Overcoming the conceptual challenge

There has been astounding growth since the establishment of the UN, not only in the adoption of international human treaties articulating, expanding, prescribing, and defining human rights but also in the range and number of international bodies with powers to supervise the performance of the obligations of States under such treaties. The UN system now offers at least something for almost every member State with every inclination, whether political or otherwise. The UN system of human rights serves basically as a platform for all groupings of States to express their frustrations with any international issues and challenges facing the international order. Throughout the Cold War the UN human rights system was used by both the Warsaw Pact and NATO countries to criticise the policies of each other. Even today, the US is criticised by many countries on issues from racism to Islamophobia on various UN platforms, and the US criticises those countries which do not uphold civil and political rights of their citizens. This is one reason why no State has ever withdrawn from the UN or talked of doing so even when subjected to heavy criticism or UN sanctions. It is a broad church with not wholly consistent or coherent policy pillars. No State is opposed to the idea of human rights *per se*. The debate about human rights within the UN is not between those who have values and those who have not. It is about the competition between all these different values.

However, what is interesting is that States differ a great deal as to what human rights *are*, how they relate to *other* values and obligations, and what role the UN human rights institutions should play in promoting human rights. For most emerging powers the starting point on human rights is the principles of the post-1945 order such as sovereignty, non-interference, and cooperation rather than confrontation. Unfortunately, these are the very principles which have often been invoked to shield such emerging powers against criticism for repression at home. The approach of the emerging powers to the situation of human rights in a given country may differ from that of the Western countries as the former attach a great deal of emphasis to a thematic approach to human rights, developing standards on various issues, without singling out particular countries. Accordingly, they place a great deal of emphasis upon economic, social and cultural rights at least as much as on civil and political rights. They seek to use the UN human rights agenda to advance their own vision of development such as the right to development and human rights instruments on foreign debt and on toxic waste.

The emerging powers and the developing countries generally are also suspicious of major innovations in the UN human rights system. They point out the double standards and selectivity in the Western approach to human rights and resent the implicit Western claim of moral superiority and the West's apparent blindness to its own history of suppression and oppression during colonialism and imperialism. This is one reason why most of the UN human rights institutions are premised on a soft law approach of constructive cooperation, rather than confrontation to be found in adversarial systems of justice. A case in point is the UPR of the Human Rights Council under which every State is subjected to public scrutiny of its human rights records.

The developing countries seek to defend the predominant role of States in international affairs, including human rights, and limit the scope of NGOs and the autonomy of UN human rights mechanisms such as the OHCHR, including expert mechanisms such as the special procedures. This is one reason why established democracies in developing countries such as India do not have as vibrant civil societies as would be expected (given its size, etc.) campaigning for human rights within India itself and beyond its borders and scrutinising and exposing the discrepancy in the conduct of the government between its domestic and international policy. When the ethos of the developing countries served the interests of the socialist countries the latter joined the former in seeking to mould the UN system of human rights in their own image. Thus, the challenge for the UN system is as much about cohesion in its approach as it is about the effectiveness of the institutions created to promote human rights. Until and unless the business of protecting human rights is entrusted to a judicial body, human rights will continue to be used as a political tool by different groupings of States.

8.3.2 Overcoming the Cold War mindset

The UN human rights system is very much the result of a compromise between those countries putting a great deal of emphasis on individual liberty based on, among others, the theory of reserved natural rights of the individual and those Communist countries adhering to the idea that the sovereignty of the State is pre-eminent and there can be no international limitation on this sovereignty or that international interference in any pretext in the internal affairs of the State cannot be accepted. This was the idea that was advanced in the run up to the 1966 Covenants on Civil and Political Rights and especially the Optional Protocol to the Covenant.

The negotiations and conclusion of the 1966 Covenants were influenced by the ideological or political division of the world at the time. Owing to the opposition of the Communist countries led by the former Soviet Union, the Covenants omitted certain rights such as the right to property, a cardinal right of any individual in the free world, and included a weak provision for implementation of the rights contained in the Covenants. The fact is that this Communist idea of sovereignty died with the death of Communism in Europe and the collapse of the Soviet empire in 1990. However, much of the UN system is still stuck with the arrangements agreed upon during the Cold War period. Therefore, the UN system of protecting human rights should be revisited to reflect the triumph of individual liberty in order to ensure that there is a more effective system of protecting fundamental rights and freedoms against dictatorial or autocratic governments.

Thanks to the advances made in public international law in general and international human rights law in particular, it has now been accepted that a system of international restrictions on how the government treats the people of its country does not amount to a violation of the principle of non-interference in the internal affairs of States and even if it does, this has been accepted as a legitimate exception to the principle. The collapse of Communism in Europe and the demise of the Soviet Union was a major international political change of our time. This change should have led to the review of the UN approach to human rights and the creation of a robust international legal mechanism to protect human rights around the globe since it was the Soviet Union and the Warsaw Pact countries that had opposed the creation of legal and judicial international bodies for human rights invoking the provisions of non-interference in the internal affairs of States in Article 2(7) of the Charter of the UN. Indeed, some developing countries did join the Soviet Union and its satellite States at the time, but it is also true that it was the developing countries themselves who introduced exceptions to the rule in Article 2(7) when seeking to take concrete action against racism and apartheid in South Africa in the 1960s and 1970s.

8.3.3 Placing emphasis on enforcement

The setting of legal standards in the field of human rights and the establishment of mechanisms to monitor and implement those standards has been one of the primary means of achieving this objective within the UN system. The first 20 years of the UN was focused on standard setting, but when this process reached a certain peak by the 1960s, the focus was on the implementation of the human rights treaties in individual countries. Although the Commission on Human Rights was established as a subsidiary of the UN Economic and Social Council (ECOSOC) in 1946, the focus until the 1960s was on standard setting rather than enforcement or implementation. Much of the 1970s, 1980s and 1990s was devoted to putting into action the provisions of many human rights treaties. It was also the time that some new institutions such as the UN High Commissioner for Human Rights and the Special Rapporteurs for human rights were created to supplement and complement the international efforts to protect and promote human rights in individual countries. The role of these two institutions has primarily been to monitor the situation of human rights and the implementation of international human rights treaties. Nevertheless, the UN Commission on Human Rights, the main UN human rights agency, was not able to overcome its deficiencies and the Cold War political mindset lingered on in its work throughout the 1990s as some of the States with Communist systems of government or with socialist tendencies continued to pose difficulties.

The then Secretary General of the UN, Kofi Annan, outlined the weaknesses of the workings of the Human Rights Commission and proposed to replace it with a new council, the Human Rights Council, with a view to making the UN human rights system more robust and effective. Accordingly, the UN General Assembly created the Human Rights Council in 2006. However, the main mandate of the new Human Rights Council remains one of monitoring rather than enforcing human rights standards. With the rapidly developing multi-polar world in mind, the time has come to look at the workings of the laws, institutions and processes within the UN system designed to promote and protect human rights. As stated by the then US Secretary of State, Hillary Clinton, there is a need to 'update an international system designed to prevent global conflict and promote global prosperity' and that 'some international rules and institutions designed for an earlier age have to be rethought and reconfigured'.[16] This is especially so with the UN human rights system designed for an earlier age.

16 Hillary Clinton, 'The Great Power Shift', *New Statesman* (London), 16 July 2012, 28.

8.3.4 Creating a self-contained mechanism for human rights

The future of human rights will depend much on the process of implementing them and the practice of these bodies through which law on paper becomes law in action, or rights in theory become a reality for the people around the globe. As stated by Ramcharan, in the field of human rights, 'the UN's normative work has been superb but its protection role has been sadly minimal from the beginning. One of the lessons of history is that we must confront those who commit egregious human rights violations and protect and assist victims.'[17] For this, a fundamental reform of the UN system of human rights is needed and the time has come for the judicialisation of international human rights. The UN should move from simply monitoring implementation to enforcement. Regional mechanisms such as those operating under the European Convention on Human Rights and the Inter-American Convention on Human Rights have already moved in this direction.

The UN system should have its own self-contained mechanism for human rights, from fact-finding and monitoring, to examining the reports from States and fact-finding missions of Special Rapporteurs and commissions of inquiry, to entertaining individual complaints and hearing cases for gross and systematic violations of human rights. Accordingly, there should be a world charter of human rights to build on the Universal Declaration of Human Rights and to encompass the provisions contained in other core international human rights treaties to proclaim, reaffirm, and consolidate all rights. Alongside this, there should be introduced a Special Rapporteur for human rights for each country to monitor compliance and implementation. The Human Rights Council should be the focal point of human rights activities and receive reports and recommendations from (1) Special Rapporteurs, (2) treaty bodies, (3) the Office of the High Commissioner for Human Rights, and (4) commissions of inquiry.

On the basis of the reports and recommendations received from the sources just outlined, the Council should have the powers to do the following: (1) Take non-forcible preventative measures, including diplomatic and economic sanctions; (2) Recommend preventative forcible measures to the Security Council; (3) Refer cases of violations of international humanitarian law directly to the International Criminal Court; and (4) Refer serious cases of human rights violations to the International Court of Human Rights.

8.4 Judicialisation of human rights and establishment of an International Court of Human Rights

There are of course non-political expert bodies within the UN system in the form of the treaty bodies, but they are toothless entities themselves. For instance, in three cases brought before the Human Rights Committee alleging

17 Bertrand G. Ramcharan, *The UN Human Rights Council* (Routledge, 2011) 1.

disappearance of three individuals during the Maoist insurgency in Nepal (1996–2005), the Committee concluded that Nepal as party to the 1966 Covenant on Civil and Political Rights and its Optional Protocol, was under an obligation to provide the applicants with an effective remedy, including:

(1) conducting a thorough and effective investigation into the disappearance of the individuals mentioned in the applications;
(2) locating their remains and handing them over to their families;
(3) prosecuting, trying and punishing those responsible for the violations committed;
(4) providing adequate compensation to the applicants for the violations suffered; and
(5) ensuring that the necessary and adequate psychological rehabilitation and medical treatment is provided to the applicants.[18]

However, in the absence of any other follow-up mechanism of such recommendations or views of the Committee, it is up to the Committee itself to follow up on its views. Therefore, the Committee itself asked the State concerned, i.e. Nepal, to furnish information to the Committee within 180 days concerning the measures taken to give effect to its views. If Nepal does not act on the recommendations of the Committee or not provide the information that the Committee is requesting then there is not much the Committee can do about it. Of course, other member States of the UN can raise this matter during Nepal's UPR, but the UPR process itself is political and the UPR recommendations are not binding either.

Non-compliance with the views, recommendations and reports of these treaty bodies is commonplace. There is no strict requirement on the part of States to implement the recommendations of the treaty bodies. The recommendations are not judgments or decisions either. Recommendations are by their nature recommendatory and not binding and there is no proper follow-up to the recommendations. This demonstrates that the victims of human rights violations even after having the treaty bodies issue views and recommendations in their favour cannot go very far with the current UN human rights system. Therefore, it is submitted that judicialisation of human rights is the way forward to address the challenges to human rights in the multi-polar world of the twenty-first century.

When the Universal Declaration of Human Rights was adopted in 1948 by the UN it was only a 'soft law' instrument of programmatic character. The European Convention was the first major international instrument that

18 The Views of the Human Rights Committee: UN Doc. CCPR/C/112/D/2031/2011 of 10 November 2014; UN Doc. CCPR/C/112/D/20111/2011 of 10 November 2014; and UN Doc. CCPR/C/112/D/2051/2011 of 11 November 2014.

converted the 'soft law' principles into 'hard law' principles, binding on all States parties to the Convention and created the European Court of Human Rights to enforce such rights. Both the European Convention and the Court have since their inception expanded the scope of human rights and made it possible to hold European governments accountable to the violation of human rights. The European Convention was followed by the Inter-American Convention on Human Rights and the African Charter on Human and Peoples Rights. However, no such attempt to judicialise human rights at the international level has taken place.

The analysis presented throughout this study demonstrates that human rights are not taken as seriously as they should be by many governments around the world, and further, the UN mechanisms created to ensure compliance with human rights have not been as effective as they should be. At the core of this state of affairs is that most of the UN mechanisms are political and the human rights agenda has often been politicised with double standards and selectivity on the part of liberal countries, i.e. Western countries that regard themselves as the guardians of human rights or the policemen of the world. Therefore, the political human rights entities within the UN system do not command the respect that a judicial organ would do.

Since the International Court of Justice is not accessible to individuals and the International Criminal Court has jurisdiction over only limited cases of human rights violations bordering on violations of international humanitarian law (which itself has a high threshold), a vast number of cases of violations of human rights remain unanswered. The human rights treaty-bodies have no judicial power as such and in any event are ineffective even as quasi-judicial bodies with a soft-touch mandate. Therefore, there must be a provision in international human rights law for allowing victims of human rights violations to seek effective legal remedy and obtain compensation or reparation of some form.

What the UN human rights bodies such as the special procedures or commissions of enquiry or fact-finding missions can do is to investigate and document violations of human rights and make recommendations. In the absence of an international judicial body most of these recommendations end up in political bodies such as the Human Rights Council which themselves can do no more than issue appeals to the State concerned to desist from such violations or deplore them. The UN political bodies, such as the Human Rights Council or the special procedures and even the human rights treaty-bodies, may very well compile lengthy lists of human rights violations, but most of these lists and reports end up on shelves gathering dust. At most, these UN agencies may adopt repetitive and ritualised resolutions with little practical significance for the people on the ground. The power of such resolutions is based on persuasion, but when a brutal regime is not willing to listen to the voices of reason and persuasion the UN human rights agencies have little power at their disposal. At the end of the day, the victims of human rights violations are left with no effective remedy.

The idea of creating an international court of human rights has been around for some time. As early as 1946-47, Australia had proposed in the former UN Commission on Human Rights to establish an International Court of Human Rights. The Australian delegation to the UN argued in the run-up to the adoption of the Universal Declaration of Human Rights that,

> the remedy is to us as important as the right, for without the remedy there is no right. Our basic thesis is that individuals and associations as well as States must have access to and full legal standing before some kind of international tribunal charged with supervision and enforcement of the [proposed covenant on human rights]. In our view, either a full and effective observance of human rights is sought, or it is not.[19]

The idea of an international court of human rights was again suggested by Australia during the negotiations for the 1966 Covenant on Civil and Political Rights,[20] and the International Commission of Jurists sought to revive this in the run-up to the Tehran World Conference of human rights in 1968. The Secretary-General of the Commission, Sean MacBride, argued:

> the great defects of present efforts of the United Nations to provide implementation machinery are that it is piecemeal and disjointed and that it is likely to be political rather than judicial. Effective implementation machinery should conform to judicial norms, it should be objective and automatic in its operation, and it should not be ad hoc nor dependent on the political expediency of the moment. . . . If we are serious about the protection of Human Rights, the time has surely come to envisage the establishment of a Universal Court of Human Rights. . . . The reasons for the need of international judicial machinery in the field of human rights are many, the most important is to ensure objectivity and independence. . . . We all know only too well that often the political authorities – particularly in periods of stress – are not above using patronage, pressures and even coercion against judges to secure their subservience.[21]

The idea was floated again during the Vienna World Conference on Human Rights in 1993, but no serious or systematic attention has been paid to this

19 Statement made by the Australian representative on an International Court of Human Rights, quoted in Annemarie Devereux, 'Australia and the International Scrutiny of Civil and Political Rights: An Analysis of Australia's Negotiating Policies, 1946–1966', *Australian Yearbook of International Law*, Vol. 22, 2003, 56.

20 See A.H. Robertson and J.G. Merrills, *Human Rights in the World: An Introduction to the Study of the Protection of Human Rights* (Universal Law Publishing Co., 2005), 28.

21 Sean MacBride, 'The Strengthening of International Machinery for the Protection of Human Rights', *Nobel Symposium VII: The International Protection of Human Rights*, Oslo, 25–27 September 1967, pp. 16–17.

idea within the UN system. The idea was pursued once more by the Swiss Government in 2008 when it appointed a Panel of Eminent Persons with the task of drafting an Agenda for Human Rights. This Agenda entitled 'Protecting Dignity' included a proposal for the creation of a World Court of Human Rights.[22] A group of experts led by a member of the Panel of Eminent Persons, Manfred Nowak, undertook the task of even drafting a consolidated stature of the World Court of Human Rights, which was published in December 2010.[23]

Since the Council of Europe consisting of some 48 States has the European Court of Human Rights and the Association of the Americas has the Inter-American Court of Human Rights, it is certainly structurally and politically possible to have an International Court of Human Rights with powers to entertain cases relating to the application of the core international human rights treaties. A good number of States have already accepted, in principle, this idea through their ratification of a number of core international human rights treaties and the UN system has already accepted the idea of individual complaints against human rights violations. For instance, a good majority of UN member States parties to the International Covenant on Civil and Political Rights have accepted the right to individual complaints through the ratification of its Protocol. The individual complaints mechanism of the International Labour Organisation too has been in existence for decades. Thus, a large number of UN member States should have no principled objections to creating an international judicial mechanism to provide legal remedy for violations of human rights.

There seems to be some degree of support from the judges of supreme courts of some countries around the globe to the idea of creating a World Court of Human Rights. A resolution adopted at the 15th International Conference of Chief Justices of the world in 2014 urged the heads of State/Government of all countries to hold a high level meeting to deliberate on the measures required for creating an effective global governance structure, including a World Court of Human Rights.[24]

An international human rights court could be created under a treaty or a protocol giving some flexibility to States as to the inclusion of treaties within

22 A background paper on 'Strengthening the Rule of Law: The right to an effective remedy for victims of human rights violations' presented by Manfred Nowak to the Vienna + 20 Conference in Vienna, 27–28 June 2013. A copy of the paper is on file with the present author.

23 See for the text of the draft statute, Julia Kozma, Manfred Nowak, and Martin Scheinin, *A World Court of Human Rights – Consolidated Draft Statute and Commentary* (Neuer Wissenschaftlicher Verlag, 2010).

24 The full text of the Chief Justices' Resolution can be found at the following link: http://www.cmseducation.org/article51/resolutions.htm (accessed 28 December 2015). See also a report of the World Court of Human Rights Development Project at http://www.worldcourtofhumanrights.net.

the jurisdiction of the court.[25] As suggested by Meron, such a court or tribunal, 'would be empowered *ratione materiae* to supervise the application of . . . international human rights treaties adopted under the aegis of the United Nations, or at least of such enumerated instruments as each State Party to the agreement would accept. The (optional) *ratione personae* jurisdiction of the tribunal would extend to States that become parties to the special protocol'.[26] His idea was that the tribunal or the court 'would have such competence as would be accepted by each State that becomes a party to the special protocol'.[27]

If there was a proper international court of human rights the chances of it becoming political would be slim. Neither China nor Russia nor even North Korea has rejected the competence of the International Court of Justice or the Dispute Settlement Mechanism of the WTO or the International Tribunal for the Law of the Sea or international arbitral tribunals such as the International Centre for Settlement of Investment Disputes (ICSID). But States have challenged or ignored the recommendations of the UN human rights mechanisms because of the perceived political nature of human rights and of the UN human rights mechanisms.

The challenge for the international community to deal with human rights violations is to depoliticise the workings of the UN human rights mechanisms if the intention is to make these mechanisms effective in a multi-polar world. Of course, the reports of various commissions of inquiry or fact-finding missions appointed by the General Assembly, the Security Council, the Human Rights Council, and the Secretary-General may ultimately lead to criminal prosecution before the International Criminal Court or other *ad hoc* international criminal tribunals. However, a good number of reports are considered by the UN political bodies and then shelved rather than leading to concrete action to implement the recommendations contained therein.

This happens when the State under consideration is able to garner enough political support in these UN political bodies to frustrate the recommendations of such reports. A resolution of the Human Rights Council of 2009 on Sri Lanka is a case in point.[28] A more recent example is the call by the UN High Commissioner for Human Rights to refer the cases of gross violations of

25 See Manfred Nowak, 'It's Time for a World Court of Human Rights' in M. Cherif Bassiouni and William Schabas (eds), *New Challenges for the UN Human Rights Machinery: What Future for the UN Treaty Body and the Human Rights Council Procedures?* (Cambridge, 2012).

26 T. Meron, *Human Rights Law-Making in the United Nations: A Critique of Instruments and Process* (Clarendon Press, 1986) 212.

27 Ibid, 213.

28 'Report of the human rights council on its eleventh special session' S-11/1 Assistance to Sri Lanka in the promotion and protection of human rights, 27 May 2009, http://www.securitycouncilreport.org/atf/cf/%7B65BFCF9B-6D27-4E9C-8CD3-CF6E4FF96FF9%7D/Sri%20Lanka%20A-HRC-S-11-2-Advance.pdf (accessed 18 July 2014).

human rights and crimes against humanity to a 'hybrid court' involving international judges to investigate the claims.[29] However, due to political considerations the Human Rights Council was not able to act on the call of the UN High Commissioner. Instead, the Council ended up adopting a soft resolution leaving the matters to the Government of Sri Lanka.[30] The Sri Lankan Government in its letter to the UN OHCHR pointed out that the report of the OHCHR represented a human rights investigation and not a criminal investigation.[31] This and other examples demonstrate that the Human Rights Council has not been able to overcome the politicisation of its work that undermined the work of its predecessor, the Commission on Human Rights. For instance, despite a series of reports of serious violations of human rights in Belarus, the resolution on the appointment of a Special Rapporteur for the country was highly politicised and was adopted with 22 votes in favour, 5 against and 20 abstentions in the Council in June 2012.

Once the International Court of Human Rights is established, the task of monitoring the execution of its judgments could be entrusted to the UN High Commissioner for Human Rights and the task of ensuring execution to the Human Rights Council and, in some exceptional cases, ultimately to the Security Council itself. The statute of such a court could include a provision requiring the States parties to it to recognise the judgments of the court and treat them on a par with the judgments of the national judiciary. This will then require or authorise national agencies responsible for execution of the judgments of the national courts to execute the judgments of the international court of human rights too. Although the human rights treaty bodies have the powers and have occasionally recommended the award of compensation to victims of human rights violations, the victims of human rights violations have not been able to obtain effective remedy from the treaty bodies due to the non-binding character of these recommendations and poor implementation of them by States. Therefore, the creation of an International Court of Human Rights together with a provision for effective execution of its judgments would go a long way in providing effective access of victims to justice, including compensation or reparation where necessary. After all, it is a fundamental principle of law that rights must be accompanied by remedies for victims themselves. This is because in the absence of such remedies rights may be rendered mere moral or political statements, ultimately illusory and meaningless.

To ensure that such an International Court of Human Rights is not flooded by cases, the statute of such a court could require the applicants to exhaust

29 See the Report of the UN OHCHR: A/HRC/30/61 of 16 September 2015 and the Report of the OHCHR Investigation on Sri Lanka (OISL) A/HRC/30/SRP.2); 'UN calls for judges to probe Sri Lanka war "crimes"', *The Financial Times* (London), 17 September 2015 and 'Sri Lanka's ex-leader could be tried for war atrocities', *The Times* (London), 17 September 2015.

30 A/HRC/30/L.29 of 29 September 2015.

31 A copy of the letter of the Ministry of Foreign Affairs of Sri Lanka of 15 September 2015 (UN/HR/1/30) is on file with the present author.

domestic remedies prior to bringing their case to the court, thereby making the international court of human rights a complementary mechanism of remedies. This already is the case with the individual complaints to the treaty bodies. Access to the international court would be available where the national mechanisms are unavailable, ineffective, or have failed to deliver justice. Once the statute of the international human rights court is adopted and ratified by a requisite number of States to bring into effect, there will be internal and external pressure on other States to become a party to it.

Until the statute of the international court of human rights receives universal or near universal acceptance, the world could accept a two-tier system of protection of human rights. There are already examples of a two-tier system within the UN system. For instance, while some States have ratified the Option Protocol to the 1966 International Covenant on Civil and Political Rights, others have not. The UN system of human rights could cater for the needs of States at different stages of development in terms of human rights protection. Those States that wish to go further should be able, and should be encouraged, to do so even though it may be that the people of these States 'need' an international human rights court less than those that fail to ratify the statute. The creation of the international court of human rights would offer each and every State the opportunity to go further than others and benefit from best practices of other States in terms of the protection of human rights in their countries.

It should be submitted that judicialisation of international human rights alone will not bring human rights violations to an end, but the possibility of being found guilty by an international human court through its binding decisions as opposed to by a political body within the UN system will deter many people in government and positions of authority and provide better and concrete legal remedy to the victims of human rights violations. As proposed above, if the UN High Commissioner for Human Rights and the Human Rights Council are entrusted with the powers to monitor execution of the rulings of the international human rights court, and if the Council itself is accorded the powers suggested above, the court should be able to function as an effective institution protecting human rights just as the European Court of Human Rights does.

8.4.1 Adopting a new single consolidated world charter of human rights

There is a considerable body of international treaties, declarations, and general comments concerning human rights. In addition, fleshing out certain human rights principles and provisions of international human rights treaties has been carried out by the treaty bodies by way of general comments. However, there is as yet no consensus on the meaning, definition and scope of human rights. Further, while there are too many international human rights instruments proclaiming various rights, they mainly concern rights against States. Regarding the State as the sole duty bearer of the protection of rights is basically the result of the post-Second World War mindset. The world has moved on and in the contemporary world human rights are violated by a myriad of other actors too.

There is a need for a paradigm shift in the conceptual framework of human rights. Rights need to be protected not only against States, but also against other powerful entities such as multinational enterprises, snooping agencies, information technology and social media related companies such as Google and Facebook. Therefore, the time has come to streamline these instruments and adopt a single comprehensive international bill of rights in the form of a new universal declaration of human rights fit for the twenty-first century, or a 'world charter of human rights', or even a modern Magna Carta, with a single annual reporting procedure and single body to examine the reports.

Such a new millennium charter of human rights should be a consolidated document of all rights, including the right to property, which is not currently included in the International Bill of Rights, and other rights such as the right to clean water, right to a clean and healthy environment, and the rights of lesbian, gay, bisexual, transgendered, and transsexual people. It should include the new rights that have been recognised by various soft law instruments in the recent past and reflect the content of the general comments issued by various treaty bodies which flesh out the principles embodied in various human rights treaties.

8.4.2 Streamlining the human rights reporting system

At present, there are simply too many human rights treaties and too many UN bodies entrusted with political and quasi-judicial work. The UN human rights system on the whole is facing tremendous challenges, especially those relating to resources. The following statement of the High Commissioner for Human Rights indicates a rather dire situation within the UN human rights system:

> We stand at a critical juncture. To appreciate it fully, let us take a step back in time to recall the foresight and courage of the drafters of the treaties who established this extraordinary system of legally binding commitments by States undertaken voluntarily in the interest of their own people. The treaties codify universal values and establish procedures to enable every human being to live a life of dignity. By accepting them, States voluntarily open themselves to a periodic public review by bodies of independent experts. But by resigning ourselves to the "inevitability" of non-compliance and inadequate resources, the system was left to suffer a long history of benign neglect to the point where, today, *it stands on the verge of drowning in its growing workload, even when leaving aside the shocking fact that an average 23% of States parties to one treaty have never engaged in the review procedure of that treaty*. We cannot let this be.[32] (emphasis added).

32 N Pillay, 'Strengthening the United Nations human rights treaty body system: A report by the United Nations High Commissioner for Human Rights', June 2012, 94. http://www2.ohchr.org/english/bodies/HRTD/docs/HCReportTBStrengthening.pdf (accessed 18 July 2014).

The time has come to overhaul the UN human rights system. A radical response is needed to address the problems of violations of human rights. Whatever its merits, the new UPR mechanism does add yet another burden on States which are already over burdened by the reporting obligations under nine core human rights treaties. Therefore, the UPR should either replace the system of reporting to the treaty bodies or focus on review of the recommendations made by the treaty bodies and special procedures.

8.4.3 Need for a single unified treaty body

The human rights treaties should be streamlined and a single, more robust and more resourceful monitoring body should be created to replace all 10 treaty bodies. This idea has been around for some time. It was Das who proposed the establishment of a Human Rights Board through a Protocol which would receive and review all reports by States parties to the human rights treaties that they have ratified.[33] This could now be done by the Human Rights Council or by a review committee consisting of independent legal/human rights experts of the Council. This would require amending all the core human rights treaties and the optional protocols to some of them. Meron stated as far back as 1986 that, 'The time has come for rationalising reporting procedures by States in the UN context. Eventually, the international community would have to consolidate supervisory systems into a more limited number of organs.' If the time came in 1986 it is now long overdue. What is more, what the US delegate observed about the state of affairs within the UN in relation to rights in the following words in 1980 seems still to be true:

> much of the work in this area proceeds without planning, in a kind of haphazard manner, at a desultory pace and with overlapping jurisdictions. We have working groups in the Third Committee [of the General Assembly] in the Commission on Human Rights, and in the Sub-commission. It is difficult to keep track of the different drafts. There is a lack of continuity and expertise among the persons working on the drafts. It makes no sense, for example, for a body of this size to attempt to draft a convention from its inception. As it is, one often has to reinvent the wheel each time a working group reconvenes. The result is neither fast nor fruitful.[34]

33 For instance, Das proposed it in his work entitled, 'Some Reflections on Implementing Human Rights', in B. Ramcharan (ed.), *Human Rights: Thirty Years After the Universal Declaration*, 131, 146–48, as cited in T. Meron, *Human Rights Law-making in the United Nations: A Critique of Instruments and Process* (Clarendon Press, 1986) 240.

34 Verbatim text of remarks by Jerome J. Shestack (13 November 1980), summarised in UN Doc. A/C.3/35/SR.56, at 12–14 (1980), as quoted in T. Meron, *Human Rights Law-making in the United Nations: A Critique of Instruments and Process* (Clarendon Press 1986) 271.

A new protocol could be concluded to empower the Human Rights Council to receive and review all reports by States as supplementary reports to their 4-yearly national reports for the Universal Periodic Review and it should replace other reporting requirements. In the absence of a single comprehensive monitoring body to cover all areas of human rights, many countries, especially smaller developing countries, are finding it difficult to keep up with their reporting obligations.

As pointed out in a report by the High Commissioner for Human Rights, 'If a State ratifies all nine core treaties and two optional protocols with a reporting procedure, it is bound to submit in the time frame of 10 years approximately 20 reports to treaty bodies, i.e. two annually.'[35] This is rather too much for any country let alone developing and especially smaller developing countries. There is also some duplication of work by the treaty bodies, the Human Rights Council under UPR and the special procedures.

While examining the role of the UPR and treaty reporting, Rodley says, 'The current challenge will be to find ways of indeed making the two processes complementary and productive, rather than competitive and injurious to the promotion of the better enjoyment of human rights. This not insignificant dimension apart, the existence of the two systems cannot be properly understood as creating substantial duplication and overlap.'[36] Of course, since under UPR the Human Rights Council can examine all crosscutting issues across a broad range of human rights obligations of States cannot be compared with the mandate of the treaty bodies, which by their very nature focus on the implementation of an individual treaty. However, the possibility of duplication in the work of both of these mechanisms is there and should be avoided. Of course, the problem with UPR is that the reports are reviewed by a political body – the Human Rights Council. If the UPR were to develop as a robust global mechanism conducted by professional experts without political involvement it could replace the reporting and monitoring system under separate individual human rights treaties.

8.4.4 Appointing one UN Special Rapporteur for every UN member

To carry out a credible check and verify the information contained in country reports to the Human Rights Council or to other treaty bodies, there should

35 Navanethem Pillay, 'Strengthening the United Nations Human Rights Treaty Body System: A Report by the United Nations High Commissioner for Human Rights', United Nations Office of the High Commissioner for Human Rights, Geneva, June 2012, 21.

36 Sir Nigel Rodley, 'The United Nations Human Rights Council, Its Special Procedures, and Its Relationship with the Treaty Bodies: Complementarity or Competition?' in Kevin Boyle (ed.), *New Institutions for Human Rights Protection* (Oxford University Press, 2009), pp.49–73 at 71.

be a full-time and salaried UN Special Rapporteur for each of the countries, required to submit an annual report to the UN Human Rights Council. Upon receipt of a single comprehensive country report from the States concerned, the report of the Special Rapporteur for that country, and any reports from civil society organisations compiled by the OHCHR, the Human Rights Council should be able to examine the situation of human rights in the country and decide what measures would be necessary to ensure compliance with human rights standards by the State concerned and also have powers to refer, by a two-thirds majority of States voting and present, matters relating to gross and systematic patterns of violation of human rights to a 'world court of human rights', and matters relating to war crimes or crimes against humanity to the International Criminal Court. The country Special Rapporteurs should be able to recommend to the Human Rights Council the course of action it should take in cases of gross and systematic patterns of violations of human rights and humanitarian law.

Access to the International Court of Human Rights and its jurisdiction could be defined as narrowly, judiciously and prudently as possible to ensure that the court is able to function in an effective manner and as a final resort. The country-specific rapporteurs could also be entrusted with the task of following up the recommendations of the UPR, execution of the rulings of the international court of human rights and treaty-bodies. There already are approximately 74 UN independent human rights experts working under the special procedures and 175 UN human rights experts working for various human rights treaty bodies. Bringing the number to a total of 193, therefore, one Special Rapporteur for each country working full-time, would not be a significant additional expense, particularly if they can do the job of both thematic and country-specific rapporteurs for the country concerned and replace several other fact-finding and follow-up mechanisms within the UN system.

8.5 Reforming, empowering and elevating the status of the Human Rights Council

If the recommendations made above, such as the adoption of a world charter of human rights and the establishment of a new international court of human rights, are implemented, the role of the current Human Rights Council would need to be changed. It could become an executive council similar to the UN Security Council, with powers to refer matters to the Security Council, the International Criminal Court and the International Court of Human Rights. The Human Rights Council should also be entrusted with the powers to take some measures not involving the use of force to ensure compliance with the recommendations of treaty bodies, Special Rapporteurs and commissions of inquiry.

The UN Charter should be amended to elevate the position of the Human Rights Council as a principal organ of the UN with the powers and functions that it requires to function as an effective global human rights body. Since the members of the UN have regarded human rights as one of the three principal pillars of the UN system, there should be a principal UN human rights body enjoying a status similar to that of the Security Council.

The Human Rights Council should be given the power to refer matters relating to serious violations of human rights and humanitarian law directly to the International Criminal Court. It could be done under a mechanism similar to that which exists currently between the Security Council and the International Criminal Court. The threshold to decide on such a referral could be higher and the Human Rights Council could be required to have a two-thirds majority in favour. A more appropriate organisation to refer the matters relating to human rights and humanitarian law to the International Criminal Court would be the Human Rights Council rather than the Security Council. Of course, the Human Rights Council also suffers from politicisation, but if it is required to do so by a two-thirds majority and informed by reports of independent commissions of inquiry or the independent UN human rights experts such as the Special Rapporteurs it would assist in obviating this.

In spite of having credible and concrete evidence presented to it by the High Commissioner for Human Rights, by various commissions of inquiry or by the special procedures mandate holders and being urged by them to refer the matters relating to gross and systematic violations of human rights and rules of international humanitarian law to the International Criminal Court, the Council is currently unable to do so. At most what the helpless Human Rights Council can do is to transmit the evidence received to all relevant bodies of the United Nations, including the General Assembly, and the Secretary General for appropriate action. This it did through a resolution adopted in September 2014 in the face of the mounting concrete and credible evidence submitted to it by the Commissions of Inquiry and investigations teams on the atrocities committed in Syria.[37] Even after the Human Rights Council's recommendation of a similar nature to the General Assembly in relation to the situation in North Korea the Assembly has not been able to do much about it except for urging the Security Council to take appropriate action, including referring the matter to the International Criminal Court. This anomaly and a major weakness of the international system should be remedied.

37 In a resolution (A/HRC/27/L.5/Rev.1) on the continuing grave deterioration in the human rights and humanitarian situation in the Syrian Arab Republic, adopted by a vote of 32 in favour, 5 against and 10 abstentions. See more at: http://www.ohchr.org/EN/NewsEvents/Pages/DisplayNews.aspx?NewsID=15110&LangID=E#sthash.uy8vZf9o.dpuf (accessed 1 October 2014). The Independent International Commission of Inquiry on the Syrian Arab Republic published its report on 11 February 2016 stating that 'flagrant violations of human rights and international humanitarian law continue unabated, aggravated by blatant impunity'. A/HRC/31/68, p. 1 (Summary). See also the report entitled 'Out of sight, Out of Mind: Deaths in Detention in the Syrian Arab Republic', A/HRC/31/CRP.1 of 3 February 2016.

The Human Rights Council itself should have powers to impose, by two-thirds majority and on the basis of reports of independent commissions of inquiry or the independent UN human rights experts such as the Special Rapporteurs, economic and diplomatic sanctions not involving the use of force on States engaged in gross and systematic patterns of human rights violations and to recommend to the Security Council, where necessary, to impose forcible sanctions under Chapter VII of the Charter of the UN against those States which fail to protect their people from gross and systematic violations of human rights and commit crimes against humanity.

Both the Security Council and the Human Rights Council could agree a system, a formal mechanism, whereby the latter could recommend to the former that it impose sanctions that would make issues open, public, formal and, most importantly, difficult for the former to ignore. If the Human Rights Council were to be entrusted with at least non-military enforcement powers, it would enhance its own standing and those of the standing of Special Rapporteurs since it would become easier for the Council to take enforcement actions to ensure that its own recommendations and those of the Special Rapporteurs are implemented.

8.5.1 De-politicising the workings of the Human Rights Council

Bearing in mind that elevating the status of the Human Rights Council to the status of the Security Council, as proposed above, would require amending the Charter of the UN, which is a difficult undertaking, it is proposed in this section to outline the reforms which can be carried out without amending the UN Charter. They can be implemented by the General Assembly through a resolution and some of them even by the Human Rights Council itself.

Similar to the former Commission on Human Rights, the Human Rights Council is not only a political organ, composed of representatives of States, but also a politicised one. The membership of the Council is by a considerable majority representative of the developing world, but many of the democracies in the developing world are lacking in leadership capability to promote human rights, rule of law and democracy in other developing countries as they are restrained by their membership of cross-cutting regional and other groupings of States such as the Non-Aligned Movement and the Organisation of Islamic Countries. For instance, when the present author submitted his report on the situation of human rights in Cambodia to the Human Rights Council in September 2012 calling for electoral reform in the country to ensure an environment conducive to the exercise of a democratic right to governance and other rights by all, the response of the governments of the neighbouring ASEAN countries was not as encouraging as it should have been. Only the Senate of the Philippines passed unanimously a resolution welcoming the report and endorsing the recommendations contained therein.

The election, composition, powers and functions of the Council should be changed. It should be comprised of a body of professionals. Not only the treaty bodies, but also the Human Rights Council should be led by people with the right expertise, background and attitude. This is primarily because countries with a poor or troubled human rights record have been members of the Human Rights Council as was the case with the former Commission on Human Rights, thereby diminishing the credibility of the institution.

The criteria set for candidate States to get elected to the Human Rights Council have not worked well. As stated by Oberleitner, 'The voluntary pledges and feebly worded duties of Council members, however, are weak compromise formulae.'[38] If there was a requirement to elect members of the Council by a two-thirds majority vote in the General Assembly, the chances of States with a poor human rights record getting elected would be minimal.

The idea of universal membership would not work either, as such a membership may turn the Council into another Third Committee of the General Assembly in sitting and meeting in Geneva. Instead of increasing membership it should be decreased and made more robust. There should be a proper mechanism for vetting the candidates for election to the Council. The General Assembly should appoint a Special Rapporteur to report to the Assembly on the human rights record of a candidate country for election to the Human Rights Council on the basis of objective, independent and impartial standards set by the Assembly itself such as the level of cooperation with the special procedures, treaty bodies and the Human Rights Council.

The individual members of the Human Rights Council should be elected by the General Assembly from a list of nominees submitted by governments, but serve in an individual capacity as persons of recognised competence in international human rights law just as the members of the UN International Law Commission do. This is how the treaty bodies are elected. This is one reason why the allegations of double standards and selectivity are reduced against the work of treaty bodies. Therefore, the Human Rights Council too should be an expert-led body and it should be made a permanent body capable of carrying out its duties all year round. Of course, by the very nature of the work involved, the Council should carry out its work in close cooperation with the political authorities of States, but the body itself should be able to command respect as an independent expert body which is less susceptible to allegations of politicisation, selectivity and double standards.

Alternatively, if the current approach continues whereby it is States that are elected rather than individuals from those countries, the elected States could be required to designate a person or persons such as serving or retired judges or distinguished academics or senior lawyers with a proven expertise in human rights to serve in the Human Rights Council rather than their ambassadors in Geneva.

Another alternative could be to establish an expert group of serving or retired judges or distinguished academics or senior lawyers with proven expertise in

38 Gerd Oberleitner, *Global Human Rights Institutions: Between Remedy and Ritual* (Polity Press 2007), 70.

human rights to assess the human rights record of candidates for election to the Human Rights Council against the criteria stipulated in the resolution of the General Assembly establishing the Human Rights Council and make public its views on it. There should be a public scrutiny of the record of human rights of the candidates for election to the Human Rights Council against the following criteria: ratification of international human rights treaties; acceptance of the individual complaints procedure under various international human rights instruments; up-to-date periodic reporting under various international human rights treaties; extension of standing invitations to special procedure mandate holders and issuance of timely visa to them, and implementation of recommendations of treaty bodies, Universal Periodic Review and special procedures where applicable.

It is acknowledged that the implementation of the recommendations of special procedures and universal periodic review might be difficult to measure since some of the recommendations are general or vague and require a long time to implement. It is also true that requiring compliance with the recommendations of the special procedures and universal periodic review might turn such soft or non-binding recommendations into effectively binding recommendations for any State seeking election to the Human Rights Council. This may be argued as undermining the sovereign right of a UN member State to participate in a UN body. However, by joining the UN, by ratifying international human rights treaties and by accepting the universal periodic review mechanism, the UN member States have already accepted limitation on their sovereign rights in the interests of the community values of the international community. It is a matter of common sense that when one decides to join a club that that person is accepting the code of conduct of that club or the consequences that flow from such membership, and the UN is no exception.

8.5.2 Reducing the number of members of the Human Rights Council

The current number of members in the Council (that is, 47) is too large to enable it to work effectively as a professional body. In principle, higher membership numbers should be regarded as positive since all members of the Council are supposed to uphold the highest standards possible and the non-renewal of membership gives all other States a chance to prove themselves in the competition. Indeed, as stated by Lord Hannay, 'a small Council consisting of squeaky-clean, mostly westernised States laying down the law for the rest of the world is not likely to advance the cause of human rights worldwide'.[39] However,

39 Lord Hannay, '2011 Review of the UN Human Rights Council: Recommendations submitted to the UK Foreign & Commonwealth Office by the United Nations Association of the UK, December 2010, 6, http://www.una.org.uk/sites/default/files/UNA-UK%20recommendations%20on%202011%20UN%20Human%20Rights%20Council%20review_0.pdf (accessed 18 July 2014).

the current number of members of the Council has not been conducive to doing business effectively and in a professional and business-like manner.

8.5.3 Empowering the UN High Commissioner for Human Rights

The terms of reference of the Office of the High Commissioner for Human Rights outlined in the 1993 resolution should be revisited and amended. The High Commissioner for Human Rights should be accorded an independent status similar to that enjoyed by an ombudsman rather than remain a part of the UN Secretariat. If an international court of human rights is created then the Office of the High Commissioner should have the powers to recommend to the Human Rights Council prosecution of government officials involved in the gross and systematic violations of human rights and referral to the International Criminal Court for serious violations of humanitarian law. Since the International Criminal Court has no competence to entertain cases of human rights violations unless they are of a grave nature and amount to violations of war crimes and crimes against humanity, both options should be at the disposal of the High Commissioner for Human Rights.

In order to maintain and enhance the stature and authority of the position, the power to appoint the High Commissioner should be taken out of the hands of an individual, in this case the Secretary General, and given to an expert search and appointment body appointed by the Security Council or made an elected position similar to the judges of the International Court of Justice or the members of the International Law Commission. The appointment process should incorporate transparency, accountability, fairness, and inclusiveness for the selection and appointment of a qualified and effective candidate with human rights credentials and must be on merit and through open competition.

The procedures for appointment or selection should include the publication of an official candidate list at the end of the nomination or application phase, distribution of candidate CVs, statements from candidates specifying how they fulfil the requirements of the post, and panel interviews and question/answer sessions with UN member States and, where possible, key relevant stakeholders. Much of this is already in place regarding the appointment of UN Special Rapporteurs, but these procedures or expectations do not currently seem to apply to the appointment of the UN High Commissioner. This was the experience of the present author when he was a candidate for appointment to this position in 2014 on the nomination of the Government of Nepal, as discussed in more detail in Chapter 5. Once elected through a transparent and competitive process the High Commissioner should have an independent status with investigative or fact-finding powers.

8.5.4 Streamlining the human rights law-making process

The human rights law-developing or proposing function has been largely concurrent or shared among various agencies within the UN including the

General Assembly, the Human Rights Council and the ECOSOC etc. Although the UN General Assembly is the lead organ in this respect, empowered by the UN Charter to exercise an overall authority, the law-making or law-developing activity within the UN has been very much a decentralised and disorganised activity. As stated by Schaefer, 'human rights expressed in treaties, Treaty Body General Comments, and resolutions passed in the [Human Rights] Council and the General Assembly have grown enormous, complex, and specialised to the point where they are impossible to monitor or apply consistently.'[40] Therefore, the Human Rights Council should be regarded as the lead agency with an overall authority in respect of the law-developing and monitoring implementation of those laws by States. The Human Rights Council should also have the primary role of coordinating further development and codification of international human rights law within the UN system.

The Human Rights Council should have its own sub-commission on international human rights law to review the existing international human rights treaties in the context of a changed world and to prepare new human rights treaties as and when needed. This sub-commission should consist of independent experts in international human rights law just as the members of the International Law Commission. Since international human rights law-making and international law-making are similar, the process and procedure for both of these should also be similar. There are so many treaties and other international legal instruments that an expert sub-commission is needed to review them and recommend timely amendments along the lines suggested in this study.

At present, there is some degree of duplication of functions between the Human Rights Council and the Third Committee of the General Assembly. After the establishment of the Human Rights Council the Third Committee has become largely an unnecessary additional layer within the UN system as far as human rights matters are concerned. There should be a clearer definition of the relationship between the two and the status of the Council should be higher than that of the Third Committee. Civil society representatives should be allowed to participate in the debate of the Third Committee on human rights and humanitarian matters in the manner in which they are able in the meetings of the Human Rights Council. Although this Committee would still have a role of coordination of the resolutions of the General Assembly concerning human rights (which is roughly one-third of all the resolutions passed by the Assembly), it should not duplicate the work of the Human Rights Council since the Council already works as a mini-General Assembly on human rights matters.

8.5.5 An annual human rights index and annual global report of the UN

At the moment, the UN human rights mechanisms have only political sticks for non-compliant States and no carrots to offer to encourage compliance. The

40 Brett D. Schaefer, 'The Human Rights Council's Failings Should Lead to Reassessment', Bulletin of the Universal Rights Group, Geneva, August 2015.

reason the present author was able to persuade, cajole and encourage the government of Cambodia to implement many of his recommendations in his capacity as the UN Special Rapporteur for the country was that he was willing to give credit to the government for the good human rights work it had done. By praising the government for some of its good deeds, they began to crave further recognition of their work from the UN and the present author used the opportunity to push the door more widely open. Those who have been in power for long and consolidated both power and money into their hands do eventually clamour for international recognition and are often willing to sacrifice something in return for such endorsement, and Cambodia is a particular case in point. One such means of offering carrots along with sticks would be to have a league table of human rights indicators in which the place in the table could be improved by good work.[41]

The Millennium Development Goals and other targets demonstrate that the rulers of a given country, no matter how autocratic they are, do wish to present a case of improvement to the outside world and strive to this effect. Indeed, human rights violations are committed by autocratic rules often not knowing what human rights are and whether they are violating them. It is also the case with some countries, especially those that have come out of autocratic regimes, that they are enthusiastic about ratifying a UN human rights treaty in order to demonstrate that they are committed to democracy and human rights and to do everything possible to institutionalise democracy so that history does not repeat itself. But they do not seem to have prepared themselves well enough to become party to such a treaty and the obligations that flow from such ratification. The enthusiastic ratification by Nepal of many human rights treaties after the people's movement for democracy in 1990 is a case in point. The new government ratified a number of human rights treaties without apparently making appropriate preparations and without realising the legislative and administrative measures needed to be adopted to bring the treaties into full implementation. A global human rights index would have guided Nepal as to what would be needed to ratify a treaty and what measures would be needed to comply with its provisions.

Despite having 130 or so international instruments and a plethora of UN human rights mechanisms, the UN does not produce an annual report on the global situation of human rights. Nor is there a generally agreed meaning,

41 See for human development index of the UNDP: http://hdr.undp.org/en/content/human-development-index-hdi/. Also, there is the Fragile States index that includes an indicator relating to the human rights and the rule of law and data on States can be sorted accordingly http://ffp.statesindex.org/. There are of course obvious challenges with any such data in terms of collection, accuracy, etc. However, through the periodic reporting by States to treaty bodies, to the Human Rights Council for UPR and through the work of the special procedures and the High Commissioner for Human Rights, the UN is generally in possession of a great deal of information to compile such a league table of human rights.

definition and scope of human rights. Some States such as the UK and US produce their own annual human rights reports. So do leading international human rights organisations such as Amnesty International and Human Rights Watch. Various agencies within the UN such as UNDP and the World Bank produce their own annual global reports on the state of economic development and there is an abundance of information collected by UN Special Rapporteurs, treaty bodies and Charter-based bodies about the situation of human rights in any given country. If all this information were collated, compiled and summarised for public consumption, such a publicly available record of human rights of each and every country would put the States concerned under considerable pressure to improve their record.

Most States, with the exception of a handful of recalcitrant States such as Iran and North Korea, want to be seen as law-abiding nations doing their utmost to improve the situation of human rights and do not wish to be in the spotlight of the world. What the present author has proposed above is something that could be done without needing to expend much in the way of additional financial resources, but may work as an effective tool to encourage States to strive their hardest to live up to the expectations of their people and the international community. The OHCHR could be entrusted with the task of producing a factual annual audit of human rights of every country on a non-selective manner. Few States would have a plausible argument to oppose the production of such a report on the basis of the information already available in the public domain. A more objective annual UN human rights index would be regarded as more acceptable and credible by different actors and stakeholders than the rather superfluous reports currently produced by individual States and would serve as an important source of reference for States, international organisations, donor agencies, human rights defenders, academics, researchers, and ordinary citizens both within and outside of the States concerned. Such a report has the potential for working as an effective human rights tool.

8.6 Conclusions

As the world has moved on, the complexities involved in promoting and protecting human rights have become manifold. However, the attempts made thus far within the UN system and proposals for reform of human rights institutions, whether the treaty body system or the Human Rights Council itself, have sought to essentially only tinker with the system with the hope of making a marginal difference. They have sought only to make an inefficient system a little more efficient when in reality the need is actually for a complete overhaul of the system. The time has come to de-politicise the workings of human rights mechanisms and judicialise human rights at the international level. This is not to imply that human rights law-making or its implementation should be apolitical, since both of these processes are inextricably linked to the political reality of the day. The point is that some of the activities of some of the UN agencies should be judicial rather than political, politicisation of the process of implementation of human rights treaties should be avoided, and there should be better streamlining of the activities of these agencies and better coordination between them under the leadership of independent experts to give them the weight that they deserve to be effective and to be seen to be effective.

The whole UN human rights system would work better if there was a better balance between the participation of independent experts and that of generalist diplomats. This is because, as seen throughout this study, the present system is inadequate, and reform is needed to usher the world into the next stage of development. As stated by Hillary Clinton, the established and emerging powers have to work together 'to renovate the global architecture to reflect better the dynamics of today's world'.[42]

The present author is of the view that the UN human rights agenda is a humane project, which is neither just Western, Eastern or African but is universal; it is for the whole of humanity and as humanity evolves it brings its own challenges and opportunities to the UN system and these challenges must be addressed by reforming the UN human rights system. Even if the reform suggested in this study is carried out it may not make much immediate difference to the situation of human rights in countries such as Iran, North Korea or Syria, but it will have a much greater impact on these and many other States. When the workings of the UN human rights mechanisms is depoliticised it will enhance the credibility and standing of these mechanisms and they will be immune from allegations of double standards or selectivity and put more effective pressure on recalcitrant States to abide by the international human rights norms.

42 Hillary Clinton, 'The Great Power Shift', *New Statesman* (London), 16 July 2012, 28.

9 Conclusions

9.1 Human wrongs and human rights

Human wrongs have been committed since time immemorial, especially by those in power and positions of public authority. The history of human civilisation is replete with brutalities and atrocities. Consequently, it is also replete with attempts to introduce checks on the excesses of people in power and positions operating under the umbrella of the State. Development of the concept of the rule of law, democracy and human rights are examples of attempts to restrain the State and those in power. While periodic elections were introduced to enable the electorate to throw out of power those committing human wrongs and those political parties with whom the public was dissatisfied for failing to keep to their pre-election promises, etc., human rights were introduced to set standards for life and dignity for all, with UN human rights mechanisms being designed to protect the people against human wrongs. The human rights treaties are part of an international code of conduct for States, that is, for people in power and position on how to protect the dignity of the individuals.

States have their own national laws, procedures and mechanisms to check human wrongs. All three main branches of the State have a role to this effect. The legislative body, elected by the people, is mandated to enact the laws to this effect, the executive to implement the will of the legislative body, and the judiciary to bring people to account for human wrongs committed. When the national system is inadequate in doing so, international law and the UN come into play. If States establish robust domestic mechanisms to uphold the international code of conduct and punish the wrong-doers there will be no need for international law and the UN to intervene. But since that is not the case in many countries the UN has to intervene not only to protect and promote human rights but also to fulfil the promise made by this world organisation to the people around the globe. It is the package of human rights that the UN promised, as mandated by its member States, to the people around the globe through the Universal Declaration of Human Rights of 1958 and other human rights treaties and it has an obligation to fulfil this promise.

9.2 Democracy and human rights

No State, no matter how advanced its democracy is, has a perfect record of human rights, as demonstrated in the Universal Periodic Review carried out by the UN Human Rights Council. Nor is any country a perfect democracy. True democracy is a utopian ideal. But there are fewer human wrongs committed in mature democracies and more human wrongs committed in countries with less developed democracies. However, since States are sovereign, no other States can impose their will or standards on another State, whether human rights or otherwise. Therefore, States agreed through the adoption of the Charter of the UN and the Universal Declaration of Human Rights to have a set of common values for the international community so that everybody living anywhere can enjoy their basic rights and have their dignity protected. Various subsequent human rights treaties have codified, solidified, and consolidated these common values and mechanisms have been created to ensure their compliance. Thus, the promotion and protection of human rights became one of the fundamental objectives of the United Nations and one of the 'common fundamental values' of the international community.[1]

9.3 Strengths and weaknesses of the international system

While the international system is more advanced than national systems in defining a code of conduct or setting standards, it is less developed than national systems in implementing and upholding such standards and even less developed in bringing to account those who violate the code or international standards. This is where the problem lies. The culture of impunity is a reality in many countries. For many cases of human rights violations there is no mechanism for prosecution either. The international system has no effective judiciary with compulsory jurisdiction. Justice or redress has not been a prominent element within the UN human rights system. A raft of international institutions with limited judicial, quasi-judicial and administrative functions has tried to fill the gap to a certain extent, but the gap still remains wide open. Since there is no world government, there is no world executive body either. The UN Security Council seeks to fill the gap to a certain extent, but it is handicapped by its limitations, both constitutional and regarding the composition of its membership. Thus, the international human rights agenda seeks to protect the dignity of each and every individual within these imperfect conditions.

1 Through the 2005 World Summit Outcome document the Heads of State and Government outlined the common fundamental values of the international community in the following words: 'We reaffirm that our common fundamental values, including freedom, equality, solidarity, tolerance, respect for all human rights, respect for nature and shared responsibility, are essential to international relations.' A/RES/60/1 of 24 October 2005, para 4.

However, many of those who have violated human rights or the international code of conduct have not been brought to account. Except for the International Court of Justice and the International Criminal Court, both of which have limited powers to entertain cases of human rights violations, all other UN human rights bodies are either political or quasi-political and toothless. Even the human rights treaty bodies are quasi-judicial at best with no powers of enforcement. The rest of the UN institutions are political and their decisions are influenced by political considerations. Therefore, even when a State in question is in violation of its human rights obligations the reaction of the UN bodies is more political than legal. Hence, there is no proper mechanism to police the violation of human rights even though much of the human rights obligations are in fact legally binding. What is more, even when there is a political will to act on the part of the majority of the states within such political bodies they are lacking in enforcement powers. Not having the political will to act is one thing, but not having the power to act is another thing and this is particularly the case with the Human Rights Council, a principle UN agency responsible for protecting and promoting human rights.

This is not to say that the UN human rights institutions have not been effective at all. They have played an important role in expanding and expounding human rights values and in protecting the human rights of people around the globe. The UN human rights system has worked better than international environmental law-related mechanisms and similar mechanisms. At the end of the day one UN agency or another will have done something about violations of human rights in a given country. For instance, when a resolution was passed by the UN General Assembly in October 2014 recommending to the Security Council that the matters relating to the gross and systematic violations of human rights in North Korea be referred to the International Criminal Court, the North Korean authorities indicated that they may allow an unprecedented visit by the UN Special Rapporteur for the country.[2] Rather than rejecting the work of the UN human rights agencies altogether North Korea remains engaged, so much so that the country circulated a draft UN resolution in October 2014 praising its own human rights record in a rare effort to counter the international community's growing condemnation of its human rights record.[3]

While the UN human rights agenda and the mechanisms have had limited impact in countries with traditional autocratic regimes such as in the Middle-east or countries with socialist systems, it has had a major impact on countries in transition. Even in countries with established democracies the UN agenda has helped to expand human rights and make the rights more meaningful. The international human rights agenda has contributed to advancing civilisation not

2 'Kim welcomes UN to dodge trial', *The Times* (London), 29 October 2014, p. 37.

3 'N. Korea Praises Rights Record in Draft Resolution', Associated Press, 15 October 2014.

only in so-called second and third world countries but also in first world countries. The brutalities, atrocities and slavery prior to and during the colonial period by the Western countries have now come to an end. The Western countries themselves have been encouraged to protect the minorities in their own countries, eliminate racial discrimination, empower women and accord them equal treatment, and work towards a fairer society for all to live in. For instance, even in the aftermath of the Second World War and after the adoption of the Universal Declaration of Human Rights people were being prosecuted in Britain for homosexual activities under a Victorian law, the Criminal Law Amendment Act of 1885. The prosecution of Alan Turing (the father of modern computer science and breaker of the enigma code, which is said to have shortened the course of the Second World War by 2 years) in 1952 is an example. It is his very own country, Britain, which now leads the international campaign for respect for LGBTI rights (lesbian, gay, bisexual, transgender and intersex) and has recently pardoned Turing, 60 years after his suicide and 62 years after his conviction.[4]

The concept of human rights is a social phenomenon and a social movement based on cooperative ideas for their implementation. That is why the UN mechanisms created for their implementation have been cooperative rather than coercive or adjudicatory. A duty to assist each other in the achievements of the purposes and objectives of the UN, which include human rights, is implied in Articles 55 and 56 of the Charter of the UN. Thus, what has been built within the UN system thus far provides an excellent platform to carry out serious reform to face the challenges of a multi-polar word. The establishment of the new UN Human Rights Council in 2006 to replace the former Commission on Human Rights was a major step, but it should have gone much further than it did. It was an attempt to tinker with the system to make it better rather than a bold move to carry out a serious reform of the UN human rights system, demanded by the dawn of the new millennium and the new century.

The UN was created to promote harmony among nations and has thus tried to reconcile the differences among States in its activities, including in the substantive provisions in treaties as well as procedural matters. The exclusion of the right to property in the 1966 Covenant on Civil and Political Rights and the adoption of the Optional Protocol to the Covenant allowing for individual petitions rather than incorporating the right to individual petition in the Covenant itself are some examples. The 1966 Covenant and many other human rights treaties included soft provisions involving submission of periodic reporting by States parties to these treaties and review of such reports by the treaty-bodies created by such treaties as a means of ensuring compliance with them.

4 'Father of modern computer science Turing is pardoned for being gay, 60 years after suicide', *The Financial Times*, London, 24 December 2013, 1.

Since most of the UN mechanisms for monitoring and implementing human rights were developed in the second half of the last century and in a political context marked by the Cold War of a bi-polar world, they reflect that mind-set. The main mechanism relied upon to ensure compliance of human rights has been a system of state reporting. Although significant progress has been made in terms of reporting requirements since their inception in terms of both the quality and content of the national reporting of human rights to various UN bodies,[5] thanks to technology, media access to the proceedings of UN human rights agencies and space for civil society participation in the process, the reporting mechanism remains weak as the UN treaty bodies are essentially toothless and able only to rely on soft power.

9.4 Addressing the challenges brought about by a multi-polar world

The world has transformed from being bi-polar in terms of world politics to unipolar (briefly and mainly in the 1990s) followed then by the emergence of a multi-polar world marked by the rise of emerging powers such as BRICS (Brazil, Russian Federation, India, China and South Africa), and the more recent talk of the emerging economies of the MINT countries (Mexico, Indonesia, Nigeria and Turkey). The decline of the economic power of the West which wielded mainly some soft power and in rare cases hard or military power (the operation in Libya in 2011 being an example of this) to support the UN human rights machinery, has brought to the fore the question as to whether the UN system of protecting human rights is fit for the purposes of the new era where 'the geometry of global power is becoming more distributed and diffuse', to borrow the words of Hillary Clinton, the then US Secretary of State.[6]

The expectations of the UN human rights system are high but the institutions created are not able to meet with the challenges brought about by violations of human rights. Therefore, this study has argued for a timely reform of the UN system in order to address the current challenges and in anticipation of those that lie ahead. It is premised on the idea that even if more serious reform of the UN system, such as democratisation of the UN Security Council, is not possible, some other reforms which would be politically acceptable should be carried out. Even if BRICS countries such as China and India stake their claim, perhaps further down the road, to leadership of the world they will have no

5 See for an analysis how poor the content and quality of the reports submitted even by advanced democracies such as the UK was as late as the 1980s and to certain extent even in the 1990s, Francesca Klug, Keir Starmer and Stuart Weir, *The Three Pillars of Liberty: Political Rights and Freedoms in the United Kingdom – The Democratic Audit of the United Kingdom* (Routledge, 1996), pp. 60–61.

6 Hillary Clinton, 'The Great Power Shift', *New Statesman* (of London), 16 July 2012, 28.

alternative but to keep and strengthen a rule-based system at the international level and consequently the UN and current regime of human rights. This is because human rights are already part of the core of the international rule-based system and they would want to continue with it with some modifications just as the leaders of independent post-colonial India such as Gandhi and Nehru saw the merit in adopting the ready-made British system of government known as the Westminster system but with some adjustment to suit the Indian situation.

Most of the BRICS countries in general and China in particular have benefitted a great deal from the rule-based system of international trade under the auspices of the World Trade Organisation and the relative political stability brought about by the present international legal order based on the rule of law, democracy and human rights and they will see the merit in strengthening and continuing this system. The rise in multi-polarism is not likely to pose a challenge to the international human rights agenda led by the UN. Rather, it offers an opportunity to the UN system to assist countries such as China in their process of reform by further developing international jurisprudence on human rights, setting new standards on new areas and adopting guidelines on how certain concepts and principles of human rights should be interpreted and applied by the State institutions and especially the judiciary in such countries.

Even if the UN human rights agenda has its origin in Western political thought it has now been embraced by all States thereby making it a global agenda. Countries like China and Saudi Arabia are not challenging the UN human rights agenda. While China makes a plea to the international community to understand its 'national realities' and make an allowance to its status as a developing country seeking to accelerate the process of political reform and embrace the rule of law and human rights, Saudi Arabia makes a similar plea of understanding on the part of the international community that it is a traditional Muslim society and is seeking to reform its system of governance and embrace human rights and the rule of law rather than invoking Islam to reject human rights.

Even if there is an economic decline followed perhaps by a diminished capacity of the West to champion human rights, those States whether BRICS, MINT or otherwise which seek to project their power internationally and assert global leadership will see the merit in strengthening the existing and ready-made rule-based international system built around the UN and its human rights system rather than start conceiving a new political architecture for the world. Power will have to come with responsibility. Therefore, whatever happens to the world politically, the UN in a reformed form and its human rights system is likely to stay for a long time to come. The human rights campaign has a long way to go. Protecting human rights is a long-term objective and defining human rights is a time-sensitive act. The notion of human rights itself is an organic or living phenomenon. It is not something that can be accomplished even after implementing the recommendations made in this study. The Universal

Declaration of Human Rights is not a reality in many societies, not only in North Korea or Syria or the slums of India or Brazil but also in the inner cities of countries such as the US, UK and France where black, ethnic minorities or undereducated and disadvantaged white or other minorities and working class populations live lives devoid of many social and economic rights.

9.5 The need for reform of the UN system

As the UN has celebrated its 70th anniversary, the world has to take stock of the developments thus far and devise appropriate means to address the challenges ahead. There is not only the rise of the BRICS countries taking place to take into account, but the old division between the East and West is resurfacing and is manifesting itself in the workings of the UN human rights agencies and especially the UN Human Rights Council. Although the current trend in the East–West division is not based on an ideology as was the case during the old Cold War period, the formation of new alliances within the UN system along political and strategic lines is undermining the effectiveness of UN human rights mechanisms.

As stated by Donovan and Andersen, since the establishment of the UN, the human rights agenda has indeed made 'remarkable strides forward – in law, in politics, in institutions. Starting with just the bare-bones Declaration of 65 years ago, we now have a raft of regional and global treaties and conventions specifying conditions for most aspects of human rights.' They go on to add that 'at the same time, in practice, the scale of deprivation of certain basic rights remains shocking, very real new challenges loom on the horizon, and the institutions of enforcement, though many, are weak and under threat . . . the mechanisms and institutions we have to respond [to human rights violations] are, to say the least, challenged.'[7]

The world needs a global machinery to uphold global values, including human rights. However imperfect its institutional structure may be and however undemocratic some of its decision making processes may be (such as the veto power) the UN is the only global political organisation the world has. Individual States, no matter how powerful they may be, lack the ability to command the trust and respect of other States since it is in the nature of individual States to put their national interests above international interests. Along with the reform of the UN system of human rights, States will have to embark upon a campaign for religious tolerance, non-discrimination against minorities and people of different colour, creed and race and human rights education at all levels. This is needed not only in politically developing countries but also in more established democracies.

7 Donald Donovan and Elizabeth Andersen, 'Toward the Effectiveness of International Human Rights Law', vol. 29 (4) *Newsletter of the American Society of International Law*, October–December 2013, 1.

Although the UN appears divided on issues relating to countries and territories such as Syria, North Korea, Ukraine, Palestine and Iran, it is less divided than during the Cold War period. The deep division during the Cold War period was along ideological lines. That is not the case today. The global North–South divide is not on ideological grounds. It is on economic grounds. Whatever division there is today is tactical and along the national interests of individual countries. There are no major global agendas at this juncture that divide nations within the UN. Therefore, this is a new and opportune period in history to overhaul the UN system of human rights. The leadership of the UN human rights agenda has been for too long in the hands of UN bureaucrats who are used to backroom dealings. The time has come to take the leadership out of their hands and give it to human rights professionals and experts and de-politicise the workings of the UN human rights mechanism and judicialise human rights at the international level. Far too many resources have been spent on trying to tinker with a system that is inefficient and outdated at its core.

The challenge for us today, when the world is at a crossroads, is to chart a path of reform so that the deficiencies that exist in the current rule-based international system are addressed and the UN human rights system is able to evolve in a manner which can keep pace with the political changes taking place around it. This has been the endeavour of this study. There is still a great deal of work to do to protect and promote human rights. Georg Schwarzenberger, a preeminent international lawyer, once remarked that 'It is the intellectual birthright of those engaged in research freely to throw out challenges to others, and the duty of those addressed to respond, if not necessarily with enthusiasm, to such threats to their peaceful vegetation.'[8] Thus, the present author has, in exercise of his 'birthright', thrown out some ideas via this book and it can be hoped that those who are addressed will respond in some way.

8 Georg Schwarzenberger, *The Inductive Approach to International Law* (Stevens & Sons, 1965), 1.

Select bibliography

Books

Ackerly, A.B., *Universal Human Rights in a World of Difference* (Cambridge University Press, 2008)

Alfredsson, G., Grimheden, J., Ramcharan, B.G. and Zayas, A. (eds), *International Human Rights Monitoring Mechanisms: Essays in Honour of Jakob Th. Möller* (2nd edn, Martinus Nijhoff Publishers, 2001)

Alston, P. *Promoting Human Rights Through Bill of Rights: Comparative Perspectives* (Oxford University Press, 1999)

—— *The United Nations and Human Rights: A Critical Appraisal* (Oxford University Press, 2nd edn, 2013)

Alston, P. and Crawford, J. (eds), *The Future of UN Human Rights Treaty Monitoring* (Cambridge University Press, 2000)

Alston, P. and Goodman, R. *International Human Rights* (Oxford University Press, 2012)

Alston, P. and Megret, F. (eds), *The United Nations and Human Rights: A Critical Appraisal* (Oxford University Press, 2nd edn, 2013)

Alston, P. and Robinson, M. *Human Rights and Development: Towards Mutual Reinforcement* (Oxford University Press, 2005)

An-Na'im, A.A and Denh F (eds), *Human Rights in Africa: Cross-Cultural Perspectives* (The Brookings Institution, 1990)

Aung san Suu Kyi, *Letters from Burma* (with a new introduction by Fergal Keane) (Penguin Books, 2010)

Baderin, M. and McCorquodale, R. *Economic, Social, and Cultural Rights in Action* (Oxford University Press, 2007)

Bagefsky F.A. (ed.), *The UN Human Rights Treaty System in the 21st Century* (Martinus Nijhoff Publishers, 2000)

—— *United Nations Human Rights Treaty System: Universality at the Crossroads* (Martinus Nijhoff Publishers, 2001)

Baghel, I. and Yadav, S.N. *Human Rights in the 21st Century* (Jnanada Prakashan, 2009)

Bantekas, I. and Oette, L. *International Human Rights Law and Practice* (Cambridge University Press, 2013)

Bassiouni, M.C. and Schabas W.A. (eds), *New Challenges for the UN Human Rights Machinery. What Future for the UN Treaty Body System and the Human Rights Council Procedures?* (Intersentia, 2011)

Baum, R. *Burying Mao: Chinese Politics in the Age of Deng Xiaoping* (Princeton University Press, 1994)
Baxi, U. *The Future of Human Rights* (Oxford University Press, 3rd edn, 2006)
Bayefsky, A.F. (ed.), *The UN Human Rights Treaty System in the 21st Century* (Kluwer, 2000)
Beardson, T. *Stumbling Giant: The Threat to China's Future* (Yale University Press, 2013)
Becker, M.S. and Schneider, J.N. (eds), *Human Rights Issues in the 21st Century* (Nova Science Publishers, 2008)
Bellamy, J.A. *Global Politics and the Responsibility to Protect: From Words to Deeds* (Routledge, 2011)
Bernstein, T. and Xiaobo Lu, *Taxation without Representation in Contemporary Rural China* (Cambridge University Press, 2003)
Bingham, T. *The Rule of Law* (Allen Lane, London 2010)
Black, K.J. *The Politics of Human Rights Protection: Moving Intervention Upstream with Impact Assessment* (Rowman & Littlefield, 2008)
Boyle, K. *New Institutions for Human Rights Protection* (Oxford University Press, 2009)
Brems, E. and Gerards, J. *Shaping Rights in the ECHR: The Role of the European Court of Human Rights in Determining the Scope of Human Rights* (Cambridge University Press, 2014)
Brownlie, I. *Basic Documents on Human Rights* (3rd edn, Clarendon Press, 1992)
Buchanan, A. *The Heart of Human Rights* (Oxford University Press, 2014)
Buchanan, R. and Zumbansen, P. *Law in Transition: Human Rights, Development and Transitional Justice* (Hart Publishing, 2014)
Burke, C. *Equitable Framework for Humanitarian Intervention* (Hart Publishing, 2013)
Carby-Hall, J. *Essays on Human Rights: A Celebration of the Life of Dr Janusz Kochanowski* (Ius et Lex Foundation, 2014)
Cassimatis, A. *Human Rights Related Trade Measures Under International Law* (Martinus Nijhoff, 2007)
Chang, G.G. *The Coming Collapse of China* (Random House, 2001)
Charlesworth, H. and Larking, E. (eds), *Human Rights and the Universal Periodic Review: Rituals and Ritualism* (Cambridge University Press, 2015)
Clapham, A. *Human Rights Obligations of Non-State Actors* (Oxford University Press, 2006)
—— *Human Rights: A Very Short Introduction* (Oxford University Press, 2007)
Clark, R. *A United Nations High Commissioner for Human Rights* (Martinus Nijhoff, 1972)
Cottier, T., Pauwelyn J. and Burgi, E. *Human Rights and International Trade* (Oxford University Press, 2005)
Craven, M. *The International Covenant on Economic, Social, and Cultural Rights: A Perspective on Its Development* (Oxford University Press, 1998)
Davis, J. *Seeking Human Rights Justice in Latin America: Truth, Extra-Territorial Courts and the Process of Justice* (Cambridge University Press, 2013)
De Schutter, O. *International Human Rights Law: Cases, Materials, Commentary* (2nd edn, Cambridge University Press, 2014)
Deva, S. and Bilchitz, D. *Human Rights Obligations of Business: Beyond the Corporate Responsibility to Respect* (Cambridge University Press, 2013)

Dupuy, M.P., Petersmann, U.E. and Francioni, F. (eds), *Human Rights in International Investment Law and Arbitration* (Oxford University Press, 2009)
Eden, P. and O'Donnell, T. *September 11, 2001: A Turning Point in International and Domestic Law?* (Transnational Publishers, 2005)
Egan, S. *The United Nations Human Rights Treaty System: Law and Procedure* (Bloomsbury Professional, 2011)
Eide, A., Alfredsson, G., Melander, G., Rehof, A.R. and Rosas, A. (eds), *The Universal Declaration of Human Rights: A Commentary* (Scandinavian University Press, 1992)
Emberland, M. *The Human Rights of Companies: Exploring the Structure of ECHR Protection* (Oxford University Press, 2006)
Fenby, J. *Will China Dominate the 21st Century?* (Polity Press, 2014)
Fleck, D. *The Handbook of International Humanitarian Law* (2nd edn, Oxford University Press, 2013)
Føllesdal, A., Schaffer, K.J. and Ulfstein, G. *The Legitimacy of International Human Rights Regimes: Legal, Political and Philosophical Perspectives* (Cambridge University Press, 2013)
Franck, T. *Human Rights in Third World Perspective, Vol I–III* (Oceana Publications Inc, 1982)
Freedman, R. *The United Nations Human Rights Council: A Critique and Early Assessment* (Routledge, 2013)
Freeman, M. *Human Rights: An Interdisciplinary Approach* (2nd edn, Polity Press, 2011)
Friedman, E. and McCormick, L.B. *What If China Doesn't Democratize? Implications for War and Peace* (M.E. Sharpe, 2000);
Fukuyama, F. *The End of History and the Last Man* (Free Press, 1992).
Gaer, F.D. and Broecker, C.L. *The United Nations High Commissioner for Human Rights Conscience for the World* (Martinus Nijhoff Publishers, 2013)
Genser, J. and Cotler, I. *The Responsibility to Protect: The Promise of Stopping Mass Atrocities in our Time* (Oxford University Press, 2012).
Gertz, W. *The China Threat: How the People's Republic Targets America* (Regnery, 2000)
Ghandi, R.P. *The Human Rights Committee and the Right of Individual Communication: Law and Practice* (Dartmouth Publishing Co Ltd, 1998)
Ghazi, B. *IMF, The World Bank Group and the Question of Human Rights* (Transnational Publishers, 2005)
Glenn, H.P. *Legal Traditions of the World: Sustainable Diversity in Law* (2nd edn, Oxford University Press, 2004)
Goldman, M. and MacFarquhar, R. *The Paradox of China's Post-Mao Reforms* (Harvard University Press, 1999)
Goodman, S.G.D. and Segal, G. *China Deconstructs: Politics, Trade and Regionalism* (Routledge, 1994)
Hague, W. *William Pitt the Younger* (Harper Press, 2004)
—— *William Wilberforce: The Life of the Great Anti-Slave Trade Campaigner* (Harper Perennial, 2008)
Hannan, D. *How We Invented Freedom and Why It Matters* (Head of Zeus, 2013)
Harris, D. and Joseph, S. (eds), *The International Covenant on Civil and Political Rights and United Kingdom Law* (Clarendon Press, 1995)

Harrison, J. *The Human Rights Impact of the World Trade Organisation* (Hart Publishing, 2013)
Hegarty, A. and Leonard, S. *Human Rights: An Agenda for the 21st Century* (Cavendish Publishing, 1999)
Heir, A. *The Responsibility to Protect: Rhetoric, Reality, and the Future of Humanitarian Intervention* (Palgrave Macmillan, 2012)
Henkin, L. and Lawrence, J. *Human Rights: An Agenda for the Next Century (Studies In Transnational Legal Studies)* (American Society of International Law, 1994)
Herman, A. *How the Scots Invented the Modern World: The True Story of How Western Europe's Poorest Nation Created Our World & Everything in It* (Three Rivers Press, 2001)
Heyns, C. H. and Viljoen, F. *The Impact of the United Nations Human Rights Treaties on the Domestic Level* (Martinus Nijhoff Publishers, 2002)
Hillebrecht, C. *Domestic Politics and International Human Rights Tribunals: The Problem of Compliance* (Cambridge University Press, 2013)
Huntington, S. *The Clash of Civilizations and the Remaking of World Order* (Simon & Schuster, 1996)
International Commission of Jurists, *Reforming the United Nations Human Rights System: A Chance for the United Nations to Fulfil its Promise* (International Commission of Jurists, 2005)
Ishay, R.M. *The History of Human Rights: From Ancient Times to the Globalization Era* (University of California Press, 2004)
Jackson, J. *The Jurisprudence of GATT and the WTO: Insights on Treaty Law and Economic Relations* (Cambridge University Press, 2007)
Jacques, M. *When China Rules the World: The Rise of the Middle Kingdom and the End of the Western World* (Allen Lane, 2009)
Jeffery, R. and Hun, J.K. *Transitional Justice in the Asia-Pacific* (Cambridge University Press, 2013)
Jolly, R., Emmerij, L. and Weiss, G.T. *UN Ideas That Changed the World* (Indiana University Press, 2009)
Joseph, S. and Castan, M. *The International Covenant on Civil and Political Rights: Cases, Materials, and Commentary* (3rd edn, Oxford University Press, 2013)
Keller, H. and Ulfstein, G. (eds), *UN Human Rights Treaty Bodies: Law and Legitimacy* (Cambridge University Press, 2012)
Kenny, A. *The Oxford Illustrated History of Western Philosophy* (Oxford University Press, 1994)
Kesby, A. *The Right to Have Rights: Citizenship, Humanity, and International Law* (Oxford University Press, 2012)
Klug, F., Starmer, K. and Weir, S. *The Three Pillars of Liberty: Political Rights and Freedoms in the United Kingdom – The Democratic Audit of the United Kingdom* (Routledge, 1996)
Koskenniemi, M. *The Politics of International Law* (Hart Publishing, 2011)
Kozma, J., Nowak, M. and Scheinin, M. *A World Court of Human Rights – Conslidated Statute and Commentary* (Neuer Wissenschaftlicher Verlag, 2010)
Langer, L. *Religious Offence and Human Rights: The Implications of Defamation of Religions* (Cambridge University Press, 2014)
Langford, M., Sumner, A. and Yamin, E.A. *The Millennium Development Goals and Human Rights: Past, Present and Future* (Cambridge University Press, 2013)

Lardy, R.N. *Integrating China into the Global Economy* (Brookings Institution Press, 2002)
Lauren, G.P. *The Evolution of International Human Rights: Visions Seen* (University of Pennsylvania Press, 1998)
Lauterpacht, H. *An International Bill of the Rights of Man* (Oxford University Press, 2013)
—— *International Law and Human Rights* (Archan Books, 1968)
Legg, A. *The Margin of Appreciation in International Human Rights Law Deference and Proportionality* (Oxford University Press, 2012)
Leiser, M.B. and Campbell, D.T. *Human Rights in Philosophy and Practice* (Ashgate Publishing Limited, 2011)
Lenzerini, F. *The Culturalization of Human Rights Law* (Oxford University Press, 2014)
Luard, E. *The International Protection of Human Rights.* (Thames and Hudson, 1967)
Lubman, B.S. *The Evolution of Law Reform in China: An Uncertain Path* (Edward Elgar Publishing, 2012)
Macklem, P. *The Sovereignty of Human Rights* (Oxford University Press, 2015)
Madsen, R.M. and Verschraegen, G. *Making Human Rights Intelligible: Towards a Sociology of Human Rights* (Hart Publishing, 2013)
Mahbubani, K. *The New Asian Hemisphere: The Irresistible Shift of Global Power to the East* (Public Affairs, 2008)
Marks, S. and Clapham, A. *International Human Rights Lexicon* (Oxford University Press, 2005)
Matsushita, M., Schoenbaum, J.T. and Mavroidis, C.P. *The World Trade Organization Law, Practice, and Policy* (2nd edn, Oxford University Press, 2006)
McGoldrick, D. *The Human Rights Committee: Its Role in the Development of the International Covenant on Civil and Political Rights* (Clarendon Press, 1991)
Meisner, M. *The Deng Xiaoping Era: An Inquiry into the Fate of Chinese Socialism, 1978–1994* (Hill & Wang, 1996)
Mendes, P.E. *Global Governance, Human Rights and International Law: Combating the Tragic Flaw* (Routledge, 2014)
Meron, T. *Human Rights in International Law* (Oxford University Press, 1984)
—— *Human Rights in International Law: Legal and Policy Issues* (Clarendon Press, 1986)
—— *Human Rights Law-Making in the United Nations: A Critique of Instruments and Process* (Clarendon Press, 1986)
—— *Human Rights and Humanitarian Norms as Customary Law* (Clarendon Press, 1991)
Mertus, J. *The United Nations and Human Rights: A Guide for a New Era* (2nd edn, Routledge, 2005)
Milanovic, M. *Extraterritorial Application of Human Rights Treaties: Law, Principles, and Policy* (Oxford University Press, 2013)
Minkle, L. *The State of Economic and Social Human Rights: A Global Overview* (Cambridge University Press, 2013)
Minxin Pei, *China's Trapped Transition: The Limits of Developmental Autocracy* (Harvard University Press, 2006)
Moyn, S. *The Last Utopia: Human Rights in History* (Harvard University Press, 2010)
Muller, L. *The First 365 Days of the United Nations Human Rights Council* (Lars Müller, 2007)

Murray, R. *The Role of National Human Rights Institutions at the International and Regional Levels* (Hart Publishing, 2007)
Neier, A. *The International Human Rights Movement: A History* (Princeton University Press, 2012)
Nifosi, I. *The UN Special Procedures in the Field of Human Rights* (Intesentia, 2005)
Nolan, A., O'Connell, R. and Harvey, C. *Human Rights and Public Finance: Budgets and the Promotion of Economic and Social Rights* (Hart Publishing, 2013)
Normand, R. and Zaidi, S. *Human Rights at the UN: The Political History of Universal Justice* (Indiana University Press, 2007)
Nowak, M. *Introduction to the International Human Rights* (Martinus Nijhoff Publishers, 2003)
Oberleitner, G. *Global Human Rights Institutions: Between Remedy and Ritual* (Polity Press, 2007).
Odello, M. and Seatzu, F. *The UN Committee on Economic, Social and Cultural Rights: The Law, Process and Practice* (Routledge, 2012)
O'Flaherty, M., *Human Rights and the UN: Practice Before the Treaty Bodies* (Martinus Nijhoff, 2002)
Open Society Foundations, *From Judgment to Justice: Implementing International and Regional Human Rights Decisions* (Open Society Justice Initiative – Open Society Foundation, 2011)
Orford, A. *International Authority and the Responsibility to Protect* (Cambridge University Press, 2011)
Parekh, B. *Gandhi* (Oxford University Press, 1997)
Pattison, J. *Humanitarian Intervention and the Responsibility to Protect: Who Should Intervene?* (Oxford University Press, 2010)
Paupp, E.T. *Redefining Human Rights in the Struggle for Peace and Development* (Cambridge University Press, 2014)
Ramcharan, B.G. *The United Nations High Commissioner for Human Rights: The Challenges of International Protection* (Martinus Nijhoff Publishers, 2002)
—— *A UN High Commissioner In Defence Of Human Rights: No License To Kill Or Torture* (Martinus Nijhoff Publishers, 2005)
—— *Contemporary Human Rights Ideas* (Routledge, 2008)
—— *The Protection Roles of UN Human Rights Special Procedures* (Koninklijke Brill NV, 2009)
—— *The UN Human Rights Council* (Routledge, 2011)
Rangarajan, L.N. *Kautilya: The Arthasastra* (edited, rearranged, translated and introduced) (Penguin Books, 1992)
Reus-Smit, C. *Individual Rights and the Making of the International System* (Cambridge University Press, 2013)
Risse, T. Ropp, C.S. and Sikkink, K. *The Persistent Power of Human Rights: From Commitment to Compliance* (Cambridge University Press, 2013)
Rodley, N. *The Treatment of Prisoners Under International Law* (2nd edn, Oxford University Press, 1999)
Sceats, S. and Breslin, S. *China and the International Human Rights System* (Chatham House, London, 2012)
Schabas, A.W. *The Universal Declaration of Human Rights: The Travaux Preparatoires* (Cambridge University Press, 2013)
Sen, A. *Development as Freedom* (Oxford University Press, 1999)
Shambaugh, D. *China Goes Global: The Partial Power* (Oxford University Press, 2013)

Shelton, D. *The Oxford Handbook of International Human Rights Law* (Oxford University Press, 2013)
—— and Carozza, G.P. *Regional Protection of Human Rights* (Oxford University Press, 2014)
Smith, J., Baehr R.P., Van Hoof, F. and Tao, Z. *Human Rights: Chinese and Dutch Perspectives* (Martinus Nijhoff Publishers, 1996)
Stacy, M.H. *Human Rights for the 21st Century: Sovereignty, Civil Society, Culture* (Stanford University Press, 2009)
Stahn, C., Easterday, S.J. and Iverson, J. *Jus Post Bellum: Mapping the Normative Foundations* (Oxford University Press, 2014)
Subedi, S.P. *International Investment Law: Reconciling Policy and Principle* (3rd edn, Hart Publishing, 2016)
Tan, H-L. *The ASEAN Intergovernmental Commission on Human Rights Institutionalising Human Rights in Southeast Asia* (Cambridge University Press, 2011)
Tusa, A. and Tusa, J. *The Nuremberg Trial* (Skyhorse Publishing Company, Inc, 2010)
Tyagi, Y. *The UN Human Rights Committee: Practice and Procedure* (Cambridge University Press, 2011)
United Nations High Commissioner for Human Rights, *The High Commissioner for Human Rights: An Introduction: Making Human Rights a Reality (Notes of the United Nations High Commissioner for Human Rights)* (United Nations, 1993)
United Nations Publications, *The Core International Human Rights Treaties* (United Nations, 2006)
van Banning, R.G.T. *The Human Right to Property* (Intersentia, 2002)
Vasak, K. (ed.) *The International Dimensions of Human Rights* (Greenwood Press, 1982)
Verziji, J.H.W. *International Law in Historical Perspective* (Martinus Nijhoff Publishers, 1998)
Viljoen, F. *International Human Rights Law in Africa* (2nd edn, Oxford University Press, 2012)
Vincent, R.J. *Human Rights in International Relations* (Cambridge University Press, 1986)
Weeramantry, G.C. *Justice Without Frontiers: Furthering Human Rights. Volume 1* (Martinus Nijhoff Publishers, 1997)
—— *Justice Without Frontiers: Furthering Human Rights in the Age of Technology Volume 2* (Kluwer Law International, 1998)
Winter, J. and Prost, A. *René Cassin and Human Rights: From the Great War to the Universal Declaration* (Cambridge University Press, 2013)
Wu, G. and Lansdowne, H. *Zhao Ziyang and China's Political Future* (Routledge, 2008)
Wu, X. 'China: Security Practice of a Modernizing and Ascending Power' in M. Alagappa (ed.), *Asian Security Practice* (Stanford University Press, 1998)
Yasuaki, O. *A Transcivilizational Perspective on International Law* (Martinus Nijhoff, 2010)
Zakaria, F. *The Future of Freedom: Illiberal Democracy at Home and Abroad* (N.W. Norton & Company, 2007)
Zhang, Q. *The Constitution of China: A Contextual Analysis* (Hart Publishing, 2012)
Zhao, S. *China and Democracy, the Prospect for a Democratic China* (Routledge, 2000)
Ziegler, S.K. and Huber, M.P. *Current Problems in the Protection of Human Rights: Perspectives from Germany and the UK* (Hart Publishing, 2013)

Articles

Ai, W.W. 'China's growth cannot last without freedom', *The Times*, 17 December 2012

Alston, P. 'Hobbling the monitors: should U.N. human rights monitors be accountable?' (2011) 52 (2) *Harv.Int'l L.J.* 561

—— 'The United Nations High Commissioner for Human Rights', *ASIL Insight*, Sept–Oct 1995

Amnesty International, 'Facing up to the failures: proposals for improving the protection of human rights by the United Nations' *Amnesty Doc.* IOR41/16/92 of December 1992

Anderlini, J. 'Pressure builds on ruling party for political reform' *The Financial Times*, 8 November 2012

BBC News: Asia, 'Vietnam officials to face parliamentary confidence votes', 22 November 2012. Online. Available HTTP: http://www.bbc.co.uk/news/world-asia-20442922

BBC News: China, 'Amnesty: China forced evictions in "significant rise"', 11 October 2012. Online. Available HTTP: http//www.bbc.co.uk/news/world-asia-china-19894292

Bossuyt, J.M. 'The development of Special Procedures of the United Nations Commission on Human Rights' (1985) 6 HRLJ 179

Buergenthal, T. 'New customary law: taking human rights seriously', 1993, 87th Annual meeting of the American Society of International Law

Cerna, M.C. and Stewart P.D. 'The United States before the UN Human Rights Council' 14 (32) *ASIL Insight* (1 November 2010)

Clapham, A. 'Creating the High Commissioner for Human Rights: the outside story' (1994) 5 *EJIL* 556

Clinton, H. 'The great power shift', *New Statesman*, 16 July 2012, 28

Committee on International Human Rights Law and Practice of the International Law Association, *Final report on the impact of findings of the United Nations human rights treaty bodies* (2004)

Cook, M.H. 'The role of the Special Procedures in the protection of human rights: the way forward after Vienna' (1993) 50 *ICJ Rev* 31

Donnelly, J. 'Cultural relativism and universal human rights' (1984) 6 (4) *Hum.Rts.Q* 400

Donovan, D. and Andersen, E. 'Toward the effectiveness of international human rights law', 2013 vol. 29 (4) October–December, *Newsletter of the American Society of International Law*

Doyle, L. 'Clinton wants UN to take on tyrannical rules', *The Independent* 14 July 1993

Ferguson, N. 'The Human Hive', *The BBC Reith Lectures: The Rule of Law and Its Enemies*, 19 June 2012. Online. Available HTTP: http://www.bbc.co.uk/programmes/b01jmx)p/features/transcript (accessed 28 June 2012)

Foreign & Commonwealth Office, *Human Rights and Democracy: The 2012 Foreign & Commonwealth Office Report* (London, April 2013)

Ghai, Y. 'Human Rights and Governance: The Asia Debate' (1994) 15 *Aust YBIL* 1

Gutter, J. 'Special procedures and the Human Rights Council: achievements and challenges ahead' (2007) 7 *HRLJ* 93

Hathaway O, 'Do human rights treaties make a difference?' [2002] *Yale L.J.* 1938

Kalin, W. and Jimenez, C. 'Reform of the UN Commission on Human Rights: Study commissioned by the Swiss Ministry of Foreign Affairs' (Institute of Public Law, University of Bern, 2003)

Kamminga, T.M. 'The Thematic Procedures of the UN Commission on Human Rights' (1987) XXXIV *NILR* 299

Lewis, L. 'New freedom of speech battle erupts as China's censors try to crack down', *The Times*, 5 January 2013

Li, Z. 'Legacy of modern Chinese history: its relevance to the Chinese perspective of the contemporary international legal order' (2001) 5 *S.G. Jl. Int. Comp. Law* 314

Limon, M. and Piccone, T. 'Human Rights Special Procedures: determinants of influence' (Policy Report of the Brookings Institute and Universal Rights Group, March 2014)

Lord Hannay, '2011 Review of the UN Human Rights Council: recommendations submitted to the UK Foreign & Commonwealth Office by the United Nations Association of the UK', December 2010

MacBride, S. 'The strengthening of international machinery for the protection of human rights', *Nobel Symposium VII: The International Protection of Human Rights*, Oslo, 25–27 September 1967

Mejia-Lemos, G.D. 'Venezuela's denunciation of the American Convention on Human Rights', *ASIL Insights*, 17 (1), 9 January 2013

Open Society Foundations 'Strengthening the Rule of Law: The right to an effective remedy for victims of human rights violations' presented by the OHCHR to the Vienna +20 Conference in Vienna, 27–28 June 2013

Pinheiro, S.P. 'Musings of a UN Special Rapporteur on Human Rights' (2003) 9 *Global Governance* 7

Power, C. 'No more broken promises' *Time*, 7 April 2014, 33

Sohn, L.B. 'A short history of United Nations documents on human rights', in *The United Nations and Human Rights: Eighteenth Report of the Commission to Study the Organisation of Peace*, New York, 1968, 70

Subedi, S.P. 'The UN human rights mandate in Cambodia: the challenges of a country in transition and the experience of the UN Special Rapporteur for the country' (2011) 15 (2) *IJHR* 247

—— 'The doctrine of objective regimes in international law and the competence of the UN Security Council to impose territorial or peace settlements on States' (1994) 37 *German Y. B. Intl. L.* 162

—— 'The legal competence of the international community to create "safe havens" in "zones of turmoil"' (1999) 12 (1) *J.R.S.* 23

—— 'Are the principles of human rights "Western" ideas? an analysis of the claim of the "Asian" concept of human rights from the perspectives of Hinduism' (1999) 30 (1) *Cal. W. Int'l L. J.* 45

Waldron, A. 'Religious revivals in communist China' (Spring 1998) Vol 42 *ORBIS* 325

Weissbrodt, D. 'The three "theme" Special Rapporteurs of the UN Commission on Human Rights' (1986) 80 *AJIL* 685

United Nations Department of Public Information, 'The High Commissioner for Human Rights: An Introduction: Making Human Rights a Reality (Notes of the United Nations High Commissioner for Human Rights)' (1996)

—— 'A more secure world: our shared responsibility' (December 2004) UN Doc. A/59/565Office of the United Nations High Commissioner for Human Rights,

'In larger freedom: towards development, security, and human rights for all' U.N. doc. A/59/565 of 21 March 2005'
—— 'National Report of China to the Human Rights Council as part of the UPR' A/HRC/WG.6/4/CHN/1 of 10 November 2008
—— 'National Report of the Russian federation to the Human Rights Council as part of the UPR' A/HRC/WG.6/4/RUS/1 of 10 November 2008
—— 'National Report of Saudi Arabia submitted to the Human Rights Council as part of the UPR' A/HRC/WG.6/4/SAU/1 of 4 December 2008
—— 'Report of the Working Group on the Universal Periodic Review: China.' A/HRC/11/25 of 5 October 2009
—— 'Report of the Working Group on the Universal Periodic Review: Russian Federation' A/HRC/11/19 of 5 October 2009
—— 'Report of the Working Group on the Universal Periodic Review: Russian Federation' A/HRC/11/19 of 5 October 2009
—— 'Report of the Human Rights Council on its eleventh session' A/HRC/1137 of 16 October 2009
—— 'United Nations Special Procedures: facts and figures, 2009' (Geneva, 2010)
—— 'Report of the Secretary-General, Measures to improve further the effectiveness, harmonization and reform of the treaty body system' UN Doc. A/66/344 of 7 September 2011, p. 5

Index

For Product Safety Concerns and Information please contact our EU
representative GPSR@taylorandfrancis.com
Taylor & Francis Verlag GmbH, Kaufingerstraße 24, 80331 München, Germany

www.ingramcontent.com/pod-product-compliance
Ingram Content Group UK Ltd.
Pitfield, Milton Keynes, MK11 3LW, UK
UKHW020016200926
475702UK00014B/1911

* 9 7 8 0 3 6 7 2 2 4 2 4 0 *